BLACKSTONE'S GUIDE TO

The Domestic Abuse Act 2021

BLACKSTONE'S GUIDE TO

The Domestic Abuse Act 2021

Edited by
Susan Edwards
David Malone
and
Gillian Jones KC

OXFORD
UNIVERSITY PRESS

OXFORD
UNIVERSITY PRESS

Great Clarendon Street, Oxford, OX2 6DP,
United Kingdom

Oxford University Press is a department of the University of Oxford.
It furthers the University's objective of excellence in research, scholarship,
and education by publishing worldwide. Oxford is a registered trade mark of
Oxford University Press in the UK and in certain other countries

First Edition published in 2023

Published in the United States of America by Oxford University Press
198 Madison Avenue, New York, NY 10016, United States of America

British Library Cataloguing in Publication Data
Data available

Library of Congress Control Number: 2023932764

ISBN 978–0–19–287051–3

DOI: 10.1093/oso/9780192870513.001.0001

Printed and bound by
CPI Group (UK) Ltd, Croydon, CR0 4YY

Foreword

I am delighted to write the foreword to *Blackstone's Guide to the Domestic Abuse Act 2021.* I have been involved in seeking reform of the law on domestic abuse since the 1970s. Change has been a long time coming; for too long, our institutions totally failed to understand the nature of such abuse, and while of course it is not experienced exclusively by women, it is usually the product of deeply embedded power relations, which still work largely against women. The Domestic Abuse Act 2021 is a much needed and important piece of legislation striving as it does to address many aspects which affect the lives of domestic abuse victims who are largely women and girls. The inclusion of the new offence of non-fatal strangulation is an important advance. A common theme in the experience of victims is the feeling of suffocation as pressure is applied to the neck. Yet perpetrators were rarely prosecuted by the police. The Act is not a panacea and more needs to be done to combat domestic abuse in all its forms. During the progress of the Domestic Abuse Bill, I urged the Government to create two new statutory defences the first to extend the current law on self-defence where there is a history of abuse to accommodate the victims of abuse accused of assault or murder. The second to provide a statutory defence for survivors of domestic abuse, in some circumstances, who commit an offence closely modelled on section 45 of the Modern Slavery Act 2015. Sadly, those reforms were a bridge too far at this time. I hope a future government will be more courageous.

This Guide is greatly needed. It is edited by an expert team and contributors are drawn from across the sector ensuring that all voices are heard and represented. It provides a blend of practical guidance and advice for practitioners in the court room, for front line workers, for charities, for local authorities and for government departments and where relevant provides a context and background to domestic abuse, legal reforms and remedies. Importantly, it also sets out what further reform is needed and provides a road map for building the future protection of victims of domestic abuse.

This is, and always has been, my priority.

Baroness Helena Kennedy KC

Preface

The problem of domestic abuse is not new. It has long been part of family and intimate partner life. Over the years, domestic abuse has been regulated in disparate pieces of criminal and civil legislation, none devoted to the problem of domestic abuse itself. It has taken the commitment and unmitigated resolve of practitioners, campaigners, politicians, front-line workers, researchers, and academics to bring the Domestic Abuse Act (DAA) 2021 to fruition.

The Act has been hailed by some as a piece of landmark legislation, whilst others rather mutedly declare it a step in the right direction and for some it is disappointing and discriminatory. It is perhaps significant that the Act came into force following the exponential rise in cases of domestic abuse due to lockdown and restrictive measures during the Covid-19 pandemic from March 2020 to September 2021, which effectively blocked off escape routes for those experiencing abuse.

For the main part, the DAA is an amending and consolidating Act improving on existing provisions and measures which, having been previously road tested, required amendment by introducing measures to strengthen court procedure, and enhancing the responsibility and accountability of local authorities and public bodies through the creation of a Domestic Abuse Commissioner's office.

It is especially significant that its most important contribution to furthering understanding and providing remedies for those experiencing domestic abuse lies in the introduction of two amendments which although not part of the government's original vision were pressed for by Harriet Harman KC, MP and Mark Garnier MP and unanimously embraced by both Houses of Parliament. The first new provision included the creation of a new offence of 'strangulation or suffocation', whilst the second placed on a statutory footing the position in common law which asserted that consent should not be a defence for sado-masochistic sexual activity, which has come more recently to be described as 'rough sex'.

The Act for the first time provides a statutory definition of domestic abuse, recognising that abuse extends beyond physical violence to encompass emotional, coercive and controlling behaviour, and economic abuse, both during and after separation. Children are given statutory recognition as 'victims' rather than 'witnesses' if they see, hear, or experience abuse in the home.

The creation of the Domestic Abuse Commissioner role provides an independent voice and point of oversight, through whom data can be gathered nationally to seek to measure the effects of the legislation and to provide challenge and momentum to push the continued need for change to ensure all victims of domestic abuse are protected, irrespective of their background.

The introduction of domestic abuse protection orders (DAPOs) and domestic abuse protection notices (DAPNs) will improve the courts and multi-agency management of perpetrators. DAPOs allow courts to include positive requirements such as attending at a perpetrator's programme. The orders will be available in criminal, family, and civil courts and can be applied for by victims, third parties, solicitors, or made of the court's own motion. Breach of the conditions of a DAPO is a criminal offence with a maximum penalty of five years' imprisonment or dealt with by way of a civil penalty as contempt of court.

The Act also extends the scope of 'revenge porn' (disclosing intimate images without the consent of the individual) by extending the scope of the offence to include the threat to disclose intimate images with the intent to cause distress.

The Act provides a long overdue and much needed clarification of the law that recognises the vulnerability of witnesses by placing on a statutory footing a presumption that victims and witnesses of domestic abuse are automatically eligible for special measures in the criminal, family, and civil courts and that perpetrators are prohibited from cross-examining victims in person in family and civil courts.

This Guide is divided into three Parts. Part I introduces the Domestic Abuse Act and provides a more detailed and contextual background to domestic abuse and remedies.

Part II considers in sequence each section of the Act. The contributors to this Part are drawn from the voluntary and statutory sectors, from academics, and from practitioners who operate in the courts, and each provides, where relevant, a background commentary to the particular section being addressed and a discussion of the section itself. Some sections of the Act require a rather more detailed exegesis than others, especially where the section is new or where there are several complex technical aspects or where the reader is likely to require some further background in order to understand an amending section.

In Part III of the Guide, contributors consider some of the limitations of the Act and set out selected areas which require further legislation, including two chapters which detail some of the proposed amendments which were dropped from the DAA including the need to include migrant women, and the separate concerns of the need to extend existing criminal defences including the 'householder defence' and duress to victims of domestic abuse. Notwithstanding this, the Act has made really significant strides in consolidating earlier legislation, the creation of new offences, and in policing and court procedures. The Guide also provides readers with copy of the Act itself.

The editors of the Guide include Professor Susan Edwards, David Malone, and Gillian Jones KC, who each bring a considerable wealth of experience from the field of academic research and practice in defending and prosecuting in the criminal courts.

Susan Edwards served on the very first Metropolitan Police Domestic Violence Consultative Committee in 1984 which was set up in response to her work on domestic violence which found that police 'no crimed' (effectively wrote off and removed from statistics) those cases where the complainant did not wish to support a prosecution. She served again in 1992 on the second Metropolitan Police Domestic Violence Consultative Committee. She has trained police officers in domestic abuse protection in Bramshill, South Wales and in Europe and was a project developer in 2002 for four Home Office projects aimed at enhancing domestic violence prosecutions. She has conducted research for the Crown Prosecution Service (CPS) and 'Standing Together Against Domestic Violence' on expert witnesses. She has published several books and numerous articles on domestic violence homicide and co-authored a leading family law textbook. Her research and publications on strangulation and the 'rough sex' defence has had a significant impact on changing the law. She draws on her practice experience as a barrister and expert witness. She is currently a door tenant at Red Lion Chambers and Professor Emerita in Law at the University of Buckingham.

David Malone, a leading criminal barrister, has championed several ground-breaking issues around domestic abuse. He has defended in cases where women who are fearful of the repercussions of giving evidence against abusers have been proceeded against for perverting the course of justice. Memorably, David challenged the high-profile conviction in *R v A* [2012] EWCA Crim 43, also known in the media as 'Sarah's Case', the case of a woman who withdrew her truthful rape complaint against her husband and was convicted for perverting the course of justice for that false retraction. The Director of Public Prosecutions subsequently accepted that 'Sarah' should never have been prosecuted and CPS policy was changed. David also successfully challenged the original decision of the Criminal Injuries Compensation Authority in *RT v (1) The First-tier Tribunal (Social Entitlement Chamber), (2) Criminal Injuries Compensation Authority* [2016] UKUT 0306 (AAC) JR/1440/2015, in which Susan Edwards provided the expert opinion), which had deducted 70 per cent of an award for Sarah, paving the way for many other awards for victims of domestic abuse and sexual violence. Much of David's work in the field of domestic abuse has been on a *pro bono* basis and he was formally commended by the Bar Council for leading the Eve's Law campaign to 'influence a change in the law, protecting all victims of domestic abuse', by ensuring that the addresses of victims were kept secret in court. David also acted *pro bono* for the Centre of Women's Justice, notably alongside Gillian Jones KC, his former Red Lion Chambers colleague, in *R v B* [2019] EWCA Crim 665. In 2021, he became the first self-employed barrister to be directly appointed as a deputy chief crown prosecutor (DCCP), as DCCP for CPS London South, following a successful secondment in a similar senior leadership role. He has also been appointed the Domestic Abuse and Stalking Lead for this CPS area, one of the busiest in the country, responsible for all such prosecutions and leading on improvements.

Gillian Jones KC brings her experience especially in murder and serious sexual offences, often dealing with vulnerable defendants and witnesses to an understanding of the need to improve criminal procedure and especially to the need for the better development of special measures in the criminal, family, and civil courts. She is joint Head of Chambers at Red Lion Chambers, named in the Hot 100 list 2021 by *The Lawyer* magazine, won Crime Silk of the Year 2020 at Legal 500's UK awards, was highly commended in the Women-in-Law category at the British Legal Awards 2019, and is cited as Leading Silk by Chambers UK and Legal 500. She has prosecuted and defended in cases involving vulnerable persons including *R v B* [2019] EWCA Crim 665, an appeal against conviction raising two novel points of law, the first challenging the way the accused is prosecuted in trial for alleged false allegations of rape and jury directions and, secondly, as to when and in what circumstances anonymity should be lost. She has prosecuted and defended in cases of domestic homicide. She is a Course Director for the Vulnerable Witness Advocacy Training Course, Inns of Court College of Advocacy (2017–2019) and a lead facilitator on behalf of Lincoln's Inn. She is also a contributor to the Advocates Gateway and currently acts *pro bono* for the Centre for Women's Justice and is on the developmental board of the charity Clean Break.

It has been our pleasure as the editors of this Guide to have worked with all the specialist contributors who represent just some of the many stakeholders working towards the protection of victims of domestic abuse and whose involvement and commitment to this project have together brought this volume to fruition.

The Editors
Professor Susan Edwards
David Malone
Gillian Jones KC
The law is stated as at October 2022

Contents

PART II OF GUIDE THE DOMESTIC ABUSE ACT 2021

PART 1 OF THE ACT—DEFINITION OF DOMESTIC ABUSE (SECTIONS 1–3)

PART 2 OF THE ACT—THE DOMESTIC ABUSE COMMISSIONER (SECTIONS 4–21)

PART 5 OF THE ACT—PROTECTION FOR VICTIMS, WITNESSES, ETC IN LEGAL PROCEEDINGS (SECTIONS 62–67)

PART 6 OF THE ACT—OFFENCES INVOLVING ABUSIVE OR VIOLENT BEHAVIOUR (SECTIONS 68–71)

Table of Cases

United Kingdom

Table of Legislation

Table of Legislation, Treaties and Conventions

Statutes

Statutory Instruments

Other National Legislation

Tasmania

European Regulations

International Instruments

Section List

Sections 1–3	Vanessa Bettinson
Sections 4–16	Susan Edwards
Section 17	Frank Mullane
Sections 18–21	Susan Edwards
Sections 22–27	Martin O'Neill
Sections 28–38	David Malone
Sections 39–43	Martin O'Neill
Sections 44–50	David Malone
Section 51	Martin O'Neill
Sections 52–56	Gillian Jones KC
Section 57	Gill Hague
Sections 58–61	Sophie Jarrett and Tina Hemingway
Sections 62–67	Gillian Jones KC
Section 68	Vanessa Bettinson
Section 69	Andy Phippen and Emma Bond
Section 70	
Context and Background	Nogah Ofer
The Section	Felicia Davy
Section 71	
Context and Background (i)	Jonathan Herring
Context and background (ii)	Susan Edwards
The Section	Felicia Davy
Sections 72–74	David Malone
Section 75	Martin O'Neill
Section 76	Matthew Bland and Vicki McLellan
Section 77	Martin O'Neill
Sections 78–79	Stephanie Harrison KC and Marina Sergides
Section 80	Susan Edwards
Sections 81–82	Pragna Patel and Janaya Walker
Section 83	Fazeela Ishmael and Rob George
Sections 84–91	Susan Edwards

Schedule 1—Martin O'Neill

Schedule 2—Susan Edwards

Schedule 3—David Malone

List of Contributors

Vanessa Bettinson, Professor of Criminal Law and Criminal Justice, De Montfort University.

Matthew Bland PhD, Associate Professor in Evidence Based Policing, University of Cambridge.

Emma Bond, Pro Vice-Chancellor Research and Professor of Socio-Technical Research, University of Suffolk.

Felicia Davy, Barrister, Red Lion Chambers, London.

Susan Edwards, Barrister, Emerita Professor University of Buckingham and Door Tenant, Red Lion Chambers.

Rob George, Barrister, Harcourt Chambers, London and Professor of Law and Policy, Faculty of Laws UCL.

Gill Hague, Emerita Professor of Violence Against Women Studies, University of Bristol.

Stephanie Harrison KC, Joint Head of Garden Court Chambers, London.

Jonathan Herring, Professor of Law, University of Oxford.

Tina Hemingway, Senior Commissioning Manager for Domestic Abuse, Gloucestershire County Council.

Fazeela Ishmael, Barrister, Harcourt Chambers, London.

Sophie Jarrett, County Domestic Abuse and Sexual Violence (DASV) Strategic Coordinator, Crime Command, Gloucestershire Constabulary.

Gillian Jones KC, Joint Head of Red Lion Chambers, London.

David Malone, Barrister, Deputy Chief Crown Prosecutor for CPS London South.

(assisted by Mr Malone's pupil Mr Andreas Malekos)

Vicki McLellan, Trial Manager Domestic Abuse Polygraph Pilot, Cambridge Centre for Evidence Based Policing Ltd.

Frank Mullane, Director, AAFDA, Advocacy After Fatal Domestic Abuse.

Nogah Ofer, Solicitor, Centre for Women's Justice, London.

Martin O'Neill PhD, Senior Lecturer in Criminal Investigation, School of Law, Criminal Justice and Policing, Canterbury Christ Church University.

Andy Phippen, Professor of Digital Rights, Bournemouth University.

Pragna Patel, Solicitor, former Director, Southall Black Sisters, London

Marina Sergides, Barrister, Garden Court Chambers, London

Katy Swaine Williams, Solicitor, Centre for Women's Justice, London.

Janaya Walker, Public Affairs Manager, End Violence Against Women Coalition (EVAW).

List of Abbreviations

AAA	Aggravated Assaults Act 1853
ABH	actual bodily harm
ACA	Adoption and Children Act 2002
APP	authorised professional practice
ASBOs	anti-social behaviour orders
BCE	bad character evidence
BME	Black and Minority Ethnic
CA	Children Act 1989
CAJA	Coroners and Justice Act 2009
CCR	coordinated community response
CDA	Crime and Disorder Act 1998/2003
CJCA	Criminal Justice and Courts Act 2015
CJA	Criminal Justice Act 1988, Criminal Justice Act 2003
CRUs	central referral units
CSA	Crime and Security Act 2010
CSODS	Child Sex Offender Disclosure Scheme
CSPs	community safer partnerships
CWJ	Centre for Women's Justice
DAA	Domestic Abuse Act 2021
DAC	Domestic Abuse Commissioner
DAPN	domestic abuse protection notice
DAPOs	domestic abuse protection orders
DCCP	Deputy Chief Crown Prosecutor
DDV	destitution and domestic violence
DHRs	domestic homicide reviews
DLUHC	Department of Levelling Up Housing and Communities
DPA	Data Protection Act 1998
DPP	Director of Public Prosecutions
DV	domestic violence
DVCVA	Domestic Violence, Crime and Victim's Act 2004
DVDS	Domestic Violence Disclosure Scheme
DVMPA	Domestic Violence and Matrimonial Proceedings Act 1976
DVPO	Domestic Violence Protection Order
ECHR	European Convention on Human Rights

EEA	European Economic Area
EM	electronic monitoring
EVAW	End Violence Against Women coalition
FLA	Family Law Act 1996
FOIA	Freedom of Information Act 2000
GBH	grievous bodily harm
GBV	gender-based violence
GDPR	General Data Protection Regulation 2018
HRA	Human Rights Act 1998
HRBs	homelessness reduction boards
IC	Council of Europe Convention on Preventing and Combating Violence against Women and Domestic Violence 2011
IE	Immigration Enforcement
IOPC	Independent Office for Police Conduct
LASPO	Legal Aid, Sentencing and Punishment of Offenders Act 2012
LAWRS	Latin American Women's Rights Service
LPB	local partnership board
MAPPA	multi-agency public protection arrangements
MARAC	Multi-Agency Risk Assessment Conference
MASHs	multi-agency safeguarding hubs
MCA	Matrimonial Causes Act 1878
MCA	Malicious Communications Act 1988
MHCLG	Ministry for Housing Communities and Local Government
MoJ	Ministry of Justice
NAO	National Audit Office
NRPF	no recourse to public funds
OAPA	Offences against the Person Act 1861
OOs	occupation order
PACE	Police and Criminal Evidence Act 1984
PCSC	Police, Crime, Sentencing and Courts Act 2022
PCSOT	Post-conviction sex offender testing
PFHA	Protection from Harassment Act 1977/1997
POQOs	prospective only quashing orders
Ros	restraining orders
RUI	released under investigation
SA	Sentencing Act 2020
SBS	Southall Black Sisters
SCA	Serious Crime Act 2015
SOA	Sexual Offences Act 2003

SPOs	stalking protection order
SROs	sexual risk orders
STADV	Standing Together Against Domestic Violence
YJCEA	Youth Justice and Criminal Evidence Act 1999

PART I OF GUIDE
THE DOMESTIC ABUSE CONTEXT

1
THE DOMESTIC ABUSE ACT 2021: A SNAPSHOT AND UPDATE

Susan Edwards

Susan Edwards, *The Domestic Abuse Act 2021: A Snapshot and Update* In: *Blackstone's Guide to the Domestic Abuse Act 2021*. Edited by Susan Edwards, David Malone, and Gillian Jones KC, Oxford University Press. © Susan Edwards 2023.
DOI: 10.1093/oso/9780192870513.003.0001

1. INTRODUCTORY REMARKS

It has been nearly two years since the Domestic Abuse Act 2021 (DAA) received royal assent on 29 April. The Act has given an impetus to all stakeholders involved in the prevention of domestic abuse to set in place strategies for improving the response to domestic abuse and the protection of victims. The government published its action plan on 30 March 2022.[1]

The Domestic Abuse Bill 2019–21 was announced in the Queen's Speech on 19 December 2019 and introduced to the House on 3 March 2020. It was a product of extensive public consultation and considerable parliamentary debate, delayed by Brexit and interrupted by the Covid-19 pandemic. In March 2018, the Home Office consulted on proposals for a draft bill for pre-legislative scrutiny published in January 2019,[2] which set out nine measures upon which the government delivered in April 2021. The measures included providing for a statutory definition of domestic abuse (ss 1–2), an amended domestic abuse protection notice (DAPN) and domestic abuse protection order (DAPO) (ss 22–56), establishing the office of the Domestic Abuse Commissioner (DAC) (ss 4–21), prohibiting perpetrators of domestic and other forms of abuse from cross-examining their victims in person in the family courts and in civil proceedings (ss 65–66), creating a statutory presumption entitling domestic abuse victims to special measures in the criminal courts (ss 62–64), enabling domestic abuse offenders to be subject to polygraph testing as a condition of their licence following release from custody (s 76), placing the guidance supporting the Domestic Violence Disclosure Scheme (DVDS) on a statutory footing (s 77), ensuring secure lifetime tenancies to domestic abuse victims (s 79), and extending the extra-territorial jurisdiction of the criminal courts in England and Wales to other violent and sexual offences (ss 72–74). By way of Lord's amendments, section 70 and section 71 were late additions, creating entirely new statutory provisions section 70 criminalising 'strangulation or suffocation', and section 71 aimed at regulating the so-called 'rough sex' excuse.

Reducing the prevalence of domestic abuse is a priority concern. The Crime Survey for England and Wales recorded, for the year ending March 2019, an estimated 2.3 million persons affected by domestic abuse.[3] For the year ending March 2021, the police recorded 1,459,663 'domestic abuse-related incidents and crimes' in England and Wales.[4] The

---

[1] HM Government 'Tackling Domestic Abuse Plan 2022' 46. https://assets.publishing.service.gov.uk/government/uploads/system/uploads/attachment_data/file/1064427/E02735263_Tackling_Domestic_Abuse_CP_639_Accessible.pdf (accessed 29 April 2022).

[2] See 'Transforming the Response to Domestic Abuse Consultation Response and Draft Bill' (January 2019) https://assets.publishing.service.gov.uk/government/uploads/system/uploads/attachment_data/file/772247/Transforming_the_response_to_domestic_abuse_-_consultation_response_and_draft_bill_-print.pdf?msclkid=dffe15bbc7e411eca964287b8fa06aac (accessed 29 April 2022).

[3] See Domestic abuse in England and Wales overview (November 2020) https://www.ons.gov.uk/peoplepopulationandcommunity/crimeandjustice/bulletins/domesticabuseinenglandandwalesoverview/november2020. See also https://assets.publishing.service.gov.uk/government/uploads/system/uploads/attachment_da/file/1013128/Domestic_homicides_and_suspected_victim_suicides_during_the_Covid-19_Pandemic_2020-2021.pdf at 24 (accessed 20 January 2022).

[4] Domestic abuse prevalence and trends, England and Wales: year ending March 2021. https://www.ons.gov.uk/peoplepopulationandcommunity/crimeandjustice/articles/domesticabuseprevalenceandtrendsenglandandwales/yearendingmarch2021 (accessed 20 January 2022).

Metropolitan Police in London, for this same period, recorded 249,986 'domestic abuse-related incidents and crimes'[5] and recorded 75,982 'domestic abuse related crimes'.[6] This was an increase over 1985 when 384 domestic violence crimes were recorded.[7] At that time the Metropolitan Police, as well as other police forces, only submitted, for data collection purposes, those cases that proceeded to prosecution. The increase in police recorded domestic violence/abuse reflects changes in police recording practice and in victim reporting. However, the period of lockdown during Covid-19 from March 2020 to September 2021 resulted in a real increase in domestic abuse and domestic homicide[8] as escape routes for victims were blocked and victim services affected.

Whilst the focus in tackling domestic abuse has concentrated on violence against women and girls as they are the more likely victims, the Act is gender neutral, applying to any person who may inflict abuse on any other person within the context of those 'personally connected' as defined within the act which is intended to include persons of any gender. Although section 84(3) Secretary of State Guidance states: 'Any guidance issued under this section must, so far as relevant, take account of the fact that the majority of victims of domestic abuse in England and Wales (excluding children treated as victims by virtue of section 3) are female.'

2. PART 1 OF THE ACT: STATUTORY DEFINITION OF 'DOMESTIC ABUSE' (SECTIONS 1–3)

Section 1 of the DAA introduces a statutory definition of 'domestic abuse'. This new language of 'abuse' is intended to reflect a wider range of behaviours beyond physical or sexual abuse, which were otherwise encompassed within the former term 'domestic violence', and to emphasise that domestic abuse is not reducible to one physical event but may more appositely be understood as a process or pattern of conduct. Domestic abuse includes violent or threatening behaviour; controlling or coercive behaviour; economic abuse; psychological, emotional, or other abuse. The term 'other' abuse is deliberately inserted to allow police, prosecutors, and the courts a wide discretion. The reference to 'controlling or coercive conduct' is already a specific offence under section 76 of the Serious Crime Act 2015 (SCA).

Section 1(4)(a) and (b) provide some examples of economic abuse but, unlike the other categories of abuse, economic abuse must have a 'substantial adverse effect' on, for example, the victim's ability to acquire, use, or maintain money or other property, or obtain goods or services. The ambit and threshold of 'substantial adverse effect' will be a matter for the courts. Section 1(3) extends the definition of 'domestic abuse' to children, and specifically

---

[5] See https://www.ons.gov.uk/peoplepopulationandcommunity/crimeandjustice/datasets/domesticabuseinenglandandwalesdatatool (accessed 29 April 2022).

[6] Table 3: Number of domestic abuse-related violence against the person offences recorded by the police and percentage of violence against the person offences that were domestic abuse-related, by police force area, England and Wales, year ending March 2016 to year ending March 2021, https://www.ons.gov.uk/peoplepopulationandcommunity/crimeandjustice/datasets/domesticabuseprevalenceandvictimcharacteristicsappendixtables (accessed 29 April 2022).

[7] Susan Edwards, *Policing Domestic Violence* (Sage 1989) ch 4.

[8] See https://www.ons.gov.uk/peoplepopulationandcommunity/crimeandjustice/articles/domesticabuse-duringthecoronaviruscovid19pandemicenglandandwales/november2020 (accessed 29 April 2022).

identifies as abuse a situation where children, who are related to the perpetrator or victim, 'see, hear, or experience' the effects of the abuse. This mirrors the provision in the Adoption and Children Act 2002 (ACA), which recognises such circumstances as potentially qualifying for a finding of 'significant harm' in care proceedings, inserting subsection (9) into section 31 of the Children Act 1989 (CA). It is reported that one in five children is living with domestic abuse.[9]

Section 2 extends the definition of those 'personally connected', and section 68 amends section 76 SCA to include parties who are not living together. This section was the subject of vigorous parliamentary debate reflecting a concern that many victims of abuse continued to be victimised even after relationships had ended (post-separation abuse) and also affected parties who were living apart.[10]

3. PART 2 OF THE ACT: ACCOUNTABILITY AND A STATUTORY FRAMEWORK, THE DOMESTIC ABUSE COMMISSIONER

Sections 4 to 21 establish the office of the Domestic Abuse Commissioner (DAC), providing a framework for oversight by the DAC of both public authorities and government ministers requiring the promotion of good practice in respect of domestic abuse protection by holding them to account. The function of the DAC is to advise and consult with public authorities, voluntary organisations, and other persons; to produce an annual report and to make recommendations to the Secretary of State. Public authorities are under a duty to respond to and cooperate with the Commissioner. Section 15(2) asserts: 'A specified public authority must, so far as is reasonably practicable, comply with a request made to it under this section.' It remains to be seen whether failure to do so by a public authority or failure to exercise its functions under sections 57 and 58 will be subject to judicial review given the tempering of the 'must' requirement with 'as is reasonably practicable' thereby situating the obligation somewhere in between 'must' and 'may'. Concerns were expressed at the consultation stage with regard to whether the Commissioner would have enough resources, powers, and independence. It remains unclear what would happen, for example, if there were a disagreement between the Secretary of State and the DAC. One year on, the DAC has called on the government to provide £18.7 million over three years to ensure that victims of domestic abuse with 'no recourse to public funds' (NRPF) can access support, accommodation, and subsistence. The DAC explains: 'Many people were concerned that migrant survivors were not given the protection they need and deserve in the Domestic Abuse Act and it's more than time that this was rectified.'[11]

[9] See https://www.actionforchildren.org.uk/support-us/campaign-with-us/domestic-abuse/?msclkid=1e95c26dc7eb11ec8f852c53e713004a (accessed 29 April 2022).

[10] See www.refuge.org.uk/our-work/forms-of-violence-and-abuse/domesticviolence/barriers-to-leaving/ (accessed 29 April 2022).

[11] DAC, 'One year on from the Domestic Abuse Act: successes and next steps', https://domesticabusecommissioner.uk/blogs/one-year-on-from-the-domestic-abuse-act-successes-and-next-steps/?msclkid=efd69849c7bc11ec93d766625545952a (accessed 29 April 2022).

Section 17 places on a statutory footing the requirement to report conclusions of any domestic homicide review to the DAC to allow for a central oversight and coordination of conclusions drawn from all DHRs in England and Wales to ensure a more collaborative action.

4. PART 3 OF THE ACT: POWERS FOR DEALING WITH DOMESTIC ABUSE; DOMESTIC ABUSE PROTECTION NOTICE AND DOMESTIC ABUSE PROTECTION ORDER

Amended provisions in the DAA include the domestic abuse protection notice (DAPN) and the domestic abuse protection order (DAPO), which are introduced under Part 3 repealing the former domestic violence protection notice (DVPN) and the domestic violence protection order (DVPO), originally introduced under the Crime and Security Act (CSA) 2010. Under sections 22 to 26 the DAPN, 'the notice'—a civil provision, may now be issued by a senior police officer 'to a person who is over the age of 18 and who is abusive to a person over the age of 16' without court proceedings and conditions may be attached, for example, that no contact between the stated parties may be made (s 23(1)(a)), or that a party must leave the premises (s 23(2)(c)). Section 29(8) provides for arrest without warrant and remand in custody, if breached. The police must bring the matter to court by applying for a DAPO (s 29), which is granted where, on the balance of probability, the alleged perpetrator has been abusive (s 32(2)) and that it is necessary and proportionate to protect a person from abuse or the risk of abuse (s 32(3)). A DAPO may be granted 'on application' or during proceedings. Regarding 'without notice' applications (s 34), the court must be satisfied that, if the order is not made immediately, 'P' will cause significant harm to the person for whose protection the order would be made (s 34(3)(a)). An order 'on application' (with stipulated exceptions) must be applied for in the family court by police, the victim, or third parties (s 28) and can be made ancillary to proceedings in criminal, family, and civil courts (ss 31 and 52). It is wide and prohibits 'doing things' and/or requires the party concerned 'to do things' (s 27). In order to enhance compliance, sections 35(6) and 37 provide for electronic monitoring as a condition of the order. A breach is a criminal offence (s 39(5)), punishable with a fine or imprisonment up to five years.

5. PART 4 OF THE ACT: LOCAL AUTHORITY SUPPORT

In order to ensure a better collaborative approach to domestic abuse and its prevention, Part 4 of the Act sets out a statutory framework specifying the duties of local authorities. These duties include: providing support to victims of domestic abuse (ss 57–61); devising, monitoring, and assessing a strategy with regard to accommodation services in their area; setting up local domestic abuse partnership boards with whom to consult (s 58); and submitting a report on how they have exercised their functions to the Secretary of State (s 59(1)). To ensure wide and relevant representation, section 58(2) stipulates that representatives to serve on the local partnership board must include police, victims, children's representatives, charities, the health sector, and the local authority. Guidance on the exercise by local authorities of functions under this Part will be issued by the Secretary of State, who must consult with the DAC (s 60(4)(a)) in the preparation of any such guidance.

6. PART 5 OF THE ACT: PROTECTION FOR VICTIMS, WITNESSES ETC. IN LEGAL PROCEEDINGS; SPECIAL MEASURES

Section 62(2)(c) extends the special measures provisions in the Youth Justice and Criminal Evidence Act (YJCEA) 1999 to cases involving domestic abuse in family and civil matters to correct the mischief where the alleged perpetrator could cross-examine the witness in family and civil proceedings. Section 65 prevents cross-examination of a witness who is a victim or alleged victim in family proceedings by an alleged perpetrator.[12] The Act makes clear that victims of domestic abuse will be automatically eligible for special measures, but it will remain a matter for the court to decide which (if any) of the available measures are necessary in the particular circumstances.

7. PART 6 OF THE ACT: OFFENCES INVOLVING ABUSIVE OR VIOLENT BEHAVIOUR, STRANGULATION OR SUFFOCATION, AND 'ROUGH SEX' EXCUSE

Part 6 of the Act, 'Offences involving violent or abusive behaviour', extends some existing offences and also introduces new offences. Section 68 DAA amends section 76 SCA (offence of controlling or coercive behaviour in an intimate or family relationship) to incorporate the new definition of 'personally connected' provided in section 2 DAA. Section 69 criminalises threats of disclosure of private sexual photographs where there is intention to cause distress by so doing. This extends section 33 of the Criminal Justice and Courts Act (CJCA) 2015, referred to as the 'revenge porn' offence, which created a criminal offence where there was a deliberate disclosure of private sexual images with intent to cause distress, to those who make threats to do so.

The creation of two new offences which were not part of the government's original reforming vision are section 70 and section 71. Section 70 prospectively inserts section 75(4)(a) into the SCA 2015, creating a new criminal offence of 'strangulation or suffocation'.[13] This crime is committed where 'A intentionally strangles another person ('B'), or A does any other act to B that affects B's ability to breathe, and constitutes battery of B'. A defence is open to A if sufficient evidence of B's consent is adduced to raise an issue (s 75(4)(a)), but not if B suffers serious harm and A intended or was reckless as to that harm.

A compelling case for this new offence gathered further momentum following the murder by strangulation of Grace Millane in New Zealand by Jesse Kempson.[14] The strangulation

[12] Home Office Policy Paper, 'Special measures in family proceedings' Updated 31 January 2022, https://www.gov.uk/government/publications/domestic-abuse-bill-2020-factsheets/special-measures-in-family-proceedings?msclkid=4c24f84bc7b911ec8ed98a06dc818934 (accessed 29 April 2022).

[13] It has been the subject of much discussion. See Rory Kelly and David Ormerod, 'Non-fatal strangulation and suffocation' (2021) 7 *Crim LR* 532. Recent case law includes *R v Solomon (Ben Sean)* [2022] EWCA 1333, where the victim was 'throttled to the point of unconsciousness'; *R v Jones (Michael George)* EWCA 1346, where the victim 'struggled to breath'.

[14] See *R v Kempson* [2020] NZSC 158.

motion was first introduced in the Commons in June 2020 and withdrawn[15] and brought back after protracted 'ping pong' debate in a House of Lords Amendment.[16] The non-fatal strangulation provision will ensure that such acts are dealt with by police, prosecutors, and by the courts. However, the provision will have little impact no homicide cases and defendants will not be prohibited as part of their defence from arguing that the strangulation that caused or may have caused death was an accident, and the act which the defendant alleges 'went wrong' was an act to which the deceased consented. The section has significantly raised the understanding and profile of such conduct and an allegation of strangulation is now considered a red flag incident and recognised as carrying a significant risk of serious and further abuse.

Section 71 establishes in statute the ruling in *R v Brown and Others*[17] that consent to 'serious harm' for sexual gratification is not a defence to charges under sections 18, 20, or 47 of the Offences against the Person (OAPA) Act 1861. Momentum for this statutory inclusion followed the death of Natalie Conolly, for which John Broadhurst[18] was deemed responsible. He claimed that she had consented during 'rough sex' to the injuries, some of which were said to have contributed to her death. This section does not preclude a defence that no injury was intended, nor does it preclude a submission that consent was given to what has come to be referred to as 'rough sex play' that accidentally caused death (as in *R v Slingsby*).[19] 'Rough sex' arguments are being relied upon with great regularity in defence submissions where victims, it is said by defendants, have consented.[20]

8. PART 7 OF THE ACT: MISCELLANEOUS AND GENERAL, EXTENDED JURISDICTION, POLYGRAPH, DISCLOSURE, HOMELESSNESS, IMMIGRATION AND PERSONAL DATA, CONTACT CENTRES AND HARM, POWERS OF SECRETARY OF STATE

Part 7 of the Act deals with a wide range of issues. Sections 72 to 75 and Schedule 3 extend jurisdiction for certain offences committed outside the UK by UK nationals or those habitually resident in the UK, thus giving effect to the Istanbul Convention and its promise of cooperation with other jurisdictions in the prevention of violence against women.[21]

---

[15] See https://hansard.parliament.uk/commons/2020-06-16/debates/3fa90c32-4bc5-4477-ab1e-aaf665da56e6/DomesticAbuseBill(TenthSitting)?msclkid=92d55446c7e911ecabc2458fbae70844 (accessed 29 April 2022).

[16] See https://bills.parliament.uk/bills/2709/stages/12653/amendments/72698 (accessed 14 November 2022). Strangulation was raised in a Lords question on 8 July 2021, https://hansard.parliament.uk/Lords/2021-07-08/debates/193F5B77-22CD-4AA7-85DF-A2039BEB176F/Non-FatalStrangulationAndSuffocation (accessed 14 November 2022).

[17] [1994] 1 AC 212.

[18] See *R v Broadhurst (John Anthony)* [2019] EWCA Crim 2026, 19.

[19] *R v Slingsby* [1995] Crim LR 570.

[20] *R v Loynes* [2022] EWCA Crim 420; *R v Corner* [2021] EWCA Crim 751; *R v Hegarty (Shaun)* [2022] NICA 31 and NICA 55. See Red Lion Chambers Webinar, 'Regulating the Rough Sex Excuse' (1 December 2021), with Jenni Dempster KC, Susan Edwards, and Felicia Davy. See https://www.youtube.com/watch?v=D7qjfHOX82o (accessed 29 April 2022).

[21] See www.coe.int/en/web/human-rights-channel/istanbul-convention (accessed 29 April 2022).

In enhancing victim safety and protection, section 76 sets out the conditions for the much-debated polygraph.[22] It is not surprising that a three-year pilot of mandatory polygraph examinations on domestic abuse perpetrators released on licence identified as being at high risk of causing serious harm is now being developed in order to build up a robust evaluation of the usefulness and reliability of this tool.

Further protection for putative victims is provided under section 77, which places on a statutory footing guidance for police disclosure of information to persons about their partner or former partner's domestic abuse offending. The Domestic Violence Disclosure Scheme, otherwise known as 'Clare's Law',[23] and the decision to disclose requires a balance between the common law powers of the police and the Data Protection Act 2018, as well as the Human Rights Act 1998. Guidance will ensure that it is more fully used by persons in making applications to police for disclosure, and by police, and by also facilitating a greater consistency in decisions that are made across all police forces.

One of the main factors that keeps a woman (or man) in an abusive relationship is the need for a home. Sections 78 and 79 address the homelessness of domestic abuse victims and make provision regarding future security of accommodation by section 79 and the grant of 'secure tenancies'. This will enable victims of domestic abuse in social housing to leave their abusive relationship without forfeiting any housing rights they may have had.

Another factor inhibiting access to justice for victims of abuse has been the charge levied by health care professionals when called upon to provide evidence of abuse to support legal aid applications on behalf of victims of abuse. Section 80 importantly places a prohibition on fee charging on relevant health professionals when consulted by victims of domestic abuse to provide a report for the purpose of accessing legal aid, the granting of which is dependent upon such evidence.

Under section 81, the Secretary of State must review and consider the processing of victims' personal data for immigration purposes and, in so doing, consider the findings of His Majesty's Inspectorate of Constabulary (HMIC), which reported the breaches of data protection regulations in the sharing of information about victims of domestic abuse by government departments with Home Office immigration, following the police super-complaint brought by Liberty and Southall Black Sisters.[24] Section 83 requires the Secretary of State to publish a report on the safety of contact centres in England and Wales, both for adult carers from domestic abuse from the other party and also for children from any harm, who use them. Sections 84 to 91 set out the power of the Secretary of State to issue guidance and deals with consequential arrangements and regulatory matters. Section 83 concerns reporting on the safety of contact centres and protection from harm.

[22] See Policy Paper, 'Mandatory polygraph tests factsheet' Updated 31 January 2022 https://www.gov.uk/government/publications/domestic-abuse-bill-2020-factsheets/mandatory-polygraph-tests-factsheet?msclkid=95fa7677c7c711eca11adc6fc7403d98 (accessed 29 April 2022).

[23] Home Office Policy Paper, 'Domestic Violence Disclosure Scheme factsheet' Updated 31 January 2022 https://www.gov.uk/government/publications/domestic-abuse-bill-2020-factsheets/domestic-violence-disclosure-scheme-factsheet?msclkid=c78f174ac7c811ecb3507446e8bcf6ad (accessed 29 April 2022).

[24] See 'Safe to share? Report on Liberty and Southall Black Sisters' super-complaint on policing and immigration status' https://www.justiceinspectorates.gov.uk/hmicfrs/publications/liberty-and-southall-black-sisters-super-complaint-on-policing-and-immigration-status/?msclkid=59f62a1dc7eb11ec931eedc5ad1a05fc, (accessed 29 April 2022).

9. CLOSING REMARKS

i. Excluded from the Act

Whilst for some the Act has been heralded as a landmark moment, for others it is disappointing and discriminatory, leaving categories of victims outside its protection. Several important tabled amendments were dropped from the Bill, including the right of migrant women to receive the same protections and services as non-migrant women (discussed in Chapter 19 of this Guide). For example, migrant women have no recourse to public funds (NRPF) and are unable to access safe accommodation. So, for example, Women's Aid reported: 'If a woman is denied recourse to public funds the spaces available to her will be limited ... only 6.3% of all vacancies listed during 2020-21 could consider women who were not eligible to access public funds.'[25] The government also refused to extend the destitute domestic violence concession to all 'migrant' women beyond women with spouse visas to allow settlement. This means that the concession which allows for access to public funds does not apply to 'migrant' women with other kinds of visas, including those with student visas, work permit holders, and domestic workers.[26] The rights of disabled women have also been marginalised, argues Ruth Bashall of Safe East, since disabled victims of domestic violence may be cared for by a person who does not fall within the definition of 'personally connected' (s 2 DAA), thus leaving disabled victims abused by carers with whom they are not 'personally connected' outside the Act. Other important concerns were debated, including an attempt to reform the law on self-defence by extending to victims of domestic abuse a similar protection as afforded men who largely benefited from the 'householder defence', and an amendment to extend the defence of compulsion in the Modern Slavery Act 2015 to victims of domestic abuse (discussed further in Chapter 20 of this Guide).

ii. Post Act Update

Since the passage of the Act, the Home Office published its 'Tackling Domestic Abuse Plan' on 30 March 2022, and issued further statutory guidance[27] in which it reiterates what has already been done and sets out an action plan for delivery on each of the sections of the DAA, the funding available, and how each issue will be tackled and delivered. Members of Parliament have continued to raise matters in the House, calling the government to account in pressing for better data including collecting disaggregated data on incidents of domestic

[25] The Domestic Abuse Report 2022: Early Release A first look at findings on the provision and usage of domestic abuse services in England in 2020-2 at 35, [5]. https://www.womensaid.org.uk/wp-content/uploads/2021/10/Domestic-Abuse-Report-2022-Early-Release.pdf?msclkid=4a4feb23c7ca11ec82ae18402c656b6a (accessed 29 April 2022).

[26] 'Safe to share?' (n 24).

See also Domestic Abuse Bill (15 April 2021) cols 543–64 https://hansard.parliament.uk/commons/2021-04-15/debates/0E322BD7-571C-4DC5-A8C8-7B29806DE067/DomesticAbuseBill?msclkid=88dc216cc7eb11ecbda15d236817ff39.

[27] See 'Tackling Domestic Abuse Plan' (n 1). See also https://www.theyworkforyou.com/wrans/?id=2022-03-30.150123.h&msclkid=d67d8166c55b11ecaeabaf4edc8038ad (accessed 14 November 2022).

violence by (a) ethnicity of the complainant, (b) immigration status of the complainant, and (c) police recorded outcome.[28]

Questions raised in the House have pressed for more prosecutions.[29] The government's own 'Tackling Domestic Abuse Plan'[30] reported: 'In 2020-21, we know that only 8% of recorded domestic abuse crimes were assigned an outcome of charged or summonsed in the same year.'[31] Questions raised have called for more support for victims[32] and specifically support for black victims of domestic abuse.[33]

Access to the courts and to effective remedies remains a key issue. On 15 March 2022, the Ministry of Justice published a consultation on proposed changes to the means test for civil legal aid, to ensure access to justice. Under the plans, domestic abuse victims would benefit from a more generous means test, including significant increases to income and capital thresholds. In addition, when applying for legal aid for a dispute about an asset, that asset will not be included in the means assessment, making it fairer for domestic abuse victims contesting a property who cannot use their equity to fund the legal proceedings. These changes will significantly widen access to legal aid for victims and will make any contributions more affordable.[34]

On 26 May 2022,[35] several honourable members asked the government what it was doing with regard to enhancing the number of prosecutions for rape and domestic abuse. The Attorney General replied: 'The Government are taking huge steps to support victims of domestic abuse. We passed a landmark piece of legislation, the Domestic Abuse Act 2021, which brought in key measures, key duties, and investment to support those who are victims of this heinous crime.'[36] Significantly, the CPS has made important strides to improve prosecutions and introduced new guidance for prosecutors.[37]

Sentencing decisions and prosecutorial assignment in some cases have raised concerns. On 5 August 2021, Harriet Harman KC, MP wrote to the Director of Public Prosecutions (DPP) regarding prosecutorial decision-making in two cases. In the case of Warren Coulton—where

---

[28] https://www.theyworkforyou.com/wrans/?id=2022-03-30.150123.h&msclkid=d67d8166c55b11eca eabaf4edc8038ad (accessed 29 April 2022). Lyn Brown's (Shadow Minister Foreign, Commonwealth and Development Affairs) question received the reply that the Home Office has begun collecting data on the ethnicity of victims of all crime from 1 April this year and these data will be published in due course. Information on the immigration status of the complainant of domestic abuse-related offences are not collected centrally.

[29] Vol 708: debated on Tuesday 8 February 2022 https://hansard.parliament.uk/Commons/2022-02-08/debates/03A7FE43-EA82-4297-BC2C-8CD06E1E74BA/a?msclkid=d67cfadec55b11ec925524ea0ef8c15a (accessed 29 April 2022).

[30] 'Tackling Domestic Abuse Plan' (n 1) 46.

[31] ibid 11, 46.

[32] Vol 707: debated on Monday 17 January 2022, https://hansard.parliament.uk/Commons/2022-01-17/debates/E4E5582C-D3BB-46C3-8C57-86841C0EDE19/details?msclkid=d67d212ac55b11eca02b48dcb ccf3cef (accessed 29 April 2022) See also https://hansard.parliament.uk/Commons/2022-07-05/debates/F38C46A8-604F-42A8-9E1B-BCFF6326DF9E/SupportForVictimsOfCrime.

[33] Vol 711: debated on Monday 28 March 2022. Support for black victims of domestic abuse. https://hansard.parliament.uk/Commons/2022-03-28/debates/D20803B5-4171-469A-BDD5-971CB74BE918/SupportForBlackVictimsOfDomesticAbuse?msclkid=31fdc785c7ec11ec86db71a58f66da17 (accessed 29 April 2022).

[34] 'Tackling Domestic Abuse Plan' (n 1) 43.

[35] See 'Violence against Women and Girls: Prosecutions' which was debated for five minutes at https://hansard.parliament.uk/commons/2022-05-26/debates/609A1254-49B2-471B-BF33-DE2C1EB7DBDC/ViolenceAgainstWomenAndGirlsProsecutions (accessed 27 May 2022).

[36] ibid col 415.

[37] https://www.cps.gov.uk/legal-guidance/domestic-abuse (accessed 8 June 2022).

there had been asphyxiation and death—where Coulton in his defence claimed it was consensual 'rough sex', the prosecution accepted a plea of gross negligence manslaughter. In the case of Sam Pybus—where there had been asphyxiation and death—the prosecution accepted a plea of unlawful manslaughter, where Pybus claimed the deceased had consented to 'rough sex'. Harriet Harman KC MP also submitted an appeal to the Attorney General following Pybus's's[38] sentence of four years and eight months for unlawful manslaughter, which the Court of Appeal did not find to be 'unduly lenient'.

Since the introduction of the DAA 2021, the Police, Crime, Sentencing and Courts Act (PCSC) 2022 has introduced reforms to pre-charge bail to better protect vulnerable victims and witnesses, making it possible for victims to bring a complaint later than six months. From 28 June 2022, section 39A Criminal Justice Act 1988 was introduced changing the statutory time limit for common assault in domestic abuse cases committed on and after 28 June 2022. The increase in time to charge an offence of domestic or common assault is now up to two years, provided it is charged within six months of a victim giving a statement or video recorded interview.[39]

The PCSC also introduces a 'serious violence duty' on specified authorities to work together to prevent and reduce serious violence, which includes domestic abuse and sexual offences within that definition.[40]

However, the Judicial Review and Courts Act 2022 section 1 has the potential to further limit judicial review. The 'prospective only quashing orders' (POQOs) which would have weakened judicial review and therefore the accountability of government[41] were removed when the 'presumption' in clause 1 of the Bill, which would have required judicial review judges to use 'suspended' or 'prospective-only' quashing orders unless there was a good reason not to, was defeated. This has implications for judicial review of public authority duties in respect of domestic abuse. It remains to be seen how section 1 is used by the judges. The factors set out in section 1(8) to be considered in exercising the power under section 1(1) are akin to the reasoning already used by judges when exercising the discretionary remedies under judicial review which takes into account unique public law concerns such as impact on third parties (s 1(8)(d)).

The DAA 2021 has made important amendments to existing legislation, put in place procedural changes, and introduced significant new offences. The government's pledge to protect victims of domestic abuse will continue to be scrutinised, further reforms pressed, and the government and public authorities held to account.

---

[38] *R v Pybus* [2021] EWCA Crim 1787.

[39] See Police, Crime, Sentencing and Courts Act 2022 (legislation.gov.uk) https://www.legislation.gov.uk/ukpga/2022/32/section/49/enacted. See also https://www.gov.uk/government/news/public-safety-boost-as-major-justice-reforms-come-into-force, also at https://www.gov.uk/government/publications/circular-0052022-police-crime-sentencing-and-courts-act-2022/circular-0052022-police-crime-sentencing-and-courts-act-2022

[40] Policy paper Police, Crime, Sentencing and Courts Bill 2021: overarching factsheet https://www.gov.uk/government/publications/police-crime-sentencing-and-courts-bill-2021-factsheets/police-crime-sentencing-and-courts-bill-2021-overarching-factsheet?msclkid=747493ecc7e411ecac10a144ea9cab7c Updated 31 March 2022 https://www.gov.uk/government/publications/police-crime-sentencing-and-courts-bill-2021-factsheets/police-crime-sentencing-and-courts-bill-2021-overarching-factsheet (accessed 29 April 2022).

[41] Justice 'Judicial Review and Courts Bill (Part 1—Judicial Review) House of Lords Committee Stage Supported Amendments' (February 2022) 4 https://files.justice.org.uk/wp-content/uploads/2022/02/22100642/JUSTICE-JR-and-Courts-Bill-Briefing-HoL-Committee-Part-1-Judicial-Review.pdf?msclkid=f7ebd0d7c7a911eca1c3d7a1b65c7f7d (accessed 29 April 2022).

2

DOMESTIC VIOLENCE AND ABUSE: CONTEXT AND BACKGROUND

Susan Edwards

Susan Edwards, *Domestic Violence and Abuse: Context and Background* In: *Blackstone's Guide to the Domestic Abuse Act 2021*. Edited by Susan Edwards, David Malone, and Gillian Jones KC, Oxford University Press. © Susan Edwards 2023.
DOI: 10.1093/oso/9780192870513.003.0002

1. INTRODUCTION

This chapter provides context and background to the problem of domestic violence (and abuse) and to the evolution of protective remedies. It considers (where relevant) the background to some provisions introduced by the Domestic Abuse Act (DAA) 2021. This chapter also considers, as does Part III of this Guide, areas which require reform.

i. A Historic Infamy

The risk of violence behind closed doors is real. For several decades approximately one-fifth of recorded homicides in England and Wales were committed against female intimate partners by male partners.[1] For those who survived domestic violence and abuse there was little public interest and certainly no adequate legal redress. Domestic violence was regarded as 'only a domestic'. Chester and Streather's study on cruelty and divorce found that of 8,800 English divorces granted in 1967, 94 per cent were granted to wives and one-third of those divorces were granted on 'cruelty' grounds. In 90 per cent of these cases, repeated physical violence was reported.[2] At that time, police were reluctant to proceed with charging husband/cohabitants with criminal assault and in those cases that were proceeded with charges of breach of the peace were more typically brought where upon conviction a bind over and/or a fine followed. Mrs X, in oral evidence to the *Select Committee on Violence in Marriage* (1976) said:

> I have had ten stitches, three stitches, five stitches, seven stitches, where he has cut me. I have had a knife stuck through my stomach; I have had a poker put through my face; I have no teeth where he knocked them all out; I have been burnt with red hot pokers; I have had red hot coals slung all over me; I have been sprayed with petrol and stood there while he has flicked lighted matches at me ... I have been to the police ... and they held him in over the weekend and he came out on Monday. He was bound over to keep the peace ... On the Tuesday he gave me the hiding of my life.[3]

Jo Richardson MP, when presenting the Domestic Violence Bill 1975–76 in the Commons, which was later to become the Domestic Violence and Matrimonial Proceedings Act 1976 (DVMPA), reported a case where a husband with two previous convictions for assaulting his wife, evaded punishment for non-fatal strangulation:

> During one attack, he tied a flex so tightly round her throat that her larynx was damaged, and she had to be fed through a tube in hospital. The man was taken to court, fined £2 and told to behave himself.[4]

The DVMPA (s 1(2)) gave judges in the county courts the power to grant to those married or living together a matrimonial injunction which could include a non-molestation or

[1] See Susan Edwards, *Policing Domestic Violence* (Sage 1989) 124–27.

[2] Robert Chester and Jane Streather, 'Cruelty in English Divorce: Some Empirical Findings' (1972) 34(4) *Journal of Marriage and Family* 706, 708–709.

[3] Select Committee on Violence in Marriage, together with the Proceedings of the Committee, Session 1974–75, vol 2 (HMSO 1975) 25.

[4] See Domestic Violence Bill (13 February 1976) vol 905, col 862 https://www.theyworkforyou.com/debates/?id=1976-02-13a.857.1#g857.2 (accessed 5 January 2022).

exclusion/ouster injunction against an abusive spouse/cohabitee. The exclusion injunction contained the power to exclude an abuser from the family home for a defined period.

This marginalisation of domestic violence by society and the law is historically habituated and instituted. During the nineteenth century under the Aggravated Assaults Act 1853 (AAA), domestic violence and sexual offences against women and girls were down-crimed as 'aggravated assaults' and heard only before magistrates with their limited jurisdiction and powers. Section 43 of the Offences Against the Person Act 1861 (OAPA) consolidated the AAA and provided for 'assault and battery'[5] but continued to downgrade the seriousness of violence against women driving the prosecution of such assaults into the summary courts. In 1878, the Matrimonial Causes Act (MCA) enabled a wife to leave a violent husband by obtaining a separation order and receiving maintenance. Mabel Sharman Crawford noted at the time that the 1878 Act required the wife to be beaten and assaulted to the point of near death before an order was ever granted.[6]

When women in attempting to defend themselves from a violent husband killed him, like Rene Duffy, they were convicted of murder.[7] Her appeal against conviction in 1949 was refused and she was sentenced to death by hanging. A petition (organised by her solicitor, Frank R Johnson) and supported by 12,000 signatures succeeded in securing her reprieve.[8]

By 1974, Erin Pizzey published *Scream Quietly or the Neighbours Will Hear*,[9] and in that year Chiswick Family Aid and the National Women's Aid Federation were established to provide support and safe housing for victims/survivors of domestic violence. Other legal provisions under the Family Law Act (FLA) 1996, which repealed the DVMPA amending non-molestation and occupation/ouster orders, were introduced. In 2004, section 1(1) of the Domestic Violence Crime and Victims Act (DVCVA) made a breach of a non-molestation order a criminal offence, established a new offence of causing or allowing a child or vulnerable person serious harm or death (s 5), and introduced domestic homicide reviews (s 9; see further s 17 DAA in Part II of this Guide). In 2009, the Coroners and Justice Act (CAJA) turned its attention to addressing the gendered inequity in the defence of manslaughter/provocation abolishing the common law defence of provocation (s 56) and in recognising that women in fear of violence from an abusive partner may kill introduced (fear/loss of control manslaughter (s 55 (3)). In 2010, the Crime and Security Act (CSA) introduced Domestic Violence Protection Notices (DVPNs) and orders (DVPOs), which allowed immediate protection for victims/survivors from domestic abuse (see further ss 22 to 56 DAA in Part II of this Guide). In 2015, section 76 of the Serious Crime Act (SCA) created a stand-alone offence of 'coercive and controlling conduct' for those 'personally connected' (s 76(1)(b)) (see further s 1, and s 68 DAA in Part II of this Guide). In recent years, the Malicious Communications Act (MCA) 1988, has been used to prosecute in cases of online abuse which is so frequently part of a campaign of domestic abuse.

---

5 See Nancy Tomes, 'A torrent of abuse crimes of violence between working class men and women in London 1840–1875' (1978) 11(3) *Journal of Social History* 328.

6 Mabel Sharman Crawford, 'Maltreatment of Wives' (1893) 3 *The Westminster Review* 139, 292–303. https://archive.org/details/in.ernet.dli.2015.21686/page/n311/mode/2up?msclkid=eb7fa56cc59011eca387d72cff3a8fd2 (accessed 26 April 2022).

7 *R v Duffy* [1949] 1 All ER 932.

8 Susan Edwards, 'Justice Devlin's legacy: Duffy—a battered woman "caught" in time' (2009) 12 *Crim LR* 851. Women were labouring under other difficulties too. In *R v Millar* [1954] 2 QB 282, it was decided that a husband could not be guilty of rape on a wife but guilty only of common assault. This legal position persisted until *R v R* [1991] UKHL 12.

9 Erin Pizzey, *Scream Quietly or the Neighbours Will Hear* (Penguin 1974).

On 29 April 2021, the DAA became law. On 2 December 2021, it was announced that domestic abuse and sexual offences would be treated as seriously as knife crime under the 'serious violence duty' to be made via an amendment to the Police, Crime, Sentencing and Courts Bill (now the Police, Crime, Sentencing and Courts Act 2022).[10] A Lords amendment on 17 January 2021 voted in favour of adding misogyny to the current list of hate crimes and to include misogyny as an aggravated feature permitting a sentencing uplift.[11] The government, however, was not in favour of any changes to the current law.

2. DEFINING DOMESTIC VIOLENCE AND DOMESTIC ABUSE

A word on terms. Historically, 'domestic violence' has been the term used to capture a variety of forms of abuse committed in the domestic context largely by men on women, albeit that legal remedies have required evidence of physical assault. Non-physical abusive conduct in the domestic context has not been recognised as a criminal offence, although defined as 'cruelty' for the purposes of divorce, recognised in non-molestation injunctions, and also in harassment offences which require a 'course of conduct' and 'putting a person in fear' (Protection from Harassment Act (PFHA) 1977).

i. Definitions: 'Domestic Violence'

Prosecution of domestic violence in the past required evidence of physical injury even though official definitions were expanding. By 2005, the Home Office defined domestic violence to include 'any incident of threatening behaviour, violence or abuse [psychological, physical, sexual, financial, or emotional] between adults who are or have been intimate partners or family members, regardless of gender or sexuality'.[12] In 2009, Sir Mark Potter P, in the Family Division, issued a Practice Direction,[13] which stated that '"domestic violence" includes physical violence, threatening or intimidating behaviour and any other form of abuse which, directly or indirectly, may have caused harm to the other party or to the child or which may give rise to the risk of harm'. In 2009, the Crown Prosecution Service (CPS), building on its earlier guidance issued in 1995 and 2002, recognised 'controlling and coercive' behaviour in its 'Policy for Prosecuting Cases of Domestic Violence':

There is no specific statutory offence of domestic violence 'Domestic violence' is a general term that describes a range of controlling and coercive behaviours, which are used by one person to

---

[10] See Home Office, 'Domestic abuse and sexual offences to be treated as seriously as knife crime' (2 December 2021) https://www.gov.uk/government/news/domestic-abuse-and-sexual-offences-to-be-treated-as-seriously-as-knife-crime (accessed 5 January 2022).

[11] See Police, Crime, Sentencing and Courts Bill vol 817 (17 January 2022) cols 1362–92 https://hansard.parliament.uk/lords/2022-01-17/debates/D4DCBA9B-3C6A-4F1C-B932-5E04908DF13C/PoliceCrimeSentencingAndCourtsBill (accessed 5 January 2022).

[12] Government (Home Office) in 2005, defined domestic violence. In 2006, the Secretary of State for Communities and Local Government issued new guidance. https://assets.publishing.service.gov.uk/government/uploads/system/uploads/attachment_data/file/696636/Supplementary_guidance_on_domestic_abuse_and_homelessness_archived.pdf (accessed 5 January 2022).

[13] Practice Direction (*Residence and Contact Orders: Domestic Violence) (No 2)* [2009] 1 WLR 251 (at para 28).

maintain control over another with whom they have, or have had, an intimate family relationship. It is the cumulative and interlinked physical, psychological, sexual, emotional or financial abuse that has a particularly damaging effect on the victim.[14]

In other areas of the law, access to housing for example, Baroness Hale in *Yemshaw v Hounslow London Borough Council*[15] said that: 'even by 1996 ... it is clear that both international and national governmental understanding of the term had developed beyond physical contact'.[16] In construing the term 'violence' she said: '"Violence" is a word very similar to the word "family". It is not a term of art. It is capable of bearing several meanings and applying to many different types of behaviour. These can change and develop over time.'[17]

Nevertheless, successful criminal prosecutions of domestic assault continued to rely on evidence of physical injury. In *Caetano v Commissioner of Police of Metropolis*,[18] the female claimant who had accepted a caution for hitting/slapping her male partner challenged the caution by way of judicial review on the grounds that she had accepted a caution following the advice given to her by the duty solicitor who had said that if she did not accept a caution she would be prosecuted. She also challenged the police's disregard of the fact that her partner had tried to strangle her subsequent to her slapping him. After an extensive review of CPS procedure and police cautioning guidance, the court concluded that this case was one of the rare cases where the court should intervene. Strangulation in 2013, although a habituated feature of domestic assault, was rarely reported by victims to police as it did not constitute an offence, often left no corroborative marks of injury and was not recognised as an aggravating feature of domestic violence/abuse, although a prevalent method of killing in intimate partner homicide.[19]

In *Earl*,[20] the victim alleged that her boyfriend had held her head under water until she lost consciousness. The police, having attended the scene, reported that they had been called to the house at 11.30 pm and found the victim naked, curled up on the floor of the bathroom with marks to her neck and hair floating in the bath water. The CPS decided against a prosecution for assault occasioning actual bodily harm because the complainant withdrew her support, and the prosecution accepted a guilty plea to common assault. The court noted:

At the first hearing, the Crown Prosecution Service did not proceed with that charge because the complainant no longer supported the prosecution. Pausing there, that is not an unusual circumstance in cases of domestic abuse. The learned judge characterised the decision of the Crown Prosecution Service as 'pusillanimous'.[21]

---

[14] Cited in *Caetano v Commissioner of Police of the Metropolis* [2013] EWHC 375 (Admin)) [33], with reference to CPS Policy for Prosecuting Cases of Domestic Violence 2009 [2.1] https://equation.org.uk/wp-content/uploads/2012/12/CPS-Policy-for-Prosecuting-cases-of-Domestic-Violence.pdf (accessed 5 January 2022).

[15] [2011] 1 WLR 433.

[16] ibid 441 [21].

[17] *Yemshaw* (n 15) [27].

[18] [2013] EWHC 375 (Admin).

[19] Susan Edwards, 'Abolishing Provocation and Reframing Self-Defence: The Law Commission Options for Reform' (2004) *Crim LR* 181; see Tables 1, 2, and 3.

[20] [2014] EWCA Crim 261.

[21] ibid [2], [3].

ii. Definitions: 'Domestic Abuse'

By 2015, the term and definition of 'domestic abuse' was given statutory approval, recognising the wider context and characteristics of domestic violence as abusive conduct in its own right. Section 76 of the SCA introduced the offence of 'coercive and controlling conduct' defined as 'a continuing act or a pattern of acts of assault, threats, humiliation, and intimidation or other abuse that is used to harm, punish, or frighten their victim and acts to control isolating them from family and friends'.[22] Coercive and controlling conduct' must be repeated or continuous (s 76(4)), and cause the victim to fear on at least two occasions that violence will be used, or else is such as to cause serious alarm or distress and has a substantial serious effect on day-to-day activities. The alleged perpetrator must know their behaviour will have a serious effect. The offence carries a sentence on summary conviction of up to twelve months' imprisonment and on indictment of up to five years. Statutory guidance sets out examples of the types of evidence anticipated which include for example: isolating a person from their friends and family; depriving them of their basic needs; monitoring their time and online communication.

Such coercive and controlling conduct has long been part of a wider pattern of violent and abusive conduct. Hedda Nussbaum,[23] the victim of physical abuse from partner Joel Steinberg, was beaten by him with a broomstick handle, a metal exercise bar, had her teeth knocked out several times, suffered a broken nose, had her hair pulled out, had her ribs broken and required a splenectomy. In her evidence she also described his controlling behaviour and how she had to ask him for permission to eat and drink, bathe, and go to the bathroom. Kiranjit Ahluwalia, who in self-defence killed a violent and abusive husband, had written a letter to her husband which was submitted in evidence at her trial. It demonstrated her coerced and subjugated state under his control:

> Deepak, if you come back, I promise you I won't touch black coffee again, I won't go town every week, I won't eat green chilli, I ready to leave Chandikah and all my friends, I won't go near Der Goodie Mohan's house again. Even I am not going to attend Bully's wedding ... I won't laugh if you don't like, I won't dye my hair even, I don't go to my neighbour's house, I won't ask you for any help.[24]

By 2018, 'domestic abuse' was also recognised in the Domestic Abuse Definitive Sentencing Guideline.[25] The Guideline stated: 'Domestic abuse is rarely a one-off incident, and it is the cumulative and interlinked physical, psychological, sexual, emotional or financial abuse that has a particularly damaging effect on the victims and those around them.'[26] In *Dewhurst*,[27] the appellant was convicted of assault, common assault, and coercive behaviour, which included keeping the victim hostage, telling her she was worthless, head-butting, and

---

[22] See 'Controlling or coercive behaviour in an intimate or family relationship: Statutory Guidance 2015' 3–4 https://www.gov.uk/government/publications/statutory-guidance-framework-controlling-or-coercive-behaviour-in-an-intimate-or-family-relationship (accessed 5 January 2022).

[23] *People v Steinberg* 79 NY2d 673 (1992).

[24] *R v Ahluwalia* [1992] 4 All ER 892h.

[25] Sentencing Council Overarching Principles Sentencing Guideline, 2 https://www.sentencingcouncil.org.uk/wp-content/uploads/6.4143_SC_Domestic_Abuse_Paper_WEB.pdf (accessed 5 January 2022).

[26] ibid 3.

[27] *R v Dewhurst* [2021] EWCA Crim 663. See also *R v LMM* [2020] EWCA Crim 1614 [3]; *R v Widdows* [2011] EWCA Crim 1500; *R v Conlon (Robert Joseph)* [2017] EWCA Crim 2450; *R v Qais Iftikhar Ahmed* [2020] EWCA Crim 1646.

threatening her with a weapon and taking control of her phone and Facebook account. He received a sentence of three years and four months' imprisonment, which was upheld on appeal. In the family courts in *H-N* the court recognised: 'It is now accepted without reservation that it is possible to be a victim of controlling or coercive behaviour or threatening behaviour without ever sustaining a physical injury.'[28] When the DAA was being debated in the Commons at the Bill stage, Rosie Duffield MP[29] spoke of her experience of being in a relationship marked by coercion and control that left her continuously fearful.

iii. Definitions: Domestic Abuse—'Control and Coercion'

Section 1 of the DAA builds on the understanding of coercive conduct set out in the SCA and recognises domestic abuse as a process and pattern of behaviour rather than a single incident and establishes a statutory definition which includes physical, sexual, threatening, coercive, psychological, economic, and financial abuse (see further s 1 of the Act in Part II of this Guide).[30] The statutory guidance provides examples of financial abuse which includes the control of finances, such as only allowing a person a punitive allowance.[31] 'Dowry abuse' is for example also such a form of abuse.[32] Unnecessary and vexatious litigation is also used as a weapon of domestic abuse through exerting control and coercion on a partner or former partner, for example by obstructing financial settlement and continually challenging financial schedules of shared assets. In family matters regarding 'child arrangements orders' (s 8 Children Act 1989) the abusive party also uses litigation to control and coerce. Section 67 of the DAA places a statutory restriction on such vexatious litigation by amendment to section 91(14) of the Children Act (CA) 1989, adding section 91(A) requiring the court to consider any risk of harm to a child or an individual and any change of circumstances before making an order[33] (see further s 67 of the Act in Part II of this Guide).

'Controlling or coercive behaviour' (DAA, s 1(3)(c))[34] between those who are 'personally connected' (see further s 1 Part II of this Guide) may be part of any form of abuse and part of a pattern of behaviour which often, but not always, includes violence. For the purpose of a specific crime under section 76(1)(a) of the SCA 'controlling or coercive conduct' must be repeated or continuous. DAA s 2 extends the groups of parties protected within the definition of 'personally connected' set out in SCA s 76(2)(b) by removing the requirement for

[28] *Re H-N and Others (children) (domestic abuse: finding of fact hearings)* [2021] EWCA Civ 448 [27].

[29] See Rosie Duffield MP on her experience of domestic abuse https://www.youtube.com/watch?v=D2hqzC4-YYc (accessed 5 January 2022).

[30] See Elissa Da Costa-Waldman, 'Economic abuse: its impact on financial remedy cases and how to manage it' (2022) (Nov) *Fam Law* 1394.

[31] See 'Controlling or coercive behaviour' (n 2) 3. See also 'Domestic abuse draft statutory guidance' (2021) https://assets.publishing.service.gov.uk/government/uploads/system/uploads/attachment_data/file/1007814/draft-da-statutory-guidance-2021-final.pdf (accessed 5 January 2022).

[32] Hanisha Patel and Jasvinder Sanghera, 'Dowry abuse' [2009] *Fam Law* 1092. See also *R S (AP) v The Secretary of State for the Home Department* [2011] CSOH 6 2011 WL 197251. CPS, 'Policy on Prosecuting Cases of Domestic Violence' https://www.cps.gov.uk/legal-guidance/domestic-abuse (accessed 5 January 2022).

[33] For a contrary view see eg *Re C3 and C4 (Child Arrangements)* [2019] EWHC B14 (Fam), where Keehan J concluded that: 'there is no authority to support the principle that a non-molestation injunction can be made to prevent a parent commencing litigation: that is solely the purpose and objective of s. 91(4) of the Children Act 1989'. The applicant's application was dismissed. Cited by Martha Holmes, 'Non-molestation orders revisited' [2021] *Fam Law* 866.

[34] 'Controlling or coercive behaviour' (n 22).

parties to be 'living together'. 'Personally connected' does not include carers of disabled persons who are not related. At the Bill stage, pressure to include such carers within the definition was rejected.[35] Pressure to include this group and extend protection to disabled persons continues to be a matter for needed reform.

iv. Children

Section 1(3) recognises children as victims of domestic abuse if they witness by seeing, hearing, or experiencing the abuse where section 1(2)(a) the person is a parent of, or has parental responsibility for, the child, or (b) the child and the person are relatives.[36] This extends the provision in section 31 of the CA, following the amendment in section 120 of the Adoption and Children Act 2002 (ACA), which recognises that witnessing domestic abuse may result in 'significant harm' to the child concerned (see further s 1(3) Part II of this Guide).

3. THE NUMERICAL EXTENT OF DOMESTIC VIOLENCE AND ABUSE

The actual prevalence of domestic violence and abuse year on year is difficult to determine as such data is impacted by the willingness of victims/survivors to report and police recording practices and data collection and changes to definitions over the years.

i. Non-fatal Violence and Abuse

a. *'Domestic abuse-related incidents and crimes'*
For the year ending March 2021, the police recorded, 1,459,663 'domestic abuse-related incidents and crimes' in England and Wales. This category includes crimes and also cases where there is no discernible crime.[37] In earlier years, for example, a domestic incident not considered as a crime or otherwise unlikely to proceed to prosecution would have more likely been recorded in the police incident report book and not officially logged. For example, Edwards' London Study at Hounslow and Holloway police stations for 1985 found out of 773 crimed cases of domestic violence examined, only sixteen resulted in police initiating a criminal prosecution all of which did not necessarily proceed to trial.[38] Of the 2021 figures, 845,734 were 'domestic abuse-related crimes'[39] including violence against the person, sexual offences, criminal damage, and arson. These offences and incidents show an increase over the previous year (2020) when 1,288,018 'domestic abuse-related incidents and crimes' and

---

[35] See Domestic Abuse Bill vol 692, col 519 (15 April 2021) https://hansard.parliament.uk/commons/2021-04-15/debates/0E322BD7-571C-4DC5-A8C8-7B29806DE067/DomesticAbuseBill (accessed 20 January 2022).

[36] *Re A (Supervised Contact Order: Assessment of Impact of Domestic Violence)* [2015] EWCA Civ 48.

[37] Domestic abuse prevalence and trends, England and Wales: year ending March 2021 Domestic Abuse and Victim Characteristics 2 Main points https://www.ons.gov.uk/peoplepopulationandcommunity/crimeandjustice/articles/domesticabuseprevalenceandtrendsenglandandwales/yearendingmarch2021 (accessed 20 January 2022).

[38] See Edwards (n 1) chs 3, 4, cited in Police Monitoring Group Briefing Paper No 1 'Police Response to Domestic Violence' London Strategic Policy Unit (1986) 40.

[39] See 'Domestic abuse prevalence and trends' (n 37).

758,941 'domestic abuse-related crimes' were recorded.[40] The victim was female in 73 per cent of domestic abuse-related crimes in the year ending March 2021. Of those domestic abuse-related crimes proceeded with 4,354 (9 per cent) involved female suspects and 50,090 (91 per cent) male suspects.[41]

With regard to controlling and coercive conduct, 33,954 offences were recorded in the year ending March 2021, compared with 24,856 for the year ending March 2020 and 17,616 for the year ending March 2019.[42] The rise in coercive control offences over recent years may be attributed to improvements by police in recognising incidents of coercive control and in the application of section 76 of the SCA 2015. However, case attrition remains a significant concern with only 1,403 prosecutions commenced in the magistrates' court for the year ending March 2021[43] and 374 convictions for the year ending March 2020.[44]

Turning to the more specific category of 'domestic abuse related violence against the person', the police recorded 672,912 offences for the year ending March 2021[45] compared with, 327,565 offences year ending March 2016. It is significant to note that of all violence against the person offences recorded in 2021, 37.8 per cent were domestic related.

b. *Unreliability of police data*

Police recorded statistics can only provide a very rough estimate of the prevalence of domestic violence and abuse. Many victims/survivors do not report to police for reasons of fear of further abuse, distrust of police (only increased by recent police misconduct and crimes against women), financial dependency on the aggressor, hopelessness and entrapment amongst other factors.[46] In addition, the several measures used, the stages of the process recorded, changes in recording practices and divers other variables examined across the datasets make prevalence and trends difficult to interpret and any new legislation and policy difficult to evaluate and call to account.

---

[40] Domestic abuse prevalence and trends, England and Wales: year ending March 2020. NB (statistics excluding Greater Manchester Police) 1 https://www.ons.gov.uk/peoplepopulationandcommunity/crimeandjustice/articles/domesticabuseprevalenceandtrendsenglandandwales/yearendingmarch2020 (accessed 20 January 2022).

[41] See Domestic abuse prevalence and victim characteristics, England and Wales: year ending March 2021. 2. Main points and Table 8: Proportion of domestic abuse related crimes recorded by the police by sex of victim. Domestic abuse prevalence and victim characteristics—Office for National Statistics (ons.gov.uk) https://www.ons.gov.uk/peoplepopulationandcommunity/crimeandjustice/datasets/domesticabuseprevalenceandvictimcharacteristicsappendixtables (accessed 30 October 2022).

[42] See 'Domestic abuse prevalence and trends' (n 37) 5.

[43] See 'Domestic abuse and the criminal justice system' (2021) Table 1: Number of arrests, arrest rate and voluntary attendances for domestic abuse-related crimes and child protection referrals for domestic abuse-related incidents and crimes, by police force area, England and Wales, year ending March 2021. Table 15: Number of controlling and coercive offences that reached a first hearing in the magistrate's court https://www.ons.gov.uk/peoplepopulationandcommunity/crimeandjustice/datasets/domesticabuseandthecriminaljusticesystemappendixtables (accessed 20 January 2022).

[44] ibid Table 16. Criminal justice outcomes for engaging in controlling or coercive behaviour in an intimate or family relationship, England and Wales, year ending December 2020.

[45] https://www.ons.gov.uk/peoplepopulationandcommunity/crimeandjustice/datasets/domesticabuseprevalenceandvictimcharacteristicsappendixtables Table 3: Number of domestic abuse-related violence against the person offences recorded by the police and percentage of violence against the person offences that were domestic abuse-related, by police force area, England and Wales, year ending March 2016 to year ending March 2021. (For 2021 only) (accessed 3 May 2022).

[46] 'Domestic Abuse Draft Statutory Guidance Framework' (n 31) 35 [88].

The vagaries of police recording practice over the decades is illustrated in this following example. With regard to 'domestic violence incidents and crimes' recorded by the police, until the last two decades, police forces submitted for official record only those cases that proceeded to a prosecution since only these cases could be resulted by them as having been 'cleared up' (the 'clear up' rate being a key performance indicator). Clear up rates were and still are interpreted as a measure of police performance and therefore politically malleable. Since victims/survivors of domestic violence were reluctant to support a prosecution because of fear of further abuse any initial recording of such incidents as crimes impacted on police 'clear up' rates. The prospect of a low clear up rate was circumvented by police either not recording such cases or else declassifying cases initially made the subject of a crime report by using the 'no crime' classification resulting in discontinuance by removing offences from the official record, thus distorting the true reported crime statistic.[47] For the year 1985, the Metropolitan police (MPD) reported only approximately 384 domestic violence cases as crimes to the Home Office statistics department (then C3).[48] Edwards' research found that this figure represented approximately only 5 per cent of domestic violence cases originally made the subject of a crime report.[49] In 1998, improvements in police response and reduced use of the 'no crime' classification resulted in 38,465 'domestic violence crimes' being recorded,[50] rising to 75,982, in 2021.[51]

Notwithstanding, yearly trends provide some indicator of fluctuations in criminal behaviour, the impact of legislation and policing and prosecution practice and initiatives.

c. *The Crime Survey for England and Wales (CSEW)*

The Crime Survey for England and Wales (CSEW), includes recorded crime from police, from a number of several different organisations and also from the victim survey (formerly known as the household survey). The CSEW[52] is considered to provide a more accurate and reliable picture of long-term trends in crime and in domestic violence/abuse. The victim survey component was introduced due to victim reluctance to report crimes including domestic violence to police and an under recording by police of cases of domestic violence/abuse reported to them.

---

47 See Susan Edwards, 'Violence Against Women: feminism and the law' in Lorraine Gelsthorpe and Alison Morris (eds), *Feminist Perspectives in Criminology* (Open University Press 1990) 157. Susan Edwards, 'Domestic violence and sexual assault' in Mike Stephens and Saul Becker (eds), *Police Force Police Service* (Macmillan 1994) 131, 135. Susan Edwards, *Sex and Gender in the Legal Process* (Blackstone Press Limited 1996) 200–201.

48 Edwards (n 1) reports 384 for 1985.The Police Monitoring Group Briefing Paper No 1 'Police Response to Domestic Violence' London Strategic Policy Unit (1986) 13 cites Edwards' research.

49 Edwards (n 1) ch 4.

50 See Susan Edwards, 'New directions in prosecution' in Julie Taylor-Browne *What works in reducing domestic violence?* (Whiting and Birch 2000). Followed Home Office circular 60/1990 and introduction of minimum standards of operational performance Metropolitan Police Service 1996 p. 218.

51 Op cit. n. 45. Table 3: Number of domestic abuse-related violence against the person offences recorded by the police and percentage of violence against the person offences that were domestic abuse-related, by police force area, England and Wales, year ending March 2016 to year ending March 2021 [n 1]. https://www.ons.gov.uk/peoplepopulationandcommunity/crimeandjustice/datasets/domesticabuseprevalenceandvictimcharacteristicsappendixtables

52 See https://www.ons.gov.uk/peoplepopulationandcommunity/crimeandjustice/bulletins/crimeinenglandandwales/yearendingseptember2021 (accessed 20 January 2022).

For year ending March 2018,[53] 1.23 million women and 695,000 men were recorded as experiencing 'domestic abuse incidents and crimes' rising to 1.6 million women and 757,000 males (n=2.3 million) year ending March 2020.[54] These are the latest figures because the crime survey could not conduct face to face interviews during Covid-19. This is a much higher figure than that found in police statistics of 1,288,018 (see above). Some of this yearly increase is attributable to the Covid-19 pandemic[55] and the impact of lock down where victims/survivors had less opportunity to leave abusive partners and abuse intensified.

ii. Recording Intimate Partner Homicide

Domestic 'violence' may result in homicide. Since 1980, at least, homicide of female intimate partners in England and Wales accounted for approximately 20 per cent of all homicides. More recently on average, two women are killed each week by a current or former partner.[56] This statistic has been relatively static for several decades. For year ending March 2016 to the year ending March 2018,[57] (three years) 216 females and three males were killed by a male intimate partner/former partner. By comparison, forty males and one female were killed by a female intimate partner/former partner. There is, however, a significant difference in the background context of male on female and female on male intimate partner homicide. When men kill female intimate partners it is frequently an escalation of prior violence and abuse. When women kill male partners, it more likely arises from self-defensive efforts to survive a partner's coercion and violence.[58]

The real risk to a woman's life is from being killed in the home from a man they know. For the year ending March 2020, 46 per cent of all adult female homicide victims were killed by an intimate partner (n=81).[59] For the year ending March

[53] Domestic Abuse in England and Wales: Year Ending March 2018, Office for National Statistics (22 November 2018) Main pointshttps://www.ons.gov.uk/peoplepopulationandcommunity/crimeandjustice/bulletins/domesticabuseinenglandandwales/yearendingmarch2018(accessed 20 January 2022).

[54] See Domestic abuse in England and Wales overview (November 2020) https://www.ons.gov.uk/peoplepopulationandcommunity/crimeandjustice/bulletins/domesticabuseinenglandandwalesoverview/november2020 . Main points. See also at 24 https://assets.publishing.service.gov.uk/government/uploads/system/uploads/attachment_data/file/1013128/Domestic_homicides_and_suspected_victim_suicides_during_the_Covid-19_Pandemic_2020-2021.pdf (accessed 20 January 2022).

[55] See Family Court Statistics Quarterly (April–June 2020) Main point 1 https://www.gov.uk/government/statistics/family-court-statistics-quarterly-april-to-june-2020/family-court-statistics-quarterly-april-to-june-2020 (accessed 20 April 2022).

[56] See Office for National Statistics, Crime Statistics, Focus on Violent Crime and Sexual Offences, 'Year ending March 2016' ch 2: Homicide (2016) https://www.ons.gov.uk/peoplepopulationandcommunity/crimeandjustice/compendium/focusonviolentcrimeandsexualoffences/yearendingmarch2016 (accessed 26 April 2022).

[57] Dataset-Domestic abuse prevalence and victim characteristics. Tables 22 link to Table 18: Relationship of victim to principal suspect in domestic homicides of adults aged 16 and over, by type of relationship and sex, England and Wales, year ending March 2018 to the year ending March 2020 combined https://www.ons.gov.uk/peoplepopulationandcommunity/crimeandjustice/datasets/domesticabuseprevalenceandvictimcharacteristicsappendixtables (accessed 20 January 2022).

[58] See Centre for Women's Justice, 'Women Who Kill' https://www.centreforwomensjustice.org.uk/women-who-kill. The methodology involved 20 case studies following interviews with women who had killed abusive partners, court transcripts, interviews with counsel and legal practitioners. See also Sophie Howes, Katy Swaine Williams, and Harriet Wistrich, 'Women who Kill: Why Self-defense rarely works for women who kill their abuser' (2021) *Crim LR* 945.

[59] Homicide in England and Wales: year ending March 2020. See point 4 'The relationship between victims and suspects' https://www.ons.gov.uk/peoplepopulationandcommunity/crimeandjustice/articles/homici

2021,[60] this figure was 37 per cent (n=57, investigations are ongoing) and 49 per cent of adult female homicide victims were killed in a domestic homicide'.[61]

The DVCVA statutory requirement to investigate domestic homicides with a view to identifying risk and improving the response of public authorities in domestic abuse and domestic homicide prevention was the subject of much discussion at the Bill stage[62] (discussed further under DAA, s 17 in Part II of this Guide).

a. *Method of killing*

A further significant difference between these two types of homicide is the method of killing. When women are killed by men in intimate partner homicide the method of killing is gender and relationship specific where strangulation and suffocation are used to kill in nearly one third of cases. The prevalence of this method has remained fairly constant since the 1980's when method of killing in intimate partner homicide was systematically researched.[63] This method of killing is not a feature of homicide outside the intimate partner context. In 2019, around one in six (17 per cent) of all female victims of homicide were killed by 'strangulation, asphyxiation' (forty-one victims), this was the second most common method of killing for female victims. In contrast, a much smaller proportion (3 per cent) of male victims were killed in this way,[64] and in these cases there was either an accomplice or men were already incapacitated by drink or drugs prior to the killing as strangling and suffocating a victim requires considerable body force. It is to be noted that non-fatal strangulation, although a criminal offence of recent origin under section 70 of the DAA, has been a habitual feature of domestic violence and abuse and has been discussed in some of the literature for several decades prior to the DAA (discussed further in s 70 in Part II of this Guide).

---

deinenglandandwales/yearendingmarch2020 (accessed 20 January 2022). A domestic homicide is defined as an offence of murder or manslaughter where the relationship between a victim aged 16 years and over and the suspect charged falls into one of the following categories: spouse, common-law spouse, cohabiting partner, boyfriend or girlfriend, ex-spouse, ex-cohabiting partner or ex-boyfriend or girlfriend, adulterous relationship, son, or daughter (including step and adopted relationships), parent (including step and adopted relationships), sibling, other relatives.

[60] See Homicide in England and Wales: year ending March 2021. See point 4 'The relationship between victims and suspects' https://www.ons.gov.uk/peoplepopulationandcommunity/crimeandjustice/articles/homicideinenglandandwales/yearendingmarch2021 (accessed 20 January 2022).

[61] ibid. Homicide in England and Wales: year ending March 2021. See point 4. The relationship of victims to suspects. See for further detail Table 31 https://www.ons.gov.uk/peoplepopulationandcommunity/crimeandjustice/datasets/appendixtableshomicideinenglandandwales (accessed 30 April 2022).

[62] See Written evidence submitted by Frank Mullane MBE, CEO of Advocacy After Fatal Domestic Abuse (AAFDA), Registered Charity 1125973 (DAB78) to the Domestic Abuse Bill https://publications.parliament.uk/pa/cm5801/cmpublic/DomesticAbuse/memo/DAB78.htm Domestic Abuse Bill (16 June 2020) (parliament.uk). See also Home Office—Domestic Homicide Reviews—Key Findings from Analysis of Domestic Homicide Reviews https://assets.publishing.service.gov.uk/government/uploads/system/uploads/attachment_data/file/575232/HO-Domestic-Homicide-Review-Analysis-161206.pdf (accessed 20 March 2022).

[63] Edwards (n 19) Tables 1, 2, 3.

[64] Homicide in England and Wales: year ending March 2019. See point 6 'What were the most common methods of killing?' https://www.ons.gov.uk/peoplepopulationandcommunity/crimeandjustice/articles/homicideinenglandandwales/yearendingmarch2019 (accessed 20 January 2022). See also Susan Edwards, 'The Strangulation of Female Partners' (2015) 12 *Crim LR* 949. Susan S M Edwards and Heather Douglas, 'The Criminalisation of a dangerous form of coercive control : Non-fatal strangulation in England and Wales and Australia' (2021) 8(1) *Journal of International and Comparative Law* 87.

4. THE LEGISLATIVE FRAMEWORK: ENGLAND AND WALES

In recent years there has been an increasing hybridisation of criminal and civil measures designed to provide greater protection for victims of domestic violence and abuse. The DAA attempts to rationalise a complex system of remedies across civil and criminal courts especially with the amendment to the regime of domestic abuse protection notices and orders (see further ss 22–56 in Part II of this Guide).

i. Civil Remedy Orders and Trends

The civil remedies (protective orders) include non-molestation and occupation orders under sections 33 to 42 (FLA), restraining orders under section 5 (Protection from Harassment Act 1997 (PFHA) following section 12 of the DVCVA 2004, which introduced section 5A into the PHA 1997), and domestic violence protection notices (DVPNs) and orders (DVPOs) under sections 24 to 33 (Crime and Security Act (CSA) 2010). Applications for these several remedies have been increasing each year. The domestic abuse protection notices (DAPNs) and domestic abuse protection orders (DAPOs) under DAA ss 22 to 48 will supersede these remedies following the piloting in a number of areas across England and Wales of the DAPN and DAPO. The pilot is expected to commence in 2023 and will run for approximately two years ahead of national roll-out (see further ss 22–56 in Part II of this Guide).

a. *Non-molestation and occupation orders*

Non-molestation order The non-molestation order (NMO), issued under the FLA s 42 prohibits a party from behaving towards another in a way that amounts to 'molestation'. The courts have defined 'molestation' to include threats, vexatious behaviour, stalking, and harassment. Conditions of exclusion from a certain area etc., can also be attached to these orders. However, Bates and Hester[65] found that evidence of physical molestation still continues to be prioritised in the decision to grant such applications. The court in its consideration of an application must have regard to all the circumstances of the case, including the need to secure the health (physical or mental), safety, and well-being of the applicant and any relevant child (s 42(5)).

When considering an ex parte, without notice, application the court must consider 'any risk of significant harm to the applicant or a relevant child, attributable to conduct of the respondent, if the order is not made immediately' (s 45(2)(a)).[66] Ex parte orders are particularly draconian on the respondent. Mr Justice Mostyn asserted: 'It has been stated time and again that ex parte relief of this nature must be very much the exception rather than the rule because it offends a fundamental principle of natural justice which is that judicial decisions should be made after having heard both sides.'[67]

[65] Lis Bates and Marianne Hester, 'No longer a civil matter? The design and use of protection orders for domestic violence in England and Wales' (2020) 42(2) *Journal of Social Welfare and Family Law* 133, 145.

[66] See *JM v CZ* [2014] EWHC 1125 (Fam).

[67] *Re W (Minors)* [2016] EWHC 2226 (Fam).

Ex parte orders are to be listed for a return hearing within 14 days of the application so as to allow the other party, to give his/her version.[68] However, this is not happening in many cases and research needs to be conducted on this point as my Freedom of Information Act (FOIA) 2000 request[69] revealed that the Ministry of Justice (MoJ) does not collate information on return hearings.

Furthermore, the respondent is not entitled to legal aid and therefore in many cases will be unable to contest the allegations made. This is concerning because confidence in ex parte remedies requires fairness to both parties. The DVCVA 2004 creates a criminal sanction for breach of a non-molestation order.[70]

Occupation order An occupation order (OO) (ss 33–41 FLA) allows for removal of an alleged abuser from the home for a period. Further conditions and terms may be attached including placing restriction on movement, for example, prohibiting him/her from being in the vicinity of the residence of the victim. When considering applications for occupation orders and ousting a party from the home the 'balance of harm' test applies and section 33(7) requires the 'significant harm' suffered by the applicant to be as great or greater than the harm to the other party from being excluded. In balancing the applicant's need for safety and protection against the other party's right to residence consideration must be given to housing needs, financial resources, and the likely effect of any order on the health, safety or well-being of the parties and 'the conduct of the parties in relation to each other and otherwise' (s 33(6)(d)). In *Chalmers v Johns*,[71] refusing an occupation order for exclusion, Thorpe LJ asserted: '[t]he order remains draconian, particularly in the perception of the respondent. It remains an order that overrides proprietary rights and it seems to me that it is an order that is only justified in exceptional circumstances.'[72] Orders may be made for a duration of up to twelve months.

b. *Trends in non-molestation and occupation orders*

In 2020, 35,984 applications were made in the family court for domestic abuse remedies (including non-molestation and occupation orders), and 39,427 orders were granted.[73] (Note that the number of orders granted do not necessarily correspond to applications made in any given period.) This reflects an increase on 2019[74] when 29,877 applications were made,

[68] See Practice Guidance Family Court: Duration of Ex Parte (Without Notice) Orders (18 January 2017) https://www.judiciary.uk/wp-content/uploads/2017/01/pfd-practice-guidance-ex-parte-orders.pdf (accessed 30 January 2022). The author is pursuing this point under a FOI request.

[69] FOI Request 220401011 (1 April 2022).

[70] Breach of a protective order (restraining and non-molestation orders): Sentencing (sentencingcouncil.org.uk) https://www.sentencingcouncil.org.uk/offences/magistrates-court/item/breach-of-a-protective-order-restraining-and-non-molestation-orders/ (accessed 30 January 2022).

[71] *Chalmers v Johns* [1999] 1 FLR 392.

[72] ibid.

[73] Family Court Statistics Quarterly, England and Wales (October–December 2020). See 9: 'Domestic violence remedy orders' Figure 7 https://www.gov.uk/government/statistics/family-court-statistics-quarterly-october-to-december-2020/family-court-statistics-quarterly-october-to-december-2020 (accessed 30 January 2022).

[74] Family Court Statistics Quarterly, England and Wales (October–December 2019). See 2019 Annual trends s 7, 14. https://assets.publishing.service.gov.uk/government/uploads/system/uploads/attachment_data/file/874822/FCSQ_October_to_December_final.pdf (accessed 30 January 2022).

and 33,671 orders were granted. In 2018,[75] 25,135 applications were made compared with 24,912 in 2017.[76]

Non-molestation applications and orders granted Applications for non-molestation orders alone increased year ending March 2021, to 30,943, from 25,167 applications for March 2020, 21,218 for 2019, and 20,406 applications for the year ending March 2018.[77] The number of orders granted rose similarly with 38,349 for the year ending March 2021, 32,070 orders for the year ending March 2020, 27,911 orders for the year ending March 2019, and 26,381 orders for the year ending March 2018.[78] In 2020, where the gender was recorded there were 33,649 female and 3,190 male applicants for non-molestation orders and 1,993 female and 318 male applications for occupation orders.[79]

Ex parte orders are recorded in a different data set according to calendar year and so the numbers of orders are not directly comparable. Of all non-molestation order applications for January to December 2020 (n=29,856), 87 per cent, (n=26,058) were made ex parte, and of all ex parte applications (16,808), 65 per cent were granted.[80] The proportion of ex parte applications made and the proportion granted does not reflect Mr Justice Mostyn's remark (noted above) that such orders should be the exception, or else this proportion reflects the seriousness of the evidence in cases where an application is made. This compares with 2011, when 85 per cent (13,737) of non-molestation order applications (16,135) were ex parte and of those ex parte applications 84 per cent (11,484) were granted. In 1998,[81] 62 per cent of all non-molestation applications were ex parte.

Occupation applications and orders granted Whilst applications for occupation orders have increased year on year, the number of orders granted during that time has remained fairly

[75] Family Court Statistics Quarterly, England and Wales, Annual 2018, including October to December 2018. See Main points 7 (Please note orders granted are not given in figures so only applications given) https://assets.publishing.service.gov.uk/government/uploads/system/uploads/attachment_data/file/789792/FCSQ_October_to_December_2018_-_final.pdf#:~:text=There%20were%2064%2C331%20new%20family%20court%20cases%20in,matrimonial%20%289%25%29%20and%20Private%20law%20%288%25%29%20cases%20started (accessed 30 January 2022).

[76] Family Court Statistics Quarterly, England and Wales, Annual 2017 including October to December 2017. Main points 7 (Please note orders granted not given in figures so only applications given) https://assets.publishing.service.gov.uk/government/uploads/system/uploads/attachment_data/file/695363/family-court-stats-oct-dec-2017.pdf (accessed 30 January 2022).

[77] 'Dataset Domestic abuse and the criminal justice system' (2021) Table 18: Number of applications and orders made for domestic violence remedies https://www.ons.gov.uk/peoplepopulationandcommunity/crimeandjustice/datasets/domesticabuseandthecriminaljusticesystemappendixtables (accessed 30 January 2022).

[78] ibid.

[79] Dataset Domestic abuse and the criminal justice system 2021 (n 77) Table 19: Number of domestic violence orders in Family Courts by gender of applicant.

[80] Family Court Tables. This data set provides ex parte data. Table 16: Applications and Orders for Domestic Violence Remedies Annually and quarterly. https://www.gov.uk/government/statistics/family-court-statistics-quarterly-july-to-september-2021). See https://view.officeapps.live.com/op/view.aspx?src=https%3A%2F%2Fassets.publishing.service.gov.uk%2Fgovernment%2Fuploads%2Fsystem%2Fuploads%2Fattachment_data%2Ffile%2F1041006%2FFamily_Court_Tables__Jul_to_Sep_2021_.ods&wdOrigin=BROWSELINK (accessed 30 January 2022).

[81] Lord Chancellor's Department Judicial statistics, cited in Edwards, 'Domestic violence and harassment: An assessment of the civil remedies' (n 47) 187–210 in Julie Taylor-Browne, *What Works in Reducing Domestic Violence?* (Whiting and Birch 2000).

static. Applications numbered 5,993 for the year ending March 2021, 5,551 for the year ending March 2020, 4,866 for the year ending March 2019, and 4,629 for the year ending 2018. Orders granted numbered 2,384 year ending March 2021, 2,525 for 2020, 2,346 for 2019, and 2,313 for 2018, respectively.[82]

Considering ex parte applications and orders for the calendar year 2020, of all occupation order applications (6,129), 72 per cent (4,412) were ex parte, and of all ex parte occupation orders applied for only 7 per cent (292) were granted, maintaining a consistently low percentage granted over the last years.[83] Compared to 2011, when 3,577 orders were applied for ex parte 29 per cent (1,034) were granted, reflecting the increasingly held view that ex parte orders, occupation orders especially, are draconian.[84]

c. *Limitations of non-molestation and occupation orders: commentary*

These remedies are limited, and unless made ex parte, victim/survivor safety is compromised by waiting for a court hearing. ACPO noted 'there is no readily available, consistent, affordable and timely access to the civil orders at this risky time'.[85] In addition, there are recognised problems with enforcement with some police forces failing to accurately record non-molestation orders.[86] Available data shows a wide regional variation which defies a simple explanation of geographical prevalence. For example, Wales recorded some 515 orders, the southwest region 3,884, and London 6,472, for the year ending March 2021.[87]

Research by Bates and Hester[88] report that during lockdown there were problems with personal service and a judicial divergence of opinion around the country about what amounted to proper service such that the Family Procedure Rules committee made recommendations that have been incorporated into Practice Direction 36U, which came into effect on 3 August 2020 (due to cease to have effect on 3 May 2021). This clarifies that the court can order an alternative method of service of both applications and orders under Part Four of FLA.

The lack of immediate protection, delay in court hearings and, in the courtroom, the ongoing control by an alleged aggressor in cross-examination of the victim/survivor has deterred many from seeking remedy. The potential for litigation control by coercive partners has likely increased in private law hearings where in the family courts the number of

---

82 'Dataset Domestic abuse and the criminal justice system' (n 77) Table 18: Number of applications and orders made for domestic violence remedies.

83 Family Court Tables (n 80) Table 16: Applications and Orders for Domestic Violence Remedies Annually and quarterly.

84 *G v G (Occupation Order)* [2000] 3 FCR 53; *Dolan v Corby* [2011] EWCA Civ 1664.

85 Association of Chief Police Officers ACPO, *Tackling Perpetrators of Violence Against Women and Girls—ACPO Review for the Home Secretary* (ACPO 2009) 48 [6.1.3] https://www.npcc.police.uk/documents/crime/2009/200909CRIVAW01.pdf (accessed 1 February 2022).

86 See PD 36H—Pilot Scheme Procedure for Service of Certain Protection Orders on the Police https://www.gov.uk/government/publications/pilot-practice-directions-july-2020-update (accessed 1 February 2022).

87 Domestic Abuse and the Criminal Justice System 2021 dataset, Table 2: Number of domestic violence protection notices, domestic violence protection orders and domestic violence disclosure schemes applied for and granted by police force area, England and Wales, year ending March 2021 (Note that there is a double counting in the Midlands and Southeast regions) (accessed 1 February 2022). https://www.ons.gov.uk/peoplepopulationandcommunity/crimeandjustice/datasets/domesticabuseandthecriminaljusticesystemappendixtables. See also Bates and Hester (n 65).

88 Bates and Hester (n 65).

represented applicants fell from 59 per cent in 2012 to 30 per cent[89] in 2021 prior to the DAA sections 65 and 66. For the year ending December 2020, there were 2,634 convictions for a breach of a non-molestation order and 424 defendants received a custodial sentence.[90]

The more recent rise in applications for non-molestation, occupation orders, and DVPOs is probably due to lockdown restrictions from March 2020 due to Covid-19 and the increase in domestic violence and abuse where victims have no support or routes to safety. Holmes notes that, at the time of writing, hearings are routinely dealt with remotely and in some cases initial NMOs are made on paper without a hearing.[91] Another factor influencing the rise in applications may also be attributable to victims/survivors pursuing civil rather than criminal remedies given the bail presumption 'released under investigation' (RUI), Policing and Crime Act 2017 (PCA) s 60 (under s 24A of CJA 2003), thereby removing an important protection for victims. In the year ending April 2019, an estimated 3,559 persons were released RUI[92] where the record had an element of domestic abuse, although it may not necessarily have been related to the matter for which they were released. There were 2,118 cases where there was a RUI where those arrested were arrested for at least one offence relating to 'rape' or 'sexual assault'. Research conducted by the Centre for Women's Justice (CWJ) found that in the first three months of the PCA the use of bail conditions in domestic abuse cases dropped by 65 per cent.[93]

Research into victim experiences concluded that RUI negatively impacted on a victim's safety and on feelings of safety.[94] The CWJ launched a super complaint (PCA, s 25), challenging the bail measures which placed domestic abuse victims at risk.[95] New measures to be called 'Kay's Law', after Kay Richardson was murdered by her former partner in August 2019 when he was released without bail conditions, are to be introduced under the Police, Crime, Sentencing and Courts Act 2022, making changes to pre-charge bail and the use of RUI by removing the statutory presumption to release without bail. This had also placed those accused in limbo. Sir David Amess commented during a Commons debate: 'I cannot stress too much to my Hon. Friend the Minister that the time the accused waits for a decision is a

[89] Family Court Statistics Quarterly (April–June 2021) s 7 'Legal Representation' https://www.gov.uk/government/statistics/family-court-statistics-quarterly-april-to-june-2021/family-court-statistics-quarterly-april-to-june-2021 (accessed 1 February 2022).

[90] Domestic Abuse and the Criminal Justice System 2021 dataset Table 17: Criminal justice outcomes for breach of a non-molestation order, England and Wales, year ending December 2020.

[91] Martha Holmes, 'Non-molestation orders revisited' [2021] *Fam Law* 866.

[92] Released under investigation domestic violence: Mayor's Question Time (london.gov.uk) https://www.london.gov.uk/questions/2020/0525 (accessed 5 February 2022).

[93] Further written evidence submitted by the Centre for Women's Justice (DAB08) to the Domestic Abuse Bill [2] https://publications.parliament.uk/pa/cm5801/cmpublic/DomesticAbuse/memo/DAB08.htm#:~:text=Since%20April%202017%20suspects%20are%20very%20frequently%20%E2%80%98released,domestic%20abuse%20cases%20dropped%20by%2065%25.%20%5B2%5D%203 (accessed 5 February 2022).

[94] Research into victim and suspect experiences of changes to the Policing and Crime Act 2017: Research commissioned by Her Majesty's Inspectorate of Constabulary and Fire and Rescue Services. See 19 https://www.justiceinspectorates.gov.uk/hmicfrs/wp-content/uploads/research-into-victim-suspect-experiences-changes-policing-crime-act-2017.pdf (justiceinspectorates.gov.uk). See also 'Impact of Covid-19: Women's Aid Release under investigation and pre-charge bail: The Law Society' https://www.lawsociety.org.uk/campaigns/criminal-justice/release-under-investigation (accessed 5 February 2022).

[95] CWJ, 'Domestic Abuse Bill' (11 June 2020) [6].

time when that individual suffers enormous stress and strain from all points of views ....'[96] The Justice Inspectorate's report found that a decision can take months or even years.[97]

d. *Restraining orders*

These orders are provided by section 5 of the PFHA[98] and may be made upon conviction or acquittal for any criminal offence.[99] These orders are intended to be preventative and protective and to restrain behaviour.[100] The standard of proof is the civil standard, and a court makes the order and should provide the factual basis for so doing. Additionally, the views of the victim should be considered. In some cases, a victim may not want a restraining order to be imposed on a defendant.[101] Orders may last between six and twelve months and a breach of an order is a criminal offence. Restraining orders can be issued on conviction for any offence.

As for trends in restraining orders Bates and Hester in their examination of several sources of available data note that restraining orders issued on conviction for harassment offences for 2017 numbered 6,820, for conviction for stalking offences numbered 941, on conviction for other offences numbered 11,455, and those issued on acquittal numbered 1,932, totalling 21,148 such orders, with 48 per cent of orders being breached.[102]

e. *Domestic violence protection notices (DVPNs) and domestic violence protection orders (DVPOs) and trends*

In response to the delay in NMOs securing immediate protection for victims of domestic abuse,[103] the domestic violence protection notice (DVPN) and domestic violence protection order (DVPO) was introduced by sections 24 to 33 of the Crime and Security Act 2010 (CSA), which allow police and magistrates' courts, where there is insufficient evidence to charge a perpetrator with a criminal offence, 'to remove the alleged perpetrator from the home for a short period and to prohibit the perpetrator from molesting the person for whose protection it is issued'.

The DVPO is of short duration and remains in force for between fourteen and twenty-eight days. DVPOs, otherwise than on application, can be made as an ancillary order in family

---

[96] Release under Investigation: Metropolitan Police—Hansard—UK Parliament. See col 77 per Sir David Amess, https://hansard.parliament.uk/Commons/2021-03-16/debates/FA94A466-54E2-4BCE-A66D-01F0E57732BA/ReleaseUnderInvestigationMetropolitanPolice (accessed 5 February 2022).

[97] Pre-charge bail and released under investigation: striking a balance (justiceinspectorates.gov.uk) https://www.justiceinspectorates.gov.uk/hmicfrs/wp-content/uploads/pre-charge-bail-and-released-under-investigation-striking-a-balance-1.pdf (accessed 5 February 2022).

[98] Crown Prosecution Service, 'Restraining Orders—section 5, Protection from Harassment Act 1997' (cps.gov.uk) https://www.cps.gov.uk/legal-guidance/restraining-orders-section-5-protection-harassment-act-1997 (accessed 5 February 2022).

[99] Sentencing Act 2020, s 360 https://www.legislation.gov.uk/ukpga/2020/17/contents/enacted?msclkid=a3e0e22bc60711eca3b16cbe728fd42c (accessed 27 April 2022). See also *R v Camara* [2022] EWCA Crim 542.

[100] Restraining Orders (n 98). See also *R v Major* [2010] EWCA Crim 3016); *R v Brown* [2012] EWCA Crim 1152; *R v Pearson* [2021] EWCA Crim 784; *R v Khellaf (Bilal)* [2016] EWCA Crim 1297; *R v Garratt* [2021] EWCA Crim 814; *R v Litwinko (Piotr)* (2016) [2016] EWCA Crim 74.

[101] *R v Brown* [2012] EWCA Crim 1152.

[102] Bates and Hester (n 65) 142.

[103] Home Office Consultation Paper, 'Together We Can End Violence Against Women and Girls', which prioritised the need to ensure the safety of women and girls https://www.refworld.org/pdfid/4b13a3472.pdf (accessed 5 February 2022).

(s 31(2)), criminal (s 31(3)), and civil proceedings (s 31(4) CSA).[104] However, this remedy is limited.[105] First, an[106] officer of the rank of superintendent is authorised to 'issue' the original DVPN[107] which is impractical. The twenty-eight-day limitation on the DVPO also leaves applicants little time to secure further protection through applications for other longer-term orders. There is no criminal sanction for any breach of the order but a breach would constitute a civil contempt of court, although a power of arrest exists for both a breach of a DVPN and a DVPO.

Trends in domestic violence protection notices (DVPNs) and domestic violence protection orders (DVPOs) For the year ending March 2020, 4,468 DVPNs were issued and 6,267 DVPOs granted[108] and rising for the year ending March 2021 to 10,046 DVPNs issued and 7,995 DVPOs granted.[109] Year ending March 2022, 11,336 DVPNs were issued and 10,167 DVPOs granted.[110] This very significant leap in notices and orders granted from 2020 to 2021 suggests the potential of a real increase in applications but also reflects a more accurate collection of data by police forces and an enhanced understanding by police of police powers to protect in domestic abuse situations. However, there is wide variability in use of these orders across the regions. The Metropolitan Police issued 1,771 notices, Greater Manchester 608, South Yorkshire 775, while Hertfordshire issued thirteen notices.[111] Wiltshire, which was part of the original domestic violence protection pilot, issued thirty-one notices.[112] Police use of these notices and orders clearly requires further qualitative interpretation alongside orders under the FLA (above).

f. *Limitations of DVPNs and DVPOs: commentary*

In reviewing the several limitations of these notices and orders, the DAA ss 22–49, repeals the DVPN and DVPO by introducing a Domestic Abuse Protection Notice (DAPN) and a Domestic Abuse Protection Order (DAPO) changing the nomenclature from 'violence' to

[104] Claire Bessant, 'Protecting Victims of Domestic Violence—Have We Got the Balance Right?' (2015) 79(2) *Journal of Criminal Law* 102.

[105] Domestic violence protection notices (DVPNs) and domestic violence protection orders (DVPOs) guidance—GOV.UK (www.gov.uk) https://www.gov.uk/government/publications/domestic-violence-protection-orders/domestic-violence-protection-notices-dvpns-and-domestic-violence-protection-orders-dvpos-guidance-sections-24-33-crime-and-security-act-2010 (accessed 5 February 2022).

[106] Domestic violence protection notices (DVPNs) and Domestic Violence Protection Orders (DVPOs) Guidance, ss 24–33 Crime and Security Act 2010 December 2016 https://assets.publishing.service.gov.uk/government/uploads/system/uploads/attachment_data/file/575363/DVPO_guidance_FINAL_3.pdf (accessed 5 February 2022).

[107] Charlotte Bishop, 'Prevention and protection: will the Domestic Abuse Act transform the response to domestic abuse in England and Wales?' [2021] *Child and Family Law Quarterly* 163.

[108] Domestic Abuse Protection Notices/Orders factsheet—gov.uk (www.gov.uk) Domestic Abuse Protection Notices/Orders factsheet—gov.uk key facts (Data from 25 forces for DVPN's and data from 37 forces for DVPOs.) (www.gov.uk). https://www.gov.uk/government/publications/domestic-abuse-bill-2020-factsheets/domestic-abuse-protection-notices-orders-factsheet (accessed 12 February 2022).

[109] 'Domestic abuse and the criminal justice system' (ons.gov.uk) Table 2: Number of domestic violence protection notices, domestic violence protection orders and domestic violence disclosure schemes applied for and granted by police force area, England and Wales for the year ending March 2021, https://www.ons.gov.uk/peoplepopulationandcommunity/crimeandjustice/datasets/domesticabuseandthecriminaljusticesystemappendixtables.

[110] ibid for the year 2022 'Domestic abuse and the criminal justice system' (ons.gov.uk) Table 2: Number of domestic violence protection notices, domestic violence protection orders and domestic violence disclosure schemes applied for and granted by police force area, England and Wales for the year ending March 2022.

[111] ibid Table 2: 'Number of domestic violence protection notices' for 2021.

[112] ibid.

'abuse' to reflect current thinking whilst updating the definition of those 'personally connected' to include those not living together. A DAPN can now be 'given' (this word replaces 'issued') by a senior police officer (s 22(1)) of at least the rank of inspector). It must be served personally by a constable (s 25(3)) and if it is breached a constable may arrest without warrant. The DAPO may be applied for under section 28(2) by (a) the person for whose protection the order is sought; (b) the appropriate chief officer of police; (c) a person specified by regulation from the Secretary of State; (d) any other person with leave of the court, and can be applied for in the civil, family, and criminal courts. Section 38 places no limit on its duration.

Unlike the earlier DVPOs, section 36(1) establishes further and new considerations for the court when making a DAPO: '(1) Requirements imposed on a person by a domestic abuse protection order—must, as far as practicable, be such as to avoid—(a) conflict with the person's religious beliefs; (b) interference with the person's work or with the person's attendance at an educational establishment; (c) conflict with the requirements of any other court order or injunction to which the person may be subject.'

The interpretation of 'as far as is practicable' leaves much discretion to the courts' consideration of the human rights obligations of the respondent. Hester and Bates from their research found that women value NMOs over DAPOs as NMOs allow them some control over the process. The Home Office in 2019 announced that DAPNs and DAPOs were intended to replace NMOs and OOs in domestic abuse cases. (See further and detailed discussion on sections 22–56 in Part II of this Guide.)

g. *Special measures civil*

DAA, sections 63 and 64 provide for a special measures direction in family or civil proceedings where a party or witness to the proceedings is, or is at risk of being, a victim of domestic abuse. DAA s 65(1)(2) and section 66 prohibit the alleged perpetrator from putting questions to the victim/survivor with regard to allegations made.[113] Both measures will have a significant impact on supporting victims/survivors and encouraging them to pursue civil remedies (discussed further in ss 62–67 in Part II of this Guide).

ii. Criminal Remedies, Sanctions, and Trends

The legal sanctions and remedies available in circumstances of domestic violence/abuse related conduct include homicide, murder, manslaughter, voluntary and involuntary, and gross negligence, and assault charges, including sections 47, 20, and 18 OAPA, common assault and battery (s 39 Criminal Justice Act (CJA)1988), and PHA s 4, fear of serious violence.

Until fairly recently, police and prosecutors gave insufficient consideration to domestic violence and even less consideration to domestic abuse. Professor Robert Reiner's 1985 finding that domestic violence was considered as 'not real police work'[114] insinuated at every level of the criminal justice process. The Assistant Chief Commissioner of the Metropolitan Police in 1994 proposed that domestic disputes might best be dealt with by civilians.[115] Serving

[113] Inserted into the Matrimonial and Family Proceedings Act 1984, after Pt 4A https://www.legislation.gov.uk/ukpga/1984/42/contents?msclkid=6d3352fbc60a11eca548ba44d22b1e41 (accessed 27 April 2022).

[114] Robert Reiner, *The Politics of the Police* (Harvester 1985).

[115] See Edwards, 'Domestic violence and sexual assault' (n 47) 133. See also Susan Edwards, 'Police Attitudes and Dispositions in Domestic Disputes: The London Study' (1986) *The Police Journal* 230, 238.

police officers remarked at the time: 'I am reluctant to arrest, usually because of the withdrawing. It creates a hell of a lot of work for no good reason.'[116] In the very early 1990s, the CPS declined to prosecute a police officer husband for buggery (the offence at that time) and violence against a wife on the ground that it was not in the 'public interest' to do so since the matter was 'better dealt with in the matrimonial courts'.[117]

Since that time, there have been improvements in policing and prosecution, although with some notable exceptions. In *R v A*[118] a wife was convicted for perverting the course of justice when she withdrew an allegation of rape against a husband. She pleaded not guilty to the first statement (the original allegation of rape) for which she was acquitted and pleaded guilty to perverting the course of justice regarding her second retraction statement for which she was convicted and sentenced to eight months' imprisonment. The sentence of imprisonment was subsequently quashed, and a non-custodial community-based order substituted. The Court of Appeal said, 'On the facts, the court was not entitled to interfere with the conviction.'[119]

Improvements in judicial understanding[120] and sentencing in domestic violence cases are noted.[121] For example, in both the criminal and family courts domestic violence and abuse is now understood as a pattern of behaviour rather than one incident. In *H v N*[122] the court gave general guidance on enhancing understanding of domestic abuse and the importance of focusing on a pattern of behaviour as opposed to a specific incident. Non-fatal strangulation is now seriously regarded as an aggravating factor in cases of abuse and violence even prior to the enactment of DAA, s 70, which criminalises non-fatal strangulation. In *R v Allen*[123] the appellant was convicted for the offences of common assault (s 47 OAPA) and false imprisonment in that he grabbed the victim by the throat with both hands, pushed her back towards the kitchen where she hit her head on the corner of the wall and then tripped and fell backwards. In another incident he punched her in the face, pushed her on to the bed, and began to strangle her. The judge in dismissing the appeal against sentence, said that to call this a 'family tiff' was simply not appropriate and that strangulation is an effective and cruel way of asserting dominance and control over a person through the terrifying experience of being starved of oxygen. In *R v Jex and others*[124] the judge criticised the charging decision as 'incomprehensible' and said there had been a failure to give adequate consideration as to the mechanism of the assault where the victim had been strangled four times by the defendant and placed in a headlock for something approaching a minute.

---

[116] Edwards (n 1) 103.

[117] *R v Director of Public Prosecutions, ex parte Tasmin C* [1994] Lexis Citation 3165, [1995] 1 Cr App Rep 136.

[118] *R v A* [2012] EWCA Crim 434.

[119] ibid [3].

[120] Crown Court Compendium Part I (July 2019). See 20-1 para 1 https://www.judiciary.uk/wp-content/uploads/2021/08/Crown-Court-Compendium-Part-I.pdf (accessed 12 February 2022).

[121] Overarching principles—Domestic abuse: Definitive guideline—Sentencing https://www.sentencingcouncil.org.uk/publications/item/overarching-principles-domestic-abuse-definitive-guideline/ (accessed 12 February 2022).

[122] *Re H-N and others (children) (domestic abuse: finding of fact hearings)* [2021] EWCA Civ 448 [78].

[123] [2020] NICA 25. See also *R v Hughes* [2022] NICA 12, where strangulation of a partner was considered an aggravating factor and the defendant was sentenced to fifty months' imprisonment upheld on appeal.

[124] EWCA Crim 1708 [8]. See also *R v Carrigan* [2021] EWCA Crim 1553.

a. *Prosecuting domestic violence and abuse*

Police and case attrition The increase in police recorded 'domestic abuse related incidents and crimes' year ending March 2018, 1,198,094,[125] rises in 2021 to 1,459,663.[126] Similarly, 'violence against the person domestic abuse related crimes' has risen from 327,565 in 2016 to 672,912 in 2021[127] (noted above). Such increases may reflect a real increase in these incidents and crimes and also reflect a change in policing practice and recognition of domestic abuse.

Concerningly, case attrition has risen.[128] The following statistical profile is drawn from a number of sources some of which are incomplete such that figures need to be treated with some caution; however, an overall trend of case attrition is found across all data bases consulted.

The arrest rate for domestic abuse-related offences dropped from fifty-two arrests per 100 (in the twelve months to 30 June 2016) to forty-five arrests per 100 in 2017,[129] thirty-two arrests per 100 in 2019,[130] thirty-two arrests per 100 in 2020,[131] and thirty-two arrests per 100 in 2021.[132] The charging rate also dropped from 23.2 per cent in the twelve months to June 2016,[133] to 18.6 per cent in 2017.[134] The volume of suspects charged fell to 53,659 in the first quarter of 2020–21 from 67,462 in the same quarter in 2018–19.[135] Further analysis would need to consider this against the rise in number of recorded offences during this period.

---

[125] Domestic abuse in England and Wales—Appendix tables—(ons.gov.uk) (2018) https://www.ons.gov.uk/peoplepopulationandcommunity/crimeandjustice/bulletins/domesticabuseinenglandandwales/yearendingmarch2018 (accessed 12 February 2022).

[126] Domestic abuse prevalence and trends, England and Wales—(ons.gov.uk) (2021) https://www.ons.gov.uk/peoplepopulationandcommunity/crimeandjustice/articles/domesticabuseprevalenceandtrendsenglandandwales/yearendingmarch2021 (accessed 12 February 2022).

[127] 'Domestic abuse and the criminal justice system' (2021) Table 3: Number of domestic abuse-related violence against the person offences recorded by the police and percentage of violence against the person offences that were domestic abuse-related, by police force area, England and Wales, year ending March 2016 to year ending March 2021. (accessed 12 February 2022).

[128] The police response to domestic abuse: An update report—HMICFRS (justiceinspectorates.gov.uk) 2019 update report https://www.justiceinspectorates.gov.uk/hmicfrs/publications/the-police-response-to-domestic-abuse-an-update-report/. See also the earlier 2014 report, 'Everyone's business: Improving the police response to domestic abuse' (2014) https://www.justiceinspectorates.gov.uk/hmicfrs/wp-content/uploads/2014/04/improving-the-police-response-to-domestic-abuse.pdf (accessed 12 February 2022).

[129] 2019 update report (n 128) 31.

[130] 'Domestic abuse in England and Wales (ons.gov.uk) 2018' (n 53). See Main point 1.

[131] Domestic abuse and the criminal justice system—(ons.gov.uk) 2020. Table 1: Number of arrests, arrest rate, bails, and voluntary attendances for domestic abuse-related crimes and child protection referrals for domestic abuse-related incidents and crimes, by police force area, year ending March 2020. https://www.ons.gov.uk/peoplepopulationandcommunity/crimeandjustice/datasets/domesticabuseandthecriminaljusticesystemappendixtables/november2020 (accessed 12 February 2022).

[132] Domestic abuse and the criminal justice system—(ons.gov.uk) 2021. Table 1: Number of arrests, arrest rate and voluntary attendances for domestic abuse-related crimes and child protection referrals for domestic abuse-related incidents and crimes, by police force area, England and Wales, for the year ending March 2021 https://www.ons.gov.uk/peoplepopulationandcommunity/crimeandjustice/datasets/domesticabuseandthecriminaljusticesystemappendixtables (accessed 12 February 2022).

[133] 2019 update report (n 128) 35 (a review of 978 crime files).

[134] ibid.

[135] Crown Prosecution Service, CPS data summary Quarter 1 2020–2021 https://www.cps.gov.uk/publication/cps-data-summary-quarter-1-2020-2021 (accessed 12 February 2022). See also https://www.endviolenceagainstwomen.org.uk/cps-data-shows-women-still-being-failed-by-justice-system/(accessed 12 February 2022).

Domestic violence/abuse referrals from police to the CPS have also dropped[136] from 126,461 in 2014–15 to 79,965 in 2019–20. In 2016, the police were discontinuing about a third of domestic abuse prosecutions[137] with a discontinuance variation between forces from 15 to 58 per cent of cases. Figures for 2021 show that the police decided not to continue to investigate three in every four domestic abuse crimes reported to them.[138] This, reported His Majesty's Inspectorate of Constabulary and Fire & Rescue Services (HMICFRS) 'Review of policing domestic abuse during the pandemic', was considered to be most commonly due to the Home Office defined 'outcome 15', where the victim wants to proceed but the police consider there is insufficient evidence to do so, or 'outcome 16', where the victim no longer wants to proceed with the case. In 2021, 54.8 per cent of victims were recorded as not supporting a prosecution, police forces recorded this as a reason for discontinuance in 36 to 71 per cent of cases and in a further 20 per cent the police did not proceed because of evidential difficulties, although the victim did support a prosecution.[139] The report also noted that in cases where victim withdrawal was anticipated such cases were less likely to be thoroughly investigated.

It is not known to what extent police induce 'de facto withdrawals' certainly victim reluctance should not be the only or primary factor in determining case outcome and other evidence should be robustly considered.

CPS and case attrition Pre-charge decisions have decreased following police referrals, from 110,562 in 2017–18 to 98,690 in 2018–19. The number of domestic abuse related prosecutions completed fell from 100,930 in 2015–16 to 93,590 in 2016–17 and to 78,624 in 2018–19. For the period 2020–2021 it is reported: 'Over the past quarter and owing to the impact of Covid-19 on the CJS, there was a significant decrease in volume of completed prosecutions, from 14,227 in Quartile 4 2019/20, to 8,744 in Quartile 1 2020/21'.[140]

The number of convictions for domestic abuse also fell from 68,098 in 2017–18 to 60,160 in 2018–19, falling to 54,515 in the year ending March 2021.[141]

However, the percentage of prosecutions leading to a conviction increased from 74.5 per cent in 2015–16 to 78 per cent in the year ending March 2021.[142] It is important to note that

---

136 ibid.

137 2019 update report (n 128) 10.

138 Police response to violence against women and girls Final inspection report 2021. https://www.justiceinspectorates.gov.uk/hmicfrs/publications/police-response-to-violence-against-women-and-girls/ (accessed 12 February 2022).

139 Review of policing domestic abuse during the pandemic—2021—HMICFRS. See p. 6. https://www.justiceinspectorates.gov.uk/hmicfrs/wp-content/uploads/review-of-policing-domestic-abuse-during-the-pandemic-2021.pdf See also: Victims' Commissioner and Domestic Abuse Commissioner express concerns about the drop in domestic abuse and rape prosecutions and cases charged. https://domesticabusecommissioner.uk/victims-commissioner-and-domestic-abuse-commissioner-express-concerns-about-the-drop-in-domestic-abuse-and-rape-prosecutions-and-cases-charged/(accessed 12 February 2022). See also Final inspection report 2021 (n 138) 81–83.

140 CPS data summary (n 135).

141 See 2019 update report (n 128) 'Domestic abuse in England and Wales (November 2021) Responses to and outcomes of domestic abuse-related cases in the criminal justice system' See Main point 2 https://www.ons.gov.uk/peoplepopulationandcommunity/crimeandjustice/articles/domesticabuseandthecriminaljusticesystemenglandandwales/november2021 (accessed 12 February 2022).

142 ibid Main point 2.

the conviction rate is a product of the nature of the cases prosecuted 'success' merely suggests that those cases put forward for prosecution are evidentially strong cases.

Reasons for discontinuance Cases are discontinued for several reasons. First, the rules governing section 39 common assault CJA (1988) required a case to be brought within six months. The number 'timed out' in 2016–17 was 1,451 rising to 3,763 in 2020–21.[143] The Police, Crime, Sentencing and Courts Act (PCSCA) 2022, however will allow victims of domestic abuse more time to report incidents of common assault or battery against them.[144] Secondly, there is some evidence that delays in CPS advice, particularly during Covid-19, resulted in victims withdrawing support for prosecutions.[145] Thirdly, there is as there has always been a reluctance to make use of hearsay provisions including section 116(2)(d) CJA (2003) and police-enhanced evidence including cameras and 999 calls which could otherwise support a criminal prosecution.

CPS domestic abuse and recent developments The CPS[146] has recently published interim Domestic Abuse Legal Guidance ('the Guidance')[147] for prosecutors to apply in all domestic abuse cases from 4 April 2022, whilst a public consultation takes place.[148] The Guidance recognises both the serious challenges brought by the investigation and prosecution of such cases. It also acknowledges the changes brought by the DAA with further sections due to come into force in 2022[149] and 2023. The Guidance will be updated and published as a final Guidance after a full review and consideration of the consultation responses.

The Guidance seeks comprehensively to set out how prosecutors should apply the Code for Crown Prosecutors when considering offences which fall within the definition of domestic abuse as set out in the DAA. In doing so, the Guidance underlines the CPS intention that domestic abuse cases are amongst the highest priority work they deal with in the criminal justice system and that the safety of victims and children is a paramount concern to them.

The Guidance importantly promotes a new offender-centric approach to case building and prosecuting domestic abuse cases. This ensures that the overall case is stronger and not overly reliant on the victim. This type of case building strategy is known in the CPS as an 'evidence led' prosecution. This term has replaced the phrase 'victim-less' prosecution, as all domestic abuse prosecutions have a victim(s) whether or not they give witness evidence at the trial.

In addition, the Guidance tackles myths and stereotypes head-on to help prosecutors challenge misconceptions and build the strongest possible case. Also, the Guidance contains a major change meaning any child who witnesses domestic abuse will also be treated as a victim. Alongside the Guidance the CPS have published a Domestic Abuse Policy Statement[150] for consultation, which sets out how the CPS approaches their responsibilities to domestic

[143] See 'Huge rise in domestic abuse cases being dropped in England and Wales' https://www.bbc.co.uk/news/uk-politics-58910802 (accessed 12 February 2022).

[144] See 'Domestic abuse victims in England and Wales to be given more time to report' assaults https://www.gov.uk/government/news/domestic-abuse-victims-in-england-and-wales-to-be-given-more-time-to-report-assaults (accessed 12 February 2022).

[145] Review of policing domestic abuse during the pandemic (n 139) 6.

[146] This short section up to, but not including, 'Reducing case attrition' has been written by David Malone.

[147] https://www.cps.gov.uk/legal-guidance/domestic-abuse (accessed 8 June 2022).

[148] The 12-week consultation closed on 26 June 2022: https://www.cps.gov.uk/domestic-abuse-feedback (accessed 8 June 2022).

[149] Including non-fatal strangulation and non-fatal suffocation, s 70 DAA.

[150] https://www.cps.gov.uk/publication/domestic-abuse-policy-statement (accessed 8 June 2022).

abuse cases and their ambition to secure justice in every possible case and improve outcomes for victims.

In launching this consultation, the CPS have acknowledged the critical need to increase the numbers of prosecutions and convictions, including by setting out the ways they work with the police and exploring how they can make sure victims are receiving consistent treatment.[151] How will the success of the CPS domestic abuse initiative be measured? One such measure, recently introduced, are the government-led Local Criminal Justice Scorecards.[152] None of the Criminal Justice agencies work in isolation and the scorecards aim to bring together key data from the various agencies (police, CPS, and the courts) to increase transparency, increase understanding of the Criminal Justice System and support collaboration, particularly at a local level. There are currently two scorecards, for all crime and for all recorded adult rape offences. However, given the importance of domestic abuse it is envisaged that a Domestic Abuse Scorecard, with a number of key metrics cited, will be developed at some point in the future. Indeed, in many quarters, this would be seen as a welcome development to help drive a major increase in the number of prosecutions reaching court. That said, scorecards and data alone are not enough—they do not tell the full story—and the concerns of victims must still be heeded in individual cases[153] and via continued engagement with victims' champions,[154] community groups and scrutiny panels.

5. REDUCING CASE ATTRITION

On 8 February 2022, Laura Farris MP tabled a question in Parliament asking what was being done to improve the number of successful prosecutions of domestic abuse.[155] The government responded drawing the attention of the house to the increase in government funding for support services and the removal of the time limit for bringing cases of common assault but saying little more.

A reduction in case attrition also depends on better gathering of all the available evidence and a use of hearsay provisions. This was urged by the Court of Appeal as long ago as 1996 where in *R v Holt; R v Bird*[156] the appellants were held to be in contempt of court. Sarah Holt was sentenced to three months' detention in a Young Offender Institution, and Sophie Bird, to two months' imprisonment. They refused to give evidence on the day of the trial of Alex Fryatt who seriously injured Holt, who was rendered unconscious as a result of being punched, kicked in the head, stamped on, and sprayed with CS gas. The case against Fryatt was dismissed and 'not guilty' recorded. In mitigation for Holt and Bird counsel said that

---

[151] https://www.cps.gov.uk/cps/news/there-no-typical-victim-domestic-abuse-cps-says-it-revises-its-legal-guidance-challenge (accessed 8 June 2022).

[152] https://www.endviolenceagainstwomen.org.uk/rape-scorecards-show-broken-justice-system-for-rape-survivors/ (accessed 8 June 2022).

[153] As enshrined in the Victims' Code: https://www.gov.uk/government/publications/the-code-of-practice-for-victims-of-crime. See also CPS Legal Guidance: https://www.cps.gov.uk/legal-guidance/victims-and-witnesses-cps-commitments-support

[154] For example: https://domesticabusecommissioner.uk/ and https://victimscommissioner.org.uk/

[155] Domestic Abuse: Prosecutions Vol 708: 8 February 2022 House of Commons. https://hansard.parliament.uk/Commons/2022-02-08/debates/03A7FE43-EA82-4297-BC2C-8CD06E1E74BA/a (accessed 27 April 2022).

[156] [1996] Lexis Citation 5009.

they were in fear of what might happen to them and their family members if they gave evidence. The Court of Appeal commented:

[d]espite indications by the appellants in the week before the trial that they wished to withdraw their statements, the Crown Prosecution Service's sensible procedure did not operate. Had it done so it might have resulted in the trial proceeding, following a successful prosecution application under s, 23(3)(b) of the Criminal Justice Act 1988 for the witnesses' s. 9 statements to be used as evidence because the appellants were witnesses who did not give oral evidence through fear. We would draw attention to this provision and express the hope that greater use will be made in future of it in cases like the case from which these proceedings emerge.[157]

i. Improving Police Evidence Gathering at Scene

In 2000, following recommendations from the Home Office Crime Reduction Programme Violence Against Women Initiative, police and prosecutors accepted the need for enhanced evidence gathering including body worn camera evidence and hearsay evidence. Yet nearly twenty years later, in 2019, the HMICFRS justice inspectorate's report still found delay in the police response, poor evidence taking, and a variation across forces in evidence gathering, including the use of body worn cameras.[158]

There have been several recent initiatives to improve the overall police response and evidence gathering. In March 2018, the CPS approved the national rollout of the domestic abuse best practice framework including establishing multi-agency safeguarding hubs (MASHs) and central referral units (CRUs) bringing together police and partner organisations. The DAA 2021, s 58 will build upon these partnerships (see further s 58 in Part II of this Guide).

The College of Policing has also developed a programme to improve police understanding of coercive and controlling conduct to enhance the skills, knowledge, and effectiveness of first responders in dealing with domestic abuse which will impact on both criminal and civil remedy uptake.[159] The Final inspectorate report on 'Police response to violence against women and girls' recommendation 1 asserts:

There should be an immediate and unequivocal commitment that the response to VAWG offences is an absolute priority for government, policing, the criminal justice system, and public-sector partnerships. This needs to be supported at a minimum by a relentless focus on these crimes; mandated responsibilities; and sufficient funding so that all partner agencies can work effectively as part of a whole-system approach to reduce and prevent the harms these offences are causing.[160]

a. *Using hearsay evidence at trial*

Case attrition can be reduced, and the number of successful prosecutions increased if the hearsay provisions are more widely used. Historically, the common law adopted a laissez

[157] Susan Edwards, 'The Duplicity of Protection: Prosecuting Frightened Victims: An Act of Gender-based Violence' (2012) 76 *The Journal of Criminal Law* 29.

[158] 2019 update report (n 128).

[159] A training programme has been developed by the College of Policing with the support of SafeLives. See Final inspection report (n 138) 43 https://www.justiceinspectorates.gov.uk/hmicfrs/wp-content/uploads/police-response-to-violence-against-women-and-girls-final-inspection-report.pdf?msclkid=1aa564bfc61711ec9625f9d1633e06cd (accessed 12 May 2022).

[160] ibid 16.

faire attitude to the vulnerable victim of domestic violence and abuse. In an appeal case, where a wife who had been physically assaulted by a husband and refused to give evidence against him, Lord Salmon said: '[i]f she does not want to avail herself of [the law's] protection, there is, in my view, no ground for holding that the common law forces it upon her'.[161] In that same case, Lord Wilberforce reiterated the common law position and said that to compel and allow her to give evidence 'would give rise to discord and to perjury and would be, to ordinary people repugnant'.[162] The habituated non-prosecution of abusive and violent husbands and partners (where victims have been reluctant and unsupported witnesses) has allowed intimate partner violence to continue and escalate in prevalence and seriousness. The golden thread of the need to protect was voiced by Lord Edmund Davis who in *Hoskyn* in a dissenting judgment said:

> Such cases are too grave to depend simply upon whether the injured spouse is, or is not, willing to testify against the attacker. A wife who has once been subjected to a 'carve-up' may well have more reasons than one for being an unwilling witness against her husband. Their investigation and where sufficiently weighty, their prosecution is a duty which the agencies of law enforcement cannot dutifully neglect.[163]

In 1984, the Police and Criminal Evidence Act (PACE), s 80 made spouses compellable witnesses placing them in the same position as intimate partners. The hearsay provisions (CJA, (2003) s 114, s 116, res gestae s 118, bad character provisions s 101) and special measures (Youth Justice and Criminal Evidence Act (YJCEA) s 17 and s 28) should be more fully used to support prosecutions of domestic violence and abuse.

b. *Hearsay*

Section 114 CJA 2003 provides for the admissibility of hearsay evidence '(1) in criminal proceedings a statement not made in oral evidence in the proceedings is admissible as evidence of any matter stated.' Section 116 deals with unavailable witnesses and section 116(2)(e) and (3) allows for admissibility of oral and documentary hearsay and permits the use of a witness statement in court in place of oral testimony where the witness is in fear. Fear is to be widely construed (s 116(3))[164] and whilst proof of fear does not require an objective test based on reasonableness,[165] every effort must be taken to secure the witness's attendance at court to evaluate the issue of fear[166] and/or persuade the victim to give evidence with the assistance of special measures[167] to satisfy fair trial objections. Section 116(4)(b) requires the judge to consider 'any risk that its admission or exclusion will result in unfairness to any party to the proceedings (and in particular to how difficult it will be to challenge the statement if the relevant person does not give oral evidence)' repealing the earlier provision CJA 1988 section 25(2)(d), where the judge in considering unfairness was required to considered unfairness to the prosecution only.

In *R v Boulton*[168] convictions for rape, false imprisonment, and putting witnesses in fear were upheld where the court ruled that it was right to allow evidence to be read under section

161 *Hoskyn and Metropolitan Police Commissioner* [1979] AC 474, 495.
162 ibid 488.
163 *Hoskyn* (n 161) 507.
164 *Blackstone's Criminal Practice* (2022) F17.8, 3169.
165 *Acton Justices, ex parte McMullen* (1990) 92 Cr App R 98.
166 *Shabir* [2012] EWCA Crim 2564.
167 *Riat* [2012] EWCA Crim 1509.
168 [2007] EWCA Crim 472.

116(d). In *R v Horncastle; R v Marquis; R v Carter*[169] the appellants challenged the fairness of convictions (under ECHR Article 6(3)(d)), where the statements of witnesses were read in court. Upholding the convictions and establishing general principles the court held that the right to confront witnesses was not absolute but were permissible provided that reliable counterbalancing measures in the manner of reliable hearsay are in place and all possible efforts are made to bring the witness to court.

The need to follow a clear procedure is illustrated in *R v Baldwin*[170] where the defendant was charged with offences of making threats to kill, assault occasioning actual bodily harm (against a former partner) theft, and criminal damage. The factual circumstances comprised of recorded footage from police body worn cameras of injury to the complainant, and damage to the property, two police statements, and a pre-recorded statement from the victim who said she had been choked, punched, and hit with several objects. The defendant denied all charges and said the complainant had injured herself. No police officers attended, nor did the complainant, and the application for an adjournment by the prosecution was refused. The judge then imposed a post acquittal restraining order section 5A of the 1997 PFHA (inserted by the DVCVA 2004) which he was entitled to do. The court said: 'The failure to identify what was the evidential status of the materials before the judge did affect the findings made by the judge. As did the fact that the complaint was eighteen months old, and it was necessary . . . to assess fairly the need to protect the complainant against the risk of future conduct . . . [and] to know more about the complainant's current situation.'[171] However, as earlier, body worn cameras are still under used in domestic violence/abuse cases.[172]

c. *Res gestae*

Under section 118(1) of the CJA (2003), the common law rules on res gestae are preserved. Section 118(4)(a) deals with the admission of hearsay evidence where a person is so emotionally overpowered by events that the possibility of concoction or distortion can be disregarded. In such circumstances where victim/survivors of domestic abuse decline to support a prosecution, 999 call transcripts may be admitted as res gestae hearsay evidence.[173] This provides vital evidence in these evidentially challenging cases where victims frequently withdraw allegations due to subtle pressures, coercion, and fear. Res gestae evidence does not provide an open door to such prosecutions as appropriate safeguards must be in place. In *Barnaby v DPP*[174] the complainant in a 999-call said: 'I'm so scared he has just strangled me' and made statements to the police officer who attended the call and saw the state of the victim and her injuries. The High Court found the justices had correctly admitted the evidence as *res gestae* and that it was not necessary to establish whether the victim was in fear.

A series of unsuccessful challenges to res gestae submissions followed which have further clarified the procedure to be applied. In *Ibrahim v Crown Prosecution Service*[175] the court upheld a conviction and ruled that res gestae was properly admitted of a 999-phone call where the victim said, 'my partner has attacked me' and was in fear of a risk of harm

[169] [2010] 2 AC 373. See [56], [57], [87].

[170] [2021] EWCA Crim 703.

[171] ibid [42] and [45].

[172] See *Ashford Magistrate's Court, ex parte Hilden* [1993] 2 All ER 154; and *McGillivray* (1992) 97 Cr App R 232.

[173] *Blackstone's Criminal Practice* (n 164) F17.56 p 3193.

[174] [2015] ECHC 232 (Admin).

[175] [2016] EWHC 1750 (Admin).

following co-operation with the police.[176] The court held that the appropriate route to vindicate the defence case was via section 78 of PACE. However, in *Wills v CPS*,[177] where the complainant unexpectedly failed to appear, the court held that before considering admission under the res gestae principles, it was essential for the justices to have discovered, so far as it was possible, why the witness had not attended. This could not be satisfactorily established, and the conviction was quashed.

In *McGuinness v The Public Prosecution Service for Northern Ireland*[178] the court upheld the conviction for common assault and held that it was right to proceed with a prosecution and admit 999 tape and bodycam footage where a victim said she did not want to give evidence because the parties had reconciled.[179] In *Morgan (Martin Edward) v Director of Public Prosecutions*,[180] a 999 tape of the call made by the complainant and bodycam footage taken by a police officer who attended the scene was properly admitted and the district judge's verdict was reasonably found on the evidence.

The importance of following clear procedure in cases where witnesses are silent and unwilling to support a prosecution is indicated in the case of *Boota v Gwent Magistrates Court*[181] where a judicial review was allowed. In this case the claimant was convicted of assaulting his wife who alleged that she was beaten and dragged by her hair. She made a complaint to the police, she did not support the prosecution and gave no evidence, neither did two neighbours who had previously given statements to the police. There was no direct evidence from witnesses who saw what happened and the defendant gave 'no comment' interviews. The judge refused to state a case. The prosecution proceeded on the basis of circumstantial evidence.

d. *Bad character*

Bad character evidence (BCE) of propensity of domestic violence/abuse can also be admitted to support a prosecution.[182] Sections 101 and 103 of the CJA provide for a matter 'in issue' between the parties as one which the court ought to take into account (s 101(1)(d)). In considering whether to admit such evidence, the trial judge must consider fairness, likely prejudice of the evidence (s 101(3)), and the relevance/prejudice of old evidence. Domestic violence either towards the same victim or other victims has been held to fall under a 'general propensity for violence' and has, depending on the circumstances, been both included[183] and excluded.[184] *R v Hanson*[185] guides admissibility of propensity evidence. In *R v Brough (Alan)*[186] where the victim was strangled, and the defendant charged with attempt murder, BCE of texts to a previous partner were admitted in evidence of his general violence towards women, resulted in the conviction being quashed. Propensity for a particular kind of violence or sexual violence is, however, considered righty admitted.

176 ibid [28].
177 [2016] EWHC 3779 (Admin).
178 [2017] NICA 30.
179 ibid [42].
180 [2016] EWHC 3414 (Admin).
181 [2012] EWHC 3550 (Admin).
182 *Blackstone's Criminal Practice* (n 164) F 13.4, F 13.39.
183 *R v Bailey* [2017] EWCA Crim 35; *R v Baldwin* [2021] EWCA Crim 703. See also *R v Khan* [2021] EWCA 1526.
184 *R v Rees* [2007] EWCA Crim 1837.
185 [2005] EWCA 824.
186 [2018] EWCA Crim 1903.

So where propensity to strangle is in issue and the charge is one of murder or attempted murder especially BCE has been admitted.[187] In *Williams*, the Court of Appeal held that BCE had been properly admitted:

The material, if true, established that this particular appellant was prone to a continuing propensity, long standing, not only to use violence against his female partners, but also and specifically to use violence of the type which resulted in the death of the deceased when he strangled her. The violence had to be considered as a whole.[188]

In *R v W (S)*[189] where the assault involved varying forms and degrees of neck grabbing or strangulation where the applicant would routinely asphyxiate KS to the point where she would lose consciousness and he would rape her anally and orally; propensity evidence was admitted of indecent assault with a vibrator relating to a conviction in 2006 for assault by penetration of the anus. The judge was satisfied that the evidence was relevant to whether the applicant had a propensity to penetrate the anus with an object against the wishes of his partner. He allowed the Crown also to rely on two convictions for common assault involving varying forms or degrees of neck grabbing or strangulation. He said that so far as strangulation is concerned, the evidence was highly probative, and it would be wrong to deprive the jury of hearing about it and letting them make up their mind whether the Crown were right to say that it establishes propensity as claimed. In the end, evidence of the previous convictions on the part of the applicant was adduced by way of agreed facts.

e. *Special measures*

The use of special measures under sections 17 and 28 of the YJCEA including pre-recorded interviews (s 28)[190] can also support prosecutions where the victim does not wish to come to court. (See further discussion in sections 62 to 67 in Part II of this Guide). Section 28 allows for the use of pre-recorded cross examination of vulnerable witnesses. Schemes piloting the use of section 28 to be extended to include victims of domestic violence are being established in the Northeast of England.[191] As section 62 of the DAA 2021 has now been brought into force (25 October 2022), complainants of domestic abuse offences will be included as section 17(4) witnesses.[192]

[187] See *Rees* (n 184). See also *Foster and others* [2007] EWCA Crim 2869; *R v Moore* [2009] EWCA Crim 821; *R v McCarry* [2009] EWCA Crim 1718; *R v McGrory* [2013] EWCA Crim 2336.

[188] See also *R v Williams* [2006] ECWA Crim 2052.

[189] [2016] EWCA Crim 2180.

[190] See Guidance HMCTS services: s 28 pre-recorded cross-examinations https://www.gov.uk/guidance/hmcts-services-section-28-pre-recorded-cross-examinations (accessed 12 February 2022).

[191] See Press release 'Major funding boost for victim services as local criminal justice scorecards published' https://www.gov.uk/government/news/major-funding-boost-for-victim-services-as-local-criminal-justice-scorecards-published (accessed 12 February 2022).

[192] See Daniel Flury, 'Changes within section 28 provision for victims and witnesses'. https://assets.publishing.service.gov.uk/government/uploads/system/uploads/attachment_data/file/1033962/Changes_within_section_28_provision_for_victim_and_witnesses.pdf (accessed 12 February 2022).

6. SENTENCING

i. Background

Historically, sentencing outcomes in domestic violence/abuse cases and domestic violence/abuse murders has been derisory. In such cases, until recently, sentencing judges have regarded the domestic violence/abuse of women in private, in the home, as less serious than violence between men, in public, on the street.

In assessing culpability in domestic abuse cases both parties, victim and aggressor, were often regarded as equally culpable. When women are killed by male intimate partners their characters have been traduced as bad mothers, bad partners, and bad wives. In the case of Joseph McGrail, the judge was reported to have said of the deceased: 'This lady would have tried the patience of a saint.'[193] By 2002, following intervention by Harriet Harman KC MP, when Solicitor General, a number of domestic abuse sentences for assault and for manslaughter were made the subject of AG references[194] and, although leave was granted in the cases of *Suratan* and *Wilkinson* and their sentences were not increased, the AG references in focusing on domestic abuse homicides and sentencing[195] prompted significant changes in the judicial approach to sentencing. However, in the case of *Attorney General's Reference (No 24 of 2003)*, where a man killed his wife, the sentencing judge echoed the public/private divide in approaching sentencing in domestic abuse cases and said that the husband 'was not a risk to the general public'.[196]

Whilst there have been significant improvements in recognising the seriousness of domestic abuse, Horder and Fitzgibbon[197] found that following the 2009 Coroners and Justice Act (CAJA) 2009, which expressly excludes sexual infidelity as a ground for loss of self-control manslaughter (s 55(6)(c)), sexual infidelity-related evidence continued to have a bearing on mitigation in murder cases where men killed intimate female partners where it is 'part and parcel of a—necessarily rare—claim of "prolonged stress" bordering on mental disorder'.[198] Lord Judge LCJ in *Attorney General's Reference (No 23 of 2011)*, in interpreting the 2009 Act provision, said:

> [55(6)(c)] is concerned with the substantive criminal offence of murder, not with the determination of the minimum term where murder is admitted or proved. Paragraph 11 of Schedule 21 remains in force ... provocation may provide relevant mitigation to murder [and] mitigation for an offence of murder [is] not closed as a result of section 55 of the 2009 Act.[199]

---

[193] Joseph McGrail, *Guardian* (1 August 1991). See *Crim LR* (March 2004).

[194] *Attorney General's References (Nos 74, 95 and 118 of 2002) Suratan, Humes and Wilkinson* [2002] All ER (D) 366 (Dec), [2002] EWCA Crim 2982. Note that Suratan's conviction was subsequently quashed on appeal: *R v Suratan*: [2004] All ER (D) 238.

[195] See Susan Edwards, 'Injustice that puts a low price on a woman's life' *The Times* (2 September 2003).

[196] [2003] EWCA 2451 [8].

[197] Jeremy Horder and Kate Fitz-Gibbon, 'Where sexual infidelity triggers murder: Examining the impact of homicide law reform on judicial attitudes in sentencing' (2015) 74(2) *Cambridge Law Review* 307.

[198] ibid 326.

[199] [2012] 1 Cr App R(S) 45, 268.

ii. Overarching Principles Domestic Abuse: Domestic Abuse Definitive Guideline

By 2018, the Sentencing Guidelines Council introduced the 'Domestic Abuse Definitive Guideline' containing overarching principles for sentencing in domestic abuse cases[200] and now is revised in accordance with domestic abuse as defined in Part 1 of the DAA. The Guideline recognises the nature of domestic abuse and the risk it poses to life and identifies factors for assessing seriousness and aggravating and mitigating factors (noting, for example, the vulnerability of a victim of domestic abuse per se as an aggravating factor. Additionally, the Guidance recognises that any sentence imposed should not be influenced by the wishes of the victim and that pleas made for leniency by the victim are to be disregarded as they are likely to have been induced by threats made by, or fear of, the offender.[201]

The guidance also states that the court, in appropriate circumstances, should make a restraining order.

iii. Revised Sentencing Guidelines for Assault Offences and Attempted Murder

The revised guideline for assault offences and attempted murder[202] includes a new sentence range of up to forty years, introduced to ensure that sentences reflect the gravity of the most serious offences. The new guideline for common assault (s 39 CJA 1988 and s 47 assault OAPA) introduces a new aggravating factor of deliberate spitting or coughing.[203] A new high culpability factor of strangulation to include asphyxiation and suffocation is also included in all guidelines except attempted murder and a revised high culpability factor of vulnerability and harm assessment is also recognised.

iv. Sentencing for Murder

With regard to sentencing in cases of murder, the statutory framework is found in sections 269 to 277 CJA 2003 (repealed by the Sentencing Act 2020 (SA) ss 321 and 322 and schedule 21).[204] The Sentencing Code in schedules 21 [2-10] mirrors sch 21 in the CJA 2003 [4-11]. There are three starting points for offenders to include those aged twenty-one years or over, those aged eighteen–twenty years old and offenders under eighteen years. Guided by schedule 21 CJA/SA, the starting points for offenders aged twenty-one years and over is a whole life order, thirty years, twenty-five years, and fifteen years. Starting points for eighteen to twenty-year-olds is thirty years, twenty-five years, and fifteen years, and for those under

200 Overarching principles—Domestic abuse: Definitive guideline—Sentencing (sentencingcouncil.org.uk) https://www.sentencingcouncil.org.uk/publications/item/overarching-principles-domestic-abuse-definitive-guideline/(accessed 12 February 2022).

201 ibid [10].

202 Courts and Tribunals Judiciary, 'Revised sentencing guidelines for assault offences and attempted murder'(2021) https://www.judiciary.uk/announcements/revised-sentencing-guidelines-for-assault-offences-and-attempted-murder/May (accessed 12 February 2022).

203 See *R v Coull* [2012] EWCA 2893 [25]; *R v Townsend (Jordan)* [2017] EWCA 1623.

204 *Blackstone's Criminal Practice* (n 164) E17.

eighteen years, a twelve-year starting point. A complex schema of culpability, seriousness, and aggravating and mitigating factors determine sentence length.

Considering seriousness of murders committed in the domestic context, a whole life term is applicable where the offence is of 'exceptionally high seriousness', for example where the killing involved [2](2) (a) two or more persons ... or, for example, (e) a murder is committed by an offender previously convicted of murder. Where the offence is of 'particularly high seriousness' and the defendant is over the age of eighteen years, a starting point of thirty years applies where there is: [3](2)(b) murder with the use of a firearm or explosive, [3](2)(e) murder involving sexual or sadistic conduct. [3](2)f the murder of two or more persons.

Since women are less able to use body force to repel male violence and may resort to using a firearm, this mandatory sentence length may work to injustice. In the *Hodges* case, the deceased had ended the relationship, the female defendant used a shotgun to kill, and entered a guilty plea to murder. In this case, the court imposed a minimum sentence of twenty-four years. The sentencing powers of the judge are determined by a mandatory starting point of thirty years for killing with a firearm.[205]

Where the offender is over eighteen years and uses a knife or a weapon, a starting point of twenty-five years normally applies [4](1)(d),4(2)). The use of a weapon attracts a longer sentence, and the different sentencing outcomes regarding weapons versus body force has been a continual point of conjecture, and concern, especially where women whose size and strength frequently result in them resorting to the use of a weapon when defending themselves from violent and sexually violent men.

Paragraph 7-10 of Schedule 21 (SA) sets out further factors, which the sentencing court may take into consideration once a minimum term has been decided, these include aggravating and mitigating factors. Aggravating factors [9] include preplanning, vulnerability of the victim, suffering before death, and concealment of the body. Mitigatory factors [10] include an intention to cause serious bodily harm rather than to kill, lack of planning, offender mental disorder, evidence of provocation, self-defence, act of mercy, and age of defendant.

The sentencing guidelines for manslaughter are also relevant.[206]

Recent sentencing decisions reflect the application of the guidelines in assault cases.[207] Where men have killed women in the domestic context judges at the sentencing stage now must take evidence of strangulation more seriously discretion, however, is still left to judges where there are considered to be exceptional circumstances.[208]

---

[205] See 'Stratton Strawless murder: Catherine Hodges jailed for 24 years' *BBC News* (26 August 2011) https://www.bbc.co.uk/news/uk-england-norfolk-14683744 (accessed 14 March 2022).

[206] https://www.sentencingcouncil.org.uk/crown-court?s&collection=manslaughter (accessed 14 March 2022).

[207] *R v Hughes* [2022] NICA 12. A sentence of four years was upheld for domestic assault where there had been 'sustained' domestic violence. See also *R v Dewhurst* (n 27). In *R v TJN* [2021] EWCA Crim 2023, where there was controlling and coercive behaviour including several incidents of strangulation a sentence of twenty-four months was handed down. In *R v Carrigan* [2021] EWCA Crim 1553, '[11]. Most importantly, it included a period of strangulation when her breathing was interrupted. The judge observed that that particular characteristic must inevitably take the offence into the top category of seriousness for the purposes of applying the relevant guideline. He therefore indicated that the appropriate starting point for that offence was 18 months' imprisonment with a range of between one—and three-years' imprisonment.'

[208] See eg *R v Williams* [2021] EWCA Crim 738 where a five-year sentence was handed down where the defendant was nearly seventy years old and was depressed and snapped killing his wife. Compare with *R v Sampford* [2014] EWCA Crim 1560, where nine years was given for a woman of seventy-six years of age who was caring for her elderly, sick, and terminally ill husband, snapped. She pleaded guilty to murder and appealed

In the cases of Sam Pybus[209] (who received a four-year and eight-month sentence following a guilty plea to manslaughter) and Warren Coulton[210] (who received five years for gross negligence manslaughter), both defendants alleged that the female deceased had consented to 'rough sex', in *Pybus* to strangulation, in *Coulton* to suffocation. Both cases were raised by Harriet Harman KC MP in letters to the Director of Public Prosecutions (DPP)[211] concerning the leniency of the sentences (discussed further in Part II of this Guide at sections 70 and 71).

7. THE INTERNATIONAL HUMAN RIGHTS LEGISLATIVE FRAMEWORK

The protection of victims of domestic abuse and the prosecution of offenders operates within the broader international human rights framework. The European Convention on Human Rights (ECHR) and the Istanbul Convention are of particular relevance to cases of domestic abuse. It is to be noted that no recognition of the Istanbul Convention is given in the DAA with regard to the office and obligations of the Domestic Abuse Commissioner. By comparison, the Children's' Commissioner under section 107 [2A](1) Children and Families Act 2014 must have regard to the United Nations Convention on the Rights of the Child (see Part II Part 2 of the Act in this Guide).

i. ECHR

The ECHR Articles 2, 3, 6, 8, 12, and 14 are of special relevance in the context of domestic abuse protection.[212] In *Opuz v Turkey*,[213] where a domestic violence perpetrator went on to kill his wife's mother, the European Court of Human Rights (ECtHR) held in conjunction with Article 2 (right to life), Article 3 (degrading and inhumane treatment), and Article 6 (right to a fair trial) that this was an act of 'gender-based violence' because of the state's failure to protect. The ruling recognises the failure of public authorities to prosecute domestic violence perpetrators and ultimately protect victims of domestic violence as an act of gender-based violence. The obligation of public authorities to protect was tested in *Michael and others v Chief Constable of South Wales Police and another (Refuge and others intervening)*,[214] where the police were called but

the sentence length of nine years. Refusing permission to appeal, the single judge said: 'This is clearly a tragic case that has caused me to review the papers with considerable anxiety.' Following a renewed appeal application, a sentence of nine years was upheld. See Wayne Couzens sentencing remarks at https://www.judiciary.uk/wp-content/uploads/2021/09/Wayne-Couzens-Sentencing-Remarks.pdf and his subsequent appeal against sentence appeal in *R v Stewart and others; R v Monaghan; Rv Tustin and another* [2022] EWCA Crim 1063 [53].

[209] *R v Pybus* [2021] EWCA Crim 1787.

[210] *R v Coulton* https://www.bbc.co.uk/news/uk-wales-56999895

[211] https://www.theguardian.com/uk-news/2021/sep/08/unduly-lenient-jail-term-for-killing-during-sex-considered-for-appeal.

[212] Article 2(1): 'Everyone's right to life shall be protected by law'. Article 3: 'No one shall be subjected to torture or to inhuman or degrading treatment or punishment'. Article 6(1): 'In the determination of his civil rights and obligations or of any criminal charge against him, everyone is entitled to a fair and public hearing within a reasonable time by an independent and impartial tribunal established by law.' Article 8(1): 'Everyone has the right to respect for his private and family life, his home and his correspondence.' Article 12 (Right to marry and found a family), and Article 14 (Prohibition from discrimination).

[213] [2010] 50 EHRR 28.

[214] [2015] AC 1732. See also *MLIA and another v Chief Constable of Hampshire Police* [2017] EWHC 292 (QB) (no finding in support of claimants).

the victim was stabbed to death before police arrived. The court concluded that the police were not liable since the common law does not impose liability for pure omissions.

ii. Istanbul

The Istanbul Convention is the Council of Europe Convention on preventing and combating violence against women and domestic violence. The UK government signed the Istanbul Convention on 8 June 2012 but has yet to ratify it in legislation despite the Preventing and Combating Violence against Women and Domestic Violence (Ratification of Convention) Act 2017.

It is of particular relevance to domestic abuse and violence and whilst the Istanbul Convention has been part of legal argument in cases involving immigration status[215] it has not similarly figured in legal argument in criminal cases. Article 1 sets out the purpose of the Convention as follows:

> [t]o protect women against all forms of violence, and prevent, prosecute and eliminate violence against women and domestic violence; design a comprehensive framework, policies and measures for the protection of and assistance to all victims of violence against women and domestic violence; provide support and assistance to organisations and law enforcement agencies to effectively co-operate in order to adopt an integrated approach to eliminating violence against women and domestic violence.

Article 2 of the Convention asserts that it applies to all forms of violence against women, including domestic violence, which affects women disproportionately, but that the states parties are encouraged to apply it to all victims of domestic violence.

The courts in England and Wales already have extraterritorial jurisdiction for some of the offences required by the Convention (for example, female genital mutilation (by virtue of s 4 of the Female Genital Mutilation Act 2003) and forced marriage (by virtue of s 121 of the Anti-social Behaviour, Crime and Policing Act 2014)). The DAA extends this jurisdiction. (See further ss 72–74 and Schedule 3 DAA in Part II of this Guide.) The Preventing and Combating Violence Against Women and Domestic Violence (Ratification of Convention) Act 2017 requires the government to lay an annual report before Parliament on progress toward ratification of the Convention. The fourth such report was laid before Parliament on 22 October 2020. This will be the responsibility of the Secretary of State.[216]

It is incumbent on all those involved in the protection of victims of domestic abuse to use the power of these conventions in litigation and in the delivery of services. It is incumbent on all those involved with protecting victim/survivors from domestic abuse to hold individuals and public authorities, police, prosecutors, and the courts and the UK government and its laws to account. The DAA 2021 is an important contribution to that wider endeavour.

[215] See for example *A v Secretary of State for the Home Department* [2016] CSHI 38; *R (on the application of FA(Sudan) v Secretary of State for the Home Department* [2021] EWCA Civ 59; *R (on the application of SWP) v Secretary of State for the Home Department* [2022] EWHC 2067.

[216] See Lisa Grans, 'The Istanbul Convention and the Positive Obligation to Prevent Violence' (2018) 18(1) *Human Rights Law Review* 133. See also Kayliegh Richardson and Ana Speed, 'Two Worlds Apart: A Comparative Analysis of the Effectiveness of Domestic Abuse Law and Policy in England and Wales and the Russian Federation' (2019) 83(5) *The Journal of Criminal Law* 320.

PART II OF GUIDE
THE DOMESTIC ABUSE ACT 2021

PART 1 OF THE ACT: DEFINITION OF DOMESTIC ABUSE (SECTIONS 1–3)

3
DEFINITION OF 'DOMESTIC ABUSE' (SECTIONS 1–3)

Vanessa Bettinson

1. DEFINITION OF 'DOMESTIC ABUSE'

i. Context and Background

This provision has the important role of defining domestic abuse in law for the first time.[1] The legislative definition allows the Domestic Abuse Act DAA to fulfil its objective of providing clear information about all forms of this abuse leading to its greater identification by statutory and non-statutory practitioners and the general public.[2] It is supported by statutory guidance, required by section 84 DAA, which sets out standards and promotes best practice

[1] See Vanessa Bettinson, 'Adding to the Domestic Abuse Criminal Law Framework: The Domestic Abuse Act 2021' (2022) 2 *Crim LR* 88.

[2] HM Government, 'Transforming the Response to Domestic Abuse: Consultation and Draft Bill' (2019) 5 https://assets.publishing.service.gov.uk/government/uploads/system/uploads/attachment_data/file/772247/Transforming_the_response_to_domestic_abuse_-_consultation_response_and_draft_bill_-print.pdf (accessed 21 April 2022).

Vanessa Bettinson, *Definition of 'Domestic Abuse' (Sections 1–3)* In: *Blackstone's Guide to the Domestic Abuse Act 2021*. Edited by Susan Edwards, David Malone, and Gillian Jones KC, Oxford University Press. © Vanessa Bettinson 2023.
DOI: 10.1093/oso/9780192870513.003.0003

among agencies.[3] Prior to this legal reform, domestic abuse and violence was defined in a Home Office Circular providing agencies with a consistent definition to assist with identifying and responding appropriately to the abuse.[4] This policy definition placed non-physical forms of abuse including coercive and controlling behaviours on an equal footing with physical harms, albeit that under the Offences Against the Person Act 1861 (OAPA) evidence of physical abuse was required, whilst introducing coercive and controlling behaviours into policy lexicon. Section 1 reflects much of this policy definition, retaining a gender-neutral approach with the statutory guidance explaining that women are disproportionately victims of domestic abuse.[5] The provision substitutes financial abuse with the broader term of economic abuse and specifies that the abuse occurs between individuals who are 'personally connected', a term explained in section 2.

The existence of the policy definition prior to the enactment of the DAA has meant that agencies do not expect their working practices to change. However, respondents to the government's *Transforming the Response to Domestic Abuse Consultation* considered that the legal definition would prompt organisations to update their training packages, guidance, and responses.[6] The statutory guidance emphasises that the ability correctly and promptly to identify domestic abuse allows public authorities to protect victims, thereby preventing escalation and recurrence of the abuse by providing the right response.[7] A legal definition of domestic abuse is intended to prevent 'myths and stereotypes [that] lead to victims receiving negative responses, [and] poor advice which exacerbates suffering'.[8]

ii. The Section

Section 1 of the DAA introduces a statutory definition of 'domestic abuse' with the new terminology of 'abuse' to encompass a wide range of circumstances and behaviours. Subsection 6 requires all references in the DAA to being abusive towards another person to be read in accordance with this section. Subsection 2(a) specifies that the 'domestic abuse' occurs between parties who are 'personally connected' to each other and both are over the age of 16. The term 'personally connected' is defined in section 2 DAA. As both parties must both be aged 16 or over, teenage relationships and adolescent to parent abuse are recognised by the provision. The age parameter has been added to preserve the distinction between domestic abuse and child abuse, which is governed by a separate legal framework and agencies.[9]

Under ss 3 behaviour is 'abusive if it consists of any of the following— (a) physical or sexual abuse; (b) violent or threatening behaviour; (c) controlling or coercive behaviour;

[3] Home Office, 'Domestic abuse: draft statutory guidance framework' (2021) https://www.gov.uk/government/consultations/domestic-abuse-act-statutory-guidance/domestic-abuse-draft-statutory-guidance-framework (accessed 21 April 2022).

[4] Home Office Circular 003/2013 https://www.gov.uk/government/publications/new-government-domestic-violence-and-abuse-definition/circular-0032013-new-government-domestic-violence-and-abuse-definition.

[5] Home Office (n 3) ch 2.

[6] HM Government (n 2) 6.

[7] Home Office (n 3) ch 1.

[8] HM Government, 'Transforming the Response to Domestic Abuse: Government Consultation' (2018) 11 https://consult.justice.gov.uk/homeoffice-moj/domestic-abuse-consultation/ (accessed 21 April 2022).

[9] Home Office (n 3) ch 2.

(d) economic abuse (see ss (4)); (e) psychological, emotional, or other abuse. It does not matter whether the behaviour consists of a single incident or a course of conduct.

Significantly the term 'other abuse' is inserted to allow police, prosecutors, and the courts a wide discretion. Breadth is also captured by physical, violent, and threatening abuse, and the statutory guidance makes reference especially to the needs of disabled victims who are harmed when access to medical aids, equipment, medication, or food are denied.[10] The violence or threats could be 'towards' another family member and not solely the primary victim of the abuse, as stated in section 5. The statutory guidance also extends this principle to violence or threats towards household pets.[11]

Controlling or coercive behaviour is an offence under section 76 Serious Crime Act (SCA) 2015 and is included within section 1. The behaviour is not further defined in either statute and practitioners are advised to refer to the statutory guidance issued by the government under section 77 of the SCA.[12] Here, controlling behaviour is defined as 'a range of acts designed to make a person subordinate and/or dependent by isolating them from sources of support, exploiting their resources and capacities for personal gain, depriving them of the means needed for independence, resistance and escape and regulating their everyday behaviour'. Coercive behaviour is defined as 'an act or a pattern of acts of assault, threats, humiliation and intimidation or other abuse that is used to harm, punish, or frighten their victim'. For further discussion, see section 68 DAA.

Subsection 4 explains that 'economic abuse' means any behaviour that has a substantial adverse effect on the victim's ability to (a) acquire, use, or maintain money or other property, or (b) obtain goods or services. This captures a wider range of behaviours than the term 'financial abuse' used in the Home Office policy definition, which is limited to the use and misuse of the victim's money by the perpetrator through the means of spending it or 'using credit cards or pressuring the victim to apply for loans, which are then used to fund activities for the perpetrator'.[13] Financial abuse is included within 'economic abuse'.

iii. Critical Commentary

This section may not change current practice dramatically as local authority agencies have worked with a consistent definition of domestic violence and abuse since 2013 as a matter of policy. These agencies include those providing front-line domestic violence and abuse services, e.g., police, prosecutors, children services, independent domestic violence advocates, etc.[14] The statutory definition of domestic abuse is expected to be adopted by any organisation working with either victims, including children, or perpetrators of domestic abuse and

[10] Home Office (n 3) ch 2 at 24 para 47, 26 para 94, and 37 para 173.

[11] Home Office (n 3) ch 2, 23 at para 47.

[12] Home Office, 'Controlling or Coercive Behaviour in an Intimate or Family Relationship. Statutory Guidance Framework' (2015) s 2 https://assets.publishing.service.gov.uk/government/uploads/system/uploads/attachment_data/file/482528/Controlling_or_coercive_behaviour_-_statutory_guidance.pdf (accessed 21 April 2022).

[13] See Women's Aid https://www.womensaid.org.uk/information-support/what-is-domestic-abuse/financial-abuse/ (accessed 21 April 2022).

[14] For further information on the policy definition of domestic violence and abuse see Home Office, 'Information for Local Areas on the Change to the Definition of Domestic Violence and Abuse' (2013) https://assets.publishing.service.gov.uk/government/uploads/system/uploads/attachment_data/file/142701/guide-on-definition-of-dv.pdf (accessed 21 April 2022).

the statutory guidance issued pursuant to section 84 DAA provides a non-exhaustive list of them.[15]

Section 1(3) explains that 'domestic abuse' can consist of a single incident or a course of conduct. In policing and prosecuting terms this means that single incidents of physical abuse can continue to be pursued as offences under the Offences Against the Person Act 1861. However, where the time limit of six months for a summary offence has passed,[16] investigators and prosecutors should include physical assaults within a charge for a controlling and coercive behaviour offence under section 76 SCA 2015. Controlling and coercive behaviour is not an offence that consists solely of non-physical abuse by the perpetrator. It involves a pattern that is frequently, although not exclusively, characterised by physical harms in addition to psychological and non-physical forms of abuse.[17] Given the time restraints of bringing OAPA offences to court, it is expected that police and prosecutors will proceed in cases of domestic violence and abuse on the basis of a section 76 SCA charge as a matter of course. Where there is evidence to support a serious non-fatal offence or sexual assault, these should be charged as separate offences alongside a section 76 offence.

There are some concerns that submerging 'domestic violence' into the legislative definition of 'domestic abuse' could lead to authorities downplaying the seriousness of the conduct and minimising victims' experiences.[18] Whilst the term domestic abuse allows forms of non-physical abuse and coercive and controlling behaviours to be more visible to victims who may not relate to the term domestic violence, there is little reason to have absorbed domestic violence entirely within its parameters.[19] Practitioners should seek to avoid this pitfall by aligning their responses to domestic violence and abuse with their national Violence Against Women and Girls' strategies,[20] and following the statutory guidance issued under section 84 DAA.[21] It is unsurprising that the provision has opted for a gender-neutral approach, given that victims are not exclusively women and legislation should be available to protect all victims. However, the problems associated with legal gender neutrality in an area that is embedded within violence against women and girls are hoped to be alleviated with the detailed statutory guidance introduced under section 84 DAA and updated training packages and responses prompted by the guidance. In particular, practitioners should take note that domestic abuse disproportionately effects women as victims, who are more likely to experience repeat abuse, be physically injured or killed by a partner or former partner, and be coerced or controlled by them.[22] Consequently, practitioners will need to take into account women's responses to the abuse they have experienced and their specific needs when they come into contact with front-line domestic abuse services.

[15] Home Office (n 3) ch 1.

[16] Magistrates' Court Act 1980; Criminal Procedure Rules, r 7.2(10).

[17] Evan Stark, *Coercive Control: How Men Entrap Women in Personal Life* (OUP 2007).

[18] Jo Aldridge, '"Not an Either/or Situation": The Minimization of Violence Against Women in United Kingdom "Domestic Abuse" Policy' (2020) 27(11) *Violence Against Women* 1823.

[19] ibid 1823–24.

[20] In Wales see the Welsh Government, 'National Strategy on Violence Against Women, Domestic Abuse and Sexual Violence—2016-2021' (2016) https://gov.wales/sites/default/files/publications/2019-06/national-strategy-2016-to-2021.pdf; in England see Home Office, 'Tackling Violence Against Women and Girls Strategy' (2021) https://www.gov.uk/government/publications/tackling-violence-against-women-and-girls-strategy/tackling-violence-against-women-and-girls-strategy (accessed 21 April 2022).

[21] Home Office (n 3) chs 1, 2.

[22] Bettinson (n 1) 94.

The statutory guidance is greatly concerned with ensuring that all victims of domestic abuse are identified and that agencies understand the different challenges that are faced by those who have an additional vulnerable characteristic such as immigration status, race, religion, gender, sexuality, or disability. These challenges relate to the abusive tactics of the perpetrator; for example, the perpetrator may convince the victim that a complaint to the police could lead to her deportation[23] or poverty or threaten to 'out' a person's sexuality to family and friends.[24] Equally, additional vulnerable characteristics can inhibit the victim's ability to access support. For example, minoritised women fear that they will face racism, misunderstandings about their parenting that stem from their cultural practices, or fear of authority on the basis of their immigration status.[25] Overall, the section, accompanied by statutory guidance, supports the aims of the DAA by outlining what forms domestic abuse can take, providing a clear statutory definition of domestic abuse to assist statutory organisations to better understand and respond to this abuse and placing importance on the training or retraining of government agencies, including police and prosecutors. More broadly, this legal clarity will enable wider society to understand and identify all forms of domestic abuse and alert the police and local authorities where they see or experience such behaviour, giving the opportunity to protect victims and prevent further abuse.

2. DEFINITION OF 'PERSONALLY CONNECTED'

i. Context and Background

Section 2 adds further detail to section 1 by defining who is considered to be 'personally connected' for the purposes of a domestic abuse relationship. The Home Office policy definition of domestic violence and abuse did not use the term 'personally connected', instead merely describing the parties to the relationship as having been or are intimate partners or family members.[26]

The first legislative appearance of 'personally connected' is found in section 76 SCA 2015, which establishes the offence of controlling or coercive behaviour in an intimate or family relationship. The offence requires that the perpetrator and victim of the prohibited behaviour are personally connected; however, concerns were raised about its exclusion of former partners who were no longer living together.[27] Weiner explains that the rationale for excluding separated partners who no longer lived together was based on concerns that the new offence, section 76 SCA, would overlap with existing offences under the Protection from Harassment Act 1997.[28] As explained in the discussion of section 68 DAA (later in this Part of the guide),

[23] Sisters for Change, 'Unequal Regard, Unequal Protection: Public authority responses to violence against BME women in England' (2017) 24 https://www.sistersforchange.org.uk/2017/11/20/unequal-regard-unequal-protection/ (accessed 21 April 2022).

[24] Catherine Donovan and Rebecca Barnes, 'Domestic violence and abuse in lesbian, gay, bisexual and/or transgender (LGB and/or T) relationships' (2017) 22(5–6) *Sexualities* 1.

[25] Sisters for Change (n 23).

[26] Home Office Circular 003/2013 (n 4).

[27] Home Office, 'A Review of the Controlling or Coercive Behaviour Offence' (March 2021) 7 https://assets.publishing.service.gov.uk/government/uploads/system/uploads/attachment_data/file/982825/review-of-the-controlling-or-coercive-behaviour-offence.pdf (accessed 21 April 2022).

[28] C Wiener, 'From social construct to legal innovation: The offence of controlling or coercive behaviour in England and Wales' in M McMahon and P McGorrey (eds), *Criminalising Coercive Control* (Springer 2020).

coercive control can take many forms. The pattern of coercive control may also be generated by psychological, physical, and non-physical tactics, including sexual and emotional abuse.[29] The behaviour, particularly post-separation, may not fall within the ambit of harassment and stalking offences, but would equate to exercising control in order to adversely interfere with the victim's day to day life. In fact, leaving an abusive relationship is the most dangerous time for a female victim[30] and a common trigger identified by Monckton-Smith on her eight-stage homicide timeline.[31]

The Femicide Census evaluated femicides in England and Wales between 2009 and 2018 and found that 43 per cent of the women killed in intimate domestic homicides were either separated or had taken steps to separate from their partner.[32] Statistics from the year ending March 2017 to the year ending March 2019 show a lower figure of 22 per cent of intimate domestic homicides of women by their former partners.[33] However, as the Femicide Census highlights, it is difficult to determine the actual numbers, because the data is reliant on the narrative of the living perpetrators, and not the dead victim, leading them to conclude that the figures demonstrate an undercount. In addition, the ending of relationships tends to be a process rather than a single event, and the abuser may refuse to accept their partner's decision to separate from them.[34] Finally, the Femicide Census study also showed that the majority of intimate homicides of women by ex-partners took place within a year of the relationship ending (89 per cent), illustrating just how dangerous this period of time is to a female victim of domestic abuse.[35] With this background, the limitation contained in section 76 SCA that excluded former intimate partners who no longer resided with each other from the term 'personally connected' seems highly problematic and it is to be welcomed that this anomaly is not repeated in section 1 DAA.

This exclusion of former partners who no longer lived with each from the meaning of domestic abuse does not mirror the policy definition, which refers to both current and former partners or the proposed definition of domestic abuse contained in the government's *Transforming the Response to Domestic Abuse Consultation*.[36] Section 2 ensures that 'domestic abuse' applies to relationships that have ended with a new definition of 'personally connected' and section 76 SCA has been amended to reflect the same wording as section 2 under section 68 DAA.

---

[29] Stark (n 17).

[30] WHO, 'Understanding and addressing violence against women: Information Sheet' 4 https://apps.who.int/iris/bitstream/handle/10665/77421/WHO_RHR_12.38_eng.pdf;jsessionid=4DD39FB77FD32FE6CC03FE9%208F3A27D79?sequence=1 (accessed 21 April 2022).

[31] J Monckton-Smith, 'Intimate Partner Femicide: Using Foucauldian Analysis to Track an Eight-Stage Progressions to Homicide' (2019) 26(11) *Violence Against Women* 1267.

[32] Femicide Census, 'UK Femicides 2009-2018' (2019) 30 https://www.femicidecensus.org/wp-content/uploads/2020/11/Femicide-Census-10-year-report.pdf (accessed 21 April 2022).

[33] ONS, 'Domestic abuse victim characteristics, England and Wales; year ending March 2020' 11, Table 2: Domestic homicide victims by sex of victim and relationship to suspect https://www.ons.gov.uk/peoplepopulationandcommunity/crimeandjustice/articles/domesticabusevictimcharacteristicsenglandandwales/yearendingmarch2020#domestic-homicide (accessed 21 April 2022).

[34] Femicide Census (n 32) 30.

[35] ibid 31.

[36] HM Government (n 2) 5.

ii. The Section

By introducing the definition of 'domestic abuse', section 1(2)(a) states that the parties involved must be 'personally connected' to each other. Section 2 states that two people are 'personally connected' to each other if any of the following applies: (a)they are, or have been, married to each other; (b) they are, or have been, civil partners of each other; (c) they have agreed to marry one another (whether or not the agreement has been terminated); (d) they have entered into a civil partnership agreement (whether or not the agreement has been terminated); (e) they are, or have been, in an intimate personal relationship with each other; (f) they each have, or there has been a time when they each have had, a parental relationship in relation to the same child (see subsection (2)); (g) they are relatives.

The section therefore seeks to include all current and former intimate relationships and family relationships with no requirement that the parties must be living together at the time the abusive behaviour occurs.

A parental relationship in respect of a child is considered to be present under subsection 2 where (a) the person is a parent of the child, or (b) the person has parental responsibility for the child.

Subsection 3 clarifies the meaning of a child for the purpose of the provision and the wider DAA as a person under the age of 18 years. A 'civil partnership agreement' has the meaning given by section 73 of the Civil Partnership Act 2004, which includes agreements made within any part of the United Kingdom's jurisdictions or abroad.

'Parental responsibility' has the same meaning as in the Children Act (CA) 1989. Section 3 CA explains parental responsibility as having all the rights, duties, powers, responsibilities, and authority which by law a parent of a child has in relation to the child and his property.

A 'relative' is a person who falls within the meaning ascribed by section 63(1) of the Family Law Act 1996, which is: (a) a parent, step parent, child, stepchild, grandparent, grandchild of that person or of that person's spouse, former spouse, civil partner, or former civil partner; or (b) a sibling, uncle, aunt, niece, nephew or first cousin (whether of the full blood or of the half blood or by marriage or civil partnership) of that person or of that person's spouse, former spouse, civil partner, or former civil partner. It further includes a person who is cohabiting or has cohabited with another person, any person who would fall within paragraph (a) or (b) if the parties were married to each other or were civil partners of each other.

Sections 1 and 2 of the DAA therefore encompass both a wide range of behaviours and relationships within the definition of domestic abuse.

iii. Critical Commentary

Implemented from 1 October 2021, section 2 provides practitioners with a full list of individuals who can be involved in domestic abuse relationships. As it differs from the previous policy definition of domestic violence and abuse by adopting the phrase 'personally connected', local authorities, police, prosecutors, and other domestic abuse agencies will need to update local policies to reflect this new list. Section 2 places domestic abuse firmly within domestic relationships and is not predicated on a domestic location. Whilst the term 'personally connected' has previously arisen in the context of the controlling and coercive behaviour offence, section 76 SCA, section 2 DAA does not restrict the term to domestic abuse relationships which are ongoing, or where ended the parties remain living together. Section 68 amends section 76 SCA to align with the approach taken in section 2 DAA, coming into effect from Autumn 2022. Ensuring that the provisions within the DAA applies to both current and former intimate relationships and to relatives who do not live together reflects the experiences of many victims of domestic abuse.

The broad definition in section 2 is to be welcomed, as it provides a means to fulfil the objectives of the Act, both to prevent domestic abuse and to protect victims from it. Leaving relationships are dangerous times for victims; recognising that abuse continues post-separation allows practitioners to develop and implement appropriate responses to it.

3. CHILDREN AS VICTIMS OF DOMESTIC ABUSE

i. Context and Background

Children aged under 18 who are the direct recipients of abusive behaviour by a parent or relative and children aged 15 or under abused by an intimate partner are understood to be victims of child abuse.[37] As such, agencies employ statutory frameworks governing child abuse, even though the circumstances also amount to domestic abuse. However, evidence suggests that between a quarter and a third of children are victims of domestic abuse where they witness it within their home and see their parent's ongoing distress resulting from the abuse.[38] Children are also harmed trying to protect the parent suffering the abusive behaviour. Exposure to domestic abuse in this way causes a range of emotional impacts upon the child, which can persist into their adult lives,[39] with Walby estimating the overall cost of domestic violence to mental healthcare to be £176 million.[40] In addition, there is evidence to suggest that witnessing domestic abuse as a child is a factor that many adult victims of domestic abuse have experienced and section 120 Adoption and Children Act 2002 includes these circumstances within the meaning of harm for the purposes of the Children Act 1989.[41] During the Consultation process of the Domestic Abuse Bill the government noted the significance of recognising the impact of domestic abuse on children as witnesses to it and the need to improve the support available to them.[42] An amendment to include children who witness domestic abuse as direct victims of domestic abuse was introduced in July 2020 after a number of MPs encouraged the government to do more to recognise these children as victims of domestic abuse.[43] Section 3 is therefore intended to be employed by statutory and non-statutory agencies responding to domestic abuse, supporting commissioned services to address the impact of domestic abuse on children.

[37] Home Office (n 3).

[38] HM Government (n 2) 16

[39] Women's Aid, 'Domestic abuse and your mental health' https://www.womensaid.org.uk/the-survivors-handbook/domestic-abuse-and-your-mental-health/; HM Government (n 2) Annex 6 (accessed 21 April 2022). https://www.basw.co.uk/system/files/resources/costs_domestic_abuse.pdf

[40] Sylvia Walby, 'The Cost of Domestic Violence Research Summary' (Women & Equality Unit 2004) paladinservice.co.uk/wp-content/uploads/2013/07/cost_of_dv_research_summary-Walby-2004.pdf (accessed 21 April 2022).

[41] Office for National Statistics (2017) ('People who were abused are more likely to be abused as an adult: Exploring the impact of what can sometimes be hidden crimes') https://www.ons.gov.uk/peoplepopulationandcommunity/crimeandjustice/articles/peoplewhowereabusedaschildrenaremorelikelytobeabusedasanadult/2017-09-27 (accessed 21 April 2022).

[42] HM Government (n 2) 16–17.

[43] Hansard, HC vol 678, col 701 (6 July 2020) https://hansard.parliament.uk/commons/2020-07-06/debates/CEAE6941-5DC8-4F76-9377-3DE3ED0F3553/DomesticAbuseBill (accessed 21 April 2022).

ii. The Section

Section 3 introduces for the first time a legal recognition of children as victims of domestic abuse where they witness it. A child for the purpose of section 3 is defined in subsection 4 as a person under the age of 18 years old. A child will be recognised as such under subsection 1 where the behaviour of the perpetrator towards the initial victim is domestic abuse as defined in section 1. Subsection 2 states that references to victims in the DAA includes a reference to a child who (a) sees or hears, or experiences the effects of, the abuse, and (b) is related to A or B. What amounts to being 'related' is explained further in subsection 3 and includes a parent of the child, or a person with parental responsibility for the child. In line with section 2 DAA, subsection 4 confirms that the term 'parental responsibility' in section 3(2)(a) has the same meaning adopted by the Children Act 1989. Alternatively, under section 3(b) a child is related to the perpetrator of the domestic abuse, where they are relatives to each other. A relative, as explained in section 4, shares the same meaning provided in section 63(1) Family Law Act 1996 to the Domestic Abuse Act and is consistent with section 4 of the Domestic Abuse Act.

iii. Critical Commentary

The recognition of children who witness domestic abuse as victims of the abuse in their own right is intended to raise awareness of their experiences of domestic abuse and promote better identification of them. This reform, that is supported by front-line domestic abuse agencies,[44] reflects the approach taken in Scotland under section 5(3) Domestic Abuse (Scotland) Act 2018. A provision which also recognises that a child witnessing domestic abuse is an aggravating factor of that abuse.

Where agencies understand what factors affect children specifically, it is expected that they will be better informed to meet the child's needs when considering how to respond to the domestic abuse.[45] Ensuring the safety of children in domestic households is a concern for all agencies, not just Children Services. For example, victims are made homeless by domestic abuse, or remain in an abusive situation to avoid homelessness for their children. The introduction of this provision is significant for practitioners in the family courts. Family courts must apply the guidance in Practice Direction 12J[46] when dealing with fact finding hearings involving domestic abuse. *Re H-N and Others (Children) (Domestic Abuse: Finding of fact hearings)*[47] emphasised the importance of allowing sufficient evidence of controlling and coercive behaviour to be presented at fact finding hearings and section 3 DAA now elevates the importance of the issue with children to be seen as direct recipients of abuse upon witnessing it. In conjunction with sections 1 and 2 DAA, section 3 is also a reminder to the family courts that domestic abuse continues post-separation, and a child remains a victim of domestic abuse where the perpetrator uses coercive and controlling behaviours towards the other parent even where the family are no longer living within the same household.

---

[44] See Women's Aid Briefing for Domestic Abuse Bill (2021) https://www.womensaid.org.uk/wp-content/uploads/2021/03/Womens-Aid-Briefing-for-Domestic-Abuse-Bill-Lords-Report-Stage.pdf (accessed 21 April 2022).

[45] Home Office (n 3) ch 3.

[46] Practice Direction 12J: Child Arrangements and Contact Orders: Domestic Abuse and Harm www.justice.gov.uk/courts/procedure-rules/family/practice_directions/pd_part_12j (accessed 21 April 2022).

[47] [2021] EWCA Civ 448.

Prosecutions should be considered where a child is harmed from witnessing domestic abuse in the household. The statutory guidance issued under section 84 Domestic Abuse Act, highlights that the offence of neglect and violence under section 1 Children and Young Person Act 1933 includes causing emotional or psychological suffering to a child, since it was amended in 2015 by section 66 SCA. Local authorities who become aware of domestic abuse in a household where children reside should consult with police and prosecution authorities to consider whether bringing charges for this offence would be appropriate. Caution should be exercised, ensuring that the parent victim of the abuse is not subject to prosecution or the threat of it. Authorities must be mindful not to become complicit in the perpetrator's abuse of the parent and child victim.

Section 3 raises the profile of the plight of children who are in households where domestic abuse is taking place and should ensure that more attention is placed on the needs of such children in multi-agency practices. Section 3 is supported by statutory guidance which explains the impact of witnessing all forms of domestic abuse on a child, including coercive and controlling behaviours. For some agencies, section 3 will not be expected to change their current working practices. However, for others, for example schools, they will need to develop domestic abuse policies and working practices. Organisations that work with children must be trained in how to identify young victims of domestic abuse and provide them with or signpost them to appropriate support. Overall, this section furthers the purpose of the Domestic Abuse Act as it seeks to improve the responses to domestic abuse experienced by children who are too often hidden from view.

PART 2 OF THE ACT
THE DOMESTIC ABUSE COMMISSIONER (SECTIONS 4–21)

4

THE DOMESTIC ABUSE COMMISSIONER (SECTIONS 4–21)

Susan Edwards, Frank Mullane*

1. SECTIONS 4–16 THE DOMESTIC ABUSE COMMISSIONER

i. Context and Background

Sections 4–16, establish the public office of the Domestic Abuse Commissioner (DAC) and set out a framework for the responsibilities, duties, and powers of the Commissioner. Sections 8, 9, 11, 13, and 14 set out the responsibilities of the DAC to the Secretary of State and sections 15–18 set out the responsibilities of the DAC and specified public authorities to each other. Sections 57 and 58 (discussed later in Part II of this Guide) set out the responsibility of public authorities to the DAC (s 57(9)) and local authority powers under section 57(7). Sections 4, 5, 6, 8, 9, 11, 14, and 15 set out the responsibilities of the Secretary of State. This inter-relationship

* Sections 4–16, 18–21 by Susan Edwards, section 17 by Frank Mullane.

Susan Edwards, Frank Mullane, *The Domestic Abuse Commissioner (Sections 4–21)* In: *Blackstone's Guide to the Domestic Abuse Act 2021*. Edited by Susan Edwards, David Malone, and Gillian Jones KC, Oxford University Press.
DOI: 10.1093/oso/9780192870513.003.0004

of duties and obligations is mandated to promote good practice regarding domestic abuse protection and to facilitate the development of plans and strategies for better understanding and prevention of domestic abuse at local and governmental level through consultation with statutory and voluntary bodies. Requirements (duties) are placed on specified public authorities, voluntary organisations, and other persons, to produce an annual report on domestic abuse and their responsibilities and submit these to the DAC. Having considered these reports, the DAC is then under a duty to make recommendations to the Secretary of State.

The purpose of the statutory appointment by the Secretary of State of the office of Commissioner is to promote and steer change and raise awareness in particular areas of public concern and importance. The appointment of Commissioners, who are quasi government bodies, independent, but appointed by Secretary of State, across a broad range of areas of social and legal concern is a demonstration of devolving functions from the state and central government to specified public authorities making specified bodies more accountable.

In 2004, the Domestic Violence, Crime and Victims Act (DVCVA) (s 48) established a Commissioner for Victims and Witnesses with the general purpose to promote the interests of victims and witnesses (s 49) and to review practice establishing a victim's code of practice (s 32). Significantly, the DVCVA creates the role and function of Parliamentary Commissioner with a responsibility to investigate complaints of failure to perform a relevant duty (s 47 and Sch 7, s 2(2)(1A)(a)).

A Children's Commissioner was also established under the Children Act 2004 (s 1 and Sch I, s 3(1)) with similar functions further developed in sections 107–116 of the Children and Families Act 2014.

Equality and Human Rights Commissioners[1] were established under the Equality Act 2006 (ss 1–43 and Sch 1). With regard to Equality and Human Rights Commissioners a different model is found and between ten and fifteen appointed Commissioners serve on the government established Equality and Human Rights Committee, a statutory body established under the Equality Act 2006. Under the section heading on 'judicial review', section 30(3), the Equality Act 2006 makes reference to human rights obligations: 'The Commission may, in the course of legal proceedings for judicial review which it institutes (or in which it intervenes), rely on section 7(1)(b) of the Human Rights Act 1998 (c. 42) (breach of Convention rights).' International human rights obligations are also embedded within the statutory requirements and functions of the Commissioner with regard to the Children's Commissioner (s 107[2A](1) Children and Families Act 2014), where the Commissioner must have regard to the United Nations Convention on the Rights of the Child: 'The Children's Commissioner must, in particular, have regard to the United Nations Convention on the Rights of the Child in considering for the purposes of the primary function what constitute the rights and interests of children (generally or so far as relating to a particular matter).'

The Modern Slavery Act (MSA) 2015 (ss 40–44) established the Independent Anti-Slavery Commissioner with similar powers, functions, and duties to work with public authorities. In the case of the Anti-Slavery Commissioner, Schedule 3 of the Act sets out the detail. The MSA especially provides a model upon which the provisions regulating the DAC is built.

Unlike the Equality Act 2006 and the Children and Families Act 2014, no international convention obligations are considered within the DAA or with regard to the duties of the DAC. The failure of the UK government to ratify the Istanbul Convention (Council of

[1] See https://www.gov.uk/government/news/new-equality-and-human-rights-commissioners-appointed (accessed 19 April 2022).

Europe Convention on preventing and combating violence against women and domestic violence),[2] a landmark treaty, is of particular significance. Article 4 of that treaty requires implementation of measures to protect the rights of victims, without discrimination on any ground such as sex, gender, race, colour, language, political or other opinion, national or social origin, association with a national minority, property, birth, sexual orientation, gender identity, age, state of health, disability, marital status, migrant or refugee status, or other status. Chapter 19 in Part III of this Guide deals with a failure on the part of the UK government to provide measures to protect migrant women.

Since the purpose of the office of the DAC is also to hold the executive and public bodies to account, including specified public authorities and presumably central government in the provision of services to victim/ survivors of domestic abuse, judicial review is theoretically available. This is an important mechanism for individuals[3] to challenge government and public authorities who may fail to exercise their duties, and particularly with regard to their duties under this Act.[4]

2. THE SECTIONS

i. Sections 4–6 Appointment, Funding, Staffing of Domestic Abuse Commissioner Office

The Secretary of State has duties he/she 'must' perform (ss 4(1), 6, 8(5), 9(7), 11(1), (4), (5a), (6a), (7a), (7b),(8a)–(8c), 14(5), and 15(5), and those he/she 'may' perform (ss 5, 8(4), 9(6), 11(4) (5b), (6b), 14(4), and 15(4).

Under section 4(1) the Secretary of State must appoint a person as the Domestic Abuse Commissioner ('the Commissioner') (currently Nicole Jacobs) to make payments (s 5), provide staff (s 6), and consult the Commissioner (s 6(2)(a)), as well as (s 6(2)(b)) obtain the Commissioner's approval as to the persons to be provided as staff for the DAC office. Under section 4, the DAC is appointed by the Secretary of State and, whilst the Commissioner is intended to be independent, matters of funding, staffing and what the Commissioner can say in the annual report is, to an extent, determined by the executive who has veto over content.

Funding for the DAC's office is provided by the Secretary of State under section 5. The budget was expected to be £1 million per annum for staff costs, with an additional budget to support other events and projects. The Joint Committee on the draft Domestic Abuse bill[5] expressed concern about whether the Commissioner would have sufficient resources to deliver what is expected, especially given what it considered an inadequate overall budget for the office and the intention that the post of Commissioner should be part-time. Nazir Afzal

---

[2] See https://www.coe.int/en/web/impact-convention-human-rights/council-of-europe-convention-on-preventing-and-combating-violence-against-women-and-domestic-violence#/ (accessed 19 April 2022).

[3] See eg challenges to public authorities and the government: *R (on the application of Skelton and Another) v West Sussex Senior Coroner* [2021] QB 525; *R (on the application of Mullane) v West Berkshire Safer Communities Partnership*[2006] EWHC 2499 (Admin); [2006] All ER (D) 476 (Jul); *R (on the application of Grice) v HM Senior Coroner for Brighton and Hove* [2020] EWHC 3581 (Admin). See also challenges to legal aid and access to justice for victims of domestic violence and abuse; *R (on the application of Rights of Women) v Lord Chancellor and Secretary of State for Justice* [2016] 3 All ER 473.

[4] The Judicial Review and Courts Act 2022 will introduce further limitations to judicial review.

[5] See Joint Committee Pt 7, paras 285, 309, 310 https://publications.parliament.uk/pa/jt201719/jtselect/jtddab/2075/207511.htm. (accessed 19 April 2022).

said it was 'nonsense' that the government was not prepared to make the post full-time when domestic abuse was estimated to cost some £66 billion a year in terms of the gross domestic product.[6]

Section 6 makes the responsibility of the appointment of staff a matter for the Secretary of State where civil servants are either to be seconded to the Commissioner's office or specifically recruited for the posts and employed by the Home Office.[7] Whilst the Secretary of State must consult with and obtain the DAC's approval, concern has been expressed regarding the independence of the DAC office and a view has been expressed that the Commissioner should directly appoint 'her' staff.

ii. Sections 7–10 Functions of Commissioner

Section 7 sets out the general functions which includes both (duties) and obligations of the Commissioner discussed further in the Domestic Abuse Draft statutory guidance[8] and Home Office factsheet.[9] Section 7(1) sets out what the DAC 'must' do, including the duty: (1) to encourage good practice in (a) the prevention of domestic abuse; and (b) the prevention, detection, investigation, and prosecution of offences involving domestic abuse.

Obligations/powers are set out under section 7(2) where, in satisfying section 7(1), the DAC 'may' (a) assess, monitor, and publish information about the provision of services to people affected by domestic abuse; (b) make recommendations to any public authority (c) undertake or support (financially or otherwise) the carrying out of research;(d) provide information, education or training; (e) take other steps to increase public awareness of domestic abuse; (f) consult with public authorities, voluntary organisations and other persons; (g) cooperate with, or work jointly with, public authorities, voluntary organisations and other persons, whether in England and Wales or outside the United Kingdom. Whilst the word 'may' is operative throughout this subsection, obligations (d) and (g) carry a responsibility which if not met would undermine the core duty of the office. Elsewhere in the Act, public authorities are required to cooperate with the Commissioner (ss 15, 16, and 58) and, as such, the responsibility of the Commissioner with regard to consultation and cooperation with public authorities and voluntary organisations is more properly a 'duty' of the weight attaching to the general duty of 'must' specified under section 7(1).

With regard to section 7(2)(c) and the DAC's obligation to undertake or support research, the DAC has published her own views on particular matters and also supported specific research initiatives.

a. *The family courts*

Since the DAC took up office, she has set out her key concerns in several documents and publications with regard to the general function objectives.[10] With regard to the family

[6] ibid paras 416–17.

[7] ibid para 390.

[8] Domestic Abuse Draft Statutory Guidance Framework (July 2021) https://www.gov.uk/government/consultations/domestic-abuse-act-statutory-guidance/domestic-abuse-draft-statutory-guidance-framework (accessed 19 April 2022).

[9] Home Office Factsheet https://homeofficemedia.blog.gov.uk/2021/04/29/domesticabuseactfactsheet/ (accessed 19 April 2022).

[10] See https://domesticabusecommissioner.uk/ (accessed 19 April 2022).

courts,[11] the Commissioner has expressed concern with the percentage of private law Children Act cases that have involved findings or allegations of domestic abuse and the risk which flows from the use of 'parental alienation' and other contact presumptions has highlighted the need for a monitoring and reporting mechanism. The Commissioner has identified the need for training of those working in the family justice system and asserted that all survivors of domestic abuse should have access to a specialist court individual domestic violence advocate (IDVA). IDVAs should be recognised as an integral part of court system and all survivors of domestic abuse should have access to non-means tested legal aid.

b. *The criminal courts*

In January 2022, it was announced that researchers at the London School of Economics had been commissioned by the DAC to produce a report by summer 2022 on support for victims and survivors of domestic abuse who have no recourse to public funds (NRPF). NRPF is discussed in Chapter 19 of this Guide. Currently, the 'domestic violence rule' allows funding only to those on spousal visas. The exclusion of migrant women from public funding was a concern raised at the Bill stage when many agreed that the rule was in breach of Article 4 of the Istanbul Convention.

The DAC under section 8 must provide reports and, under section 14, an annual report on the exercise of the Commissioner's functions to be submitted to the Secretary of State. However, to what extent the Secretary of State is obliged to take action regarding the DAC's findings, proposals, or recommendations is left unstated. The Secretary of State has the final oversight and veto concerning the content of the DAC's reports and under section 8 (4) and section 14 (4) 'may direct' the Commissioner to omit material from any report before publication if the Secretary of State considers the publication of that material '(a) might jeopardise the safety of any person, or (b) might prejudice the investigation or prosecution of an offence'.

This power of oversight is also found in the Modern Slavery Act (s 42(14)) where: 'The Secretary of State may remove from an annual report any material whose publication the Secretary of State thinks: (a) would be against the interests of national security; (b) might jeopardise the safety of any person in England and Wales; or (c) might prejudice the investigation or prosecution of an offence under the law of England and Wales.'

Under section 9(1), the DAC must provide the Secretary of State with any advice or assistance that the Secretary of State may request. Under section 9(2), the DAC may provide advice with regard to the general functions, and to 'any other person'. The content of that advice is also scrutinised by the Secretary of State before being released. Under section 9(5), 'Before publishing any advice given under this section, the Commissioner must send a draft of what is proposed to be published to the Secretary of State'. The Secretary of State 'may direct' the removal of material under (s 9(6)). Section 10 confers incidental powers on the Commissioner to do anything that the Commisioner considers would support 'her' in carrying out the functions as set out, with the exception of borrowing money.[12]

[11] Nicole Jacobs, Comment and Opinion 'Domestic abuse and the family courts: key priorities' [2021] *Fam Law* 1113 https://domesticabusecommissioner.uk/the-family-and-criminal-court-system-retraumatises-victims-according-to-a-new-report (accessed 14 November 2022).

[12] Explanatory notes Domestic Abuse (parliament.uk) https://publications.parliament.uk/pa/bills/cbill/58-01/0096/en/20096en.pdf (accessed 19 April 2022).

iii. Sections 11–14 Framework Document, Advisory Board, Strategic Plans, and Annual Reports under this Part; Secretary of State Duties and Powers

The Secretary of State must issue a framework document under section 11(1), must keep it under review, must consult the DAC (s 11(6)(a)) and the Welsh ministers (s 11(7)) and under section 11(8)(a) arrange for any framework document issued under this section to be published in the manner which the Secretary of State considers appropriate, and (b) send a copy of the framework document to the Welsh Ministers, and (c) lay a copy of the framework document before Parliament. It remains to be seen how the relationship between the DAC and the Secretary of State will work with regard to consultation which is set out in the requirements for the agreement of a framework document under section 11. The Domestic Abuse Draft framework document[13] will set out a joint statement of how the Secretary of State and Domestic Abuse Commissioner propose to work together. The framework document sets out the process by which the Secretary of State exercises the powers including clear time limits for the required consultation with the Commissioner.[14] The framework document contains less of substance and more on governance, status, roles, reporting, process, and timescales,[15] omitting any discussion of how the delicate relationship will be negotiated.

Concern was expressed at the Bill stage that there might be a conflict between the DAC and the Home Office, thus inhibiting the DAC's independence. Andrea Simon, of End Violence Against Women Coalition, said:

> We have some concerns about categories of victims such as migrant women. Since their situation is so deeply impacted by immigration policies and the Home Office is the holder of immigration enforcement, there could be a conflict in its [DAC] representing the interests of that group of victims to its very best ability.[16]

In exercising the function of the DAC office, section 12 establishes an advisory board of at least six and not more than ten persons (s 12(4)). The members of the board must include representation from a person(s) to represent the interests of victims of domestic abuse. charitable and voluntary organisations, health care, and social care providers, policing or criminal justice, and academic expertise in relation to domestic abuse. Section 13 requires the Commissioner to prepare a strategic plan to provide Parliament, ministers, and the public with information about priorities, future work programmes, and the issues the advisory board intend to report on.

Section 14 requires the DAC to produce an annual report which is subject to executive scrutiny and, under section 14(4), the Secretary of State may direct the DAC to remove material (noted above). This was a matter of concern to the Joint Committee on the Draft Domestic Abuse bill,[17] who considered this power of the Secretary of State might lead to

[13] Domestic Abuse Commissioner Draft Framework Document https://assets.publishing.service.gov.uk/government/uploads/system/uploads/attachment_data/file/919604/Domestic_Abuse_Commissioner_Draft_Framework_Document.pdf#:~:text=1.1.%20This%20Framework%20Document%20has%20been%20drawn%20up,out%20in%20the%20Act%20or%20other%20relevant%20enactments. (accessed 19 April 2022).

[14] ibid para 82.

[15] ibid.

[16] See Joint Committee (n 5) para 304.

[17] ibid para 296; see esp paras 391, 392.

the Secretary of State omitting important material from reports and also any advice the Commissioner might otherwise wish to publish. Concerns over independence and potential interference from the Secretary of State resulted in the resignation of Kevin Hyland the Anti-Slavery Commissioner from his role.[18] The Anti-Slavery Commissioner reporting on his experience said: 'Sometimes I would select staff, and seven months later they had not arrived, or when they did arrive, they sometimes waited two or three months for pay. In my 30 years in the police, I never, ever saw that happen once.'[19]

The Anti-Slavery Commissioner also said that he would produce reports which, had to go through a long process of negotiation and modification before approval by the Secretary of State resulting in a final report which did not fully representing his views.[20] Responding specifically to the requirement of the DAC to report to the Home Office he said that it was 'a terrible idea'.[21]

iv. Sections 15–16 Duties of Public Authorities in Relation to Commissioner

Section 15 sets out the duties of specified public authorities to cooperate 'as far as is possible' with the Commissioner and sets out the relationship between public authorities and the DAC. However, the 'cooperate as far as is possible' proviso highlights the limitations of the powers of the DAC in developing and ensuring an effective strategic partnership with public authorities.[22] The specified public authorities include: police, CPS, British Transport Police Authority; Ministry of Defence Police; immigration authorities, the Parole Board; the Criminal Cases Review Commission; local authorities and NHS in England; Her Majesty's Inspectors of Constabulary; Chief Inspector of the Crown Prosecution Service; Chief Inspector of Education, Children's Services and Skills; inspectorate under section 106 of the Education and Skills Act 2008 and the Care Quality Commission. The Secretary of State under section 15(4) may by regulation add, remove, or vary a description of a public authority.

However, section 16 does require a public authority or a government minister to respond and prepare comment under section 16(2) to any report published under section 8 and propose the action to be taken or detail why no action will be taken (s 16(4)). The response must be published within fifty-six days of the publication of the DAC's report.

v. Section 17 Domestic Homicide Reviews

a. *Context and background*

Domestic homicide reviews (DHRs) became law in April 2011, seven years after being introduced in England and Wales, via section 9 of the Domestic Violence, Crime and Victims Act 2004. DHRs are multi-agency reviews focusing on applying learning from the homicide to prevent further domestic abuse and domestic homicide. The plight of many of the victims had been considered in the Multi-Agency Risk Assessment Conference (MARAC) and many

---

[18] Independent Anti-Slavery Commissioner: letter of resignation, gov.uk (www.gov.uk) https://www.gov.uk/government/publications/independent-anti-slavery-commissioner-letter-of-resignation.

[19] Joint Committee (n 5) 396.

[20] ibid 298, 396, 397.

[21] ibid 299.

[22] ibid 85.

were known to police and other public protection agencies. Yet, the deadly trajectory was unaltered. Some may wonder if learning from DHRs is being adequately applied.

Community safer partnerships (CSPs) have the responsibility to commission DHRs. Agencies taking part are typically police, health trusts, GP practices, probation, adult social care, children's social care, housing providers, and local domestic abuse specialist organisations. These agencies are normally part of the local CSP.

The Home Office published statutory guidance to assist those carrying out reviews, revising that in 2013 and 2016. Another refresh is expected in 2022. Although the original guidance could be read to mean that a DHR should be undertaken following a suicide or unexplained death where there was a domestic abuse history, it became clearer in 2016 when the revised guidance included at paragraph 18:

> Where a victim took their own life (suicide) and the circumstances give rise to concern, for example it emerges that there was coercive controlling behaviour in the relationship, a review should be undertaken, even if a suspect is not charged with an offence or they are tried and acquitted. Reviews are not about who is culpable.[23]

This obligation has led to a surge in DHRs being undertaken following suicides. This is not unexpected given that available research infers that suicides following domestic abuse outnumber homicides.[24]

Before DHRs are published they must pass a quality assurance process. The Home Office appointed several expert readers to assess each DHR against certain criteria,[25] including that the DHR followed the statutory guidance. These assessments are shared with members of the National Quality Assurance Panel[26] (drawn from the statutory and charitable sectors but chaired by the Home Office) who also receive the DHR reports. The panel decides if the DHR is suitable for publication and, in reality, it always advises the CSP what changes are required before publication can happen. These range from small changes (the CSP is trusted to make these and then publish, to more changes required and to be checked by the Home Office only, to substantial changes required, including sometimes, a rewrite (possibly requiring a new chair), which must be put before the panel again. The Home Office then writes to the CSP with the panel's decision and these letters are expected to be published.

Applying learning The statutory guidance includes:

> Completing the action plan and publishing the DHR is only the beginning of the process. To derive value from the DHR process and prevent further abuse and homicide, CSPs should satisfy themselves that there are appropriate governance mechanisms in place for monitoring delivery against DHR action plans.[27]

---

[23] Home Office, 'Multi-agency Statutory Guidance for the Conduct of Domestic Homicide Reviews' (December 2016) https://www.gov.uk/government/publications/revised-statutory-guidance-for-the-conduct-of-domestic-homicide-reviews (accessed 29 January 2022).

[24] Sylvia Walby http://openaccess.city.ac.uk/id/eprint/21681/1/The%20Cost%20of%20Domestic%20Violence.pdf (accessed 29 January 2022).

[25] Home Office, 'Criteria for considering Domestic Homicide Review reports' (June 2013) https://www.gov.uk/government/publications/criteria-for-considering-domestic-homicide-review-reports (accessed 29 January 2022).

[26] Home Office, 'Terms of Reference (June 2013) Domestic Homicide Review Quality Assurance Panel' https://www.gov.uk/government/publications/terms-of-reference-domestic-homicide-review-quality-assurance-panel (accessed 29 January 2022).

[27] Home Office (n 23).

DHRs are not adversarial processes, and their recommendations are expected to be followed, but there are no real conventional teeth behind them. It is a collaborative approach, and it will always be difficult to measure their effect. However, teeth of another kind may come from the following aspect of DHRs. A central thread in these reviews, supported by the statutory guidance, is that they are about learning and not attributing blame and that this non-hostile approach makes it more likely that we will first reveal what needs to be learned and second, we will apply that learning. This philosophy came from the USA where the fatality review movement started in the 1990s. Professor Neil Websdale of the Arizona State University wrote, in personal communication to me: 'those reviews which have led to the most profound changes in agency behaviours are those shrouded in no blame cultures'.

We have spent many years developing our review methodology and now we should invest more resource into ensuring that identifying lessons gets translated into changing behaviours, policies, and procedures. Arguably, there has been insufficient focus on this aspect. Three initiatives may assist.

b. *The Section*

First, section 17 of the Domestic Abuse Act 2021 (DA Act 2021), amended section 9 of the Domestic Violence, Crime and Victims Act 2004 (establishment and conduct of domestic homicide reviews) as follows:

(2) After subsection (3A) insert—

'(3B) A person or body within subsection (4)(a) that establishes a domestic homicide review (whether or not held pursuant to a direction under subsection (2)) must send a copy of any report setting out the conclusions of the review to the Domestic Abuse Commissioner.

(3C) The copy must be sent as soon as reasonably practicable after the report is completed.'[28]

Secondly, subject to agreement and funding from government, the Domestic Abuse Commissioner (DAC) is seeking to develop an oversight mechanism that would bring together findings, recommendations and learning from across relevant reviews relating to domestic homicides and suicides (primarily DHRs, but also coronial preventing future death reports and others). This would provide a national picture, enable analysis leading to identification of key themes and provide the evidence for the escalation of common issues to relevant agencies or government departments. The mechanism would also trigger the following up with local and national partners to understand how recommendations have been implemented and allow for tracking against progress.

Thirdly, the DAC will sit on the steering group of the DHR Network created by AAFDA with the objective of reducing domestic abuse and fatal domestic abuse via better quality DHRs.[29]

DHRs and other multi-agency reviews may not, together, bring all of the change required significantly to reduce domestic abuse and fatal domestic abuse. The inquest also has a role with its ability to challenge agencies via prevention of future death reports. More importantly, the inquest is a more independent enquiry than a DHR. It may follow, but not necessarily, that a more independent enquiry may elicit learning not previously unearthed. There have been judicial reviews of whether an inquest should be resumed where other reviews have already been held. Following the death of his mother Vittoria Baker, Silvera successfully

[28] Domestic Abuse Act 2021, s 17.

[29] https://aafda.org.uk/news/a-dhr-network (accessed 30 January 2022).

argued that the NHS Trust investigation and the DHR did not mean the inquest need not be resumed.[30]

One attempt to increase the capability of the family in the DHR which arguably also helps the reviewers (much better relationship) was conceived in the statutory guidance in 2016 after an approach from AAFDA,[31] of which I am CEO. Seven steps were suggested to the Home Office which if applied would raise the families' status from being involved to being integral to the review. The Home Office accepted these and included them in revised statutory guidance. The steps are that families should be offered: specialist and expert advocacy (and specialist help for children), opportunity to assist with the scope of the DHR, the choice of medium through which to participate, a meeting with the DHR panel (needn't be restricted to one meeting), regular updates, privacy, and time to review the draft report and opportunity to help create change after the review.

c. *Critical Commentary*

Improving DHRs A number of other initiatives should be considered to help DHRs have more impact.

The terms of reference for the Home Office Quality Assurance Panel for DHRs would benefit from development including that the panel checks that recommendations in DHRs have been implemented and have led to identifiable and positive outcomes. Best practice could be shared with under-performing CSPs. A repository of all DHRs is now being built by the Home Office. This should conceive regular and frequent thematic analyses of DHR findings, half yearly or annually should be the target as happens in Australia and Canada for example. Regular regional roadshows exhibiting best practice may improve performance of CSPs, which have different levels of knowledge of DHR best practice.

The statutory guidance for DHRs should be amended to include going beyond the date of death to identify, for example, poor investigations by police of suicides and unexplained deaths. Improving police investigations of these types of deaths is likely to increase levels of justice as unchecked criminality is identified. This includes correctly identifying where a homicide has been presented as a suicide and identifying where domestic abuse has caused, or in part caused, the person to take their own life. In 2017, Nicholas Allen was convicted of the manslaughter of his ex-girlfriend after she killed herself following his abuse.[32] The learning derived from the DHR going beyond the date of death may also help to prevent fatal domestic abuse. Police should investigate suicides where there has been a domestic abuse history (reported or not) or where there is suspicion of domestic abuse, with the same rigour that they investigate homicides. AAFDA is working with approximately 100 families bereaved by suicide/unexplained death following domestic abuse and the families often report superficial or non-existent police investigations. Police should record suspected domestic abuse suicides, so everyone understands the extent of the problem well before the inquest.

Someone with lived experience, speaking for victims of fatal domestic abuse and their families, should be on the Domestic Abuse Commissioner's Advisory Board and on every domestic abuse local partnership boards. This would ensure the interests of victims of fatal domestic abuse are considered.

[30] *Silvera v HM Senior Coroner for Oxfordshire* [2017] EWHC 2499 (Admin).

[31] www.aafda.org.uk (accessed 29 January 2022).

[32] https://www.bbc.co.uk/news/uk-40758095 (accessed 30 January 2022).

It seems a reasonable speculation that not all significant improvements to public protection stem from activities that are adversarial in nature. Although inquests are inquisitorial and about fact finding, many professionals have commented that being witnesses in a Middleton inquest feels adversarial. Perhaps DHRs provide another way to make people safer. DHRs have raised the status of domestic abuse as an affliction that CSPs must address. They encourage partnership working and raise understanding of domestic abuse and its impact on victims.

Limitations The effectiveness of DHRs as regards achieving their objectives of reducing domestic abuse and fatal domestic abuse, is in part determined by many other variables including culture and funding. DHRs often lead to numerous improvements being made to policy and practice, like a continuous audit. We may have to rely on narratives from victims and professionals to believe that those changes will be benefiting victims somewhere as it is extremely difficult, if not impossible, to measure the direct effectiveness of DHRs given that multiple other initiatives are simultaneously acting on agency practice and it is not possible to establish a control group.

Converting changes in policy and practice to improved behaviours in public protection professionals may require cultural shifts. This is where the DAC's oversight mechanism and more frequent thematic analyses from the Home Office may assist. Section 7 of the DA Act 2021 requires of the DAC that:

The Commissioner must encourage good practice in—

(a) the prevention of domestic abuse;

(b) the prevention, detection, investigation, and prosecution of offences involving domestic abuse;

(c) the identification of—
  (i) people who carry out domestic abuse;
  (ii) victims of domestic abuse;
  (iii) children affected by domestic abuse;

(d) the provision of protection and support to people affected by domestic abuse.[33]

If established, the oversight mechanism will be an exciting initiative which will hopefully help make the DAC's reports laid before Parliament compelling narratives and evidence, with which the Secretary of State will concur.

vi. Section 18 Disclosure of Information, Miscellaneous, and Supplementary

Section 18 gives the DAC the power to disclose information to assist in the delivery of the Commissioner's functions. It is envisaged that this is a two-way information sharing but any sharing of information must not override data protection legislation (see super complaint discussed in Part III Chapter One of this Guide). Under section 18(4):

But nothing in this Part requires or authorises any of the following—(a) the disclosure of any patient information (see subsection (5)); (b) the making of a disclosure which, although made

[33] DAA 2021, s 7.

in the exercise of a function under this Part, would contravene the data protection legislation (see subsection (6)); (c) the making of a disclosure which is prohibited by any of Parts 1 to 7 or Chapter 1 of Part 9 of the Investigatory Powers Act 2016.

vii. Section 19 Restriction on the DAC's Exercise of Functions

The wording of 'may not' also places limitations on the DAC role. Section 7(3), subject to subsection (4), the Commissioner may not do anything in pursuance of the general duty under subsection (1) that—(a) relates to a devolved Welsh authority, or (b) otherwise relates to Welsh devolved matters. Under section 6(b), the Secretary of State may not issue a framework document without the agreement of the Commissioner. Under section 19 the DAC 'may not' exercise any function in relation to an individual case by intervening.

viii. Section 20 Duty to Report on Domestic Services

Under section 20 the DAC is under a duty to report on the need for and the provision of domestic abuse services in England. But subsection (1) does not require the Commissioner to report on the need for, or provision of, services provided to people who reside in relevant accommodation (within the meaning of section 57(2)).

ix. Section 21 Amendments

Section 21 deals with amendments relating to the Commissioner with three consequential amendments: the Commissioner cannot be an MP, the Commissioner is subject to the Freedom of Information Act 2020, and the scrutiny of Senedd Cymru with relation to the Commissioner is amended.

PART 3 OF THE ACT
POWERS FOR DEALING WITH DOMESTIC ABUSE (SECTIONS 22–56)

5
DOMESTIC ABUSE PROTECTION NOTICES AND ORDERS, DEFINITIONS, BREACHES, AND THE POLICE ROLE (SECTIONS 22–27)

Martin O'Neill

1. SECTIONS 22–27 DOMESTIC ABUSE PROTECTION NOTICES AND ORDERS, DEFINITIONS, BREACHES, AND THE POLICE ROLE

i. Context and Background

The Domestic Abuse Act (DAA) 2021 creates new notices and orders that replace the existing domestic violence protection notice (DVPN) and domestic violence protection order (DVPO). The original orders, premised upon the use or threat of violence, were created by sections 24–33 Crime and Security Act (CSA) 2010 and have been in place since 2014.[1]

[1] Kate Blackburn and Sofia Graca, 'A critical reflection on the use and effectiveness of DVPNs and DVPOs' (2021) 22(1) *Police Practice and Research* 1 https://doi.org/10.1080/15614263.2020.1759059 (accessed 2 February 2022).

Martin O'Neill, *Domestic Abuse Protection Notices and Orders, Definitions, Breaches, and the Police Role (Sections 22–27)*
In: *Blackstone's Guide to the Domestic Abuse Act 2021*. Edited by Susan Edwards, David Malone, and Gillian Jones KC,
Oxford University Press. © Martin O'Neill 2023. DOI: 10.1093/oso/9780192870513.003.0005

Their use has been sporadic and there have been criticisms of their practical implementation and their effectiveness.[2] The notices were designed to provide short-term breathing space for domestic violence victims in order to allow them to consider their next move following an incident.[3] The DVPO was designed to have a maximum duration of twenty-eight days. Once introduced into practice in 2014, the orders joined a complex and often confusing tapestry of orders available in family, civil, and criminal court contexts where domestic abuse was a factor (i.e., non-molestation orders (NMOs), restraining orders (ROs), and occupation orders (OOs).[4] Concerns have been raised about the judicial attitude to some of these orders, in particular reluctance of family courts to interfere with property rights,[5] as well as unequal enforcement of some orders over others, which in effect creates a dual system of protective measures enforced differently depending upon the court of origin.[6] Bates and Hester found, for instance, that ROs issued in criminal proceedings were enforced more than civil court issued NMOs.[7] The attraction of DVPNs and DVPOs was their 'in principle' similarity to other civil orders previously utilised in England and Wales (i.e., anti-social behaviour orders (ASBOs), and extended to certain sexual offender orders (i.e., sexual risk orders (SROs), constraining individuals behaviour.[8] These other civil orders (in both interim and full forms) like breach of the DVPN and DVPO, carried a power of arrest for breach, although the sanction provided for breach of a DVPO was minimal, it being treated as a civil breach of a court order under section 63 of the Magistrates Court Act, 1980. This could entail a £50 per day fine in default (up to a maximum of £5,000) or two months' imprisonment. Breach of SROs attracts a criminal sanction in the form of potential imprisonment of up to five years.[9] Presumably this was to reflect the gravity with which some of these cases were viewed, although it is hard to discern why legislators chose a non-criminal sanction for breach of a DVPO.

The other orders discussed (ASBOs and SROs) demonstrated a legislative shift from immediate criminalisation in favour of an attempt to contain behaviour by way of a civil order, only responding with a criminal sanction where necessary (what has been labelled a 'hybridisation' of protection orders).[10] Breach of a DVPN and DVPO was arrestable, and breach of a DVPO was a contempt of court rather than a criminal offence. The other orders available (NMO, RO, and OO) also contained sanctions upon breach including arrest. However, concerns were raised by the Centre for Women's Justice (CWJ) about the effectiveness of the police use of the protective orders available in domestic abuse cases. As a result, CWJ made a super complaint to HMICFRS under the Police Super-complaints (Designation and Procedure) Regulations 2018,

---

[2] Jamie Grace, *Domestic Abuse Disclosure Schemes* (Kindle edn, 2022) 235; see also Centre for Women's Justice super-complaint (2019) https://assets.publishing.service.gov.uk/government/uploads/system/uploads/attachment_data/file/797419/Super-complaint_report.FINAL.PDF (accessed 16 February 2022).

[3] Blackburn and Graca (n 1). See also Explanatory Notes to the DAA 2021 https://www.legislation.gov.uk/ukpga/2021/17/pdfs/ukpgaen_20210017_en.pdf (accessed 16 February 2022).

[4] Roger Bird, *Domestic Abuse: Law and Practice* (8th edn, Lexis Nexis 2020) 27–34; Non-Molestation Orders: Part IV of the Family Law Act 1996, Restraining orders: the Protection from Harassment Act 1997, and Occupation Orders (Part IV of the Family Law Act 1996).

[5] Rosemary Hunter, 'Domestic abuse, a UK perspective' in John Eekelaar and Rob George, *Routledge Handbook of Family Law and Policy* (Kindle edn, Taylor & Francis 2020).

[6] Lis Bates and Marianne Hester, 'No longer a civil matter? The design and use of protection orders for domestic violence in England and Wales' (2020) 42(2) *Journal of Social Welfare and Family Law* 133.

[7] ibid 149.

[8] Terry Thomas and Daniel J Marsh, *The Sex Offender Register: Politics, Policy and Public Opinion* (1st edn, Routledge 2021) 108–109.

[9] ibid.

[10] Bates and Hester (n 6).

pointing out what they saw as deficiencies in police use of bail conditions, NMOs, Restraining Orders, DVPNs and DVPOs. In relation to NMO, the complaint contended that the police often advised victims that a NMO was suitable as an *alternative* to arrest, and then often failed to arrest for breach of a NMO.[11] That said, the police perspective identified that administrative processing failures meant that records of orders were either not kept or else difficult to locate, and problematic and vague wording in orders sometimes meant arrest was not possible.[12] In terms of DVPN and DVPO use, it has been suggested they were underused due to lack of knowledge and understanding (particularly in coercive control cases), and because the police bear the cost of applications and receive no funding to support this process (this is not the case for victims in relation to DAPOs).[13] Others identify a potential attitudinal problem, with practitioners considering low physical harm to reflect less serious cases and therefore less police intervention and order outcomes.[14] HMICFRS research found sporadic use of DVPOs, and a trend toward decreased applications. Many forces are still not using DVPOs as widely as they could, and opportunities to use them are continuing to be missed. Over half of the forces that were able to provide data on the use of DVPOs reported a decrease in the number of DVPOs granted per 100 domestic abuse related offences in the 12 months to 30 June 2016 compared to the twelve months to 31 March 2015.[15]

Data deficiency in this area, as well as lack of research was also highlighted. The research sought practitioner views as to why figures were so low. They reported:

> We asked officers from 37 forces why they think the number of DVPNs and DVPOs issued is so low. More than half reported finding DVPNs time-consuming, complicated, bureaucratic and difficult. These tended to be staff from forces where DVPN use is falling. In forces where their use is high, we found that DVPNs tend to be widely understood, embedded in processes and supported by a legal team.[16]

These views support the research on the DVPN/DVPO pilot scheme, where time and bureaucracy were seen as key barriers to their use.[17] In terms of Restraining Orders, it was argued that their use was equally sporadic. Whilst HMICFRS did not find underuse of this order, they did find that RO numbers had fallen, in line with a reduction in prosecutions for domestic abuse cases between 2016 and 2018.[18] HMICFRS pointed out there is a paucity

---

[11] See CWJ (n 2).

[12] College of Policing, Her Majesty's Inspectorate of Constabulary Fire and Rescue Service, Independent Office of Police Conduct 'A duty to protect: police use of protective measures in cases involving violence against women and girls' (HM Government) 2021. https://assets.publishing.service.gov.uk/government/uploads/system/uploads/attachment_data/file/1012890/a-duty-to-protect-police-use-of-protective-measures-cases-involving-violence-against-women-and-girls.pdf (accessed 16 February 2022).

[13] Parliamentary Select Committee on the Domestic Abuse Bill [109] https://publications.parliament.uk/pa/jt201719/jtselect/jtddab/2075/207506.htm (accessed 16 February 2022).

[14] Mandy Burton, 'Emergency barring orders in domestic violence cases: What can England and Wales learn from other European countries?' (2015) 27 *Child & Family Law Quarterly* 25.

[15] Her Majesty's Inspectorate of Constabulary and Fire & Rescue Services, 'A progress report on the police response to domestic abuse' (November 2017), https://www.justiceinspectorates.gov.uk/hmicfrs/wp-content/uploads/progress-report-on-the-police-response-to-domestic-abuse.pdf (accessed 16 February 2022).

[16] ibid.

[17] Liz Kelly and others, 'Evaluation of the Pilot of Domestic Violence Protection Orders' Home Office Research Report 76 (TSO 2013) https://assets.publishing.service.gov.uk/government/uploads/system/uploads/attachment_data/file/506148/2016-03-08_DVPO_report_for_publication.pdf (accessed 16 February 2022).

[18] ibid.

of research in relation to DVPN and DVPO usage. Blackburn and Graca[19] provide a more recent snapshot of Metropolitan Police Service use of DVPN and DVPO between 2016 and 2017 and found a high success rate in terms of securing a DVPO, which appeared to reflect what was then the national trend identified by previous reports.[20]

2. SECTIONS 22–27 DAPN AND DAPO

The new DAPN and DAPO are not yet in force (commencement indicated early 2023). At the consultation stage, the government pledged to retain protective measures but sought to align them to the new definition of abuse rather than the more limiting term 'violence'.[21] The move is consistent with the general acceptance that domestic violence is but one part of the wider abusive landscape, which includes a number of different behaviours beyond physical violence and overt injury. Currently, the government intends to pilot the measures to test the new regime.[22] Draft guidance on DAPNs and DAPOs was issued to police in January 2021.[23] The draft makes clear:

> The Government's aim in developing DAPNs and DAPOs is to bring together the strongest elements of the existing protective order regime into a single comprehensive, flexible order to afford longer-term protection for victims of domestic abuse and their children. These orders will be used to protect victims from all forms of domestic abuse, including non-physical abuse, economic abuse, psychological and emotional abuse and controlling or coercive behaviour.[24]

The orders are intended as the 'go to' order in domestic abuse cases,[25] in part to remedy the confusing array of orders available and to allow for immediate protection, thus enhancing victim safety. Most importantly, the orders are available from civil, family, and criminal courts and can be applied for by the victim, the police, and any interested parties.[26] The emergency nature of the DAPN stays, although there are some elements that have changed and are subject to discussion below. The police will be able to issue a DAPN in appropriate situations, and a hearing for a full DAPO must be scheduled in court within 48 hours of the notice being provided (s 29(2)). A DAPN is described by the Act as an order that prohibits a person aged 18 or over from being abusive towards a person with whom they are personally connected (s 22(2)). 'Abuse' is the term now used instead of 'use or threats of violence' to

---

[19] Blackburn and Graca (n 1).

[20] See Kelly and others (n 17). See also HMICFRS (n 15)

[21] HM Government, 'Transforming the Response to Domestic Abuse: Government Consultation' (2018) 34, https://consult.justice.gov.uk/homeoffice-moj/domestic-abuseconsultation/ (accessed 6 February 2022).

[22] Home Office, 'Domestic Abuse Protection Notices and Domestic Abuse Protection Orders Draft statutory guidance for the police' (January 2021) https://assets.publishing.service.gov.uk/government/uploads/system/uploads/attachment_data/file/955459/Draft_statutory_guidance_for_police_on_domestic_abuse_protection_notices_and_orders.pdf (accessed 6 February 2022).

[23] ibid 5.

[24] ibid 4.

[25] House of Commons Joint Committee on the Draft Domestic Abuse Bill Draft Domestic Abuse Bill First Report of Session 2017–19 Report, together with formal minutes relating to the report Ordered by the House of Lords to be printed 11 June 2019 Ordered by the House of Commons to be printed 11 June 2019 (Victoria Atkins) 23. https://publications.parliament.uk/pa/jt201719/jtselect/jtddab/2075/2075.pdf?msclkid=97c38a6ac18411eca311a3b62f98f0de (accessed 21 April 2022).

[26] Home Office (n 22).

broaden the circumstances in which a notice and subsequent order can be made. Whilst this has received positive feedback,[27] concerns have been raised that these other forms of abuse may not satisfy family courts in particular in family court mediation, where arguably tensions exist with an overriding concern to maintain family ties despite the abusive nature of relationships. Hunter points out that notwithstanding the DAA intention to broaden the definition of abuse beyond violence, family courts may still prioritise violence cases. It remains to be seen what the family courts attitude to new applications will be and what any new rules of court and guidance will say. If the situation remains that violence is elevated above abuse in importance, an opportunity to signal a sea change in attitudes will be lost.[28] Similar concerns relate to police attitudes to cases where violence is not used or threatened and whether this will lead to fewer DAPNs.[29] Abuse is defined within the Act. It can take place in England and Wales and anywhere else (s 22(5)) and an order has effect anywhere in the UK.

i. Section 22 Authorisation

The previous DVPN required the authorisation of a superintendent, whilst the DAPN requires at least the rank of inspector (s 22(8)). The inclusion of a significantly lower rank may well reflect pragmatism and the recognition that in future more DAPN are likely required. An officer of the rank of inspector is more likely to be available when required, and this change also pays heed to previous concerns that more junior officers might not have wanted to bother a senior officer with such cases in the past.[30] The inspector must be from one of the forty-three Home Office forces, British Transport Police, or the Ministry of Defence Police (s 22(8)). Section 22 (subsections 3 and 4), set out the statutory conditions under which a senior police officer may authorise the issuing of a DAPN:

(3) Condition A is that the senior police officer has reasonable grounds for believing that P has been abusive towards a person aged 16 or over to whom P is personally connected.
(4) Condition B is that the senior police officer has reasonable grounds for believing that it is necessary to give the notice to protect that person from domestic abuse, or the risk of domestic abuse, carried out by P.

The term 'personally connected' is defined under section 2 of the Act and relates to current or former spouses (including civil partners), those who had or currently have agreed to marry or enter into a civil partnership, those in an intimate relationship, family members, and those who have or had a parental relationship with the same child. It is clear from the definition that there is no cohabitation requirement between individuals in order for there to be a personal relationship.[31]

ii. Section 23 Provisions

Section 23 provides that the notice can contain various relevant prohibitions and terms on the immediate future conduct of the perpetrator:

[27] Hunter (n 5).
[28] Hunter (n 5).
[29] Burton (n 14).
[30] Kelly and others (n 17).
[31] Home Office (n 22).

(1) A domestic abuse protection notice may provide that the person to whom the notice is given ('P')—
  (a) may not contact the person for whose protection the notice is given;
  (b) may not come within a specified distance of any premises in England or Wales in which that person lives. 'Specified' means specified in the notice.

(2) If P lives in premises in England or Wales in which the person for whose protection the notice is given also lives, the notice may also contain provision— (a) prohibiting P from evicting or excluding that person from the premises; (b) prohibiting P from entering the premises; (c) requiring P to leave the premises.

Clearly this and other sections are designed to ensure that there is no repeat of further abuse and that where necessary the perpetrator is distanced from the victim and is made aware of the conditions and consequences of breach.

iii. Section 24 Matters to Consider before Issuing a Notice

Like the DVPN before it, the DAPN is not a finding of guilt,[32] but is used as an emergency protective measure. However, before issuing a notice, the issuing officer must take reasonable steps to seek the views and representations of any interested parties, such as the victim, the perpetrator (P), and any other relevant occupant who resides at the premises and is personally connected to P or the victim.[33] In addition, the officer must take account of the welfare of any person under 18 (s 24(1)(a)). The consent of the victim is not necessary for the issuing of the notice, but the police must consider the victims wishes (s 24(1)(b)). This allows for a notice to be given against the victims wishes, because experience has demonstrated victims have a number of compelling reasons for being against such a course of action.[34] Draft statutory guidance makes it clear that the person to be protected may also be under the coercion of the perpetrator not to agree to a DAPN (and subsequent DAPO process), and so careful consideration of the circumstances is required.[35] Any decision is likely to be informed by all the circumstances, including assessment of the level of risk to the victim and other parties. Whilst there are sound reasons for allowing police to go against victim wishes, it has been argued that where this does occur, it may render notices or orders ineffective as victims will be unlikely to report any breaches.[36] Officers are also reminded of their obligations under the Victim Code[37] and that they should consider referral of the victim to relevant supporting agencies.[38] Failing to mandate referral to supporting agencies has been criticised.[39] Guidance suggests it would be good practice for the senior officer to consider any intelligence the police and other agencies hold relating to previous incidents, and whether the giving of the notice

[32] Explanatory Notes to the DAA 2021 (n 3).

[33] Bird (n 4).

[34] ibid.

[35] Home Office (n 22) Appendix B, [2].

[36] Burton (n 14) 25.

[37] Ministry of Justice, 'Code of Practice for Victims of Crime in England and Wales' (November 2020) https://assets.publishing.service.gov.uk/government/uploads/system/uploads/attachment_data/file/974376/victims-code-2020.pdf (accessed 28 March 2022).

[38] Home Office (n 22) Appendix B, [3].

[39] Vanessa Bettinson, 'Adding to the domestic abuse criminal law framework: the Domestic Abuse Act 2021' (2022) 2 *Crim LR*, 88.

would make the perpetrator homeless or vulnerable.[40] Where homelessness is a possible consequence, the police should provide contact details and how to apply to the Local Authority for relief.[41]

iv. Section 25 What the Notice May Contain

Any notice issued must be in writing and issued to the perpetrator personally by a constable (s 25(3)). It must contain the grounds upon which the notice was given, the consequences of arrest for breach, the fact that a hearing for a full order will take place at a magistrate's court within 48 hours of the giving of the notice and what prohibition the order can contain (s 25). It must also be made clear that the notice has effect until the hearing for the Order has concluded (s 25(2)(d)). A template will be produced for this purpose.[42]

a. *Further requirements*
Within 48 hours of the giving of DAPN, a full application for a DAPO must be heard, and a clear procedure to be followed upon personal service of the notice (s 29(2)), in order to ensure that the perpetrator understands the prohibitions (as well as consequences of breach) and supplies an address so that he/she can be notified of the location and time when the full hearing is to take place (s 25). The notice of the hearing location, time, and date must be given to the perpetrator personally (s.29 (4)), but in their absence it can be left at the address provided (s 29(5)). In the event that an address was not provided, the hearing may continue in the perpetrator's absence, providing the police have taken reasonable steps to provide the notice (s 29(6)). In this situation it will fall to the police to demonstrate the reasonable steps taken to give the notice. If premises relate to a member of the Armed Forces and relevant accommodation, the police must take reasonable steps to notify the perpetrators commanding officer of the giving of the notice.[43]

v. Section 26 Breach of Notice

Section 26 of the Act sets out the consequences of a breach of the notice. Police have power to arrest without warrant and to enter premises in order to effect arrest: '(1) If a constable has reasonable grounds for believing that a person is in breach of a domestic abuse protection notice, the constable may arrest the person without warrant'.

Guidance encourages prompt action to arrest for the purposes of protection and to ensure confidence in the system is maintained.[44] This also presumably addresses previous criticisms of the poor response to breaches of the old DVPNs and DVPOs.[45] By virtue of section 26 (9), Section 17(1) of PACE is amended to allow a constable power to enter premises for the purpose of searching for and arresting someone reasonably believed to have breached a DAPN. If arrested for breach of a DAPN, that person must be held in custody and brought before the appropriate magistrates' court before the end of 24 hours elapsing after the arrest, or to the

---

[40] Home Office (n 22) 10.
[41] ibid 11 [5].
[42] ibid 11 [3].
[43] ibid 11 [8].
[44] ibid 12 [7].
[45] See Blackburn and Graca (n 1) 22. See also HMICFRS (n 15).

relevant DAPO hearing should that already have been arranged to take place earlier than the 24-hour period (s 26(2)(a) and (b)). The provision is presumably designed to dovetail perpetrators to the relevant application for an Order where possible, to minimise any delays that may occur. Christmas day, bank holidays, and Sundays are specifically excluded from calculations, so in some instances further time will elapse before the perpetrator in breach is brought before the appropriate court. Needless to say, the earliest available court date following these delays are necessary (s 26(4)). If brought before the court within 24 hours of the arrest for breach and section 26(2)(4) does not apply (i.e., not brought to the DAPO hearing because it is not occurring), then the court have power to remand the person (s 26(5)).[46] If remanding on bail, the court have power to impose what they believe to be necessary requirements to ensure there is no obstruction of justice or interference with witnesses (s 26(7)). Police guidance urges thorough investigations into breaches of DAPNs to uncover any criminal offences that the perpetrator may have committed.[47]

vi. Section 27 Domestic Abuse Protection Order

A DAPO is defined in the Act (s 27) and like the DAPN applies to conduct that relates to the broader definition of abuse rather than the former consideration which was largely limited to acts of physical violence'.[48] Again, it is a preventative measure designed to prevent the perpetrator from being abusive to a person over 16 who is to be protected. The section also makes clear that there are a number of different ways a DAPO can be issued, either by application of a number of different parties to different courts[49] (see more on this later), and in the course of proceedings such as criminal trials. The section is set out in full here:

Section 27 Meaning of 'domestic abuse protection order'

(1) In this Part a 'domestic abuse protection order' is an order which, for the purpose of preventing a person ('P') from being abusive towards a person aged 16 or over to whom P is personally connected—
 (a) prohibits P from doing things described in the order, or
 (b) requires P to do things described in the order.
(2) A domestic abuse protection order may be made—
 (a) on application (see section 28), or
 (b) in the course of certain proceedings (see section 31).
(3) Section 32 sets out the conditions for making a domestic abuse protection order.

a. *Critical Commentary*

Terms such as 'abuse' and 'personal connection' have already been discussed. However, unlike the DAPN, the DAPO can contain both prohibitions and requirements. Guidance to police officers[50] suggests this could include prohibitions preventing contact by any means, prohibiting access to premises, or setting clear geographical restrictions such as how close to the

[46] If brought before the DAPO hearing, there are separate powers available to a court for remand under s 29(8) of the Act.
[47] Home Office (n 22) 12 [8].
[48] ibid 13 [4].
[49] Bird (n 4) 39.
[50] Home Office (n 22) 13, [4].

premises the perpetrator is allowed. Requirements in an order can be negative or positive. Examples include being required to undertake a perpetrator programme, submit to electronic tagging,[51] attend a mental health assessment or attend assessment for drug or alcohol dependency.[52] Whilst there was some support for these proposals, concerns were expressed regarding the potential negative effects upon perpetrators human rights (i.e., religious beliefs, work, education, privacy, family life). It was also argued that such measures could effectively delay opportunity for victims to move on following incidents because of the delay in perpetrator completion of positive obligations.[53] It is clear that the Act provides a non-exhaustive list of examples,[54] but it is equally to be expected that there will be litigation and legal argument in relation to the human rights of the perpetrator.[55] In response to concerns raised in consultation, some provisions in the Act are designed to ensure that prohibitions or restrictions, where possible, cohere with the human rights of perpetrator, such as their religious beliefs, work or education.[56] Returning to the prohibitions though, this relies upon good inter-agency cooperation and agencies with sufficient resourcing to be able to respond to requirements in a timely fashion.[57]

[51] House of Commons Joint Committee (n 25).

[52] Home Office (n 22) 24, [5].

[53] House of Commons Joint Committee (n 25) 27.

[54] Home Office (n 22) 22, [2].

[55] Lucy Crompton, 'DVP notices and orders: Protecting victims or the public purse?' (2013) 44 *Family Law* 62; Blackburn and Graca (n 1) 29; House of Commons Joint Committee (n 25) 28.

[56] DAA 2021, s 36 (1); Explanatory Notes to the DAA 2021 (n 3) [162].

[57] House of Commons Joint Committee (n 25) 32.

6

DOMESTIC ABUSE PROTECTION ORDERS, THE COURT PROCEDURE (SECTIONS 28–38)

David Malone*

* This chapter has been written with the assistance of David Malone's pupil, Mr Andreas Malekos.

David Malone, *Domestic Abuse Protection Orders, the Court Procedure (Sections 28–38)* In: *Blackstone's Guide to the Domestic Abuse Act 2021*. Edited by Susan Edwards, David Malone, and Gillian Jones KC, Oxford University Press.
 DOI: 10.1093/oso/9780192870513.003.0006

1. SECTION 28 DOMESTIC ABUSE PROTECTION ORDERS ON APPLICATION

The domestic abuse protection order (DAPO) provisions are designed to make DAPOs more accessible by enabling applications to be made to a wide spectrum of courts. Section 28(2) enables applications for DAPOs to be made by the victim, the police, a relevant third party specified in the regulations, or any other person with leave of the court. Applications made by the police must be made to a magistrates' court. Applications made after a domestic abuse protection notice (DAPN) has been given to the perpetrator by the police must be made by the police force who gave that notice. However, applications made by the police for a stand-alone order without a notice should be made by the police force for the police area in which the perpetrator currently resides, or where it is believed by the chief officer of police for a police area that the perpetrator is in that police area or intends to come into that police area.

The appropriate court to which an application for a DAPO is to be made is determined by which category of person is making the application and is set out at section 28(5)–(7) DAA 2021. Applications made by the police must always be made to the magistrates' court (s 28(6) DAA 2021). An application may be made in family or civil proceedings where both the perpetrator and the victim are parties to those proceedings, and it would be open to the court to make a DAPO in those proceedings under section 31 DAA 2021 without an application being made (s 28(7) DAA 2021). In all other cases, applications must be made to the family court (s 28(5) DAA 2021). A victim cannot be compelled to attend the hearing unless they have given oral or written evidence at the hearing. This provision enables the police and other third-party applicants to make evidence-led applications which do not rely on the victim's testimony.[1]

2. SECTION 29 APPLICATIONS WHERE DOMESTIC ABUSE PROTECTION NOTICE HAS BEEN GIVEN

Section 29 deals with the steps the police must take once a DAPN has been given under section 22 DAA 2021. Where the police have given a DAPN to a person under section 22 the police must apply to the magistrates' court for a DAPO against that person within forty-eight hours, excluding Sundays and bank holidays (s 29(2) DAA 2021). This forty-eight-hour period is designed to ensure that police have sufficient time to apply for the order and that the victim is provided with breathing space away from the perpetrator until longer-term measures can be established by way of a DAPO.[2] The person against whom the application is being made (the perpetrator) must be given notice of the DAPO hearing (s 29(4) DAA 2021). Provided that the perpetrator has given an address for service of the DAPO hearing application notice (under s 25(4)), leaving the notice at that address constitutes service (s 29(5)). Where the perpetrator has not provided an address for service of the DAPO hearing application notice, the court may hear the application if it is satisfied that the police have

[1] Hansard (10 June 2020) col 189 https://hansard.parliament.uk/commons/2020-06-10/debates/23639d42-9d1f-4ef4-afa8-d6f66b70052d/DomesticAbuseBill(SixthSitting accessed 26 May 2022).

[2] ibid.

made reasonable efforts to give the perpetrator notice of the hearing (s 29(6)). This section is designed to protect victims until DAPO applications have been decided or withdrawn.[3] Consequently, the domestic abuse protection notice remains effective until the application has been determined or withdrawn (s 29(7)). The court has the power to remand a perpetrator in custody where they have been arrested for breaching a domestic abuse protection notice and the court has adjourned the hearing (s 29(8)).

3. SECTION 30 REMAND UNDER SECTION 29(8) OF PERSON ARRESTED FOR BREACH OF NOTICE

This section applies where a perpetrator has breached a DAPN and has been brought before the magistrates' court at the hearing of an application for a DAPO. This section sets out the power of the magistrates' court to remand the perpetrator in custody or on bail. Section 30(2) DAA 2021 modifies the power of the magistrates' court to remand a person for up to 8 days by enabling a perpetrator remanded on bail to be remanded for longer than eight days where the perpetrator and the senior police officer who issued the DAPN consent. The court may remand a perpetrator to enable a medical examination to take place and a report to be made where it has reason to suspect that a medical report will be required (s 30(3) DAA 2021). Such adjournments may not be for more than three weeks at a time where the perpetrator is remanded in custody (s 30(4)) and may not be for more than four weeks at a time if they are remanded on bail (s 30(5)). Where a court suspects that the perpetrator is suffering from a mental disorder it may order that they are remanded to a hospital for a report on their mental condition to be produced (s 30(6)). Such an order can be for up to twenty-eight days at a time or a total of twelve weeks if there are multiple stays in hospital (s 35(7) Mental Health Act 1983).[4] When remanding the perpetrator on bail, the court may impose any requirements that the court considers necessary to prevent the perpetrator from interfering with witnesses or otherwise obstructing the course of justice. The court may require the perpetrator to comply with these requirements before release on bail or later (s 30(7)).

4. SECTION 31 DOMESTIC ABUSE PROTECTION ORDERS OTHERWISE THAN ON APPLICATION

This provision enables a DAPO to be made on the court's own initiative in the family court, criminal court, or civil court during ongoing proceedings where the court becomes aware of the need to protect an individual from domestic abuse. In any family proceedings, the High Court or the family court may make a DAPO provided that the perpetrator and the victim are both parties to the proceedings (s 31(2)). In criminal proceedings, the magistrates' court or the Crown Court may make a DAPO on conviction or acquittal of the perpetrator. A Crown Court allowing an appeal against conviction may make a DAPO against the appellant. In order for a county court to make a DAPO against a perpetrator in civil proceedings

[3] Hansard (n 1) col 190.

[4] Explanatory Notes to the Domestic Abuse Act 2021, s 30: Remand under s 29(8) of person arrested for breach of notice [146] https://www.legislation.gov.uk/ukpga/2021/17/pdfs/ukpgaen_20210017_en.pdf (accessed 26 May 2022).

the perpetrator and the victim must both be parties to the proceedings, and the proceedings must be designated as 'relevant proceedings' in regulations made by the Secretary of State (s 31(7)). This section is designed to restrict this power to the type of civil proceedings where domestic abuse is most likely to be alleged or revealed in evidence.[5]

5. SECTION 32 CONDITIONS FOR MAKING AN ORDER

In order to make a DAPO the court must be satisfied on the balance of probabilities that the two conditions set out in section 32 DAA 2021 are met. First, the court must be satisfied that the perpetrator has been abusive towards a person aged 16 or over to whom they are personally connected. A personal connection for the purposes of this section is defined at section 2 DAA 2021. Abusive behaviour for the purposes of this section is set out at section 1(3) DAA 2021. Secondly, the court must be satisfied that the order is necessary and proportionate to protect that person from domestic abuse, or the risk of domestic abuse, carried out by the perpetrator. Once those conditions are satisfied, the court can only impose requirements that it considers necessary to protect the victim. The imposition of conditions that go beyond those necessary could constitute a breach of the European Convention on Human Rights.[6] This provision specifies that DAPOs can only be made against a person who is 18 years old or over (s 32(5)).

6. SECTION 33 MATTERS TO BE CONSIDERED BEFORE MAKING AN ORDER

When determining whether to make a DAPO the court must firstly consider the welfare of any person under the age of 18 whose interests are relevant to the DAPO (s 33(1)). The person does not have to be personally connected to the perpetrator and could, for example, be the victim's child from a previous relationship.[7] This provision is designed to ensure that any safeguarding concerns can be properly addressed.[8] Secondly, the court must also consider any opinion of the victim in relation to the making of the order of which the court is made aware (s 33(1)(b) DAA 2021). In order to enable the court to protect victims who may be coerced into withholding their consent, or are fearful of the consequences of their perceived support of action against the perpetrator,[9] it is not necessary for the victim to consent to the making of the DAPO.[10] Thirdly, where the DAPO is to include provisions relating to premises lived in by the victim, the court must consider any opinion of a person living in the premises who is personally connected to the victim, or the perpetrator (if the perpetrator also lives in the premises).[11] Consequently, the court would therefore have to consider the opinion of a family member for whom the perpetrator has caring responsibilities, when considering whether

---

[5] ibid [149].
[6] Hansard (n 1) col 194.
[7] ibid col 195.
[8] ibid.
[9] ibid.
[10] DAA 2021, s 33(3).
[11] ibid s 33(2).

to make an order excluding the perpetrator from the premises, provided that the perpetrator also lives in the premises.[12]

7. SECTION 34 MAKING OF ORDERS WITHOUT NOTICE

Under section 29(4) DAA 2021, the perpetrator must be given notice of the hearing of a DAPO application. A court may make a DAPO against a perpetrator despite the perpetrator not having been given notice of the proceedings if it would be just and convenient to do so (s 34(1)). Applications should only be made without notice in exceptional or urgent circumstances and the applicant would need to produce evidence to the court as to why the without notice hearing was necessary.[13] Where the perpetrator has not been notified of the hearing, before making a DAPO the court must consider any risk that the perpetrator will cause significant harm to the victim if the order is not given immediately, whether the applicant will be deterred or prevented from pursuing the application if the order is not made immediately, and whether there is reason to believe that the perpetrator is deliberately evading service which will result in a seriously prejudicial delay being caused to the victim (s 34(3)). If the court makes a DAPO without notice, the court must schedule a return hearing as soon as is just and convenient, to allow the perpetrator to make representations about the order (s 34(4)). It should be noted that electronic monitoring requirements may not be imposed in the perpetrator's absence (s 37(2)). Given the balance of risks addressed by this section and the rights afforded to the perpetrator to appeal, it is not envisaged that the section infringes Convention rights, but clearly this will be the subject of scrutiny by those representing individuals who are the subject of such orders.

8. SECTION 35 PROVISION THAT MAY BE MADE BY ORDERS

A court making a DAPO may impose any requirements necessary to protect the victim from domestic abuse or the risk thereof (s 35(1)). The court must consider which requirements are necessary to protect the victim from different kinds of abusive behaviour (s 35(2)), including but not limited to physical or sexual abuse, violent or threatening behaviour, controlling or coercive behaviour, psychological, emotional, or economic abuse.[14] The example requirements set out at section 35(4) are not exhaustive, and include prohibiting the perpetrator from contacting the victim, which includes online contact and all other forms of contact.[15] Other example requirements include a prohibition preventing the perpetrator from coming within a specified distance of the victim's residence and any specified premises in England or Wales, which will include any place the victim may be commonly found such as their workplace, place of worship, or children's school.[16] A DAPO may also require the perpetrator to attend programmes relating to behavioural change, and may

[12] Hansard (n 1) col 195.
[13] Explanatory Notes (n 4) 34: Making of orders without notice [154].
[14] ibid [157].
[15] ibid [159].
[16] ibid [159].

include drug and alcohol rehabilitation requirements.[17] This flexibility enables the court to tailor the DAPOs to reflect the perpetrator's behaviour on a case-by-case basis to impose requirements that protect the victim.[18] Where the perpetrator lives in the same premises as the victim, the order may also require the perpetrator to leave, and not to enter, the premises; or prohibit the perpetrator from evicting or excluding the victim from the premises (s 35(5)). These conditions may be imposed regardless of who owns or rents the premises.[19] A DAPO may impose electronic monitoring requirements on the perpetrator to monitor their compliance with other requirements imposed by the order (s 35(6)). The DAPO may monitor compliance with a requirement not to consume alcohol by electronically monitoring the perpetrator's alcohol consumption.[20] Prohibitions should, of course, be dealt with on a case-by-case basis, but in practice the authorities will rely on tried and tested prohibitions used frequently in a range of ancillary orders such as restriction orders and criminal behaviour orders. New and innovative prohibitions will continue to be challenged in the appeal courts in the usual way.

9. SECTION 36 FURTHER PROVISION ABOUT REQUIREMENTS THAT MAY BE IMPOSED BY ORDERS

The restrictions on requirements for a DAPO (s 36(1)) are not mentioned in the three European Convention on Human Rights memos pertaining to the Domestic Abuse Bill, the explanatory notes or Hansard. That said, they are clearly influenced by Convention rights and a proportionate approach to prohibitions should be adopted to prevent challenges on the basis that a perpetrator's rights to worship, or attend work/education, are not unfairly and/or unnecessarily infringed. The same applies to restrictions that lead an individual into conflict with any other court orders. This does not mean that restrictions cannot be the same, but they must, so far as practicable, be such as to avoid such conflict. In practice, where such conflict may arise and the authorities believe such restrictions are necessary, there is nothing to prevent other court orders being revisited. The various agencies should cooperate to ensure that the 'bigger picture' around risk is always well in focus. A DAPO imposing a requirement on a perpetrator must specify the person responsible for supervising compliance with that requirement (s 36(2)), this could include the local authority or a recognised provider of substance misuse recovery services.[21] Before imposing any requirement in a DAPO the compliance supervisor must provide the court with evidence about its suitability and enforceability (s 36(3)). The compliance supervisor will be subject to the duties set out at section 36(5), including a duty to inform the police where the perpetrator has complied, or failed to comply, with the relevant requirements. A perpetrator subject to a DAPO requirement must keep in touch with their compliance supervisor and notify them of any change to their home address (s 36(7)).

---

[17] ibid [158].
[18] Hansard (n 1) col 191.
[19] Explanatory Notes (n 4) s 35: Provision that may be made by orders [160].
[20] ibid [161].
[21] ibid [163].

10. SECTION 37 FURTHER PROVISION ABOUT ELECTRONIC MONITORING REQUIREMENTS

An electronic monitoring requirement may be imposed to ensure a perpetrator's compliance with DAPO requirements and usually involves fitting an electronic tag to the perpetrator's ankle.[22] An electronic monitoring requirement cannot be imposed on a perpetrator in their absence (s 37(2)). Where the cooperation of someone other than the perpetrator is required to secure the electronic monitoring, the requirement may not be imposed without their consent (s 37(3)). This may include persons living at the same premises as the perpetrator.[23] The court must ensure that electronic monitoring arrangements are available in the relevant local area before imposing an electronic monitoring requirement (s 37(4)). The court will usually be notified of any such availability by the Ministry of Justice.[24] When imposing an electronic monitoring requirement, the court must specify the person responsible for the monitoring (s 37(6)). The subject of an electronic monitoring requirement must facilitate the fitting, installation, inspection, or repair of the necessary equipment; not interfere with the equipment; and take the steps required by the person responsible for monitoring their compliance to keep the equipment in working order (s 37(8)). Any breach of these obligations would constitute a breach of the DAPO.[25]

11. SECTION 38 DURATION AND GEOGRAPHICAL APPLICATION OF ORDERS

Section 38 is designed to enable the court to be flexible when setting the effective period by explicitly prescribing a specified period or by using the occurrence of a specified event to terminate the effective period (s 38(3)). Moreover, the court may specify that a DAPO is effective until the court makes a further order which terminates the effective period (s 38(2)(c)). Where a perpetrator has been convicted, the court may make an order which exceeds the length of the sentence passed to ensure that the victim receives the necessary protection.[26]

[22] ibid 37: Further provision about requirements imposed by orders [165].

[23] ibid [167].

[24] ibid [168].

[25] ibid [171].

[26] Hansard (n 1) col 190.

7
BREACHES OF ORDERS, NOTIFICATION, AND POLICE POWERS (SECTIONS 39–43)

Martin O'Neill

1. SECTIONS 39–43

i. Context and Background

On the one hand, the domestic violence protection order (DVPO) did not carry any criminal sanction upon breach.[1] Breach of a domestic abuse protection order (DAPO), on the other hand, can lead to conviction for a criminal offence, with a maximum penalty summarily of six months' imprisonment or a fine or both, or on indictment a maximum of five years' imprisonment (s 39(5)). The government's stated intention is to send a 'strong message' about the consequences of non-compliance,[2] and, according to government minister Victoria Atkins, the purpose was to put pressure on the perpetrator to comply.[3] Due to concerns that some victims may be deterred from reporting a breach because of the ultimate criminal

[1] HM Government, 'Transforming the Response to Domestic Abuse: Government Consultation' (2018) 29 https://consult.justice.gov.uk/homeoffice-moj/domestic-abuse-consultation/supporting_documents/Transforming%20the%20response%20to%20domestic%20abuse.pdf?msclkid=800930f5c18b11eca3412074f93a9703 (accessed 21 April 2022).

[2] ibid.

[3] House of Commons Joint Committee on the Draft Domestic Abuse Bill Draft Domestic Abuse Bill First Report of Session 2017–19 Report, together with formal minutes relating to the report Ordered by the House of Lords to be printed 11 June 2019 Ordered by the House of Commons to be printed 11 June 2019, 30 [106] https://publications.parliament.uk/pa/jt201719/jtselect/jtddab/2075/2075.pdf (accessed 21 April 2022).

Martin O'Neill, *Breaches of orders, Notification, and Police Powers (Sections 39–43)* In: *Blackstone's Guide to the Domestic Abuse Act 2021*. Edited by Susan Edwards, David Malone, and Gillian Jones KC, Oxford University Press.
 DOI: 10.1093/oso/9780192870513.003.0007

sanction, courts will have discretion to deal with breaches as contempt of court instead of using the criminal sanction.[4] This can attract a maximum penalty of two months' imprisonment or a fine or both at magistrates' court, or two years' imprisonment or a fine or both in other courts.[5]

2. SECTION 39 BREACH OF ORDER

Section 39 of the Act defines the offence:

(1) A person who is subject to a domestic abuse protection order commits an offence if without reasonable excuse the person fails to comply with any requirement imposed by the order.

(2) In a case where the order was made against the person without that person being given notice of the proceedings, the person commits an offence under this section only in respect of behaviour engaged in at a time when the person was aware of the existence of the order.

(See also section 45(8) and (9), which makes similar provision where an order has been varied.)

(3) Where a person is convicted of an offence under this section in respect of any behaviour, that behaviour is not punishable as a contempt of court.

(4) A person may not be convicted of an offence under this section in respect of any behaviour which has been punished as a contempt of court.

The addition of reasonable excuse in the definition of the offence means that breach is not strict liability, and there may be some grounds for a defendant to argue that a criminal sanction should not apply. It is likely that this will be an area of contention where the courts should be the final arbiter of what is reasonable on a case-by-case basis. This should not be routinely decided as a prosecutorial decision. In similar hybrid provisions such as sexual harm orders, issues such as illness preventing compliance with requirements or family emergencies (meaning that a non-contact requirement was breached), have been determined as reasonable excuses.[6] Because of the complexities of human conduct and relationships, there may well be some genuine reasonable excuses that apply, although equally, there will be some examples where manipulating and controlling current or former partners may intentionally breach under the guise of reasonableness. The addition of subsection (2) is important because, where an order has effectively been made ex parte, and the person subject to it is unaware of its existence, it would be unfair to sanction that person for behaviour they did not know was disallowed. However, the fact that any process can occur ex parte may itself be subject to legal challenge in future. There would need to be justifiable reasons why an order has been made ex parte, for instance, where a person subject to an order has not provided an address for notification of a hearing or has otherwise been obstructive. In proceedings relating to emergency

---

[4] ibid.

[5] Explanatory Notes to the Domestic Abuse Act 2021,32 [177] https://www.legislation.gov.uk/ukpga/2021/17/pdfs/ukpgaen_20210017_en.pdf (accessed 21 April 2022).

[6] Terry Thomas and Daniel J Marsh, *The Sex Offender Register: Politics, Policy and Public Opinion* (1st edn, Routledge 2021).

protection orders, for instance, ex parte hearings have been described as 'draconian' measures that are only justifiable in exceptional circumstances and for compelling reasons.[7]

Proof of the existence of an order for police practitioners and proof of service to the perpetrator are essential components before any breach can be sanctioned.[8] There is little doubt that this section may provide further room for argument regarding when or whether notice is or was given. Who and how the order is communicated to a perpetrator in circumstances where they are not in attendance is also not discussed. It may be that having the notice sent to an address, for instance by recorded delivery, will be sufficient, although this could be problematic where there is no fixed address, or one has not been served. This may have to rely upon personal service, in which case there are resource implications involved.

Subsections 4 and 5 in effect prevent double jeopardy. Where the breach has been dealt with either as a criminal offence or a contempt of court, the provisions make it clear that defendants cannot be dealt with again for the alternative disposal (i.e., if convicted of a criminal offence upon breach, they cannot also be in contempt of court for the same behaviour, and vice versa).[9] Subsections 6 and 7 make it clear that conditional discharge is not a disposal option for courts or service courts when sentencing for breach of a DAPO, presumably to send a message to perpetrators of the serious nature of the breach and societal disapproval of such behaviour.[10]

Liberty expressed concern about the Article 6 rights (European Convention on Human Rights (ECHR)) of the perpetrator and the steps to criminal sanction based upon an order that is essentially civil in nature and which has the balance of probabilities required for its issuance by a court.[11] Whether different courts apply the same standards to issuing an order is also a concern, particularly in family courts, where Hunter suggests there have previously been tensions between the needs of domestic abuse victims and families and the family courts' overriding interests in protecting family relationships.[12] Legitimate concerns have also been raised about the ability of the police and agencies to monitor compliance and deal with breach, and there will arguably be a need for police to undertake a risk assessment to inform what action to take regarding breach of an order.[13]

3. SECTION 40 ARREST FOR BREACH OF ORDER

A person may be arrested with or without warrant for breach of an order. Section 26 of the Act provides that the police may arrest anyone where there are reasonable grounds to suspect them to be in breach of a domestic abuse protection notice (DAPN). Section 17 of the Police and Criminal Evidence Act 1984 (PACE) is also amended to allow for entry to premises to effect an arrest for breach of a DAPN. In terms of breach of a DAPO, a constable may arrest

---

[7] *X Council v B (Emergency Protection Orders)* [2004] EWHC 2015 (Fam) [57] (Munby J).

[8] Lis Bates and Marianne Hester, 'No longer a civil matter? The design and use of protection orders for domestic violence in England and Wales' (2020) 42(2) *Journal of Social Welfare and Family Law* 139.

[9] Explanatory Notes (n 5) [177].

[10] ibid [176].

[11] ibid.

[12] Rosemary Hunter, 'Domestic Abuse, a UK perspective' in John Eekelaar and Rob George (eds), *Routledge Handbook of Family Law and Policy* (Kindle edn, Taylor & Francis 2020).

[13] Vanessa Bettinson, 'Adding to the domestic abuse criminal law framework: the Domestic Abuse Act 2021' (2022) 2 *Crim LR* 88.

a person without warrant under the provisions of section 24 of PACE,[14] and has a power to enter and search premises to effect an arrest under section 17(2) of PACE if the relevant criteria apply. New Draft Police Guidance makes it clear that prompt action is required to respond to breaches of any DAPOs (whether police led or not), meeting criticisms expressed by many that in the past police have been slow to act, and concerns that police might see non-police led orders as in some way less important. On the arrest point, however, there is some evidence that police do arrest for breach of orders when they are in place, although the research relates only to domestic violence protection notices (DVPNs) and DVPOs between 2016 and 2018.[15] The guidance states:

It is vital for maintaining the confidence of the person to be protected and the efficacy of the protective order regime that all reported breaches are thoroughly investigated, and that appropriate action is taken in a timely manner. An arrest should be made at the first opportunity, as any delay may increase the risk to the person to be protected and therefore undermine the purpose of the DAPO.[16]

Importantly, guidance also suggests that the police should take steps to obtain a copy of the order and notes that this will rely upon joint agency working and liaison with courts who process orders when made.[17] This could cause issues if the police are not able to find evidence of an order, and the guidance is silent on this matter.

Section 40 of the Act also sets out conditions where a warrant for arrest can be sought from and issued by the High Court, Family Court, or the county court for a person who is in breach of a DAPO, where a DAPO has previously been issued. Draft Police Guidance suggests that where a victim wishes the breach to be dealt with as a contempt of court rather than as a criminal offence, that person can apply to a relevant court for the issuance of a warrant for arrest.[18] The process is complainant-led to a relevant judge (s 40(8)), in a relevant court (s 40(2)). The complainant can be either the person to be protected, or other relevant parties, including anyone given permission by a judge (s 40(4)). Section 40 of the DAA states:

(1) This section applies where a relevant court has made a domestic abuse protection order against a person ('P').

(3) A person mentioned in subsection (4) may apply to the relevant judge for the issue of a warrant for P's arrest if the person considers that P has failed to comply with the order or is otherwise in contempt of court in relation to the order.

(4) The persons referred to in subsection (3) are—
  (a) the person for whose protection the order was made;
  (b) where the order was made under section 28, the person who applied for the order (if different);
  (c) any other person with the leave of the relevant judge.

[14] Explanatory Notes (n 5) 39; DAA, s 40(9).

[15] Rob Ewin, Elizabeth A Bates, and Julie C Taylor, 'Domestic abuse orders: risk, vulnerability and training' (2020) 6(2) *Journal of Criminological Research, Policy and Practice* 151.

[16] Home Office, 'Domestic Abuse Protection Notices and Domestic Abuse Protection Orders Draft statutory guidance for the police' (January 2021) 38. https://assets.publishing.service.gov.uk/government/uploads/system/uploads/attachment_data/file/955459/Draft_statutory_guidance_for_police_on_domestic_abuse_protection_notices_and_orders.pdf (accessed 21 April 2022).

[17] ibid 39.

[18] Explanatory Notes (n 5) [179].

(5) The relevant judge may issue a warrant on an application under subsection (3) only if—
(a) the application is substantiated on oath, and
(b) the relevant judge has reasonable grounds for believing that P has failed to comply with the order or is otherwise in contempt of court in relation to the order.

(6) If—
(a) P is brought before a relevant court as a result of a warrant issued under this section, and
(b) the court does not immediately dispose of the matter,
the court may remand P.

(7) Schedule 1 contains further provision about remand under this section.

Subsection 5 sets out the nature of evidence that will be required for a judge to have reasonable grounds for believing that an order has been breached or the person is in contempt of court. Evidence will need to be provided on oath. The Act makes clear that if a person is brought before a relevant court having been arrested on warrant for breach, that person can be dealt with immediately or remanded with or without bail in order to dispose of the matter on another occasion (s 40(6)).[19] Once the perpetrator has been arrested and brought before the court, the court may either deal with the contempt of court then and there, or remand the perpetrator, whether in custody or on bail, in order for the case to be dealt with at a later date. Schedule 1 provides the court with further powers relating to remand, including remand for the purposes of medical, or mental health, assessment. The court also has powers to impose restrictions where it releases persons on bail (see later).[20]

4. SECTIONS 41–42 NOTIFICATION REQUIREMENTS

Sections 41, 42, and 43 of the Act create notification requirements and penalties for breach regarding individuals subject to a DAPO. Notification requirements have been a part of the sexual offences landscape for a number of years now and are a settled and well-known process within policing for individuals where a qualifying conviction and sentence apply or where they are made subject to various sex offender orders.[21] In consultation for the draft bill, respondents were in favour of having some notification requirements placed upon persons subject to a DAPO.[22] The majority of respondents (76 per cent) were in favour of having notification requirements and felt this would help the police to protect victims more effectively, although concerns were raised about the resourcing required to facilitate the new

[19] ibid.

[20] ibid [180].

[21] Thomas and Marsh (n 6).

[22] HM Government, 'Transforming the Response to Domestic Abuse Consultation Response and Draft Bill January 2019' 28–29 https://assets.publishing.service.gov.uk/government/uploads/system/uploads/attachment_data/file/772247/Transforming_the_response_to_domestic_abuse_-_consultation_response_and_draft_bill_-print.pdf (accessed 21 April 2022).

regime.[23] Knowing where a perpetrator lives will assist police if they are seeking to arrest for suspected breaches of a DAPO, and it was also suggested that the information could be utilised in disclosure should there be a 'right to ask' application, or where a situation arises for disclosure under the 'right to know' route.[24] For instance, this could apply if the person subject to a DAPO cohabits with a different partner and it is considered appropriate to disclose any information to a new partner.

Section 41(1) enacts a notification requirement for anyone subject to a DAPO. The section goes on to detail the requirements and timescales. After explaining that requirements relate to a person subject to a DAPO, the section continues:

> (2) The person must, within the period of three days beginning with the day on which the order is made, notify the police of the information in subsection (3).
>
> (3) The information referred to in subsection (2) is—
> (a) the person's name and, if the person uses one or more other names, each of those names;
> (b) the person's home address.
>
> (4) If the person uses a name which has not been notified under this section, the person must, within the period of three days beginning with the day on which the person first uses that name, notify the police of that name.
>
> (5) If the person changes home address, the person must, before the end of the period of three days beginning with the day on which that happens, notify the police of the new home address.
>
> (6) If the person ceases to have any home address, the person must, before the end of the period of three days beginning with the day on which that happens, notify the police of that fact.

These provisions are akin to notification requirements for sex offenders, in terms of name and address, and any other names that the person may use. It extends the notification requirements[25] to where new names are used (different from those originally disclosed to the police), change address, or become homeless. In such cases, the requirement is to notify the police within three days of the changes. Three days commence from the first day of any order being put in place or any of the changes to name or address occurring. Home address is defined further to include the following examples provided by the explanatory notes to the Act:

> The perpetrator's 'home address' for these purposes is defined in section 56(1) as meaning either the person's sole or main residence in the UK or, where they have no such residence, the address or location in the UK where they can regularly be found. If a person can regularly be found at two or more locations (for example at a family home at the weekend and at a flat near their work during the week) they would need to select one of these places and provide details of its address. Equally, if a person is homeless, they would need to provide details of one location where they can regularly be found.[26]

[23] ibid.

[24] See n 22.

[25] By DAA, s 42(7), a 'notification requirement' is a requirement for the person against whom the order is made to provide specified information to the police.

[26] Explanatory Notes (n 5) [185].

Because there was support for the requirements going even further than just name and address (for instance new relationship, visa applications, firearms licences),[27] there is a provision for additional regulations by the Secretary of State allowing further requirements to be made by a court upon imposing or varying a DAPO (s 41(7)). The government said it would await the pilot phase to see whether any further requirements became evident. The Act makes clear that DAPO requirements cannot exist in tandem with other DAPO, stalking protection orders (SPOs), or notification requirements under the Sexual Offences Act 2003, meaning that only one can apply at a time (i.e., the first in time that existed, provided it is still operative) (s 41(8)). This would prevent the situation of multiple orders and requirements acting upon the person at the same time. However, the Act also makes clear that if any other order expires then the present DAPO notification requirements apply from the expiry of the other order (s 41(9)).[28] Such a person would then be required to notify within three days as if the DAPO had been issued on the expiry of the other order. Effectively, this should mean a seamless set of requirements on a person who would appear to be a repeat offender from the set of circumstances described in the Act.

Section 42 provides detail about where and how a notification is given by the person subject to the DAPO. Similar to sex offender notifications,[29] notification must be provided orally, in person at a police station, to either a police officer or a person authorised (effectively allowing civilian staff and volunteers to be notified where appropriate)(s 42(1)). Notification must be given in the appropriate police area (s 42(2)), which is defined as the area where the person resides if they live in England and Wales, or if they live outside England and Wales or do not have a home address, the police station for the area where the order was made. The Act makes clear that if the person is providing notification of change of address, then the notification requirements and conditions must be made in the area relevant to the new address (s 42(3)). Police must acknowledge the notification in writing and the form the notice takes will be designated by the Secretary of State (s 42(4)). Where a person provides notification, the person must allow the person notified to take photographs, images (of them or any part of them), or fingerprints in order to allow for their identity to be verified. These subsections are again familiar territory in sex offender notifications and allow for checks to be made to confirm identity.[30] Some people might try to evade the system by sending others in their place, and so this is a logical addition to the Act to allow for confirmation of identity. In relation to notification requirements under the original Sex Offenders Act 1997, a challenge was made to the automatic nature of the registration requirements upon conviction for a sexual offence.[31] It was argued to be a breach of human rights, particularly Article 7 ECHR, a lesser known right which provides that there is

No punishment without law No one shall be held guilty of any criminal offence on account of any act or omission which did not constitute a criminal offence under national or international law at the time when it was committed. Nor shall a heavier penalty be imposed than the one that was applicable at the time.

---

[27] Consultation Response and Draft Bill (n 22) 28–29.
[28] Explanatory Notes (n 5) [187].
[29] Thomas and Marsh (n 6) 46. See now the Sex Offences Act 2003, ss 80–102.
[30] Thomas and Marsh (n 6) 46.
[31] *Ibbotson v UK* (App no 40146/98) ECHR.

The courts concluded[32] that the registration requirements were separate from sentencing procedures upon conviction and required only registration by an offender. As a result, what was required did not constitute a 'penalty' under Article 7. Instead, the court identified the requirements as a public protection measure.

5. SECTION 43 CONSEQUENCES OF FAILURE TO NOTIFY

Section 43(1)(a) creates offences for failing to notify any of the details required by the Act without reasonable excuse (i.e., name (or any name change) or address (or any address change)). It also creates an offence if false information is provided in purported compliance with any of the obligations (s 43(1)(b)). The courts will be required to decide on a case-by-case basis what constitutes a reasonable excuse for failing to comply.[33] Each offence can attract a maximum sentence of six months' imprisonment (potentially 12 months') on summary conviction (or a fine or both), but up to a maximum of five year' imprisonment if convicted on indictment (or a fine or both). The Act is silent on what offence X (a third party) would commit if they provide false information for P (the person upon whom notification requirements fall), so presumably an offence such as criminal conspiracy could apply to such circumstances, in respect of both X and P.[34] A person commits offences when they first fail without reasonable excuse to comply, and the offence is continuing. However, they cannot be convicted more than once for the same failure (s 43(4),(5), and (6)).

[32] ibid.
[33] Explanatory Notes (n 5) [188].
[34] For the offence of conspiracy see s 1 of the Criminal Law Act 1977. For perverting the course of justice see the common law.

8
VARIATION OF ORDERS, COURT PROCEDURE, AND OTHER PROVISIONS INCLUDING ELECTRONIC MONITORING (SECTIONS 44–51)

David Malone,* Martin O'Neill**

1. SECTION 44 VARIATION AND DISCHARGE OF ORDERS

The flexibility of the domestic abuse protection order (DAPO) is evidenced by the fact that the requirements imposed by a DAPO can be varied or discharged, thereby enabling the court to respond to changes in the circumstances of the victim and the perpetrator, including the perpetrator's behaviour.[1] A court can vary or discharge a DAPO of its own volition

* This chapter has been written with the assistance of David Malone's pupil, Mr Andreas Malekos.

** Sections 44–50 by David Malone, section 51 by Martin O'Neill

[1] Domestic Abuse Bill col 197 (10 June) https://hansard.parliament.uk/commons/2020-06-10/debates/23639d42-9d1f-4ef4-afa8-d6f66b70052d/DomesticAbuseBill(SixthSitting) (accessed 26 May 2022).

David Malone, Martin O'Neill, *Variation of Orders, Court Procedure, and Other Provisions Including Electronic Monitoring (Sections 44–51)* In: *Blackstone's Guide to the Domestic Abuse Act 2021*. Edited by Susan Edwards, David Malone, and Gillian Jones KC, Oxford University Press. © David Malone, Martin O'Neill 2023. DOI: 10.1093/oso/9780192870513.003.0008

(s 44(b)) or on application by the perpetrator, the victim, or the police (s 44(2)(a)). In order to vary or discharge a DAPO the court must hear from a police officer specified in section 44(5). Where the victim is seeking to discharge the order, or make it less onerous, the court must also hear from the victim in order to ensure that he or she is not being coerced or intimidated (s 44(5)).[2] When varying or discharging a DAPO, the court must consider the same factors it would have to consider when making a DAPO under section 33 (s 44(6)). A court can make any order varying or discharging a DAPO that it considers appropriate (s 44(8)). The court may only add an additional requirement to a DAPO or extend a requirement's duration if it is satisfied that it is necessary to protect the victim from domestic abuse, or the risk thereof, by the perpetrator (s 44(9)). The court can only remove a requirement from a DAPO, make a requirement less onerous, or discharge a DAPO altogether, if it is satisfied that it is no longer necessary to protect the victim from abuse by the perpetrator (s 44(11), s 44(13)). The court must remove, and may not extend the duration of, a requirement where the conditions required for imposing it, set out in section 32 DAA, are no longer met (s 44(12)).

2. SECTION 45 VARIATION AND DISCHARGE: SUPPLEMENTARY

This section sets out to which court an application to vary or discharge a DAPO should be made. Any such application must be made to the court that made the DAPO (s 45(1)). The reference to 'the court' refers to a particular legal jurisdiction, as opposed to a physical court building.[3] Where the DAPO was made by a magistrates' court, an application to vary or discharge may be made to any other magistrates' court acting in the local justice area in which that court acts (s 45(2)). Where a DAPO has been made by a family court, an application to vary or discharge that order may be made to any family court as the family courts constitute a single jurisdiction. This principle also applies to the Crown Court and the county court, respectively.[4] Where a perpetrator has not been notified of proceedings in which a DAPO was varied to include an additional requirement or extend an existing requirement, the perpetrator cannot breach the order by way of non-compliance with that order unless he or she was aware of the variation at the time of non-compliance.[5]

3. SECTION 46 APPEALS

This section sets out who is eligible to appeal a court's decision to make or decline to make, vary, or discharge a DAPO and where any such appeal should be made. Where a court hears an application for a DAPO, any decision that it makes in relation to the DAPO can be appealed by the victim, the applicant, or the perpetrator (s 46(2)). Where a court makes a DAPO otherwise than on application or varies a DAPO, the perpetrator may appeal against the making or variation of the DAPO. The making or variation of the DAPO would be

[2] Explanatory Notes to the Domestic Abuse Act, s 44: Variation or discharge of orders [197] https://www.legislation.gov.uk/ukpga/2021/17/pdfs/ukpgaen_20210017_en.pdf (accessed 26 May 2022).

[3] ibid [199].

[4] ibid.

[5] ibid [200].

treated as a sentence for the purposes of the appeal.[6] Where appeals are made in the family or civil courts, the existing rights of appeal in those courts apply.[7] Appeals made against a decision of the magistrates' court must be made to the Crown Court and appeals against a decision of the Crown Court must be made to the Court of Appeal (s 46(7)). Practitioners will need to be alive to the appellate decisions in different jurisdictions as they will clearly be of influence in the particular jurisdiction they are dealing with.

4. SECTION 47 FURTHER PROVISION ABOUT APPEALS

In any appeal relating to a DAPO, the court must hear from the police where they wish to be heard (s 47(1)). This provides a continuing voice for victims and the community. It also ensures that the appeal courts have all the information they require in relation to risk. The powers of the Crown Court and the Court of Appeal, when hearing an appeal made in relation to a DAPO are set out at section 47(4) DAA. In accordance with that section, when hearing an appeal those courts may confirm, vary, or revoke any part of the decision; refer the matter back to the court that made the decision, directing them to reconsider and make a new decision in line with its ruling; make an order which the court that made the decision could have made; or make any incidental or consequential orders that it considers just (s 47(4)). Any appeal in the Crown Court or the Court of Appeal will not constitute a rehearing but rather a review of the lower court's decision.[8] Where an existing DAPO has been confirmed or varied on appeal, the DAPO will remain an order of the court that first made it. Where a DAPO has been made by a court on appeal, the DAPO will be treated as an order made by the court whose decision was appealed against (s 47(5)). The consequence of this section is to ensure that subsequent proceedings relating to the variation or discharge of the DAPO should be issued in the lower courts.[9]

5. SECTION 48 NATURE OF CERTAIN PROCEEDINGS UNDER THIS PART

Proceedings arising out of a DAPO made in criminal proceedings, whether that be on conviction, acquittal. or on a successful appeal, constitute civil proceedings (s 48(1)). When determining whether to make a DAPO at the conclusion of criminal proceedings, the court may hear evidence that was inadmissible in the relevant criminal proceedings, including but not limited to, hearsay and bad character evidence.[10] A magistrates' court or Crown Court may adjourn proceedings after sentencing, convicting, or allowing the appeal of the perpetrator, in order to facilitate the making of further enquiries before determining whether to make a DAPO.[11] A court may make a DAPO regardless of whether the perpetrator was convicted, acquitted, or discharged in the relevant proceedings (s 48(4)).

6 ibid [202].
7 ibid.
8 ibid [205].
9 ibid [206].
10 ibid [208].
11 ibid [209].

6. SECTION 49 SPECIAL MEASURES FOR WITNESSES

This section extends the use of special measures, which can currently be provided to vulnerable and intimidated witnesses in criminal and family proceedings, to victims of domestic abuse in any proceedings in which a DAPO is being made. Special measures, which are ubiquitous and work so effectively in criminal proceedings, are designed to enable vulnerable and intimidated witnesses to give their best evidence in court and due to their flexibility can be tailored to fit the individual needs of a witness on a case specific basis. Examples of special measures that may be provided include screening the witness from the perpetrator in court to ensure that they do not feel threatened or intimidated when giving their testimony, enabling the witness to give evidence by live link, and permitting the witness to give their evidence in private by excluding individuals from the court (other than the accused, their legal representatives, or their interpreter). For a witness to be eligible for special measures on the grounds of fear or distress about testifying they must satisfy the requirements set out at section 17 of the Youth Justice and Criminal Evidence Act (YJCEA) 1999.

7. SECTION 50 GUIDANCE

i. Notices and Orders: Supplementary

This section places an obligation on the Secretary of State to issue statutory guidance, to the police and other parties that may apply for a DAPO, regarding the various pathways for applications and provide practical toolkits for applicants.[12] The relevant guidance should cover how the different application pathways for a DAPO operate, when to consider applying for a DAPO, how to prepare DAPO conditions, how to work with victims, and highlighting the importance of robust safety planning and referral to the appropriate victim support services.[13] The police or any other applicant must have regard to any such guidance when undertaking any action in relation to a DAPO. The Secretary of State must consult the Domestic Abuse Commissioner before issuing or revising this guidance to ensure that frontline practitioners have the requisite knowledge of DAPOs in order to make full use of them to protect victims of domestic abuse and their children.[14] These toolkits have worked well in similar areas of law and give added insight into the intention of the legislators.

8. SECTION 51 DATA FROM ELECTRONIC MONITORING: CODE OF PRACTICE

i. Context and Background

The use of electronic monitoring (EM) in domestic abuse cases to support requirements within a DAPO are expressly provided for under section 35(6) of the Act. This measure was

[12] ibid [212].
[13] Domestic Abuse Bill (n 1) [217].
[14] ibid.

welcomed by some as another potential fetter on the behaviour of a perpetrator,[15] designed to monitor compliance with any requirements in the DAPO. However, concerns were raised by some organisations[16] who were worried about the lack of funding and resources available to support the initiative, and the quality of equipment used. It was argued that whilst aesthetically EM seems to provide an extra layer of protection for victims, in reality it may do little more than provide a false sense of security for them. That is, unless the initiative is implemented effectively with appropriate funding and infrastructure. The nature of EM was discussed in consultation on the draft Bill, with several organisations making suggestions about the forms of EM that could be utilised beyond mere GPS monitoring (including for instance location monitoring, and radio frequency monitoring). EM was particularly supported for cases such as stalking, high risk offenders and vulnerable offenders, and repeat victimisation.[17]

However, use of EM may lead to legal challenge alleging breaches of human rights, particularly when a perpetrator is in a position of having measures put in place to restrict their lives when they are not convicted of any criminal offences. The use of EM in circumstances such as these has often been labelled 'net widening', where traditionally EM has been used to monitor individuals convicted of criminal offences.[18] Careful consideration will need to be given to the necessity and proportionality of any such restrictions. In response to the draft consultation on the Domestic Abuse Bill, the Information Commissioner's Office commented:

> Electronic monitoring (for example location or alcohol monitoring) of perpetrators is identified as one of the measures that could be attached to the new order. Under new data protection laws, it is highly likely that this would require a DPIA which would assess proportionality and unpick data protection compliance risks, for example determining whether continuous monitoring could be justifiable. Controllers with responsibility for monitoring should also ensure that they procure systems that enable them to be compliant with the law.[19]

Section 51 of the DAA requires the Secretary of State to issue a code of practice relating to the processing of data gathered in the course of electronic monitoring for DAPOs. A code already exists for community orders, suspended sentences, and licence conditions, and it is expected that the new code will contain similar provisions.[20] As the explanatory notes to

[15] House of Commons Joint Committee on the Draft Domestic Abuse Bill Draft Domestic Abuse Bill First Report of Session 2017–19 Report, together with formal minutes relating to the report ordered by the House of Lords to be printed 11 June 2019, ordered by the House of Commons to be printed 11 June 2019, 28 [99] https://publications.parliament.uk/pa/jt201719/jtselect/jtddab/2075/2075.pdf (accessed 21 April 2022).

[16] ibid 29 [100]–[101].

[17] HM Government, 'Transforming the Response to Domestic Abuse Consultation Response and Draft Bill January 2019' 30, 31 https://assets.publishing.service.gov.uk/government/uploads/system/uploads/attachment_data/file/772247/Transforming_the_response_to_domestic_abuse_-_consultation_response_and_draft_bill_-print.pdf (accessed 21 April 2022).

[18] Jyoti Belur and others, 'A systematic review of the effectiveness of the electronic monitoring of offenders' (2020) 68 *Journal of Criminal Justice* 1.

[19] ICO response to the Draft consultation: The Information Commissioner's response to Domestic Abuse consultation (2018) https://ico.org.uk/media/about-the-ico/consultation-responses/2259736/ico-response-to-consultation-on-transforming-the-response-to-domestic-abuse-bill.pdf (accessed 21 April 2022).

[20] HM Prison and Probation Service, 'Code of Practice: Electronic Monitoring Data, Electronic Monitoring Directorate' (October 2020) https://assets.publishing.service.gov.uk/government/uploads/system/uploads/attachment_data/file/926813/em-revised-code-practice.pdf?msclkid=cf4cece0ae6c11ec989d7482e9ede41e (accessed 21 April 2022).

the Act point out,[21] processing of such data is subject to both the General Data Protection Regulations and the Data Protection Act 2018. It adds:

> The code of practice issued under this section is intended to set out the appropriate tests and safeguards for the processing of such data, in order to assist with compliance of the data protection legislation. For example, it is envisaged that the code will set out the length of time for which data may be retained and the circumstances in which it may be permissible to share data with the police to assist with crime detection.[22]

Section 51(2) also provides a standard subsection clarifying that breaches of the code do not automatically mean individual liability in either civil or criminal proceedings.

[21] Explanatory Notes (n 2) 36 [214].
[22] ibid.

9

POWERS TO MAKE OTHER ORDERS IN COURT PROCEEDINGS UNDER THIS PART (SECTIONS 52–56)

Gillian Jones KC

1. SECTION 52 POWERS TO MAKE OTHER ORDERS IN PROCEEDINGS UNDER THIS PART

Section 52 DAA provides:

(1) In section 8 of the Children Act 1989 (child arrangements orders and other orders with respect to children), in subsection (4), at the end insert—

'(k) Part 3 of the Domestic Abuse Act 2021, where the proceedings are in the family court or the Family Division of the High Court.'

(2) In Part 4 of the Family Law Act 1996 (family homes and domestic violence), in section 63(2) (definition of 'family proceedings'), after paragraph (j) insert—

'(k) Part 3 of the Domestic Abuse Act 2021, where the proceedings are in the family court or the Family Division of the High Court.'

The practical effect of subsection (1) is to amend the Children Act 1989 by inserting a reference to Part 3 of the Domestic Abuse Act (DAA) which provides that proceedings under Part 3 of the DAA are 'family proceedings' for the purpose of the Children Act 1989. This

Gillian Jones KC, *Powers to Make Other Orders in Court Proceedings Under this Part (Sections 52–56)* In: *Blackstone's Guide to the Domestic Abuse Act 2021*. Edited by Susan Edwards, David Malone, and Gillian Jones KC, Oxford University Press. © Gillian Jones KC 2023. DOI: 10.1093/oso/9780192870513.003.0009

amendment enables a judge (sitting in the family court or Family Division of the High Court) hearing an application to make or vary a domestic abuse protection order (DAPO) to make an interim care order (which means the local authority would be able to make decisions as to the welfare of the child and where the child lives), or exercise other powers under the Children Act 1989, in the same set of proceedings. The aim here is to protect children who are exposed to domestic abuse without requiring the commencement of separate applications or fresh proceedings as would otherwise be the case.

Subsection (2) inserts a reference to Part 3 of the DAA into section 63(2) of the Family Law Act 1996, which amends the definition of 'family proceedings' for the purposes of Part 4 of the Family Law Act 1996. This amendment enables a judge (sitting in the family court of the Family Division of the High Court) hearing an application to make or vary a DAPO, to make a forced marriage protection order, or an occupation or non-molestation order in the same set of proceedings.

2. SECTION 53 PROCEEDINGS NOT TO BE SUBJECT TO CONDITIONAL FEE AGREEMENTS

Section 53 DAA provides:

In section 58A of the Courts and Legal Services Act 1990 (conditional fee agreements: supplementary), in subsection (2), after paragraph (fd) (but before the 'and' following it) insert—

> '(fe) proceedings under Part 3 of the Domestic Abuse Act 2021 (proceedings for domestic abuse protection order), where the proceedings are in the family court or the Family Division of the High Court'.

A conditional fee agreement allows clients to agree that their lawyer will not receive all or part of their fee or expenses if they lose the case; or if they win, that the client will pay an uplift in fees. This section adds proceedings under Part 3 of the DAA, to the list of proceedings as detailed in section 58A of the Courts and Legal Services Act 1990 that cannot be the subject of an enforceable conditional fee agreement.

3. SECTION 54 CONSEQUENTIAL AMENDMENTS OF THE SENTENCING CODE

Section 54 DAA provides:

(1) The Sentencing Code is amended as follows.

(2) In section 80 (order for conditional discharge), in subsection (3), at the end insert—

> '(f) section 39(6) of the Domestic Abuse Act 2021 (breach of domestic abuse protection order).'

(3) In Chapter 6 of Part 11 (other behaviour orders), before section 379 (but after the heading 'Other orders') insert—

> **'378A Domestic abuse protection orders**
>
> See Part 3 of the Domestic Abuse Act 2021 (and in particular section 31(3) of that Act) for the power of a court to make a domestic abuse protection order when dealing with an offender for an offence.'

The practical effect of this section is to make two amendments to the Sentencing Code. The first amendment adds breach of a DAPO to the list of circumstances in section 80(3) of the Sentencing Code in which a conditional discharge is not available. The second amendment inserts into Part 11 of the Sentencing Code (behaviour orders), the power of the court to make a DAPO.

4. SECTION 55 REPEAL OF PROVISIONS ABOUT DOMESTIC VIOLENCE PROTECTION NOTICES AND ORDERS

Section 55 DAA provides:

(1) In the Crime and Security Act 2010, omit sections 24 to 33 (which make provision for domestic violence protection notices and domestic violence protection orders).

(2) In consequence of the repeal made by subsection (1), omit the following provisions—
  (a) in Schedule 8 to the Crime and Courts Act 2013, paragraph 179;
  (b) in Schedule 14 to the Policing and Crime Act 2017, paragraph 7(g).

This section repeals the provisions of the Crime and Security Act 2010, which gave the court power to issue domestic violence protection notices and make domestic violence protection orders, which were the precursor to DAPOs. Orders made under sections 24 and 33 of the Crime and Security Act 2010 will, however, continue to have effect.

5. SECTION 56 INTERPRETATION OF PART 3

Section 56 DAA provides:

(1) In this Part—

'chief officer of police' means—

(a) in relation to a police force maintained by a local policing body, the chief officer of police of that force;

(b) in relation to the British Transport Police Force, the Chief Constable of the Force;

(c) in relation to the Ministry of Defence Police, the Chief Constable of the Ministry of Defence Police;

'domestic abuse protection notice' has the meaning given by section 22(2);

'domestic abuse protection order' has the meaning given by section 27(1);

'electronic monitoring requirement' has the meaning given by section 35(6);

'family proceedings' means—

(a) proceedings in the family court (other than proceedings under or by virtue of this Part), and

(b) family proceedings within the meaning of Part 5 of the Matrimonial and Family Proceedings Act 1984;

'home address', in relation to a person, means—

(a) the address of the person's sole or main residence in the United Kingdom, or

(b) if the person has no such residence—

(i) the address or location of a place in the United Kingdom where the person can regularly be found;

(ii) if there is more than one such place, the address or location of whichever one of those places the person selects;

'relevant police force' has the meaning given by section 22(8);

'requirement', in relation to a domestic abuse protection order, is to be read in accordance with section 35(1);

'senior police officer' has the meaning given by section 22(8).

(2) Any reference to a member of a police force includes, in the case of a police force maintained by a local policing body, a reference to a special constable appointed by the chief officer of police of that force.

(3) Any reference to changing home address includes a reference to a case where—

(a) a person acquires a home address at any time, and

(b) immediately before that time, the person did not have a home address.

(4) See also—

(a) section 1 (definition of 'domestic abuse');

(b) section 2 (definition of 'personally connected').

This section defines the terms used in Part 3.

PART 4 OF THE ACT
LOCAL AUTHORITY SUPPORT
(SECTIONS 57–61)

10

LOCAL AUTHORITY SUPPORT AND LOCAL PARTNERSHIP BOARDS (SECTIONS 57–61)

Gill Hague, Sophie Jarrett and Tina Hemingway*

1. SECTION 57 SUPPORT PROVIDED BY LOCAL AUTHORITIES TO VICTIMS OF DOMESTIC ABUSE

i. Context and Background

One of the most important things that victims and survivors of domestic violence need, if they are forced to leave home because of abuse, is access to safe, secure housing for themselves and their children. From the beginning of the current wave of activism on these issues in the early 1970s, Women's Aid and other activists and practitioners have fought tenaciously to achieve initially temporary, and later permanent, housing for abused women. In the early days they were helped by the fact that laws passed during the period were often liberal in nature, and these included the Housing (Homeless Persons) Act 1977[1] (since modified), which provided temporary and permanent housing for particular homelessness groups.

* Section 57 by Gill Hague, sections 58–61 by Sophie Jarrett and Tina Hemingway.

[1] https://www.legislation.gov.uk/ukpga/1977/48/contents/enacted?msclkid=f3f634e7c19911ec886260b21bbe54b7 (accessed 21 April 2022).

Gill Hague, Sophie Jarrett and Tina Hemingway, *Local Authority Support and Local Partnership Boards (Sections 57–61)*
In: *Blackstone's Guide to the Domestic Abuse Act 2021*. Edited by Susan Edwards, David Malone, and Gillian Jones KC,
Oxford University Press. DOI: 10.1093/oso/9780192870513.003.0010

The Women's Aid federations, the main organisations coordinating domestic violence services, played an important role in the drafting and redrafting of this vital legislation from the 1970s on. The colloquially named Homeless Persons Act (HPA) 1977 laid down provisions for who would be considered as homeless and eligible for local authority housing, and the women's organisations were key in getting experiences of domestic abuse included as an accepted cause and criteria of homelessness. This meant that women escaping violence could be regarded as 'non-intentionally' homeless under the 1977 Act and opened avenues for rehousing. Women also had to be in what is known as 'priority need', which included those who were pregnant, who had children, or were vulnerable in specific ways, but many others fell through the net due to not fulfilling these conditions. Nevertheless, hundreds of thousands of women and children have been permanently rehoused under this legislation over the years, after waiting in a refuge or other emergency and temporary accommodation.

The legislation has been modified over time. However, with large-scale decreases in social housing,[2] families made homeless due to domestic violence in many areas have often had to wait much longer in temporary accommodation and have commonly been placed in such accommodation far from family and friendship ties. Women without children have had little hope of getting help in most instances.

a. *The Domestic Abuse Act*

The Domestic Abuse Act (DAA) has made attempts to improve this situation that are broadly to be welcomed. Importantly, these include the development of Domestic Abuse Strategies on accommodation under section 57. The new provisions on accommodation came into force in July 2021 and have important ramifications for social *housing* providers—including changes under section 78, which modify Part VII of the 1996 Housing Act[3] (a successor to the 1977 Act). What the new provisions do is expand the definitions of priority need to create the *automatic* inclusion of all who are homeless as a result of domestic abuse. This is a considerable step forward and places a duty on councils to provide emergency temporary accommodation to victims of abuse, providing that they meet immigration requirements.

b. *What evidence is required that someone is a victim of domestic abuse—and do they then get priority for a permanent tenancy?*

Importantly, it will no longer be permitted for local housing authorities to carry out an evaluative assessment of whether someone has become vulnerable as a result of their experiences of violence. Rather, they will be required to carry out a purely factual assessment (i.e., not a vulnerability evaluation) as to whether or not: (i) the person has in fact experienced domestic abuse as defined by the DAA, and, if yes: (ii) whether that person is homeless as a result.

The Homelessness Code of Guidance[4] that accompanies the legislation deals in detail with the issue of domestic abuse and has been fully rewritten with effect from July 2021 to

---

[2] With regard to the last 10 years see eg Lucie Hughes, 'Number of social rent homes falls by more than 200,000 since 2012, UK Housing Review Reveals' *Inside Housing* (29 March 2021) https://www.insidehousing.co.uk/news/news/number-of-social-rent-homes-falls-by-more-than-200000-since-2012-uk-housing-review-reveals-70193 (accessed 18 December 2021).

[3] https://www.legislation.gov.uk/ukpga/1996/52/contents (accessed 21 April 2022).

[4] Department for Levelling Up, Housing and Communities, *Homelessness Code of Guidance for Local Authorities* (2021) https://www.gov.uk/guidance/homelessness-code-of-guidance-for-local-authorities/chapter-1-introduction (accessed 21 April 2022).

reflect the changes introduced. It provides advice on understanding what domestic abuse is, on carrying out inquiries and investigations in a safe manner, and on what accommodation is suitable. The Code sets out the types of evidence that may be appropriate to prove that someone is at risk of domestic abuse, including from health care and criminal justice professionals, from social services or from friends and family of the applicant. But absence of such evidence is not to be taken by the local authority as a reason to refuse assistance. This means that councils will no longer need to consider if a victim has specific issues or vulnerabilities in order to access accommodation secured by the local authority. The principal is that no victims/survivors will have to remain with their abusers for fear of not having a roof over their heads or be referred back against their will to an area where they are at risk of further domestic abuse.

The DAA does not alter the fact the local authorities are responsible for devising allocation schemes for social housing within a national framework. In framing these criteria, local authorities must consider their duties under the equalities legislation (Equality Act 2010)[5] and the requirement to give overall priority to people in the 'reasonable preference' categories, which include domestic abuse. There is a new provision in DAA section 79 for housing authorities to be obligated in qualifying circumstances to offer secure, safe, permanent tenancies to victims of domestic abuse, not flexible tenancies (discussed below). However, these positive developments do not help all victims/survivors. Women with uncertain immigration status do not qualify and are likely to be left without help if they experience domestic abuse (discussed later in Part III of this book). The many women and their children placed in poor-standard temporary accommodation may then wait there for extremely long periods of time, possibly rotating over years from one temporary accommodation to another. According to practitioners in London boroughs, this scenario is especially the case in large cities like London.

Smaller towns and cities may have more facilities. The CEO of a domestic abuse service provider, from outside London, who was interviewed for this section of the chapter, welcomed the new provisions which she considered were having a positive effect and were improving both agency collaboration and the general culture of how domestic abuse is dealt with and viewed by the local authority. Her organisation had helpful experiences of the new legislation on priority need. And they are currently using provisions for increased funding under the Act for accommodation support to finance both new independent domestic violence adviser/advocate posts to work in partnership with homelessness teams, and also other workers including a play worker and an LGBT+ specialist.

2. SECTION 57 AND DOMESTIC ABUSE HOUSING STRATEGIES

Under section 57 of the new Act, local authorities must draw up domestic abuse strategies, expanding from previous requirements. Each relevant local authority must assess (or make arrangements for the assessment of) the need for accommodation-based support in its area for victims/survivors. It must then prepare a strategy for the provision of such support, guided by regulations in the Act as to how these strategies are to be drawn up, monitored, and

[5] https://www.legislation.gov.uk/ukpga/2010/15/contents (accessed 21 April 2022).

evaluated. Practitioners consulted suggested that domestic abuse strategies on accommodation are likely to have positive impacts for future service commissioning policies by the local authority concerned and for resultant service provision. However, in practice, domestic abuse organisations also pointed out for this section that there may be a danger of these strategies being somewhat vague or overly general.

This section of the DAA lays down the necessity for local authorities to monitor needs, to publish their strategy, and then to put the strategy into effect. It is not yet clear, however, how all this will work in practice, how far local authorities will take account of what those consulted recommend, and how fully abused women themselves will be included in the consultations. Although the new accommodation-based funding available under the Act is important, it is unclear who will then fund any wider provisions put forward in an agreed strategy. For example, should the local authority identify a need for further permanent housing for domestic abuse victims in its area, where will this come from? Local authorities only have to 'give effect to' the strategy they have drawn up, a weak provision, and not a 'duty'. This may not be a strong enough prerogative to enable challenge for perceived council failures or inadequacies in this respect, or for any such challenges to be likely to be successful. Vitally, the possible use of judicial review in these circumstances is not clear at this point. While there have of course been homelessness cases taken successfully to judicial review in the past, using the new strategies which do not include statutory duties in such reviews in the future may not be easy to accomplish.

There is an ongoing need to provide linked-up services, with a strengthening of the working together of voluntary agencies and crucially the domestic abuse sector, women's agencies, and survivors' groups to inform the strategy and its implementation locally, and also to feed into the national obligation across all authorities to meet the accommodation needs of violence survivors. There are nods in this direction in the Act and, of course, inter-agency frameworks of various types do already exist. How these new domestic abuse strategies will pan out as time goes on is an open question, however.

At the time of writing, different developments are in progress in different places. The CEO of the domestic abuse service provider, quoted above, outlined how their organisation is currently involved in consultations carried out by the local authority on its new strategy. She pointed out how important it is for the violence against women and girls' sector to be represented around the table. For example, the draft strategy in question had included inaccurate and skewed data, which only the specialist service was in a position to correct. Her organisation was now being invited to the further consultations, a positive situation. She emphasised how building relationships with housing officers helps. However, she explained how the situation varies markedly by area, and other housing authorities in the region were not consulting with specialist services for abused women. Thus, she believed the new Act and the development of domestic abuse strategies on homelessness are currently helping domestic violence organisations to argue the case for better accommodation services, but many local authorities are less receptive or proactive.

In a piece of research on housing and domestic violence by Ellen Malos and myself in the 1990s,[6] we identified a 'postcode lottery' in terms of how local authorities respond to housing and domestic violence. Some had excellent policies in place, and also held good stocks of permanent housing. Others had neither the policies nor the stock. This remains widely true

[6] Ellen Malos and Gill Hague, 'Women, housing, homelessness and domestic violence' (1997) 20(3) *Women's Studies International Forum* 397.

today but has been made infinitely worse due to the huge decrease in social housing availability since then. Thus, the postcode lottery effect is likely to be the case with the operation of the new strategies as time goes on. Ideally, the Act provides an important opportunity to make voices on housing provision heard, to provide some consistency across local authorities and to help relevant bodies work together. This does seem to be the case so far in sympathetic, responsive housing authorities. But such strategic developments can also just be window dressing.

In our later research on domestic abuse interagency initiatives,[7] we identified how initiatives of this type can be extremely effective. At worst, however, and often in reality, they can be talking shops with officers taking up a lot of time and energy in drawing up and operating what are often somewhat ineffective strategies. They may also overlook the voices of survivors. These types of strategies can look good—but can unfortunately at worst be time wasters, using up overstretched resources. And they can be smokescreens that mask and disguise lack of actual action and change.

There is little evidence yet that this grim prognosis will not be the case with these newest strategies in at least some areas, although vigilance by local domestic abuse services and the full involvement of both these services and survivor groups will enable pressure to be put on local authorities in the future. As time goes on, interviewees pointed out that there will be a need for the new funding provisions for accommodation services also to take on community services, and for longer-term provisions to be put in place, rather than year-on-year strategising with the local authority as now.

i. Critical Commentary

A 2020 report (before the new Act), *The Hidden Housing Crisis*,[8] identified an extreme shortage of affordable and public sector housing to meet the needs of abused women and children, accompanied by prohibitively high rents for private accommodation, and very long waits for social housing, coupled with rising homelessness. In terms of refuges, 64.1 per cent of women applicants were turned away due to lack of secure accommodation. In December 2019, Women's Aid in England[9] reported a study which found that only *one quarter* of abused women seeking refuge were able to be accommodated. Women's Aid point out that about one in ten refuges and one in five community-based services receive no local authority funding at all, and services led 'by and for' black and minority women have been disproportionately impacted.

Before the Domestic Abuse Bill was passed, Rights of Women, Women's Aid in England and Wales, Refuge, Southall Black Sisters, Migrant Women Speak Out, survivors' groups, and other women's organisations were tireless in their work on attempting to amend it, as discussed throughout this volume. Their hard work demonstrated the role that women's movement activists can have in influencing the law. They attempted to fill gaps, for example,

[7] Gill Hague, 'Smoke screen or leap forward: interagency initiatives as a response to domestic violence' (1997) 17(53) *Critical Social Policy* 93.

[8] Lizzie Magnussen and Sarah Davidge, *The Hidden Housing Crisis: Domestic Abuse Report* (Women's Aid 2020) https://www.womensaid.org.uk/wp-content/uploads/2020/06/The-Domestic-Abuse-Report-2020-The-Hidden-Housing-Crisis.pdf (accessed 21 April 2022).

[9] Women's Aid, 'Women's Aid report says £393 million a year is needed' https://www.womensaid.org.uk/evidence-hub/research-and-publications/funding-specialist-support-for-domestic-abuse-survivors/ (accessed 14 November 2022).

the extreme impact that immigration status has on accessing housing for homeless migrant women subjected to violence and their overall lack of protection. However, the amendments to support migrant women and those without recourse to public funds failed to pass. The Act continues to fail these women overall and many black and minority ethnic women face almost insurmountable barriers in escaping violence and securing housing.

Women's Aid in England[10] points out that, although the new legislation strengthens the statutory duties on local authorities to fund accommodation-based services, it does not once use the word, 'refuge'. Domestic abuse survivors commonly need the specialist help that refuges and domestic abuse services provide, not merely offers of housing, possibly without support. The federation strongly emphasises that it is crucial that local authorities must more adequately fund specialist women's refuges, which deliver expert support to survivors and their children. Whatever the improvements in the legislation, these realities remain for women and children homeless due to domestic abuse in many localities.

It is important to acknowledge that accessing safe, permanent accommodation after leaving home due to domestic abuse is easier in countries which have at least some provision of public sector or social housing, as the UK does (compared with, say, the many countries with no financing for such provision). Also, the UK is somewhat unusual in having specialist legislation on homelessness and domestic abuse in place.[11] It used to be fairly routine to enable families to get rehoused moderately quickly by the local council. In the last thirty years, however, with the selling-off of council housing and the catastrophic diminishing of social and public housing options, these positive provisions have become stretched almost beyond measure in many localities. Forty-two per cent of people lived in council housing in the UK in 1979. Currently, the figure is just 8 per cent.[12]

Shelter tells us[13] that there are 1.5 million fewer social housing units than in 1980, with about 2.6 million council homes sold and the building of new social homes reduced from 94,140 in 1980 to just 6,287 in 2019. There are 1.1 million people waiting. Of course, those who are statutorily homeless have some priority and the shortage is less acute in some areas. Overall, the provisions of the Domestic Abuse Act on housing are welcome, despite their shortcomings, noted above. But the harsh reality of social housing in the 2020s may override such hopeful improvements.

3. SECTIONS 58–61 LOCAL PARTNERSHIP BOARDS

i. Context and Background

Women's Aid, alongside other organisations within the women's sector, have been campaigning for a sustainable funding model that supports and maintains the refuge network across

[10] Women's Aid, 'Domestic Abuse Bill' https://www.womensaid.org.uk/get-involved/campaign/domestic-abuse-bill/ (accessed 14 November 2022).

[11] Paula Maycock, Joanne Bretherton, and Isabel Baptista, 'Women's homelessness and domestic violence: (In)visible interactions' in Paula Maycock and Joanne Bretherton (eds), *Women's Homelessness in Europe* (Palgrave Macmillan 2016) 127.

[12] John Harris, 'The end of council housing' *The Guardian* (4 January 2016) www.theguardian.com/society/2016/jan/04/end-of-council-housing-bill-secure-tenancies-pay-to-stay (accessed 18 January 2022).

[13] Shelter, *The Story of Social Housing* (Shelter 2021) https://england.shelter.org.uk/support_us/campaigns/story_of_social_housing (accessed 14 November 2022).

England, with Welsh Women's Aid advocating separately for Wales. The Save our Services (SOS) campaign[14] called for the existing national network of refuges to be protected and fully funded, ensuring the sustainability and growth of the refuge network to better meet the need for safe housing. Following the SOS campaign, the funding support required for refuge services was recognised in the 2017 general election in which the Prime Minister made a manifesto commitment to funding refuges.[15]

The Violence Against Women and Girls (VAWG) strategy 2016–2020 made a clear commitment to ensure 'no woman is turned away from the support she needs and that all victims get the right support at the right time'. This sought to drive local transformation of service provision and was supported by the publication of the VAWG National Statement of Expectations (2016).[16] From 2016 to 2018, the Ministry for Housing Communities and Local Government (MHCLG) provided funding to local areas, creating more than 2,200 bed spaces within safe accommodation[17] and funding the Women's Aid 'Routes to Support' work.[18]

In May 2019, the MHCLG released its consultation 'Future Delivery of Support to Victims and their Children in Accommodation-Based Domestic Abuse Services'.[19] This consultation and its response,[20] paved the way for the requirements placed on local authorities under Part 4 of the Domestic Abuse Act 2021, ensuring a duty to provide support within safe accommodation, and to ensure a partnership approach to assessing local need and developing strategies that outline local requirements in meeting the duty.

4. SECTIONS 58–61

Part 4 of the DAA covers a range of requirements for local authorities in England to ensure the provision of support within safe accommodation for victims of domestic abuse and their children. This part of the act was implemented upon royal assent in April 2021, placing a statutory duty on local authorities in England.

[14] See https://edm.parliament.uk/early-day-motion/47145/womens-aid-save-our-services-campaign (accessed 14 November 2022.

[15] See Conservative Party Manifesto https://general-election-2010.co.uk/2017-general-election-manifestos/conservative-manifesto-2017.pdf?msclkid=f8b8c455c19a11ecbe90b5c1a7932330 (accessed 21 April 2022).

[16] See VAWG National Statement of Expectation 2016 https://assets.publishing.service.gov.uk/government/uploads/system/uploads/attachment_data/file/574665/VAWG_National_Statement_of_Expectations_-_FINAL.PDF (accessed 21 April 2022).

[17] See https://www.gov.uk/government/news/19-million-fund-to-support-victims-of-domestic-abuse (accessed 21 April 2022).

[18] See Women's Aid, 'Access to Routes to Support' https://www.womensaid.org.uk/what-we-do/i-work-with-survivors/routes-to-support/access-to-routes-to-support/ (accessed 14 November 2022).

[19] See MHCLG, 'Future Delivery of Support to Victims and their Children in Accommodation-Based Domestic Abuse Services' Consultation Response (2019) https://safelives.org.uk/sites/default/files/resources/MHCLG%20Consultation%20on%20the%20Future%20Delivery%20of%20Support%20to%20Victims%20and%20their%20Children%20in%20Accommodation%20SafeLives%20response.pdf (accessed 21 April 2022).

[20] See Domestic Abuse Services Future Delivery of Support to Victims and their Children in Accommodation-Based Domestic Abuse Services: Consultation Response https://assets.publishing.service.gov.uk/government/uploads/system/uploads/attachment_data/file/839171/Domestic_Abuse_Duty_Gov_Response_to_Consultation.pdf (accessed 21 April 2022).

Many parts of England have two tiers of local government:[21]

- county councils (Tier 1)
- district, borough, or city councils (Tier 2).

In some parts of the country, there is just one (unitary) tier of local government providing all the local services.

The statutory duty is the responsibility of Tier 1 or unitary authorities.[22]

Sections 58–61 set out the requirements on local authorities in meeting their duty through establishing a partnership board, assessing local need, developing a local strategy, and the ongoing implementation and monitoring of the local approach.

i. Section 58 Domestic Abuse Local Partnership Boards

Section 58(1) sets out that a relevant local authority in England must appoint a domestic abuse local partnership board (LPB) for the purposes of providing advice to the authority about:

(a) the exercise of the authority's functions under section 57, and
(b) the provision of other local authority support in the authority's area.

This requires local authorities in England to appoint a LPB to support the delivery of the statutory duty outlined in section 57 of the DAA in which local authorities must

(a) assess, or make arrangements for the assessment of, the need for accommodation-based support in its area
(b) prepare and publish a strategy for the provision of such support in its area and
(c) monitor and evaluate the effectiveness of the strategy.

This element of the DAA builds on the already existing duty placed on local authorities under the Crime and Disorder Act, section 5 (CDA) 1998[23] in which community safety partnerships were established. Whilst not specific to domestic abuse, these partnerships ensured that strategies for the prevention of crime were no longer just a police responsibility, but required joint working across criminal justice, health, and local councils. The CDA was later amended by section 6 (6)(a) to include a requirement for strategies to be formulated to address 'the reduction of crime or disorder of a particular description,' leading to the establishment of domestic abuse partnerships in many areas.

Domestic abuse partnerships have been heavily influenced by the Duluth Model,[24] originally established in Minnesota, USA in the 1980s. This model, designed to reduce domestic violence and abuse, pioneered the coordinated community response (CCR) a partnership model that brings key agencies together, including for example police, health, local authorities, and victim services, in order work together with the aim of keeping survivors safe, holding abusers to account, and preventing domestic abuse. Brought to the UK in the 1990s, the

[21] See https://www.gov.uk/understand-how-your-council-works (accessed 21 April 2022).

[22] Throughout this section of the chapter, the term 'local authority' will be used to describe the authority that holds the statutory duty within a local area.

[23] See https://www.legislation.gov.uk/ukpga/1998/37/contents (accessed 21 April 2022).

[24] See https://www.theduluthmodel.org/what-is-the-duluth-model/ (accessed 21 April 2022).

CCR has been heavily championed and developed in the UK by Standing Together Against Domestic Violence (STADV),[25] a national domestic abuse charity, and now forms the basis of partnership structures for addressing domestic abuse at a local level. This, alongside the Domestic Violence, Crime and Victim's Act (DVCVA 2004),[26] in which a further commitment to victims of domestic abuse was made, provides the basis for the new requirements as set out in the DAA, adding for the first time, a specific statutory duty to ensure the provision of support at a local level within domestic abuse safe accommodation.

In recognition of these existing partnerships, authorities can use existing boards and structures to fulfil the statutory duty but must ensure the required membership set out in section 58(2) is met. Supported by statutory guidance,[27] LPBs must include:

(a) a representative of the relevant local authority
(b) at least one person appearing to the authority to represent the interests of local authorities for areas within its area
(c) at least one person appearing to the authority to represent the interests of victims of domestic abuse
(d) at least one person appearing to the authority to represent the interests of children of domestic abuse victims
e) at least one person appearing to the authority to represent the interests of charities and other voluntary organisations that work with victims of domestic abuse in its area
f) at least one person appearing to the authority to represent the interests of persons who provide, or have functions relating to, health care services in its area
g) at least one person appearing to the authority to represent the interests of persons with functions relating to policing or criminal justice in its area.

The statutory guidance is clear that the list provided is the minimum representation required.

Given the focus of the statutory duty on the requirement to provide support within domestic abuse safe accommodation (s 57 DAA), boards should consider housing representation as well as links to existing boards such as community safety partnerships and homelessness reduction boards (HRBs).

The function of the LPB must include:

1. Assessing the scale and nature of local need

   This is specific to the statutory duty, requiring the LPB to 'conduct a local needs assessment to determine the level of need for support within safe accommodation in their area'.[28] This is an important precursor to the development of local strategies, and must be conducted at a minimum every three years, with an annual refresh to ensure any change in demand or support required is adequately captured.

[25] See 'What is a CCR? Standing Together' https://www.standingtogether.org.uk/what-is-ccr (accessed 21 April 2022).

[26] See https://www.legislation.gov.uk/ukpga/2004/28/contents (accessed 21 April 2022).

[27] See DLUHC, 'Delivery of Support to Victims of Domestic Abuse, including Children, in Domestic Abuse Safe Accommodation Services: Statutory guidance for local authorities across England' (2021) https://www.gov.uk/government/publications/domestic-abuse-support-within-safe-accommodation/delivery-of-support-to-victims-of-domestic-abuse-in-domestic-abuse-safe-accommodation-services (accessed 21 April 2022).

[28] ibid s B2.

2. Preparing and publishing a whole-area domestic abuse support in relevant safe accommodation strategy

   Local strategies must be based on a robust needs assessment, reviewed every three years and 'ensure the strategy clearly sets out its overall and holistic approach to deliver a rounded offer of support to victims in safe accommodation'.[29]

3. Giving effect to the strategy through commissioning and decommissioning

   Local authorities must ensure 'support is commissioned (directly and/or through decommissioning) in safe accommodation to meet the needs of victims and their children in line with their local strategy as soon as reasonably practicable and in line with local authority procurement rules and commissioning cycles'.[30] To support giving effect to local strategies the Department of Levelling Up Housing and Communities (DLUHC, formerly MHCLG) has identified £125 million of funding for the year 2021/2022 for local authorities to enable them to meet their statutory duties, allocated based on a local population and labour costs adjustment formula.[31] The DLUHC intends funding to be available on an annual basis whilst the duty remains in the place.

4. Monitoring and evaluating activity[32]

   The LPB must have a clear approach to monitoring and evaluating local delivery against approaches set out within their local strategies.

5. Reporting on progress[33]

   The LPB must report back to DLUHC on an annual basis in line with the intended standardised reporting format as laid out in the Regulations made under section 59(2) of the DAA.

ii. Section 59 Annual Reports

Section 59 outlines the annual reporting requirements for local authorities, detailing that a relevant local authority in England must submit to the Secretary of State an annual report in relation to the exercise of the authority's functions under this Part of the DAA.

Annual reports are expected to be made to DLUHC within three months following the end of the financial year and should demonstrate how local authorities have executed their functions, providing data and information that includes evidence that:

- a LPB has been established
- adequate needs assessments having been undertaken
- local strategies are in place and working effectively
- local commissioning decisions are informed by needs assessments and strategies

[29] DLUHC (n 27) s B4.2.
[30] ibid s B5.1.
[31] See MHCLG Funding allocation methods: new domestic abuse duty https://www.gov.uk/government/consultations/funding-allocation-methods-new-domestic-abuse-duty.
[32] See DLUHC (n 27) s C1.1.
[33] DLUHC (n 27) ss B.2.21 and C3.8.

- how allocated funding has been spent against the delivery approaches set out in local strategies, demonstrating value for money.

Local authorities will be accountable to the DLUHC, which will be establishing a ministerial led national expert steering group.

iii. Sections 60–61 Guidance and Interpretation of Part 4

Section 60 sets out the requirement on the Secretary of State to publish guidance for local authorities to support them in exercising their functions under Part 4 of the DAA. This guidance must be consulted on with the Domestic Abuse Commissioner (DAC) for England and Wales, local authorities, and any other person the Secretary of State consider appropriate. Local authorities must have regard to this guidance.

Section 61 provides a definition of what Local Authority and relevant Local Authority mean in the context of Part 4 of the DAA.

a. *Critical Commentary (ss 58–61)*

The statutory duty has been broadly welcomed following years of campaigning to ensure adequate provision of domestic abuse safe accommodation. The LPB and its required functions (ss 58–61) play a critical and necessary role in guiding local areas in implementing the duty; in particular providing the essential structure to assess need and direct commissioning activity. The limited nature of the duty does present some challenges to local areas.

Local Partnership Board The requirements around the establishment of a LPB, whilst not necessarily new, do allow local authorities to reconsider and, where necessary, refresh their partnership approach. In support of this, the required LPB membership assists local areas in compelling partner agencies to participate and provides some consistency across England.

Within Gloucestershire, as one local authority area, the requirements have enabled a new approach to be taken through the establishment of a LPB that consists of strategic, operational and consultation groups, each with their own set of aims and objectives.[34] It has also encouraged a self-evaluation against the core criteria for a CCR via 'In search of excellence',[35] placing a marker for success which the LPB can continue to monitor and develop.

Whilst there are many positives to the requirements around the LPB, its narrow focus of ensuring local areas meet the statutory duty may lead to the broader CCR aims and objectives being neglected; with accommodation-based activity being prioritised over wider community-based initiatives to tackle domestic abuse. In addition to this, whilst board members are required to attend, there is no guarantee around their or their organisation's meaningful contribution, since much partnership activity is often personality led.

Needs Assessment The development of a domestic abuse needs assessment is not a new consideration, as an assessment of this nature forms part of the commissioning process to ensure the appropriate provision of services across local areas. The requirement to assess the specific needs around support within safe accommodation is, however, new, although potentially has always been considered by areas which deliver an accommodation-based model of support.

---

[34] See https://www.gloucestershire.gov.uk/media/2110605/gcc-domestic-abuse-strategy.pdf (accessed 21 April 2022).

[35] See Standing Together, 'In Search of Excellence' (2020) https://www.standingtogether.org.uk/blog-3/in-search-of-excellence (accessed 21 April 2022).

As with the LPB, the needs assessment is only required to consider assessing need within safe accommodation. As such, it is a local decision as to whether a wider assessment of need beyond the scope of the statutory duty is undertaken; potentially making it difficult to achieve a standardised approach nationally.

Whilst the importance of safe accommodation is recognised, the LGA outlined concerns that the narrow focus of the duty may impact on the delivery of a holistic approach to domestic abuse, and therefore on broader support to victims and prevention,[36] failing to recognise the wider context of community-based support which may push local authorities into reducing, rather than sustaining, vital services through failing to assess broader community need.[37]

Conducting a needs assessment is reliant on the availability of robust and appropriate data. Many local authorities, via the LGA, expressed concerns that an absence of national data on unmet demand for domestic abuse safe accommodation makes local needs assessments challenging.[38] Alongside this, local areas will have identified gaps in data which may leave a knowledge gap in terms of actual need and will also need to consider mechanisms for ensuring the voice of victims and their children is represented. Over time, as local areas establish a robust data set, alongside a national template, the understanding of unmet need will improve. The requirement to conduct an annual refresh will allow local areas the opportunity to reflect on the impact of any commissioning decisions on the wider implementation of local strategies and the potential changing demographics of local communities.

Strategy Development Local areas are only required to publish a strategy that demonstrates its approach to the duty. As such, some local authorities may choose to focus only on their statutory requirements at the expense of a whole system approach to domestic abuse that could impact on broader provision and support options for victims. Equally, many areas may choose to widen the scope of their strategies, leading to varying approaches being taken. As 2021 is the first year in which this duty was in place, lessons can be learnt which could result in the development of a more standardised approach in the future. Alongside this, the DAC has pledged to tackle inconsistences across England and Wales.[39] Giving effect to local strategy in meeting the duty is also potentially undermined by a number of factors.

Short-term nature of funding Funding for this duty will initially be paid on an annual basis in the form of a non-ring-fenced grant under section 31 of the Local Government Act (LGA) 2003 for two years. Following this, it is intended that the duty will become part of the local government financial settlement.

These funding arrangements present challenges for commissioning, with the LGA noting that the statutory duty requires comprehensive and long-term funding in order to allow local authorities to commission and plan strategically. Without the reassurance of future funding

---

[36] See LGA's response to the government's consultation on the future delivery of support to victims and their children in accommodation-based domestic abuse services in England 2019 https://www.local.gov.uk/sites/default/files/documents/LGA%20response%20-%20MHCLG%20DA%20consultation%20%20-%20FINAL.pdf (accessed 21 April 2022).

[37] See Safe Lives Briefing for Domestic Abuse Bill—Second Reading—House of Lords https://safelives.org.uk/sites/default/files/resources/SafeLives%20briefing%20for%20DA%20Bill%20HL%20Second%20Reading%20Stage_0.pdf (accessed 21 April 2022).

[38] ibid.

[39] See https://domesticabusecommissioner.uk/domestic-abuse-commissioner-pledges-to-end-the-postcode-lottery-of-domestic-abuse-services-2/ (accessed 21 April 2022).

levels and the option for ring-fenced funding it is difficult to deliver sustainable commissioned services.[40]

In addition, the parameters of the funding do not include any capital expenditure. For local authorities who do not have sufficient relevant accommodation provision, there are challenges in identifying and funding appropriate properties where the cost of domestic abuse support could be funded through the DLUHC allocation.

Challenges facing housing sector The new duty to provide support within safe accommodation is hindered by the pressures currently facing the housing sector, with the LGA highlighting that a number of areas across the country are facing a lack of affordable housing and temporary accommodation.[41] The issues of housing supply may make it difficult to identify relevant safe accommodation in which to commission specialist support.

Monitoring implementation Whilst local areas will be required to develop their own approach to monitoring and evaluating local delivery, the DLUHC will be developing a standardised reporting form for local authorities to report back to government on the steps taken in meeting the statutory duty. This will be monitored by a ministerial led national expert steering group.

At the time of writing, the reporting requirements are unknown. The DLUHC has, however, conducted a survey with local authorities to understand the data available at a local level and we understand that reporting mechanisms and requirements with clear guidance will be issued. Local areas are broadly supportive of a standardised approach which will facilitate a shared understanding and allow for comparisons on performance and delivery. However, there is potential for this standardised approach to reporting to limit innovative approaches at a local level.

In addition to the reporting requirements, all local authorities will be expected to adhere to the statutory guidance.[42]

[40] See Safe Lives Briefing for Domestic Abuse Bill (n 37).
[41] ibid.
[42] DLUHC (n 27).

PART 5 OF THE ACT
PROTECTION FOR VICTIMS, WITNESSES, ETC IN LEGAL PROCEEDINGS (SECTIONS 62–67)

11

SPECIAL MEASURES FOR VICTIMS AND WITNESSES AND ORDERS UNDER THE CHILDREN ACT (SECTIONS 62–67)

Gillian Jones KC

1. CONTEXT AND BACKGROUND

Part 5 of the DAA from a procedural perspective is of landmark importance, as it provides much needed clarification of the law, recognising the vulnerability of witnesses by placing on a statutory footing a presumption that victims of domestic abuse are automatically eligible for special measures in the criminal courts and in family and civil proceedings. Importantly, it also prohibits alleged perpetrators in family and civil proceedings from cross-examining in

Gillian Jones KC, *Special Measures for Victims and Witnesses and Orders Under the Children Act (Sections 62–67)*
In: *Blackstone's Guide to the Domestic Abuse Act 2021*. Edited by Susan Edwards, David Malone, and Gillian Jones KC,
Oxford University Press. © Gillian Jones KC 2023. DOI: 10.1093/oso/9780192870513.003.0011

person a victim of domestic abuse as well as preventing vexatious applications by an applicant not satisfied with the decision of the court in family matters concerning children.

Discussions at the Bill stage highlighted that the initial proposals to extend special measures to include domestic abuse victims in the criminal courts were not far-reaching enough, as they did not ensure similar protections in civil and family courts. The all-party parliamentary group on domestic violence and abuse found that victims of domestic abuse reported feeling revictimised and retraumatised through the family court process. In 2012, a report by Rights of Women, a women's charity providing legal information and advice, outlined how victims of domestic abuse suffer intimidation and harassment from their former partners, and that they often feel unsafe during the court procedure in a family court. To address these concerns, an amendment was proposed to extend eligibility for the measures to family courts in cases where domestic abuse is involved.

Prior to the DAA, provision for the use of special measures in family proceedings was not dictated by statute but in the Family Procedure Rules 2010 and associated Practice Directions. In November 2017, the Ministry of Justice introduced a new practice direction 3AA, *Vulnerable persons: participation in proceedings and giving evidence*, which stated that 'the court may use its general case management powers as it considers appropriate to facilitate the party's participation'. However, evidence at the bill stage suggested that special measures were not advertised in the family court and were rarely ordered.[1] A report by Women's Aid in 2018 found that 61 per cent of domestic abuse victims who participated in a survey were not provided with special measures in a family court.[2] So, whilst special measures were available in the family courts prior to the DAA their use was not uniform, leading to an unevenness of application and a lack of protection for victims. Moreover, 'facilities such as video and audio link are not as readily available as they are in the criminal courts'.[3]

A similar lack of equality of approach between criminal and family proceedings arose in respect of the ability of an alleged perpetrator of domestic abuse to be able to cross-examine in person a victim of domestic abuse. 'In 2018, Women's Aid found that 24% of respondents had been cross-examined by their abusive ex-partner in the family court.'[4]

Part 5 of the DAA for the first time provides much needed statutory protections for victims and witnesses across criminal, family, and civil jurisdictions.[5]

2. SECTIONS 62–64 SPECIAL MEASURES

i. Section 62: Special Measures in Criminal Proceedings for Offences Involving Domestic Abuse

Section 62 DAA provides:

[1] Women's Aid Report, 'Picking up the pieces: domestic violence and child contact' Research report by Maddy Coy, Katherine Perks, Emma Scott, and Ruth Tweedale, Rights of Women and CWASU (2012) https://rightsofwomen.org.uk/wp-content/uploads/2014/10/Picking_Up_the_Pieces_Report-2012l.pdf (accessed 8 May 2022).

[2] Christine Jardine, col 256, Domestic Abuse Bill (Eighth Sitting) https://hansard.parliament.uk/commons/2020-06-11/debates/2b88e3cc-6f84-42a0-a440-136bbc9fbe0b/DomesticAbuseBill(EighthSitting)?msclkid=aa7e13decf7b11ec801505b8e71266a8 (accessed 8 May 2022).

[3] Jess Phillips, col 259, Domestic Abuse Bill (Eighth Sitting).

[4] Christine Jardine (n 2) col 258.

[5] Explanatory Notes Pt 5—ukpgaen_20210017_en.pdf (legislation.gov.uk) (accessed 8 May 2022).

(1) Chapter 1 of Part 2 of the Youth Justice and Criminal Evidence Act 1999 (giving of evidence or information for purposes of criminal proceedings: special measures directions in case of vulnerable and intimidated witnesses) is amended as follows.

(2) In section 17 (witnesses eligible for assistance on grounds of fear or distress about testifying)—

(a) in subsection (4), for 'a sexual offence or an offence under section 1 or 2 of the Modern Slavery Act 2015' substitute 'an offence listed in subsection (4A)';

(b) after subsection (4) insert—

'(4A) The offences are—

(a) a sexual offence;

(b) an offence under section 1 or 2 of the Modern Slavery Act 2015;

(c) any other offence where it is alleged that the behaviour of the accused amounted to domestic abuse within the meaning of the Domestic Abuse Act 2021 (see section 1 of that Act).'

(3) In section 25(4)(a) (evidence given in private), for 'a sexual offence or an offence under section 1 or 2 of the Modern Slavery Act 2015' substitute 'an offence listed in section 17(4A)'.[6]

Witnesses whose quality of evidence is likely to be diminished due to fear, distress, or intimidation are eligible in criminal proceedings for special measures under section 17 of the Youth Justice Criminal Evidence Act 1999. The practical effect of this section when it comes into force is to create a statutory presumption that victims of domestic abuse (as defined by s 1 of the DAA) are automatically eligible for special measures in the criminal courts on the grounds of fear or distress, unless they inform the court that they do not require special measures. This removes the need for a witness to have to satisfy the fear or distress test to be eligible.

Subsection (3) extends the circumstances in which a special measures direction can be made that provides for the witness's evidence to be given in private (with the exception of a representative of the press), to include cases where it is alleged that the behaviour of the accused amounted to domestic abuse. Currently, such a direction can only be made in cases involving sexual offences or modern slavery offences, or where it appears to the court that there are reasonable grounds for believing that any person other than the accused has sought, or will seek, to intimidate the witness in connection with testifying in the proceedings.[7]

ii. Section 63: Special Measures in Family Proceedings: Victims of Domestic Abuse

Section 63 DAA provides:

(1) This section applies where rules of court provide that the court may make a special measures direction in relation to a person ('P') who is a party or witness in family proceedings.

[6] See Policy Paper 'Special measures in the criminal courts factsheet' (Updated 31 January 2022) https://www.gov.uk/government/publications/domestic-abuse-bill-2020-factsheets/special-measures-in-the-criminal-courts-factsheet (accessed 5 May 2022).

[7] YJCEA 1999, s 25.

(2) Rules of court must provide that where P is, or is at risk of being, a victim of domestic abuse carried out by a person listed in subsection (3), it is to be assumed that the following matters are likely to be diminished by reason of vulnerability—
   (a) the quality of P's evidence;
   (b) where P is a party to the proceedings, P's participation in the proceedings.

(3) The persons referred to in subsection (2) are—
   (a) a party to the proceedings;
   (b) a relative of a party to the proceedings (other than P);
   (c) a witness in the proceedings.

(4) Rules of court may provide for an exception to the provision made by virtue of subsection (2) where P does not wish to be deemed to be eligible for the making of a special measures direction by virtue of that subsection.

(5) In this section—

'family proceedings' has the meaning given by section 75(3) of the Courts Act 2003;

'relative' has the meaning given by section 63(1) of the Family Law Act 1996;

'special measures' means such measures as may be specified by rules of court for the purpose of assisting a person to give evidence or participate in proceedings;

'special measures direction' means a direction by the court granting special measures.

On 1 October 2021, section 63 came into force.[8] The purpose of this section is to ensure that victims of domestic abuse will be automatically eligible for access to special measures in family proceedings without the need for any determination of their vulnerability, an amendment which is long overdue. Subsections (2) and (3) state that the rules of court must provide that where a party or a witness is at risk of, or a victim of domestic abuse carried out by a party to the proceedings, a relative of a party to the proceedings or a witness, then the court is to assume that the quality of the victim's evidence and (where the victim is also a party) their ability to participate in the proceedings will be diminished by reason of vulnerability. Subsection (4) provides that rules of court may provide for an exception to this general rule if the party or witness informs the court that they do not wish to have a special measures direction.

The provision of special measures in family proceedings is governed by Part 3A of the Family Procedure Rules 2010, and Practice Direction 3AA. As eligibility will be assumed, the court will proceed straight to the second part of the test in Rules 3A.4 (participation in the proceedings) and/or 3A.5 (giving evidence) and determine whether it is necessary to make one or more participation directions. Prior to making any determination, the court must consider the view of the party in respect of whom the special measure is sought. However, whilst this section amends the law concerning eligibility for special measures, which is welcomed, it does not provide automatic access or guarantee the provision of special measures in any given case.

[8] SI 2021/1038, reg 2(d). See also Policy Paper 'Special measures in family proceedings' (Updated 31 January 2022) https://www.gov.uk/government/publications/domestic-abuse-bill-2020-factsheets/special-measures-in-family-proceedings (accessed 5 May 2022).

iii. Section 64: Special Measures in Civil Proceedings: Victims of Domestic Abuse etc.

Section 64 DAA states:

(1) Rules of court must make provision enabling the court to make a special measures direction in relation to a person who is a party or witness in civil proceedings where that person—
   (a) is, or is at risk of being, a victim of domestic abuse;
   (b) is the victim, or alleged victim, of a specified offence.

(2) Rules made by virtue of subsection (1) must, in particular, provide for the court to consider—
   (a) whether—
      (i) the quality of the person's evidence, or
      (ii) where the person is a party to the proceedings, the person's participation in the proceedings, is likely to be diminished by reason of vulnerability, and
   (b) if so, whether it is necessary to make one or more special measures directions.

(3) For the purposes of this section—
   (a) a person is the victim of a specified offence if another person has been convicted of, or given a caution for, the offence;
   (b) a person is the alleged victim of a specified offence if another person has been charged with the offence.

(4) In this section—

'civil proceedings' means—
   (a) proceedings in the county court,
   (b) proceedings in the High Court, other than—
      (i) proceedings in the Family Division of the High Court which are business assigned, by or under section 61 of (and Schedule 1 to) the Senior Courts Act 1981, to that Division of the High Court and no other, and
      (ii) proceedings in the exercise of its jurisdiction under the Extradition Act 2003, and
   (c) proceedings in the civil division of the Court of Appeal;

'special measures' means such measures as may be specified by rules of court for the purpose of assisting a person to give evidence or participate in proceedings;

'special measures direction' means a direction by the court granting special measures;

'specified offence' means an offence which is specified, or of a description specified, in regulations made by the Lord Chancellor.

This section provides that Court Rules must make provision to enable the court to make a special measures direction in relation to victims and alleged victims of specified offences (to be specified in regulations made by the Lord Chancellor), and victims, or those at risk of being victims of domestic abuse. It requires the court to consider whether the quality of their evidence or their participation in the proceedings is likely to be diminished by reason of vulnerability.

3. SECTIONS 65–67: PROHIBITION OF CROSS-EXAMINATION IN PERSON AND ORDERS UNDER THE CHILDREN ACT

i. Section 65: Prohibition of Cross-examination in Person in Family Proceedings

Section 65 DAA inserts a new Part 4B (ss 31Q–31Z) into the Matrimonial and Family Proceedings Act 1984. It represents a long overdue reform introducing into family proceedings an automatic prohibition on perpetrators or alleged perpetrators of abuse from cross-examining their victims and victims from having to cross-examine their abuser themselves. In addition, it gives family courts the discretion to prevent cross-examination in person in other circumstances where it would diminish the quality of the witness' evidence or cause significant distress to the witness or party. A further welcome reform is the power to appoint a publicly funded qualified legal representative to conduct cross-examination when required.

Few things are likely to retraumatise victims more than being subject to direct cross-examination by their abuser in legal proceedings. Such an experience will inevitably cause immense stress and would of itself be a continuation of the abuse.[9]

New section 31R—Prohibition of cross-examination in person: victims of offences—provides that any person involved in family proceedings who has an unspent conviction or caution (including conditional and absolute discharges), or who is charged with a 'specified offence' cannot cross-examine in person the victim of that offence, or alleged offence, during the course of family proceedings. The 'specified offences' are to be listed in regulations to be made by the Lord Chancellor and are likely to include a comprehensive list of domestic abuse-related and other violent and sexual offences, including child abuse offences, both current and historic, as well as similar domestic abuse related, violent, or sexual service disciplinary offences. If the conviction is spent, the prohibition will not apply unless the conviction or caution is admissible, or may be required, in the proceedings (such as where justice cannot be done in a case except by admitting or requiring evidence relating to a person's spent conviction or caution). If cross-examination takes place in breach of the provision, for example, because the court was not aware of the conviction or caution at the time of the cross-examination, the validity of decisions made by the court will not be affected.

New section 31S—Prohibition of cross-examination in person: persons protected by injunctions, etc.—makes provision for a prohibition on cross-examination in person when an 'on-notice protective injunction' is in place. The person protected by the injunction may not be cross-examined directly by the person against whom the injunction is in force and vice versa. Subsection (5) sets out what is meant by 'on notice' for the purposes of this section. It is intended that 'protective injunctions' will include, for example, non-molestation orders made under the Family Law Act 1996 and domestic abuse protection orders (DAPOs) made under Part 3 of DAA. As with other prohibitions on cross-examination, provision is made for the validity of decisions made by the court to be upheld if the provision is breached as a result of the court not being aware of the on-notice protective injunction.

---

[9] Justice Secretary, Robert Buckland, Commons second reading of the Bill (October 2019) https://www.parliament.uk/business/news/2019/october/commons-domestic-abuse-bill/?msclkid=f7d875b7cf7b11ecb72c6ed942aa5f6e (accessed 5 May 2022).

New section 31T—Prohibition of cross-examination in person: evidence of domestic abuse—makes provision for a prohibition on cross-examination in person where 'specified evidence' is adduced that a witness in the proceedings has been the victim of domestic abuse[10] perpetrated by a party to the proceedings (or vice versa). Subsection (3) provides that 'specified evidence' is evidence specified, or of a description specified, in regulations to be made by the Lord Chancellor. It is understood that 'specified evidence' is intended broadly to replicate the list of evidence that is currently specified for the purposes of accessing civil legal aid.[11] Such evidence includes, for example, a copy of a finding of fact made in legal proceedings in the UK, a letter or report from a health professional, a letter from any person who is a member of a local safeguarding forum, or a letter from an independent domestic violence adviser.

New section 31U—Direction for prohibition of cross-examination in person: other cases—provides that, in addition to the automatic bar to cross-examination in person provided in sections 31R to 31T, the court has the discretion to prohibit cross-examination in person if someone involved in the proceedings applies for such a direction or if the court of its own motion raises the issue. This is to ensure that the court retains a discretion to prohibit cross-examination in person whenever it is needed, including in domestic abuse-related cases where the automatic prohibition does not apply. In determining whether to exercise its discretion the court must be satisfied that either the 'quality condition' (where cross-examination in person will diminish the quality of the evidence) or the 'significant distress condition' (where cross-examination in person would be likely to cause significant distress to the witness or the party) is met and that it will not be contrary to the interests of justice, before prohibiting cross-examination by a party in person. Subsection (5) sets out a non-exhaustive list of factors the court must consider when deciding whether the 'quality condition' or 'significant distress condition' is met, which includes how the party or witness is acting in the proceedings, any findings of fact as to the party's or witness' behaviour, the views of the witness or the party, the likely content of questions to be asked, and the relationship between the party and the witness.

New section 31V provides more detail in relation to directions given by the court under section 31U, how long they should last, and the circumstances in which such directions may be revoked.

New section 31W—Alternatives to cross-examination in person—makes provision for alternatives to cross-examination in person where a party is prevented from cross-examining in person (ss 31R–31U). The court must consider whether there is a 'satisfactory alternative' means for the witness to be cross-examined or the evidence to be obtained. If there is no satisfactory alternative, the court will ask the party who has been prohibited from cross-examining in person to arrange, within a specified time, a qualified legal representative[12] to cross-examine the witness on their behalf, and to notify the court of the arrangements. If no such arrangements are made, or the court has not received notification within the specified time, then the court must consider whether it is necessary in the interests of justice for the court to appoint a qualified legal representative to cross-examine the witness in the interests of the party. Section 31X confers a power on the Lord Chancellor to make regulations about payment out of central funds for a court appointed qualified legal representative.

[10] As defined by s 1 of the DAA.

[11] Schedule 1 to the Civil Legal Aid (Procedure) Regulations 2012 (SI 2012/3098), as amended.

[12] As defined by s 31W(8)(b).

ii. Section 66: Prohibition of Cross-examination in Person in Civil Proceedings

Section 66 DAA inserts a new Part 7A (sections 85E to 85N) into the Courts Act 2003 to make provision for the cross-examination of vulnerable witnesses in civil proceedings, including provision automatically to prohibit perpetrators or alleged perpetrators of abuse from cross-examining their victims in person in the civil court, and vice versa. It also makes provision for the court to have a discretion to prevent cross-examination in person in other circumstances where it would affect the quality of the witness's evidence or cause significant distress. As with the family courts, civil courts are to be given the power to appoint a publicly funded qualified legal representative to conduct cross-examination in the interests of the prohibited party.

Sections 85E to 85N mirror the provisions in the new Part 4B of the Matrimonial and Family Proceedings Act 1984, set out above, setting out a similar framework for the civil courts. This section is in force 21 July 2022.

iii. Section 67: Orders under Section 91(14) of the Children Act 1989

Section 67 DAA provides:

(1) The Children Act 1989 is amended as follows.

(2) In section 91 (effect and duration of orders etc.), at the end of subsection (14) insert—

'For further provision about orders under this subsection, see section 91A (section 91(14) orders: further provision).'

(3) After section 91 insert—

91A Section 91(14) orders: further provision

(1) This section makes further provision about orders under section 91(14) (referred to in this section as 'section 91(14) orders').

(2) The circumstances in which the court may make a section 91(14) order include, among others, where the court is satisfied that the making of an application for an order under this Act of a specified kind by any person who is to be named in the section 91(14) order would put—
   (a) the child concerned, or
   (b) another individual ('the relevant individual'), at risk of harm.

(3) In the case of a child or other individual who has reached the age of eighteen, the reference in subsection (2) to 'harm' is to be read as a reference to ill-treatment or the impairment of physical or mental health.

(4) Where a person who is named in a section 91(14) order applies for leave to make an application of a specified kind, the court must, in determining whether to grant leave, consider whether there has been a material change of circumstances since the order was made.

(5) A section 91(14) order may be made by the court—
   (a) on an application made—

(i) by the relevant individual;
(ii) by or on behalf of the child concerned;
(iii) by any other person who is a party to the application being disposed of by the court;

(b) of its own motion.

(6) In this section, 'the child concerned' means the child referred to in section 91(14).

Section 67 inserts a new section 91A into the Children Act 1989, which makes further provision about the circumstances in which the court may make a section 91(14) order ('barring order') preventing individuals from making further specified applications under that Act without permission of the court. The insertion of this section follows the recommendations made by the Ministry of Justice's Expert Panel in its report entitled 'Assessing risk of Harm to Children and Parents in Private Law Children Cases'.[13] Such orders are available to parents and children to protect them when further proceedings would risk causing them harm,[14] in particular where proceedings could be a form of continuing domestic abuse. Such an order can be made by the court of its own motion, or pursuant to an application by a person who could be put at risk of harm by a further application. Once a barring order is in place, the court must consider whether there has been a material change in circumstances before allowing a subsequent application.

[13] Published in June 2020 https://www.gov.uk/government/consultations/assessing-risk-of-harm-to-children-and-parents-in-private-law-children-cases?msclkid=3c1102e0cf7c11ecae6eb01c4cc8d100 (accessed 5 May 2022).

[14] A broad concept of 'harm' is used as defined in s 31(9) of the Act.

PART 6 OF THE ACT
OFFENCES INVOLVING ABUSIVE OR VIOLENT BEHAVIOUR (SECTIONS 68–71)

12

OFFENCES INVOLVING ABUSIVE OR VIOLENT BEHAVIOUR (SECTIONS 68–69)

Vanessa Bettinson, Andy Phippen and Emma Bond*

1. SECTION 68 CONTROLLING OR COERCIVE BEHAVIOUR IN AN INTIMATE OR FAMILY RELATIONSHIP

i. Context and Background

This section amends the offence of coercive or controlling behaviour in an intimate or family relationship by extending the offence's ambit to include people who are personally connected and living together. The amendment followed a Home Office consultation that asked for views on whether the offence under section 76 Serious Crime Act (SCA) 2015[1] ought to be strengthened and suggestions on how this would be achieved.[2] In the year ending March 2021, the police had recorded 33,954 offences;[3] however, the Home Office recognised that

* Section 68 by Vanessa Bettinson, section 69 by Andy Phippen and Emma Bond.

[1] https://www.legislation.gov.uk/ukpga/2015/9/contents/enacted (accessed 21 April 2022).

[2] HM Government, 'Transforming the Response to Domestic Abuse: Government Consultation' (2018) 54 https://consult.justice.gov.uk/homeoffice-moj/domestic-abuse-consultation/supporting_documents/Transforming%20the%20response%20to%20domestic%20abuse.pdf (accessed 21 April 2022).

[3] ONS Domestic abuse prevalence and trends, in England and Wales: year ending March 2021 [5] https://www.ons.gov.uk/peoplepopulationandcommunity/crimeandjustice/articles/domesticabuseprevalenceandtrendsenglandandwales/yearendingmarch2021#police-recorded-crime (accessed 21 April 2022).

Vanessa Bettinson, Andy Phippen and Emma Bond, *Offences Involving Abusive or Violent Behaviour (Sections 68–69)* In: *Blackstone's Guide to the Domestic Abuse Act 2021*. Edited by Susan Edwards, David Malone, and Gillian Jones KC, Oxford University Press.
 DOI: 10.1093/oso/9780192870513.003.0012

further awareness raising and improved understanding of the offence was needed to increase the number of cases progressing to the prosecution stage. Respondents suggested that the offence was too limited as it did not extend to controlling or coercive behaviours used by ex-partners once they were no longer living with the victim.[4] Consequently, post-separation abuse was not recognised by the offence itself where the parties no longer lived together, even though the behaviour amounted to coercive control.

Statutory guidance prepared by the Secretary of State pursuant to section 77 SCA 2015 explained that when the relationship had ended between the parties, coercive or controlling behaviours could be prosecuted under harassment and stalking offences under section 2, 2A, 4, and 4A of the Protection from Harassment Act (PFHA) 1997.[5] The rationale for limiting the offence to current intimate partners was to prevent an overlap with the harassment and stalking provisions and close a lacuna in the existing legal framework.[6] However, controlling and coercive conduct is not uncommon post-separation, such as economic abuses, which control a woman's ability to acquire, use, and maintain economic resources thereby threatening her economic security.[7] Early recognition of this form of abuse was reflected in Tasmania, which criminalised economic abuse under section 8, Tasmania Family Violence Act 2004.[8] The offence applies inter alia where the defendant withholds or threatens to withhold child maintenance support.[9] Similarly, using the court system to effect child contact arrangements is also a means for a perpetrator to continue his controlling behaviour post-separation, a consideration that can be taken into account when making an order under the Children Act 1989, section 91(14), amended by section 67 DAA.[10] The approach taken under section 76 SCA to who can be subjected to coercive control for the purposes of the offence was at odds with the Home Office policy definition of domestic abuse, which includes both current and former partners. Such differences in meaning can cause confusion for those seeking to implement both policy and legal provisions and inhibit a progressive public understanding of coercive or controlling behaviour in intimate or family relationships. Section 1 Domestic Abuse Act (DAA) 2021 (discussed in section 1 of Part II of this book) reflects the Home Office's policy definition of domestic abuse, stating that it occurs between people who are personally connected. Section 68 DAA, therefore, aligns section 76 SCA to section 1 to avoid different meanings of coercive and controlling behaviours between the provisions.

---

[4] HM Government, 'Transforming the Response to Domestic Abuse: Consultation and Draft Bill' (2019) 53 https://assets.publishing.service.gov.uk/government/uploads/system/uploads/attachment_data/file/772247/Transforming_the_response_to_domestic_abuse_-_consultation_response_and_draft_bill_-print.pdf (accessed 21 April 2022).

[5] PFHA; see https://www.legislation.gov.uk/ukpga/1997/40/contents. Home Office, 'Controlling or Coercive Behaviour in an Intimate or Family Relationship: Statutory Guidance Framework' (2015) 5. https://assets.publishing.service.gov.uk/government/uploads/system/uploads/attachment_data/file/482528/Controlling_or_coercive_behaviour_-_statutory_guidance.pdf (accessed 21 April 2022).

[6] Statutory Guidance Framework (n 5) 2.

[7] Adrienne Adams and others, 'Development of the scale of economic abuse' (2008) 14(5) *Violence Against Women* 563, 564.

[8] See https://www.legislation.tas.gov.au/view/whole/html/inforce/current/act-2004-067 (accessed 21 April 2022).

[9] Vanessa Bettinson, 'A Comparative Evaluation of Offences: Criminalising Abusive Behaviour in England, Wales, Scotland, Ireland and Tasmania' in Marilyn McMahon and Paul McGorrey (eds), *Criminalising Coercive Control* (Springer 2020). Evan Stark, 'Coercive Control: How Men Entrap Women in Personal Life' (OUP 2007).

[10] Heather Douglas, 'Legal systems abuse and coercive control' (2018) 18(1) *Criminology & Criminal Justice* 84.

ii. The Section

The expected implementation date for section 68 is expected to be Autumn 2022. Section 68 amends the offence of 'controlling or coercive behaviour in an intimate or family relationship' by inserting a new definition of the term 'personally connected'. The offence under section 76 SCA states that an offence under section 76(1) will be committed where a person A: (a) repeatedly or continuously engages in behaviour towards another person (B) that is controlling or coercive; (b) at the time of the behaviour, A and B are personally connected; (c) the behaviour has a serious effect on B; and (d) A knows or ought to know that the behaviour will have a serious effect on B.

Section 68(2) DAA amends section 76(1)(b) by inserting '(see subsection (6))' and removes section 76(2), which outlines the previous definition of the term 'personally connected'. According to section 68(4) DAA, the amended definition appears under a new section 76(6), which repeats the definition provided in section 2 DAA (discussed in Part II of this book).

The legal amendment means that there is no longer a requirement that the parties live together at the time the prohibited conduct takes place. This applies equally to current and former intimate partners and family members.

Also inserted is a subsection 6A, which explains that: a parental relationship for the purposes of subsection (6)(f) exists where—(a) the person is a parent of the child, or (b) the person has parental responsibility for the child.

This provision extends to those who no longer have parental responsibility for the child under subsection 6(f). Subsection 7 has been amended to reflect these changes.

iii. Critical Commentary

This section is an important amendment to the controlling or coercive behaviour offence, not least because it ensures the term 'personally connected' has a consistent definition throughout the DAA (see s 1). Clarification over the relationships the offence applies to gives support to the aims of the Act as it should increase awareness raising among both professionals and the public, alongside an improvement in understanding what forms this type of abuse takes. To assist criminal justice practitioners with how to implement and monitor the offence of controlling or coercive behaviour, harassment, and stalking post-separation, the Statutory Guidance Framework should be revisited.[11] As a starting point, emotional and economic abuse and activities that on the face of it appear to be non-criminal when viewed as separate incidents may be best considered under section 76 SCA. Surveillance and other activities associated with stalking (see s 2A(3) PFH, as amended by s 111 Protection of Freedoms Act 2012[12]), in some cases would be more appropriately charged under this harassment legislation. Cases which involve behaviours that began during the relationship and have since continued can be used to construct a stronger case of controlling or coercive behaviour under section 76 SCA.

For sentencers, domestic abuse cases which span beyond the life of the relationship should be assessed as more serious. This is recognised by the Sentencing Guidelines, which state that 'domestic abuse is likely to become increasingly frequent and more serious the longer it

[11] Statutory Guidance Framework (n 5).

[12] https://www.legislation.gov.uk/ukpga/2012/9/contents/enacted (accessed 21 April 2022).

continues'[13] and as the statistics discussed in section 2 DAA (see earlier in Part II of this book) illustrate can lead to death, with the first twelve months after the end of the relationship being the most dangerous for the victim.[14] Ensuring that the seriousness of coercive control and its continuance post-separation is understood by courts, continued judicial training and refresher training will be necessary. In this way, the change made by section 68 to section 76 SCA will enable the DAA to achieve its objectives of preventing domestic abuse and protecting its victims.

Debate around future legal reform of this offence should focus on the limited maximum penalty of five years' imprisonment. Scotland's equivalent offence under section 1 Domestic Abuse (Scotland) Act 2018 provides a maximum penalty of fourteen years' imprisonment, allowing different levels of serious harm and conduct to be considered at sentencing stage.

2. SECTION 69 THREATS TO DISCLOSE PRIVATE SEXUAL PHOTOGRAPHS AND FILMS WITH INTENT TO CAUSE DISTRESS

Section 69 of the DAA addresses a specific issue arising from what is sometimes unhelpfully referred to as the 'revenge pornography' legislation added to the statute books in section 33 of the Criminal Justice and Courts Act 2015 (CJCA).[15] In this legislation, the act of disclosing private sexual photographs and films with intent to cause distress is defined under section 33(1). It is an offence for a person to disclose a private sexual photograph or film if the disclosure is made—

(a) without the consent of an individual who appears in the photograph or film, and
(b) with the intention of causing that individual distress.

Section 69 of the DAA adds to this definition the harm caused by a threat to send an image as well as actual disclosure:

(1) Section 33 of the Criminal Justice and Courts Act 2015 (disclosing private sexual photographs and films with intent to cause distress) is amended as follows.
(2) In the heading, after 'Disclosing' insert ', or threatening to disclose,'.
(3) For subsection (1) substitute—
'(1) A person commits an offence if—
    (a) the person discloses, or threatens to disclose, a private sexual photograph or film in which another individual ('the relevant individual') appears,
    (b) by so doing, the person intends to cause distress to that individual, and
    (c) the disclosure is, or would be, made without the consent of that individual.

[13] Sentencing Council Guidelines (2018) 'Overarching Principles: Domestic Abuse Definitive Guideline' para. 7 https://www.sentencingcouncil.org.uk/wp-content/uploads/Overarching-Principles-Domestic-Abuse-definitive-guideline-Web.pdf (accessed 21 April 2022).

[14] Femicide Census, 'UK Femicides 2009-2018' (2019) 30–31 https://www.femicidecensus.org/wp-content/uploads/2020/11/Femicide-Census-10-year-report.pdf (accessed 21 April 2022).

[15] https://www.legislation.gov.uk/ukpga/2015/2/section/33/enacted (accessed 21 April 2022).

In adding the new wording to the legislation, it addresses a criticism levelled at the existing legislation regarding failure to consider the power of threatening to share an image or film, compared to the actual act of disclosing.

In considering this change, it is important to provide some further detail on the nature of the offence, the origins of the 2015 legislation, and how the 2021 legislation is a step in the right direction in providing greater protection, albeit with the caveat that some criticisms levelled at the 2015 Act are still not addressed.

i. Context and Background

a. *'Revenge pornography' law*

While it has been argued[16] that there are a diverse set of motivations for posting 'revenge pornography' images and films, the prevailing narrative has focused on the notion of 'revenge' as the primary motivation for the offender. Where the victim, for example, ends a relationship or does not behave in a manner pleasing to the offender, the offender seeks revenge by disclosing intimate images of the victim. The 2019 'Shattering Lives' report,[17] which spoke to both victims of image-based abuse and stakeholders in this area, makes a very clear argument that the term is a myth, and those sharing images non-consensually are not doing so for revenge. Instead, the authors state: 'The reality is that image-based sexual abuse is motivated by control, as well as misogyny, men's entitlement and "laddish" attitudes.'

Therefore, while the term is embedded in popular culture, it does little to enlighten stakeholders in the criminal justice system with regard to the actual nature of abuse and its impact on victims. If we consider the definition of revenge: 'Revenge[18]: the action of hurting or harming someone in return for an injury or wrong suffered at their hands.'

By using this term, we provide an excuse or legitimation of the conduct of the abuser. In the case of non-consensually sharing intimate images of a partner or ex-partner, this is not revenge, this is abuse. If we then consider the definition of pornography: 'Pornography[19]: printed or visual material containing the explicit description or display of sexual organs or activity, intended to stimulate sexual excitement.'

Again, this is incorrect. It is not the intention of the abuser to disclose these images for sexual gratification. The abuser is disclosing in order to harm, abuse, and/or control the victim. While sexual gratification might arise from the viewing of the images, it is not the primary motivation of the abuser.

We would suggest that using the term 'revenge pornography' in legal discussions undermines the impact on the victim and implies mitigation on the part of the abuser. We would, instead, suggest a better definition is 'image-based abuse as part of domestic abuse, exploitation, harassment, coercion and control'.

---

[16] Claire McGlynn and Erika Rackley, 'Image-Based Sexual Abuse' (2017) 37(1) *Oxford Journal of Legal Studies* 534. https://academic.oup.com/ojls/article-abstract/37/3/534/2965256?redirectedFrom=fulltext (accessed 21 April 2022).

[17] Claire McGlynn and others, 'Shattering lives and myths: a report on image-based sexual abuse' (2019) https://www.dur.ac.uk/resources/law/ShatteringLivesandMythsFINALJuly2019.pdf (accessed 21 April 2022).

[18] https://en.oxforddictionaries.com/definition/revenge (accessed 21 April 2022).

[19] https://en.oxforddictionaries.com/definition/pornography (accessed 21 April 2022).

b. *The need for new legislation*

With the introduction of the new legislation in 2015, the courts and criminal justice system had, for the first time, a well-defined piece of legislation with which to tackle crimes of image-based abuse. However, the actual acts around the non-consensual sharing of intimate images have existed for far longer. The advent of digital technology has made the production and distribution far easier (and, as discussed below, prior to the 2015 legislation the problem was tackled across diverse legislation), and acts of coercion and abuse making use of private, intimate images has existed for far longer.

Two notable cases, namely *Contostavlos v Mendahun*[20] and *AMP v Persons Unknown*[21] raised concerns around the non-consensual sharing of intimate material using digital technology, in both capture and distribution. In *Contostavlos v Mendahun*, the victim, who was in the public eye, obtained an interim injunction against the dissemination of a leaked sex tape which had been published online. While the case subsequently settled, in April 2012, an interim injunction was granted (continued in May) preventing the disclosure of photographs of a personal nature, together with text messages sent by the claimant during the course of an adulterous affair with the second defendant. The photographs and text messages, described by the judge as 'of a sexual nature, but could not be described as pornographic', had come into the control of the first defendant (with whom the second defendant had been in a relationship) in undisclosed circumstances. The court granted an order to protect the claimant's right to confidentiality and privacy, as well as to protect her from harassment.

AMP v Persons Unknown was particularly significant because the injunction in this case was against 'persons unknown' and attempted to control the spread of intimate images of the victim via digital, peer-to-peer file sharing channels online, where the sharer might only be recognised by his IP address. In this case, the applicant had lost her mobile phone, which contained intimate images of her and the series of images were subsequently shared online via peer-to-peer channels. Applying the Protection from Harassment Act (PFHA) 1997, the judge considered there was sufficient evidence that the 'unknown persons' had caused sufficient alarm and distress to the applicant and, therefore, an offence had been committed.

Subsequently, and prior to the 2015 legislation, victims of non-consensual sharing had been forced to draw upon existing legislation, none of which was specifically designed to protect them from such forms of abuse. Typically, this legislation included:

- section 1 of the Malicious Communications Act 1988[22]—Sending a communication that is grossly offensive, indecent, obscene, conveys a threat or is false, with intent to cause distress or anxiety;
- section 127 of the Communications Act 2003[23]—Sending a communication that is grossly offensive, indecent, obscene, menacing or false;
- section 2 and 4 of the Protection from Harassment Act 1997[24]; or (as discussed above) the civil tort of misuse of private information or breach of confidence.

However, other legislation has also been applied in different circumstances:

[20] [2013] EWHC 4026 (KB).

[21] [2011] EWHC 3454 (TCC), Transcript.

[22] http://www.legislation.gov.uk/ukpga/1988/27/section/1/2004-10-31 (accessed 21 April 2022).

[23] http://www.legislation.gov.uk/ukpga/2003/21/section/127/enacted (accessed 21 April 2022).

[24] http://www.legislation.gov.uk/ukpga/1997/40/contents (accessed 21 April 2022).

- section 21, Theft Act 1968[25] (blackmail)—where stolen images have been used to blackmail;
- section 154 Criminal Justice & Public Order Act 1994[26]—causing intentional harassment, alarm or distress;
- section 1 of the Computer Misuse Act 1990[27]—where the images have been obtained through unauthorised access to computer equipment.

c. *Impact on victims*

None of these pieces of legislation considered the distress caused to the victim by the sharing of such private imagery. In the 'Shattering Lives' report,[28] the authors described a 'social rupture' that occurred when someone becomes a victim of image-based abuse. The impact of the sharing affects all aspects of their lives—it is not something that can be shrugged off or ignored.

Citron and Franks[29] develop further categorisation on psychological impact, raising concerns around anxiety that can possibly lead to suicidal thoughts. They were clear that the harm that can arise from the non-consensual sharing of images should not be underestimated. Moreover, there can be further impacts such as concerns for personal safety, body image anxieties, long-term trust issues, and simply the anxiety of not knowing where images have been posted, whether further images will emerge, or how many people and who have seen them.

The growing concern around the fitness of the law to protect victims from this sort of abuse resulted in the 2015 legislation, driven in part by an adjournment debate by the Conservative MP Maria Miller[30] arriving at a broad consensus that there was a need to develop legislation specific to image-based abuse and the non-consensual sharing of images. Section 33 of the Criminal Justice and Courts Act (CJCA) 2015 came into force on 13 April 2015, creating a new criminal offence of disclosing private sexual photographs and films with intent to cause distress. As noted above, crucial to the offence are: (a) the lack of consent of the individual appearing in the photograph and film; and (b) the intent to cause that individual distress. The offence carries a maximum two-year sentence on conviction.

Section 33 states:

Disclosing private sexual photographs and films with intent to cause distress

(1) It is an offence for a person to disclose a private sexual photograph or film if the disclosure is made—

  (a) without the consent of an individual who appears in the photograph or film, and
  (b) with the intention of causing that individual distress.

Table 12.1 below charts the implementation of this section.

---

[25] http://www.legislation.gov.uk/ukpga/1968/60/section/21 (accessed 21 April 2022).

[26] http://www.legislation.gov.uk/ukpga/1994/33/section/154 (accessed 21 April 2022).

[27] http://www.legislation.gov.uk/ukpga/1990/18/section/1 (accessed 21 April 2022).

[28] See n 22.

[29] Danielle Citron and Mary Franks, 'Criminalizing revenge porn' (2014) 49 *Wake Forest Law Review* 345.

[30] Revenge Pornography vol 582: debated on Thursday 19 June 2014 https://hansard.parliament.uk/commons/2014-06-19/debates/14061947000003/RevengePornography (accessed 21 April 2022).

Table 12.1 Ministry of Justice statistics on s33 of the Criminal Justice and Courts Act 2015.

	2015	2016	2017	2018	2019	2020	2021
Proceeded against	82	267	294	224	189	167	218
Found Guilty	64	228	261	183	168	160	194
Sentenced	63	228	251	183	176	161	196

Table 12.2 Call numbers for the Revenge Porn Helpline

2015	2016	2017	2018	2019	2020	2021
521	708	1094	1300	1680	3146	4406

What is less clear from this data, however, is the proportion of complaints that result in proceedings or conviction. Research by the Revenge Porn Helpline,[31] a national service to support victims of image-based abuse, have published research on 'Intimate Image Abuse'[32] detailing the number of cases dealt with since 2015, which suggests that whilst more people are disclosing image-based abuse, the number of prosecutions in England and Wales is dropping. Table 12.2 sets out the call numbers reported by the Revenge Porn Helpline.

While direct comparisons cannot be made, given cases are likely to have increased due to an increase in awareness of the service over time, we can see that while there are clearly increases in disclosures, the same increase is not reflected in numbers prosecuted.

ii. The Section

Section 69 DAA specifically addresses culpability in the event of threat to disclose, whilst the 2015 Act required *actual* disclosure to a third party, whether to a private individual or posting to an online platform. It was the failure to acknowledge the threat to share images that raised concerns with the potential of the legislation to capture such harm.

At the same time, the Scottish Parliament was developing similar legislation, the Abusive Behaviour and Sexual Harm (Scotland) Act 2016.[33] However, while the wording of the Scottish law was very similar to that of section 33 of the 2015 Act, threat of disclosure was part of the legislation in Scotland.

Disclosing, or threatening to disclose, an intimate photograph or film

(1) A person ('A') commits an offence if—

[31] http://www.revengepornhelpline.org.uk/ (accessed 21 April 2022).

[32] Intimate image abuse https://revengepornhelpline.org.uk/assets/documents/intimate-image-abuse-an-evolving-landscape.pdf?_=1639471939 (accessed 21 April 2022), 8.

[33] Scottish Government, Abusive Behaviour and Sexual Harm (Scotland) Act 2016 (2016) https://www.legislation.gov.uk/asp/2016/22/section/2/enacted (accessed 21 April 2022).

(a) A discloses, *or threatens to disclose*, a photograph or film which shows, or appears to show, another person ('B') in an intimate situation,
(b) by doing so, A intends to cause B fear, alarm or distress or A is reckless as to whether B will be caused fear, alarm or distress, and
(c) the photograph or film has not previously been disclosed to the public at large, or any section of the public, by B or with B's consent.[34]

a. *Critical Commentary*

There are further issues with section 69.

Intent In discussions with the Revenge Porn Helpline, while threat is a consistent element of abuse brought up by their clients, the issue of *intent* to cause distress is one that presents more challenges for the police and prosecution.

Subsection 8 states: 'A person charged with an offence under this section is not to be taken to have disclosed a photograph or film with the intention of causing distress merely because that was a natural and probable consequence of the disclosure.'[35]

While the DAA updates subsection 8, it does so simply to incorporate threat: 'A person charged with an offence under this section is not to be taken to have intended to cause distress by disclosing, or threatening to disclose, a photograph or film merely because that was a natural and probable consequence of the disclosure or threat.'

Unless intent can be proven it is unlikely that the CPS will proceed. This is certainly the experience of many of the clients supported by the Revenge Porn Helpline.

Anonymity The Sexual Offences (Amendment) Act 1992[36] defines a number of sexual crimes which grant the victim anonymity during court proceedings. At present, image-based abuse remains defined as a communications crime, as confirmed in 2016 by the then Minister for Preventing Abuse, Exploitation and Crime, Karen Bradley, who said:

> Whilst victims can in some circumstances feel violated by the malicious disclosure of sexual images the offence is not a sexual one.It does not require any element of sexual contact or sexual gratification and it does not attract sex offender registration ... We do not consider automatic anonymity is necessary or desirable in the case of revenge pornography.[37]

While orders have been made in individual cases, campaigners argue that the prospect of being named in the courts is a significant barrier to victims coming forward. In June 2019,

---

[34] 421 crimes recorded against this legislation between September 2017 and September 2018, 596 for 2019, 655 for 2020 https://www.gov.scot/publications/recorded-crime-scotland-2019-2020/documents/and in 2020-21, 780 for 2021 https://www.gov.scot/publications/recorded-crime-scotland-2020-2021/documents/ (accessed 21 April 2022).

[35] See also Crown Prosecution Service, 'Revenge Pornography: Guidelines on prosecuting the offence of disclosing private sexual photographs and films' (2017) https://www.cps.gov.uk/legal-guidance/revenge-pornography-guidelines-prosecuting-offence-disclosing-private-sexual; College of Policing, 'Revenge Pornography Briefing Note' (May 2015) 2 http://library.college.police.uk/docs/appref/briefing-note-revenge-pornography-may-2015.pdf (accessed 21 April 2022).

[36] https://www.legislation.gov.uk/ukpga/1992/34/section/2 (accessed 21 April 2022).

[37] Sarah Laville, '"Revenge porn" victims should get anonymity, say 75% of people' (2016) https://www.theguardian.com/law/2016/jul/19/revenge-porn-victims-should-get-anonymity-say-75-per-cent-of-people (accessed 21 April 2022).

it was announced that the Law Commission would review anonymity for victims of image-based abuse.[38] At the time of writing, the Law Commission had not published its recommendation. However, from a victim centric perspective, as evidenced by those who work at the Revenge Porn Helpline, they are very clear that anonymity is needed in order to support victims reporting. Scotland lists image-based abuse as a sexual crime, and grants anonymity to victims. The addition to legislation of a threat to disclose around the non-consensual disclosure of intimate images is to be welcomed, bringing England and Wales legislation in line with Scotland. We would anticipate that, as a result of this change, more victims will come forward. It is likely that further changes to legislation will result from the Law Commission review.

[38] UK Government, 'Law around non-consensual taking, making and sharing of sexual images to be reviewed' (2019) https://www.gov.uk/government/news/law-around-non-consensual-taking-making-and-sharing-of-sexual-images-to-be-reviewed (accessed 21 April 2022).

13

OFFENCES AGAINST THE PERSON (SECTIONS 70–71)

Nogah Ofer, Felicia Davy, Jonathan Herring, Susan Edwards*

1. SECTION 70 STRANGULATION OR SUFFOCATION

i. Context and Background

a. The need for a new offence

Section 70 of the Domestic Abuse Act (DAA) 2021, which introduced a new stand-alone criminal offence of non-fatal strangulation and suffocation, corrects a systemic inadequacy in the way the existing law prior to the 2021 Act was applied in practice. As a result, this offending was trivialised and overlooked. The criminal law of assault in England and Wales categorises offences based upon the degree of physical injury,[1] which fails to capture the realities of, and the harms caused by, non-fatal strangulation and suffocation. This is a unique form of assault in that there is a large disparity between a high degree of violence on the one hand and a lack of corresponding visible injury on the other. This partly explains why this form of assault has been consistently minimised and under-charged in a number of jurisdictions.[2] Police officers more typically assess assaults by the immediately visible effects. In some 50 per

* Section 70(i) by Nogah Ofer, section 70(ii) by Felicia Davy, section 71(i)(a) by Jonathan Herring, section 71(i)(b) by Susan Edwards, section 71(ii) by Felicia Davy.

[1] Assault offences are broadly divided into three categories based on the level of injury: (1) common assault/assault by beating under s 39 Criminal Justice Act 1988, (2) actual bodily harm (ABH) under s 47, or (3) grievous bodily harm (GBH)/wounding (s 20) or wounding with intent (s 18) under the Offences against the Person Act (OAPA) 1861.

[2] A pattern also identified in New Zealand and the US; see New Zealand Law Commission *Strangulation: The Case for a New Offence* Report no 138 (2016). https://www.lawcom.govt.nz/sites/default/files/projectAvailableFormats/NZLC-R138.pdf (accessed 21 April 2022).

Nogah Ofer, Felicia Davy, Jonathan Herring, Susan Edwards, *Offences Against the Person (Sections 70–71)* In: *Blackstone's Guide to the Domestic Abuse Act 2021*. Edited by Susan Edwards, David Malone, and Gillian Jones KC, Oxford University Press.
 DOI: 10.1093/oso/9780192870513.003.0013

cent of cases, strangulation does not leave any visible injuries on the neck[3] and, where it does, these may be red marks or minor bruising which do not reflect the degree of harm caused.

Anecdotally, domestic abuse support workers have reported that the majority of cases they see which are charged, are prosecuted as common assault/assault by beating under section 39 of the Criminal Justice Act (CJA) 1988.[4] This is the lowest level of assault charge, equivalent to a slap or a push. As a summary offence it must be prosecuted within six months, so that some cases are not prosecuted at all where this time limit has passed (The Police, Crime and Sentencing and Courts Act proposes to extend this time period). CPS guidance that strangulation and suffocation cases can be charged as actual bodily harm (ABH)[5] (a more serious offence, without a time limit) is not well-known to police and not routinely applied by prosecutors. This anecdotal evidence triggered the campaign to introduce the new offence into the Domestic Abuse Bill, because the way in which the existing law was being implemented simply failed to capture the severity of offending or to deliver justice for victims and survivors.

b. *Strangulation and suffocation are gendered crimes*

In order to strangle or suffocate a person it is necessary to overpower them physically, and it is unsurprising that the fatal cases show this method of killing mainly in female homicides. Strangulation and asphyxiation are the second most common form of killing of female victims—29 per cent[6] of females aged over 14 and 17 per cent of females of all ages—as against only 3 per cent of male victims,[7] which includes male children and killings by male perpetrators.

Non-fatal strangulation and suffocation follow a similar gendered pattern and are widely recognised as a common feature of domestic abuse. The standard risk assessment tool used by police and domestic abuse services, the 'DASH' checklist, includes a question about attempts to strangle, choke, suffocate, or drown the victim. The questions in the DASH checklist were identified through extensive research on factors associated with serious domestic violence and homicide.[8] A leading domestic abuse charity, Safelives, reports that 41 per cent of survivors assessed as being in the high-risk category, who reported physical abuse, reported non-fatal strangulation[9] and 21 per cent of those assessed were at standard and medium risk.[10] Strangulation and suffocation are high-volume crimes in a domestic abuse context. Some

---

[3] George McClane, Gael Strack, and Dean Hawley, 'A review of 300 strangulation cases Part II: Clinical evaluation of the surviving victim' (2001) 21(3) *Journal of Emergency Medicine* 312; Catherine White and others, '"I thought he was going to kill me": Analysis of 204 case files of adults reporting non-fatal strangulation as part of a sexual assault over a 3-year period' (2021) 79 *Journal of Forensic and Legal Medicine* 8.

[4] https://www.legislation.gov.uk/ukpga/1988/33/section/39 (accessed 17 December 2021).

[5] CPS legal guidance on offences against the person https://www.cps.gov.uk/legal-guidance/offences-against-person-incorporating-charging-standard (accessed 17 December 2021).

[6] The Femicide Census for 2018 https://www.femicidecensus.org/wp-content/uploads/2020/02/Femicide-Census-Report-on-2018-Femicides-.pdf (accessed 17 December 2021).

[7] Office for National Statistics Homicides in England and Wales year ending March 2019 https://www.ons.gov.uk/peoplepopulationandcommunity/crimeandjustice/articles/homicideinenglandandwales/yearendingmarch2019 (accessed 17 December 2021).

[8] https://safelives.org.uk/sites/default/files/resources/Dash%20risk%20checklist%20quick%20start%20guidance%20FINAL.pdf (accessed 17 December 2021).

[9] Safelives Insights Idva dataset 2019/20 https://safelives.org.uk/sites/default/files/resources/Idva%20Insights%20Dataset%20201920_1.pdf (accessed 17 December 2021).

[10] Safelives Insights Outreach dataset 2019/20 https://safelives.org.uk/sites/default/files/resources/Outreach%20Insights%20Dataset%20201920.pdf (accessed 17 December 2021).

working in front-line domestic abuse work describe strangulation as being so common as to become normalised.

Non-fatal strangulation is also an increasingly prevalent form of abuse during sex, influenced by the increased easy access to pornography in the digital age. In a BBC survey of over 2,000 participants, 38 per cent of women under 40 had experienced strangulation during sex, with 42 per cent of those saying it was unwanted, and they had felt pressured, coerced, or forced.[11] Unlike strangulation during domestic violence, strangulation during sex raises issues around consent, including consent to strangulation as distinct from consent to sexual contact during the encounter more generally.

c. *Strangulation as terror, power, and control*

Reports describe strangulation as extremely painful and the inability to breathe as a 'primal fear'.[12] It has been compared to 'water-boarding', which is recognised as a form of torture based on restricting breathing.[13] The charity Stand Up to Domestic Abuse conducted a survey of 487 women who had experienced strangulation.[14] In response to an open question 'how did you feel whilst being strangled?', many respondents said they genuinely believed they were going to die. Examples of responses include:

'I thought this is it'; I was thinking about my family finding me'; and 'I felt like my head was going to explode, I was gasping for air and trying to scream and shout but could not make any real noise and felt totally helpless. I have thought on several occasions I may lose my life this way'.

Many reported sexualised verbal abuse and threats to kill from their abusers during strangulation, such as 'slut you don't deserve to live'.

Respondents described losing control of their bladder or bowels and passing out. Some were pregnant or holding small children at the time of the strangulation. Others described their children witnessing incidents, in one case a ten-year-old called the police.[15] A high proportion of women who reported strangulation during sexual assaults to an NHS Sexual Assault Referral Centre also said they had thought they were going to die.[16]

Researchers have observed that many abusers do not strangle to kill, but to show that they *could* kill,[17] using strangulation as a tool of fear and coercion during intimate partner violence, often accompanied by death threats.[18] The result is compliance and submissiveness by the victim within the relationship in the longer term.[19] A study in the US featuring

[11] BBC (2019) https://www.comresglobal.com/wp-content/uploads/2019/11/Final-BBC-5-Live-Tables_211119cdh.pdf (accessed 17 December 2021).

[12] Susan Sorenson, Manisha Joshi, and Elizabeth Sivitz, 'A systematic review of the epidemiology of non-fatal strangulation, a human rights and health concern' (2014) 104(11) *American Journal of Public Health* 1, 2. Helen Bichard and others, 'The neuropsychological outcomes of non-fatal strangulation in domestic and sexual violence: A systematic review' (2021) 32(1) *Neuropsychological Rehabilitation* 1164, 11684.

[13] Bichard and others (n 12) 1185.

[14] https://sutda.org/wp-content/uploads/Non-fatal-strangulation-Survey-June-2020-.pdf (accessed 17 December 2021).

[15] ibid 8.

[16] White and other (n 3) 5.

[17] Kirstie Thomas, Manisha Joshi, and Susan Sorenson, 'Do you know what it feels like to drown? Strangulation as coercive control in intimate relationships' (2014) 38(1) *Psychology of Women Quarterly* 1, 6–7 https://repository.upenn.edu/cgi/viewcontent.cgi?article=1190&context=spp_papers (accessed 17 December 2021).

[18] Bichard and others (n 12) 18.

[19] Thomas, Joshi, and Sorenson (n 17).

qualitative analysis of detailed interviews with survivors identified strangulation as a method of exercising power and coercive control in intimate relationships.[20] The women reported that efforts to extricate themselves largely failed and physical resistance led to an escalation of violence. They also noted that the lack of physical marks made detection more difficult and therefore strangulation was a useful tool for abusers.

d. *The medical impacts of strangulation*

Loss of consciousness can occur within ten seconds[21] and a lack of oxygen to the brain results in mild brain damage. Studies report that between 8.9 per cent and 38 per cent of those strangled lose consciousness,[22] and that some of those who lose consciousness do not recall this.[23] Numerous longer-term effects of strangulation are reported, including damaged trachea/larynx, internal bleeding, dizziness, nausea, ear bleeding, sore throat, a raspy voice, and neurological injuries such as facial and eyelid droop, loss of memory, and tinnitus. An array of symptoms is set out in a survey of a collection of studies of neurological outcomes, including increased risk of miscarriage and delayed strokes.[24]

Beyond the physical and neurological impact, not surprisingly strangulation has been found to result in long-term mental health impacts. Post-traumatic stress disorder is closely linked to experiencing fear of imminent death. Four studies report 'a sense of existential threat, a firm conviction that they were going to die'.[25] A survey of fourteen studies of delayed psychological outcomes identifies depression, anxiety, suicidality, nightmares, PTSD, dissociation, and exacerbation of existing mental health difficulties.[26] Whilst in law psychiatric injury can be a basis for a charge of ABH or GBH, anecdotal reports from domestic abuse support workers is that, in their experience, such cases are not prosecuted.

e. *Non-fatal strangulation as a red flag for homicide risk*

Non-fatal strangulation is linked to a significantly increased risk of fatality, not only by strangulation but also other methods of killing. Quantitative research in the US found that a prior history of strangulation was associated with a seven-fold increase in the risk of death, by whatever method.[27] A stand-alone offence gives this form of abuse prominence within a risk assessment process, unlike the DASH checklist, where strangulation is simply one of twenty-seven questions.

It is hoped that a new stand-alone offence will trigger increased awareness and education, not only for police and prosecutors, but for all professionals working with survivors of domestic abuse. It may also help survivors themselves to articulate the severity of their experiences and understand the risks they face. With a proper understanding of this multifaceted form of abuse it becomes all too clear why a charge of common assault cannot be an acceptable criminal justice response. If properly implemented, this offence can help shine a

---

[20] ibid.

[21] Training Institute of Strangulation Prevention, San Diego, USA, https://www.strangulationtraininginstitute.com (accessed 17 December 2021).

[22] Bichard and others (n 12) 17.

[23] ibid.

[24] ibid 16.

[25] ibid 18.

[26] ibid 18.

[27] Nancy Glass and others, 'Non-fatal strangulation is an important risk factor for homicide of women' (2008) 35 *Journal of Emergency Medicine* 3.

light on this particularly pernicious form of abuse and enable the criminal justice system to treat it with the gravity it deserves.

ii. The Section

a. *Section 70: 75A strangulation or suffocation*

Section 70 of the DAA introduces a new offence of *non-fatal strangulation or suffocation.* When one considers the case for introducing a provision to target such conduct specifically, its significance cannot be overstated, and it is arguably one of the most important provisions enacted by the DAA in terms of providing long-term protection for victims of domestic abuse. It will assist in identifying those most at risk, as well as 'red-flagging' those who engage in this particular form of abuse and, statistics suggest, pose an ongoing risk of causing even greater harm or death where the cycle of abuse is repeated.

Until now, prosecutors have had to rely upon those provisions of general application under the Offences against the Person Act (OAPA) 1861 as a catch all, or, where applicable, section 21 OAPA, which is rarely used and, in any event, limited in its scope because of the requirement that the *attempt to choke, suffocate or strangle* be *with intent to commit an indictable offence.*[28] Equally, the offence of *coercive control* introduced by section 76 of the Serious Crime Act 2015 may cover incidents of strangulation, but it is not designed to target such conduct specifically. It requires proof of repeated or continuous controlling or coercive behaviour and only applies in the context of those who are in an intimate personal relationship; or where the victim and the offender live together and are in a relevant relationship.[29] In contrast, section 70 DAA recognises the gravamen of non-fatal strangulation of itself; as a separate and distinct form of criminal conduct, worthy of recognition and protection against.

The offence was not initially included in the Domestic Abuse Bill, but was added in Committee, following an amendment tabled by Baroness Newlove, former Victims' Commissioner in the House of Lords.[30] The need for a specific offence of non-fatal strangulation was made clear[31]: victims are seven times more likely than other forms domestic abuse to go on to be killed, with more than half the victims of recurrent domestic abuse experiencing strangulation. It is estimated that 20,000 women per year—or fifty-five women every day—who have been assessed as high risk and suffer physical abuse, have experienced strangulation or attempted strangulation. Strangulation and asphyxiation are the second most common method of killing in female homicides, after stabbing, with a woman or girl being violently killed in this way every ten days.

Despite such alarming statistics, incidents of non-fatal strangulation were not being picked up adequately by the police. As attacks of this kind often leave few or no physical marks, they

[28] OAPA, s 21. Note the Law Commission recommended repeal of that section as a 'prime example of a needlessly specific offence'. *Law Commission, Reform of Offences Against the Person*, (2015) [9.27] https://www.gov.uk/government/publications/reform-of-offences-against-the-person?msclkid=596e1ba6c24011ecab5a6691eaefcfd2 (accessed 21 April 2022).

[29] As covered by s 76(6) and (7) of the Serious Crime Act 2015; namely married, civil partners, parents of the same child, etc.

[30] Amendment 19 (10 March 2021) House of Lords debates: 'They Work For You' https://www.theyworkforyou.com/lords/?id=2021-03-10b.1650.2 (accessed 21 April 2022).

[31] Domestic Abuse Bill—Hansard—UK Parliament (HL, 5 January 2021) col 45 https://hansard.parliament.uk/Lords/2021-01-05/debates/1384371F-73F4-40BC-A44A-B0358CF839B6/DomesticAbuseBill?highlight=non%20fatal%20strangulation#contribution-F5023F75-C1E6-40CA-9A5C-8F9FC67CFAD2 (accessed 22 April 2022).

are seen as less serious than other forms of violence, despite being a terrifying crime and leaving many victims feeling as if their head is about to explode and that they are about to die.[32]

In an impassioned speech addressing the House on the need for the Domestic Abuse Bill to include a specific offence targeting non-fatal strangulation, Baroness Newlove said:

> Creating a stand-alone offence presents a unique opportunity for the Government to turn the tide on this shockingly high number of victims. Importantly for this Bill, strangulations and suffocations, both fatal and non-fatal, are concentrated within domestic abuse. Victims who survive strangulation do not just survive and get on with their lives . . . To make this a stand-out Bill, and to make it what it should be, we need to change the law, as the lives of many people depend upon us making this change.[33]

Against this backdrop and a number of high-profile cases involving, more often than not, the fatal strangulation of victims, on 7 June 2021, section 70 DAA was in force and section 75A thereby inserted into Part 5 of the Serious Crime Act (SCA) 2015. It provides:

a. Section 70: 75A Strangulation or Suffocation

(1) A person ('A') commits an offence if—
 (a) A intentionally strangles another person ('B'), OR
 (b) A does any other act to B that—
  (i) affects B's ability to breathe, and
  (ii) constitutes battery of B.

(2) It is a defence to an offence under this section for A to show that B consented to the strangulation or other act.

(3) But subsection (2) does not apply if—
 (a) B suffers serious harm as a result of the strangulation or other act, and
 (b) A either—
  (i) intended to cause B serious harm, or
  (ii) was reckless as to whether B would suffer serious harm.

(4) A is to be taken to have shown the fact mentioned in subsection (2) if—
 (a) sufficient evidence of the fact is adduced to raise an issue with respect to it, and
 (b) the contrary is not proved beyond reasonable doubt.

b. *Section 70 in practice: defining strangulation*

The meaning of ***strangulation*** is not defined anywhere within the DAA 2021 (or by statute generally[34]), albeit the explanatory notes[35] state that the alternative form of the offence can

[32] See Jane Monckton-Smith, 'Non-Fatal Strangulation' Stand up to Domestic Violence (2020) 7, https://sutda.org/wp-content/uploads/Nonfatal-strangulation-Survey-June-2020-.pdf. (accessed 22 April 2022).

[33] See col 46 https://hansard.parliament.uk/Lords/2021-01-05/debates/1384371F-73F4-40BC-A44A-B0358CF839B6/DomesticAbuseBill (accessed 22 April 2022). See also *New Zealand Law Commission, Strangulation: The Case for a New Offence (2016);* https://www.lawcom.govt.nz/sites/default/files/projectAvailableFormats/NZLC-R138.pdf?msclkid=df50b64ec24111ecaeca94456766a5d9, Victims Commissioner, 'Commissioners endorse non-fatal strangulation amendment to the Domestic Abuse Bill' (2021) https://victimscommissioner.org.uk/news/commissioners-endorsenon-fatal-strangulationamendment-to-the domesticabuse-bill/: 'non-fatal strangulation is currently significantly under-charged across the UK . . . This is a systemic issue and the law as it stands is not fit for purpose.' (accessed 22 April 2022).

[34] Including 'strangulation,' 'suffocation', or 'choking' under s 21 OAPA 1861.

[35] Explanatory Notes DAA 318 at 49 https://www.legislation.gov.uk/ukpga/2021/17/pdfs/ukpgaen_20210017_en.pdf(accessed 25 April 2022).

include, but is not limited to, *suffocation*. Accordingly, any work on defining its meaning has been left to the courts and no judicial guidance on interpreting the provision is available at this stage. It is suggested that, in the absence of a statutory definition, *strangulation* will be given its ordinary meaning, applying *Brutus v Cozens*[36] to achieve that aim.[37] How is *strangulation* to be defined, even on that basis? Individual understanding and definitions vary considerably, for example, 'throttle, kill by squeezing windpipe; prevent circulation through vein by compression'.[38]

In the Northern Ireland case of *The Queen v Campbell Allen*[39] Stephens LJ offered the following definition: 'Strangulation is a form of asphyxia (lack of oxygen) characterised by closure of the blood vessels and/or air passages of the neck as a result of external pressure on the neck.'

Given the potential for inconsistency, a statutory definition would arguably have made it easier to achieve consistency, certainty, and address the intended aim of the provision. This is imperative when one considers the need for consistency of approach when potential charges are being considered by the police and prosecutors before an allegation ever reaches a court room. Further, concern has been expressed as to the effect the absence of a statutory definition may have, with the end result being that an unnecessarily narrow interpretation may be applied in practice: 'Without a clear definition of NFS [Non-fatal strangulation] in the legislation there is a risk that non-fatal strangulation will be interpreted narrowly, for example, to require complete stoppage of breath or that unconsciousness results.'[40] However, such concerns may be misplaced given the alternative route to conviction under section 75A(1)(b), which includes *any other act*, in respect of which one need only prove that A's ability to breathe is affected and that the *act* amounts to a battery, for the offence to be made out (regardless of the mechanism or nature of the act), the emphasis being on the effect of B's actions.

c. *Non-fatal strangulation: necessary* mens rea

From a practitioner perspective, when considering the *strangulation* route, once the definition to be applied has been determined, the mental element required is clear—A must *intentionally* strangle B. The alternative route requires proof of a battery and, therefore, proof of A having used unlawful force on B *intentionally* or *recklessly*. What is not clear is whether a separate mental element is required to be proved as to B's ability to breathe being affected by A's conduct. As considered by Kelly and Ormerod,[41] where, for example, A pins B to the floor by kneeling on her chest, whereas A would intend or be reckless as to the infliction of unlawful force, would A necessarily realise that he was affecting B's ability to breathe? On the one hand, the offence is of general prohibition and a serious one. Where the DAA is silent on this issue, the presumption of *mens rea* should arguably apply, so that A would not be liable

[36] [1973] AC 854.

[37] The Home Office and Ministry of Justice, 'Domestic Abuse Bill' (Second Supplemental Memorandum, 2021) [9]; House of Commons, Domestic Abuse Bill: Explanatory notes on Lords Amendments [77] https://publications.parliament.uk/pa/bills/cbill/58-01/0281/en/200281en.pdf?msclkid=1892a325c49711ec8330d69551a51e2b (accessed 25 April 2022).

[38] See *Concise Oxford English Dictionary*.

[39] [2020] NICA 25.

[40] See Heather Douglas and Robin Fitzgerald, 'Women's stories of non-fatal strangulation: Informing the criminal justice response' (2020) 22(2) *Criminology & Criminal Justice* 1 and Rory Kelly and David Ormerod, 'Non-fatal strangulation and suffocation' (2021) 7 *Crim LR* 532.

[41] Kelly and Ormerod (n 40) 544.

for the strangulation but merely for battery. On the other hand, for the very many reasons already identified, *strangulation*, particularly in an act of domestic abuse is of such concern that it is arguable that the presumption of *mens rea* should be rebutted for this offence. In due course, the precise ambit of what is required to prove an offence under the *other act* route is likely to require guidance from the Court of Appeal, as is the definition of strangulation.

By reference to section 75A(2), the defence of consent remains in cases of minor assault albeit the evidential burden will be on the defence to raise.[42] This highlights the tension between the need to respect the autonomy of the individual to choose to engage in particular conduct which risks some harm, against the need to protect individuals against more serious harm. However, even where *serious harm*[43] is caused, it remains open to the defence to argue a lack of intention or recklessness as to the likelihood of serious harm. Further, in order to demonstrate that B consented to the conduct in question, where in issue, A will inevitably seek to adduce evidence of previous sexual behaviour. This may also be relevant to the question of intent or recklessness, where, for example, no serious harm previously resulted from similar conduct. In the context of a sexual allegation, the defence would have to pass through one of the gateways under section 41 of the Youth Justice and Criminal Evidence Act (YJCEA) 1999 in order to adduce evidence of previous sexual behaviour. No such prohibition arises where the allegations are *non-sexual*, notwithstanding the context. Equally, evidence of previous instances of behaviour that would now fall to be charged under section 70 are likely to be admissible under the *Bad Character* provisions as relevant to the level of harm intended or foreseen.

One other potential issue likely to be raised in such cases is the question of A's *belief* in consent. By reference to the common law, a genuine belief in consent by A would be sufficient for the new offence. However, where allegations of non-fatal strangulation are joined on the same indictment as sexual offences, which will frequently be the case, practical difficulties may arise as to the how the jury will be directed on the differing approaches applicable to the issue of (genuine or reasonable) belief in consent.

d. *Sentencing non-fatal strangulation*

A person convicted of an offence of non-fatal strangulation under the new provisions will be liable on indictment to a maximum sentence of five years' imprisonment. This is the same as an offence contrary to section 47 or section 20 of the OAPA 1861. Whilst there are no specific sentencing guidelines in place at present, as of May 2020 new guidance was issued by the Sentencing Council for assault offences, in which *strangulation*, *suffocation*, and *asphyxiation* is included as a factor attracting *higher culpability*.

e. *Critical Commentary*

The new provision (s 70 DAA) is not without controversy and, some would argue, unnecessary, while others believe that it does not go far enough and needs further clarity. However, as a starting point, by making non-fatal strangulation an offence in its own right, it will raise public awareness; require better training for the police, prosecutors, and the judiciary; require better provision for the examination and support of victims who complain, and it

[42] Not without some controversary: see debates Baroness Newlove, 1653–54, Lord Marks, 1656, Lord Wolfson, 1660, Hansard, HL vol 810, cols 1626–1794 (10 March 2021). https://hansard.parliament.uk/lords/2021-03-10/debates/5A6B3EBE-EE46-453F-AAC8-5391793E3923/DomesticAbuseBill

[43] As defined under DAA 2021, s 71.

will go some way to ensuring that perpetrators of domestic abuse in this most serious form are identified and dealt with.

2. SECTION 71 CONSENT TO SERIOUS HARM FOR SEXUAL GRATIFICATION NOT A DEFENCE

i. Context and Background

a. *The common law*

The starting point for a discussion of the recent law's response to the concern with 'rough sex' has to be the landmark case of *R v Brown*.[44] The defendants were part of a group of men who injured each other as part of a consensual sadomasochistic encounter. Charges under section 47 and 20 of the OAPA 1861 referred to activities involving branding, burning, and nailing. Lord Templeman explained: 'The charges against the appellants were based on genital torture and violence to the buttocks, anus, penis, testicles and nipples. The victims were degraded and humiliated, sometimes beaten, sometimes wounded with instruments and sometimes branded.'[45]

In December 1990, all five defendants were convicted of offences including assault occasioning actual bodily harm (s 47 of the OAPA 1861), unlawful wounding (s 20 of the OAPA 1861), and the common law offence of keeping a disorderly house. The convictions were appealed to the House of Lords, where, by a majority of three to two, the convictions were upheld. For the majority, the consent of a victim to acts resulting in actual bodily harm or a more serious injury was not a defence, unless the activity fell within an 'exceptional category'. Sadomasochism did not fall into the existing categories and there were no good reasons to create a new one. Lord Templeman, giving the leading speech for the majority, gave examples of what kinds of consensual behaviour would be lawfully permitted: surgery, ritual circumcision, tattooing, ear piecing, and violent sports (including boxing). He indicated the list could be added to if there was behaviour which could be regarded as being in the public interest, but that sadomasochism did not do so. In fact, he went further than he needed to and made it clear that he thought sadomasochism was contrary to the public good. Such behaviour was 'unpredictably dangerous'; 'degrading to body and mind'; and involved 'the indulgence of cruelty by sadists and the degradation of victims'.[46]

The dissenting judges warned of the danger of using law to respond to matters of private morality. They emphasised the right to respect for private life under Article 8 of the European Convention on Human Rights. This aspect of the case was taken up when the case was heard by the European Court of Human Rights.[47] Perhaps surprisingly, it was held that although the criminalisation of sadomasochism did breach the applicant's Article 8 rights' such interference could be justified under Article 8(2) as being necessary to protect the health of others.

It would be fair to say that the academic response to the decision in *Brown* has been overwhelmingly negative.[48] Many commentators have detected a homophobic and moralistic flavour to the approach of the majority's speeches. Such concerns have been exacerbated by

[44] *R v Brown* [1994] 1 AC 212 (HL).

[45] ibid 230.

[46] *R v Brown* (n 44) 237.

[47] *Laskey v UK* (1997) 24 EHRR 39.

[48] See eg David Gurnham, 'Legal Authority and Savagery in Judicial Rhetoric: Sexual Violence and the Criminal Courts' (2011) 7 *International Journal of Law in Context* 117.

the treatment of the decision in later cases. But, as we shall, at the same time the later cases highlight a whole set of issues overlooked in *Brown*.

In *R v Wilson*[49] a husband branded his initials on his wife's buttocks. One might have expected following *Brown* that his conviction would be upheld. However, the Court of Appeal explained: 'Consensual activity between husband and wife, in the privacy of the matrimonial home, is not, in our judgment, normally a proper matter for criminal investigation, let alone criminal prosecution.'[50]

No explanation is offered as to why a special rule is created for married couples. There is a real concern that the case leaves wives open to being abused, with the court assuming that domestic violence does not take place between spouses. Subsequently, in *R v Emmett*[51] the Court of Appeal was clear the law drew no distinction between married and unmarried couples or opposite or same sex couples. The ruling in *Brown* applied to all instances of sadomasochism and the explanation of the outcome in *Wilson* was that the case was analogous to tattooing. The situation was plunged back into confusion when, in the most recent case, *R v BM*,[52] *Wilson* was again explained in terms of marital privacy.

What, however, is striking about these cases is the complete failure to recognise the domestic abuse angle. In *Emmett*, the defendant poured lighter fuel on his partner's breasts and set them alight, causing severe burns, measuring 24 cm^2, and put a plastic bag over her head and tightened it to the point that she could no long endure the pain and was unable to communicate with him. Notably, in both that case, and in *Wilson*, the prosecution was brought after the victim's doctor notified the police about what had happened. That would have been a breach of confidence by the doctor, although cases of domestic abuse are one of few the instances justifying such a breach. While we cannot know the truth, there must be a strong suspicion that these were simply cases of domestic violence to which the defendant gave the only defence he could: she wanted it!

Later cases backed these concerns that the courts were accepting some domestic abuse cases as consensual sadomasochism. For example, in *R v Lock*,[53] a woman had the words, 'Property of Steven Lock' tattooed around her genitals, she was chained 'like a dog' to his bedroom floor and he whipped her repeatedly with a rope. This case has all the hallmarks of domestic abuse and yet the defendant was cleared of all charges, claiming they were engaging in consensual activity. The victim explained at the trial: 'I knew there would be pain involved and I knew I wasn't going to like it, but I'd agreed to it and had to follow it through;' clearly, a statement which reveals how she did not want the activity to happen and felt she had no choice but to allow it to occur. Indeed, in her evidence she explained how she screamed and cried during the violence. Sadly, it seems there are powerful messages that violence and pain in sex should be seen as normal and indeed part of a lively and exciting sex life. These narratives are inspired by books such as *Fifty Shades of Grey*[54] and make it very hard for a victim to persuade a jury there was no genuine consent.

---

49 [1997] QB 47.

50 ibid 50.

51 *R v Emmett* [1999] All ER (D) 641.

52 [2018] EWCA Crim 560.

53 B Kendall, 'Gardener Cleared of Assault after *Fifty Shades of Grey*-inspired Sadomasochistic Sex Session,' *The Independent* (22 January 2013).

54 EL James, *Fifty Shades of Grey* (Arrow 2012).

b. *The background to section 70 of the Domestic Abuse Bill*

It is the case of *R v Broadhurst*[55]—where the defendant was convicted of the gross negligence manslaughter (GNM) of Natalie Connolly—and the case of *R v Kempson*[56]—where the defendant was convicted of the murder of Grace Millane—which acted as the catalyst in galvanising a campaign which pressed for the statutory regulation of the so-called 'rough sex' narratives and the admissibility of victim character evidence in cases where the defendant alleges that the victim died in the course of acts committed during consensual sex. Natalie Connolly died on 18 December 2016 and Grace Millane died on 1 December 2018. Whilst the common law held that consent to any assault above section 39 CJA common assault and battery was negated, that common law position (see above) did not prevent the defendants in both these and other cases from traducing the character of the dead in an effort to advance a defence of accident no intent and shift the blame and culpability onto the dead victim.

It was the case of Natalie Connolly (who died following acts committed by John Broadhurst) that resulted in the introduction of section 71 DAA codifying the common law position on consent, following lengthy debates in both Houses during the passage of the Domestic Abuse Bill (DAB). On 7 July 2020, clause 65 of the DAB (HL Bill 124), as introduced, provided that consent is not a defence where a person inflicts 'serious harm' on another for the purposes of obtaining sexual gratification.[57] 'Serious harm' means an offence under section 18 grievous bodily harm, section 20 wounding, or section 47 actual bodily harm, within the meaning of the OAPA 1861. The Justice Minister, Alex Chalk, said at the time:

No death or other serious injury—whatever the circumstances—should be defended as 'rough sex gone wrong' which is why we are making it absolutely clear that this is never acceptable. Perpetrators of these crimes should be under no illusions—their actions will never be justifiable in any way, and they will be pursued rigorously through the courts to seek justice for victims and their families.[58]

Case law over the years is replete with cases where the defendant alleged that the victim consented to the acts that caused death. In *HM Advocate v Rutherford*,[59] the accused was charged with murdering a woman by strangling her. The medical evidence showed that:

death was due to strangulation, and that severe pressure must have been used and persisted in for some time. There were linear bands of discoloration round the neck and abrasions on the skin in the region where the tie had been tightened. There were also marks of bruising under or behind the jaw on both sides of the neck, under the sterno-mastoid muscles and the tissues of the larynx, pointing in the opinion of medical experts to manual pressure of a throttling nature.

He stated in evidence that: 'she had repeatedly asked him to strangle her to death, that he had put his necktie round her neck and that he had pulled it and pulled it again, her telling him to get on with it.' Found guilty of culpable homicide, he was sentenced to seven years' imprisonment.

---

55 *R v Broadhurst* [2019] EWCA Crim 2026.

56 *Kempson v R* [2020] NZCA 656.

57 https://publications.parliament.uk/pa/bills/lbill/58-01/124/5801124en.pdf?msclkid=0af9239ec26b11ecaaa9a2160e1251e2 (accessed 22 April 2020).

58 Policy paper Consent to serious harm for sexual gratification not a defence https://www.gov.uk/government/publications/domestic-abuse-bill-2020-factsheets/consent-to-serious-harm-for-sexual-gratification-not-a-defence (accessed 22 April 2022).

59 [1947] JC 1 (HC).

In *R v Coates*,[60] seven and a half years for manslaughter was handed down where the defendant said that the deceased had practised paraphilia; and that she was responsible for putting the belt around her own neck and her death was an accident. In *R v Doblys*,[61] the defendant was convicted of manslaughter and sentenced to sixteen years' imprisonment. He said what had happened between them was consensual, which included a violent vaginal and anal rape and a ferocious attack. The appeal court made a reference to 'sadistic attack'. In *R v Tobin*,[62] the defendant was convicted of manslaughter and sentenced to sixteen years' imprisonment. He said that there had been an argument and consensual rough sex between him and the victim, who sustained thirty-six injuries. Out of these and many other cases a pattern of violence against women during the sexual act nuanced by the defendant as consensual began to emerge.

John Broadhurst evaded a conviction for both murder and manslaughter. In summarising the medical evidence in Broadhurst's trial for murder, grievous bodily harm with intent (s 18) and assault by penetration (s 2 Sexual Offences Act (SOA) 2003), the judge said that death was the result of:

> [a] combination of the alcohol level (acute alcohol intoxication) and the 40 separate physical injuries and resultant blood loss. The injuries to Natalie Connolly included bruising to the head, a blow-out fracture to the left eye socket, internal bleeding and tissue haemorrhaging on the bottom and lower back. The insertion and/or the removal of the spray bottle had caused lacerations of the vagina which resulted in arterial and venous haemorrhage.[63]

The prosecution alleged that Broadhurst had beaten her to 'teach her a lesson' because she had contacted two former boyfriends. This was, they submitted, a case of violence, anger, and jealousy by a man who beat the deceased with his fists following his discovery that she had sent explicit texts to a former boyfriend.

Broadhurst claimed that Natalie Connolly had consented to and derived sexual satisfaction from being injured in this way and that she had requested that he hit her with his hand and a boot on her breasts and buttocks and that she had requested that he insert a spray bottle into her vagina. The deceased's levels of intoxication included a blood alcohol level of 389 mg per 100 ml of blood, a cocaine level of 0.74 mg per litre of blood, and a cocaethylene level of 0.59 mg per litre, which provided the defence with an opportunity to pursue a point on causation. Broadhurst in his evidence said that he saw that she was bleeding from her vagina, that she was incoherent and largely unresponsive and said he left her, almost naked, lying on her back at the foot of the stairs and went to bed at about 3.00 am.[64] Mobile phone evidence showed that at 6.06 am he walked up the stairs and sent a text message to a friend. During this time, he did not call an ambulance or seek assistance for Natalie Connolly. At about 9.23 am, he phoned the emergency services. The 999-call evidence reported him saying that she was: 'as dead as a doughnut'.[65] At the conclusion of the prosecution case, the defence prepared to make a submission of 'no case to answer' on the grounds (i) of her consent, (ii) that the acts were lawful, (iii) the cause of death was uncertain, and (iv) the deceased's levels of intoxication may have been the proximate cause of death. The judge concluded: 'I cannot be sure she was incapable of consenting to being beaten with a shoe' and accepted that she

[60] [2012] EWCA Crim 2400.
[61] [2014] EWCA Crim 402.
[62] [2017] EWCA Crim 1235 [7].
[63] *R v Broadhurst* (n 55) [8].
[64] ibid [4], [5].
[65] https://www.bbc.co.uk/news/uk-england-46591150 (accessed 22 April 2022).

instigated 'being penetrated by the carpet cleaner bottle'.[66] Following *R v Slingsby*[67] (cited below), he held that penetration with an object was not an unlawful act (albeit potentially dangerous). However, he did find that Broadhurst had caused most of the injuries to Ms Connolly's breasts, bottom, and lower back, which, he found to be 'actual bodily harm of quite a serious type' (note not grievous bodily harm). The judge directed the jury to acquit on the charge of murder and assault by penetration (s 2 SOA 2003). Directing the jury to acquit on the charge of murder, the Crown then withdrew the charge of section 2 SOA assault by penetration and, given the judge's rulings and the possibility that a conviction for unlawful act manslaughter might fail, accepted the defence's guilty plea to GNM.

The judge imposed a sentence of three years and eight months' imprisonment to reflect the guilty plea[68] (five years and six months was the starting point). Broadhurst served half this sentence.

Natalie Connolly's MP, Mark Garnier[69] and Harriet Harman KC, MP,[70] introduced the matter to Parliament on 2 October 2019 and tabled several amendments to the second reading of the Domestic Abuse Bill. On 16 June 2020, during the Public Committee stage of the Domestic Abuse Bill,[71] clauses 4 and 5 were approved. Clause 4, 'No defence for consent to death', provides: '(1) If a person ('A') wounds, assaults, or asphyxiates another person ('B') to whom they are personally connected as defined in section 2 of this Act causing death, it is not a defence to a prosecution that B consented to the infliction of injury. (2) Subsection (1) applies whether or not the death occurred in the course of a sadomasochistic encounter.' Clause 5, 'No defence for consent to injury', provides: '(1) If a person ('A') wounds, assaults or asphyxiates another person ('B') to whom they are personally connected as defined in section 2 of this Act causing actual bodily harm or more serious injury, it is not a defence to a prosecution that B consented to the infliction of injury or asphyxiation. (2) Subsection (1) applies whether or not the actual bodily harm, non-fatal strangulation, or more serious injury occurred in the course of a sadomasochistic encounter.'

This section of the Bill was being debated with the killing on 2 December 2018, in Auckland, New Zealand, of Grace Millane (a British backpacker) also in mind. Grace Millane was strangled by the defendant Jesse Kempson (although at the time of the trial (November 2019) his identity was protected by anonymity). They had met on a Tinder date and that evening Grace Millane was killed by him by strangulation (the prosecution alleged that the strangulation lasted several minutes). Kempson later disposed of her body. At trial, he said that she had consented to 'rough sex' involving strangulation. Like Natalie Connolly, her character was traduced, the defence having been granted leave to adduce sexual history evidence. The jury convicted Kempson of murder.[72] This 'rough sex' narrative was emerging as a

---

[66] ibid [23], [31].

[67] *R v Slingsby* [1995] *Crim LR* 570.

[68] See https://www.sentencingcouncil.org.uk/offences/crown-court/item/gross-negligence-manslaughter/ (accessed 30 March 2022).

[69] Domestic Abuse Bill—Hansard—UK Parliament cols 1287–88 https://hansard.parliament.uk/commons/2019-10-02/debates/C3488538-CFEC-4670-9299-732672E2BE67/DomesticAbuseBill (accessed 22 April 2022).

[70] ibid col 1278.

[71] Public Bill Committees, Domestic Abuse Bill, Tenth Session (16 June 2020) col 339. See https://hansard.parliament.uk/ Commons/2020-06-16/debates/3fa90c32-4bc5-4477-ab1e-aaf665da56e6/DomesticAbuseBill(TenthSitting) (accessed 17 January 2022).

[72] *Kempson v R* (n 56). See also Susan Edwards and Kris Gledhill, 'Strangulation and false narratives of consent' Counsel (March 2021) https://www.counselmagazine.co.uk/articles/strangulation-false-narratives-of-consent (accessed 22 April 2022).

not infrequent defence in the last two decades, especially.[73] The government finally accepted a proposed amendment to clause 65 of the Domestic Abuse Bill (clause 72 on 17 March 2021), now section 71 DAA.

ii. Section 71 Regulating the 'Rough Sex' Defence

a. *The position before the DAA 2021*

In the case of *R v Brown*[74] (discussed above), the group of sadomasochists who participated in the commission of acts of violence against each other for sexual pleasure were prosecuted for offences contrary to section 47 of the OAPA 1861 and, initially pleading 'Not Guilty' before the Crown Court, they subsequently changed their pleas to Guilty following a ruling by the trial judge that the prosecution did not have to prove lack of consent. Appealing on the basis of the judge's ruling, the House of Lords (Lord Mustill and Lord Slynn of Hadley dissenting), held that, although a prosecutor had to prove absence of consent in order to secure a conviction for mere assault, it was not in the public interest that a person should wound or cause actual bodily harm to another for no 'good reason' and, in the absence of such a reason, the victim's consent afforded no defence to a charge under section 20 or section 47 of the Act of 1861.

For the best part of thirty years, therefore, under the common law, a person could not consent to actual bodily harm or to other, more serious, injury for no 'good reason', including 'for the purposes of sexual gratification'. Despite this, in a number of recent, high-profile cases in which women have been killed by male acquaintances or partners, including Grace Millane[75] and Natalie Connolly[76] in 2018, the narrative of consensual *rough sex* gone wrong has continued to be advanced in the criminal courts as an explanation for multiple, serious injuries, alongside a defence of lack of intent to cause really serious harm to the victim.

The government's response, galvanised by the 'We Cannot Consent to This'[77] campaign led by the Centre for Women's Justice (CWJ),[78] alongside a swell of political support, was to table an amendment to the Domestic Abuse Bill, as it then was, specifically to address this issue.

On 29 April 2021, section 71 of the DAA 2021 finally became law, the intention of Parliament being to clarify the law by restating, in statute, the broad legal principle established nearly thirty years ago in *Brown*. When one considers the data gathered by those who campaigned for change: that at least sixty females were killed in the UK between 1972 and 2020 by males who claimed that the death happened during a sex game gone wrong; that between 1996 and 2006 there has been a ten-fold increase in rough sex claims being relied upon in court, whilst, at the same time, the normalisation of bondage, domination, and

[73] *R v Coutts* [2006] 1 WLR 2154. See also Susan S M Edwards, 'Consent and the "Rough Sex" Defence in Rape, Murder, Manslaughter and Gross Negligence' (2020) 84(4) *Journal of Criminal Law* 293–311.

[74] [1994] 1 AC 212.

[75] *Kempson v R* [2020] NZCA 656.

[76] *R v Broadhurst* [2019] EWCA Crime 2026.

[77] See https://wecantconsenttothis.uk/actnow?msclkid=ca0ae1e7c49511ec939742abff99a065 (accessed 25 April 2022).

[78] https://www.centreforwomensjustice.org.uk/?msclkid=02f1a09ac49611ecbe75382f0b080c55 (accessed 25 April 2022).

sadomasochism (BDSM) across various media had generated a 'culturally approved script' for men who kill women;[79] it has been a long time coming.

b. Interpreting section 71 in practice

Section 71 of the DAA provides:

Consent to serious harm for sexual gratification not a defence

(1) This section applies for the purposes of determining whether a person ('D') who inflicts serious harm on another person ('V') is guilty of a relevant offence.
(2) It is not a defence that V consented to the infliction of the serious harm for the purposes of obtaining sexual gratification (but see subsection (4)).
(3) In this section—
'relevant offence' means an offence under section 18, 20 or 47 of the Offences Against the Person Act 1861 ('the 1861 Act');
'serious harm' means—(a) grievous bodily harm, within the meaning of section 18 of the 1861 Act, (b) wounding, within the meaning of that section, or (c) actual bodily harm, within the meaning of section 47 of the 1861 Act.
(4) Subsection (2) does not apply in the case of an offence under section 20 or 47 of the 1861 Act where (a) the serious harm consists of, or is a result of, the infection of V with a sexually transmitted infection in the course of sexual activity, and (b) V consented to the sexual activity in the knowledge or belief that D had the sexually transmitted infection.
(5) For the purposes of this section, it does not matter whether the harm was inflicted for the purposes of obtaining sexual gratification for D, V or some other person.
(6) Nothing in this section affects any enactment or rule of law relating to other circumstances in which a person's consent to the infliction of serious harm may, or may not, be a defence to a relevant offence.

In practical terms, section 71 will apply in all cases in which an offence contrary to section 18, 20, and/or 47 of the OAPA 1861 is alleged, and in which 'serious harm' is inflicted. 'Serious harm' is defined to include grievous bodily harm, wounding, or actual bodily harm. On one view, the language of the Act—'serious harm'—is confusing, given that evidence of any injury of harm, which is 'calculated to interfere with the comfort or health of [the victim]'[80] is sufficient for an offence contrary to section 47 OAPA; for example, minor cuts and bruises may suffice. However, by reference to CPS legal guidance: Offences against the Person (incorporating Charging Standard)[81] it appears to favour a charge of actual bodily harm in circumstances where there is evidence of serious (as opposed to less serious) injury. Serious injury is described as including 'damaged teeth or bones, extensive and severe bruising, cuts requiring suturing and those that result in loss of consciousness. That the injuries required medical treatment, because they could not be treated by the victim alone and required medical assessment at least, may indicate a serious injury'.

Where the injuries inflicted clearly amount to grievous bodily harm, there may be little difficulty in determining that section 71(1) is satisfied. Where, however, the injury or harm

[79] Elizabeth Yardley, 'Rough sex doesn't kill women, their abusers do' Real World Criminologist blog https://www.elizabethyardley.com/blog-1?msclkid=11f3f210c49211ecad66106197f0ac68 (accessed 24 April 2022).
[80] *R v Miller* [1954] QB 282.
[81] Updated 21 March 2022 https://www.cps.gov.uk/legal-guidance/offences-against-person-incorporating-charging-standard?msclkid=5a8d48ebc49311ecabdb17ec9e6c04f6 (accessed 25 April 2022).

falls into the grey area between what amounts to actual bodily harm or an offence contrary to section 39 of the Criminal Justice Act 1988 may be more difficult. Ordinarily, the appropriate charge will be contrary to section 39 where injuries amount to no more than grazes, scratches, abrasions, minor bruising, swellings, reddening of the skin, or superficial cuts. However, in circumstances where any number of aggravating features are present, such as the offence being repeated or forming part of a pattern of similar offending against the same complainant, the complainant is vulnerable or intimidated,[82] and/or a weapon has been used, this is likely to support a charge of actual bodily harm.

In practice, therefore, imposing a threshold on 'serious harm' of actual bodily harm is likely to exclude a whole host of conduct indicative of abuse in the context of 'rough sex', where proof of actual physical injury may be difficult to establish; for example, in cases of attempted strangulation or suffocation; or where there is evidence of spitting, hair pulling, restraints, bondage, grabbing of the neck etc, subject to the application of section 70 DAA, provided the threshold is not met, the defence of consent remains.

Where section 71(1) is satisfied, section 71(2) states that '*it is not a defence*' that V consented to the infliction of such harm *for the purposes of obtaining sexual gratification*. It matters not for whose sexual gratification the harm is inflicted (s 71(5)). Note also the exception inserted by section 71(4) in relation to offences contrary to section 47 or section 20 OAPA 1861. By reference to *Brown*, the practical effect of section 71(2) is nothing new; it merely restates the common law position. However, the extent to which it may be argued that harm was inflicted for purposes *other* than the obtaining of sexual gratification remains to be seen. Depending upon the circumstances surrounding the alleged offence, the purpose for which harm has been inflicted may be clear. Where it is not, and no admission is made by the defence, the onus will be on the prosecution to prove it is caught by the Act. Arguably the 'no good reason' test in *Brown* went further than the statute does; being undefined, it has the potential to change over time. However, one can readily see why Parliament chose to focus instead on the mischief of the so-called 'rough sex' defence, particularly where legislating expressly to *exclude* a defence.

In *R v Wilson*[83] (also discussed earlier), the Court of Appeal quashed a conviction where a husband branded his initials on his wife's buttocks with a hot knife (with her agreement). Allowing the appeal, the Court held that the case was distinct from *Brown* (also discussed earlier), since (i) there was no aggressive intent; (ii) W's wife had wanted it, not out of a desire for pain, but as an adornment, not unlike jewellery; (iii) *Brown* was merely a ruling on sadomasochism, whereas this was essentially similar to tattooing; (iv) it was not in the public interest that a husband and wife's private activities should be regulated, whereas that was not the case with violent sadomasochists.

By its absence, and consistent with *Brown*, section 71 does not preclude D relying upon V's consent to some physical force, which would amount to no more than a battery contrary to section 39 for the purposes of obtaining sexual gratification. So too, notwithstanding the introduction of section 71, even if consent does not afford a defence in the face of the harm caused, it does not prohibit or preclude reference to 'rough sex' and V's alleged consent as evidence of D's *lack of intent* to cause really serious harm or *lack of foresight* of the risk of

---

[82] Within the meaning of Youth Justice and Criminal Evidence Act 1999, s 16(2) and s 17(2) https://www.legislation.gov.uk/ukpga/1999/23/contents?msclkid=c2673271c49311ec94a0fdbfea2a33fa (accessed 25 May 2022).

[83] [1996] 3 WLR 125.

serious harm. In the context of a murder trial in which D claims to have had consensual, rough sex, the issue of consent will almost always be relevant to the question of D's intention, albeit not necessarily determinative; it is just one piece of the evidential puzzle and there will invariably be other evidence against which the plausibility of D's explanation can be measured.[84] For example, the post mortem and expert evidence of the forensic pathologists will reveal the nature and number of injuries that were inflicted; the degree of force require to cause the injuries, as well as the precise cause of death and when the deceased is likely to have died. Further, evidence of previous injuries to, or complaint by, the deceased about similar behaviour may provide evidence of rebuttal in the face of any reliance upon consensual 'rough sex' to demonstrate a lack of intent or foresight of likely injuries. In *R v Coutts*,[85] in which the defendant was initially convicted of the murder of his girlfriend's friend, both from the defence and prosecution perspective, evidence was adduced as to the defendant's interest in asphyxial sex and fascination in women's necks over a period of some twenty years. However, the prosecution also adduced evidence of the defendant allegedly having visited a number of pornographic websites, showing violence towards women, and on repeated visits by him to the storage facility where the body of the deceased had been stored to suggest that he had necrophiliac propensities.[86] Likewise, in the context of a manslaughter charge it will still remain possible for D to claim that the alleged unlawful and dangerous act that caused death was a mere battery consented to by V and that D did not envisage it involving a risk of bodily harm.[87] In *R v Slingsby*[88] the defendant claimed that, with the deceased's consent, he had penetrated her vagina and rectum with his hand. The deceased suffered cuts caused by the defendant's signet ring. She later died of septicaemia as a result of the cuts. The Crown alleged D was guilty of manslaughter. The court held: 'It would be contrary to principle to treat as criminal activity something which would not otherwise amount to assault merely because in the course of the activity an injury occurred.' Accordingly, the count of manslaughter could not be sustained on the basis of the agreed facts and, ultimately, the Crown offered no evidence.

c. *Critical Commentary*

It is difficult to see how the implementation of section 71 will put an end to the underlying narrative of 'rough sex' being advanced in all cases of sexual or physical violence any time soon. Even where the defence is precluded from relying upon consent as a defence because of the harm caused, where a complainant's consent may be relevant to a defendant's state of mind (or any other issue in the case), one can readily see a route to the admissibility of such evidence. Of course, in cases where a complainant was killed during sexual and/or physical violence, she will be unable to give an account of what occurred. In such circumstances, a jury will be left to piece together what occurred from the available evidence. Despite a clear desire to protect the character of the deceased, including evidence of previous sexual behaviour, this is likely to remain a highly contentious issue as between prosecution and defence. Whether or not section 41 YJCEA 1999 bites may depend upon what offence(s) the defendant is charged with. Where it is relevant, and when balanced against competing, fair trial

[84] Genevieve Reed, 'New Law Seeking to Ban "Rough Sex Defence" Unlikely to Change Trial Outcomes' *The Justice Gap* (10 July 2020).
[85] [2006] 1 WLR 2154, [2006] 4 All ER 353.
[86] ibid.
[87] David Ormerod, 'The Domestic Abuse Bill 2021 (Editorial)' (2021) 6 *Crim LR* 423.
[88] [1995] *Crim LR* 570.

arguments evidence of what the defence will characterise as 'rough sex' is likely to continue to be admissible in the criminal courts.

To that extent it may be argued that the new Act has failed in part to achieve its intended aim. That said, the section does succeed in shining a light on the issue of sexual violence and its consequences, which, in turn, will serve to raise awareness, redress media driven misconceptions, and alter public perception, which is of fundamental importance. Given the central role of jurors as fact finders in criminal trials, this provision it to be welcomed as a positive step in the right direction.

14
OFFENCES COMMITTED OUTSIDE THE UK (SECTIONS 72–74)

David Malone*

1. SECTION 72 OFFENCES AGAINST THE PERSON COMMITTED OUTSIDE THE UK: ENGLAND AND WALES

i. Context and Background

As a general rule, the jurisdiction of the criminal law of England and Wales does not extend to acts committed abroad, regardless of whether the individual committing the act is a British citizen.[1] For an offence to apply extra-territorially, Parliament must expressly state an intention that the relevant law should extend to conduct abroad.[2] Prior to the passing of the Domestic Abuse Act (DAA) 2021, certain offences already enjoyed extra-territorial jurisdiction, such as murder or manslaughter committed by a subject of His Majesty by way of section 9 of the Offences against the Person Act (OAPA) 1861.

The contextual background of section 72 DAA 2021, dates back to the signing by the UK of the Istanbul Convention in 2012 (The Council of Europe Convention on preventing and combating violence against women and domestic violence),[3] which provided for binding standards in international law to prevent violence against women and domestic violence, to protect victims, and to punish perpetrators. By virtue of Article 44 of the Istanbul

* This chapter has been written with the assistance of David Malone's pupil, Mr Andreas Malekos.

[1] *R v Harden* [1963] 1 QB 8.

[2] *Treacy v DPP* [1971] AC 537 (HL).

[3] https://www.coe.int/en/web/istanbul-convention (accessed 26 May 2022).

David Malone, *Offences Committed Outside the UK (Sections 72–74)* In: *Blackstone's Guide to the Domestic Abuse Act 2021*. Edited by Susan Edwards, David Malone, and Gillian Jones KC, Oxford University Press. © David Malone 2023.
DOI: 10.1093/oso/9780192870513.003.0014

Convention, the UK is now required to prosecute criminal conduct, set out in the Istanbul Convention, committed abroad by a UK national or a person who is habitually resident in the UK. Before the Domestic Abuse Act 2021 came into effect, the UK had already conferred extraterritorial jurisdiction on some of the offences prescribed by the Istanbul Convention, such as murder and manslaughter (in most circumstances), sexual offences committed against a victim under the age of 18, forced marriage, and female genital mutilation. The effect of the DAA is therefore to extend extraterritorial jurisdiction to the remaining offences prescribed by the Istanbul Convention.[4]

a. *Changes to the law*

The Act extends the jurisdiction of the courts of England and Wales, Scotland, and Northern Ireland to relevant offences committed outside the UK by a UK national or a person habitually resident in that country in accordance with Article 44(1) of the Istanbul Convention.

Under section 72(1) DAA 2021, a person who is a UK national or habitually resident in England and Wales is guilty in England and Wales of that offence provided that the offence is listed in section 72(2), the act constitutes an offence under the law of the country in which the act was committed, and the act would constitute an offence if committed in England or Wales. Offences to which this provision applies include murder; manslaughter; offences relating to bodily harm under sections 18, 20, or 47 of the OAPA 1861; offences involving the administering of poison under sections 23 and 24 of the OAPA; and child destruction contrary to section 1 of the Infant Life (Preservation) Act 1929. Offences of murder or manslaughter which have been committed abroad may not be prosecuted under this section where the perpetrator would be guilty of those offences under other laws such as sections 9 and 10 of the OAPA (s 72(3)). The description of the offence in the country where it is committed does not need to match the description of the offence in the UK (s 72(4)).

When considering whether an act constitutes an offence under the law of the country in which it was committed, the court will consider this condition met unless the defendant serves a notice on the prosecution stating that the condition is not met, showing grounds for that opinion, and requiring the prosecution to prove that it is met (s 72(5)). The court may permit the defendant to require the prosecution to prove that an act would constitute an offence in the country in which it was committed if the court sees fit to do so (s 72(6)).

b. *Decision to prosecute*

The extension of extraterritorial jurisdiction does not necessarily mean that an offence committed abroad will be prosecuted in the UK. The government's general policy on the jurisdiction of UK courts in relation to international criminal offending is that criminal offending is best dealt with by the criminal justice system of the state where the offence occurred. However, where the accused is not prosecuted in the state in which the offence was allegedly committed, they may be prosecuted in the UK provided that they are physically present in this jurisdiction, and the Full Code Test is met.

[4] Home Office Policy Paper, 'Extraterritorial Jurisdiction Factsheet' (31 January 2022) https://www.gov.uk/government/publications/domestic-abuse-bill-2020-factsheets/extraterritorial-jurisdiction-factsheet (accessed 26 May 2022).

The Full Test Code requires that there is sufficient evidence to provide a realistic prospect of conviction and that it is in the public interest to prosecute the suspect.[5] When considering the public interest stage of the Full Code Test, one of the factors to consider is the impact the offending has on the community. The Code expressly recognises that the term 'community' is not restricted to communities defined by location (para 4.14(e)).

2. SECTION 73 OFFENCES AGAINST THE PERSON COMMITTED OUTSIDE THE UK: NORTHERN IRELAND

There are no substantive differences between the provisions made under this section and those made under section 72 other than the fact that, for the purposes of this section, the provisions relate to Northern Ireland, whereas section 72 applies in respect of England and Wales. Consequently, offences listed in section 73(2) which have been committed abroad may be prosecuted in Northern Ireland where they have been committed by a UK national or a habitual resident of Northern Ireland and the offence would constitute an offence if committed in Northern Ireland and would also constitute an offence in the country in which it was committed.

3. SECTION 74 AMENDMENTS RELATING TO OFFENCES COMMITTED OUTSIDE THE UK

This section further extends the circumstances in which UK nationals or habitual residents of England and Wales, Scotland, or Northern Ireland may be prosecuted in the UK for certain violent and sexual offences committed abroad.

[5] Crown Prosecution Service, 'The Code for Crown Prosecutors' (26 October 2018) https://www.cps.gov.uk/publication/code-crown-prosecutors (accessed 26 May 2022).

PART 7 OF THE ACT
MISCELLANEOUS AND GENERAL
(SECTIONS 75–91)

15

OFFENDERS: POLICE AND PROSECUTION (SECTIONS 75–77)

Martin O'Neill, Matthew Bland and Vicki McLellan*

1. SECTION 75 STRATEGY FOR PROSECUTION AND MANAGEMENT OF OFFENDERS

i. Context and Background

Before the DAA 2021 was enacted, there was considerable pressure exerted on the government to produce a perpetrator strategy in order to have a joined-up and consistent approach, in particular towards serial domestic abuse and stalking perpetrators.[1] Criticisms suggested that perpetrators were absent from the domestic abuse narrative, and that victims sometimes felt the focus of the criminal justice process was on their behaviour and responses to domestic abuse, rather than on that of the perpetrator. The absence of the perpetrator from the narrative, and in particular a specific perpetrator strategy was described as a 'missed opportunity'. In its Call for Action,[2]

* Sections 75 and 77 by Martin O'Neill, section 76 by Matthew Bland and Vicki McLellan.

[1] Drive, A domestic abuse perpetrator strategy for England & Wales: call to action (2020) 4 http://driveproject.org.uk/wp-content/uploads/2020/01/Call-to-Action-Final.pdf (accessed 27 March 2022).

[2] ibid.

Martin O'Neill, Matthew Bland and Vicki McLellan, *Offenders: Police and Prosecution (Sections 75–77)* In: *Blackstone's Guide to the Domestic Abuse Act 2021*. Edited by: Susan Edwards, David Malone, and Gillian Jones KC, Oxford University Press.
 DOI: 10.1093/oso/9780192870513.003.0015

Drive[3] noted: 'The publication of the draft Domestic Abuse Bill and the evidence on the social and economic cost of abuse laid bare the costs of continuing with "business as usual" and the need to respond to the behaviour of perpetrators head on.'[4] For instance, evidence suggested that perpetrator intervention programmes can have an effect upon repeat offending.[5] The new strategy requirement in the Act was welcomed:

> We're delighted to see a requirement for a strategic approach to DA perpetrators set into law. This is something that we and over a hundred other organisations have been campaigning for a long time. A comprehensive strategy that centres the needs of survivors will help survivors and their families to find freedom and reduce the numbers of new victims, including children.[6]

In addition, the evidence demonstrated that the criminal justice response to perpetrators of domestic abuse was often lacking, and statistics pre-pandemic demonstrate falling referrals for prosecutions and prosecutions.[7]

ii. The Section

Section 75 of the DAA states:

(1) The Secretary of State must, before the end of the period of 12 months beginning with the day on which this Act is passed, prepare and publish a document setting out a strategy for—

 (a) detecting, investigating and prosecuting offences involving domestic abuse,
 (b) assessing and managing the risks posed by individuals who commit offences involving domestic abuse, including (among others) risks associated with stalking, and
 (c) reducing the risk that such individuals commit further offences involving domestic abuse.

Explanatory notes describe this as a duty on the Secretary of State, to prepare, consult, and keep under review the strategy, and in preparation of new or amended guidance there are further duties to consult the Domestic Abuse Commissioner and any other parties deemed appropriate.[8] Whilst that is the case, there is no duty to listen to consultees, but given the importance of the strategy it is likely to be prepared following widespread consultation between agencies. The consultation process must take place for the new strategy and any subsequent revisions[9] unless any planned changes are considered to be inconsequential.[10] In relation to Part 1(a) of the proposed strategy, it

[3] The Drive project is an initiative to develop work with high harm domestic abuse perpetrators because of the gap in the provision nationwide and low take up. See http://driveproject.org.uk/ (accessed 21 March 2022).

[4] Drive (n 1) 7.

[5] ibid 44.

[6] Jo Todd, Chief Executive Officer, Respect, Home Office, Policy Paper: 'Tackling Perpetrators' (updated 31 January 2022) https://www.gov.uk/government/publications/domestic-abuse-bill-2020-factsheets/tackling-perpetrators (accessed 21 March 2022).

[7] Office for National Statistics, Domestic abuse and the criminal justice system, England and Wales (November 2020) https://www.ons.gov.uk/peoplepopulationandcommunity/crimeandjustice/articles/domesticabuseandthecriminaljusticesystemenglandandwales/november2020?msclkid=96b95de8adf111ec86ea362f20dcb14a (accessed 21 March 2022).

[8] DAA, Explanatory Notes 54 https://www.legislation.gov.uk/ukpga/2021/17/pdfs/ukpgaen_20210017_en.pdf (accessed 21 March 2022).

[9] DAA, s 75(4).

[10] DAA, s 75(5).

has been argued that the Act has succeeded in widening the scope of domestic abuse and related offences,[11] including the addition of the offence of non-fatal strangulation, extension to offences of coercive and controlling behaviour and private images, and clarification of the so-called 'rough sex' defence, which is effectively removed irrespective of consent.[12] These clarifications and additions will add to the potential offences available to prosecutors in terms of domestic abuse. However, the strategy will need to set out the importance of a robust approach to prosecuting perpetrators, because of the very low conviction rate for domestic abuse offences. Whilst the Crown Prosecution Service (CPS) has specific and updated guidance on domestic abuse and prosecution,[13] and the police have improved training for officers,[14] it has been suggested that a range of evidence could be utilised to a greater extent in these kinds of cases, and that securing such evidence during investigation could improve prosecutions. Bishop and Bettison,[15] for instance, argued in coercive and controlling behaviour cases that more use could be made by the prosecution of the hearsay provisions, res gestae, and special measures, thereby strengthening cases. In addition, training and education of practitioners and juries was considered crucial because survivor reactions to trauma may not produce the impeccable and perfect evidence expected by those unaware that inaccuracies and inconsistencies are normal. Often, witnesses are judged negatively, and conclusions are drawn about truthfulness or accuracy without allowance for the trauma.[16]

Regarding Part 1(b) of the proposed strategy (assessing and managing risk), the government had already committed to updating multi-agency public protection arrangements (MAPPA) guidance on domestic abuse and stalking and risks posed particularly by serial offenders.[17] Previous criticisms suggested that MAPPA arrangements failed to address both stalking and domestic abuse effectively, because existing arrangements were not adequate. It was argued that even where DA and stalking were considered at MAPPA, invitations were not extended to relevant DA and stalking practitioners.[18] Assessing and managing risk of perpetrators and the appropriateness of interventions to safeguard has also been a developing area. The College of Policing has issued guidance on the 'Identification, assessment and management of serial or potentially dangerous domestic abuse and stalking perpetrators'.[19] The national risk assessment protocol, the Domestic Abuse, Stalking and Harassment tool (known as DASH, which contains 27 questions and 11 stalking related questions where appropriate), became the national risk assessment tool building upon the former separation, pregnancy, escalation, community issues, stalking, and sexual assault model (a risk assessment approach known

[11] Charlotte Bishop and Vanessa Bettinson, 'Evidencing domestic violence, including behaviour that falls under the new offence of "controlling or coercive behaviour"' (2018) 22(1) *The International Journal of Evidence & Proof* 3.

[12] DAA (n 8).

[13] CPS, Domestic Abuse https://www.cps.gov.uk/crime-info/domestic-abuse?msclkid=96b99bebadf11 1ec862716a24b2c5cf8 (accessed 21 March 2022).

[14] Todd (n 6).

[15] Bishop and Bettinson (n 11).

[16] ibid.

[17] Todd (n 6).

[18] Baroness Royall, Hansard, HL vol 811, col 79 (15 March 2021) https://hansard.parliament.uk/Lords/ 2021-03-15/debates/4ECEFBDB-E347-4F76-8DFF-604EFC5A618B/DomesticAbuseBill (accessed 28 March 2022).

[19] Todd (n 6).

as SPECSS+,) which had been developed within the Metropolitan Police).[20] The tool was developed by establishing common features of domestic violence cases and creating the tool to ask questions based upon their occurrence in a given relationship.[21] The DASH tool has, however, concentrated upon violence or threats of violence and was identified as having a lack of questions around coercive and controlling behaviour and frequency of behaviours.[22] Moreover, it has been shown that police officers tend either to prioritise cases based upon violence and injury and fail to see beyond these kinds of cases where no overt violence has been used.[23] In addition, it has been criticised by police officers due to its length and the time it takes to complete, poor completion rates, and quality of completion. The first point about coercive control and frequency are reasonable and it must be pointed out that the move from a violence to a coercive control model has only taken place in the last few years, and the importance of coercive control was not accentuated when the DASH tool was created. In terms of the lack of completion or poor completion rates, this could relate to the practicalities of response officers being able to administer it when responding to numerous calls.

It seemed obvious that completing the DASH form is something that requires patience and time, the second factor not being evident or readily available in response work. In addition, poor completion rates could demonstrate a lack of awareness of its importance and signal poor attitude to these kinds of cases, which would not fill one with significant optimism about how much any new strategy may be applied in practice. A national trial is now being undertaken for a new risk assessment tool, known as domestic abuse risk assessment (DARA) to replace DASH.[24] This new tool asks fewer questions but, importantly, asks questions about coercive and controlling behaviour and frequency of occurrences.[25] Expectations of tools such as this do, however, need to be managed as they can never be 100 per cent accurate. Often, they are as good as the information provided/obtained and dependent upon the level of knowledge, understanding, and professional competence of those making professional judgments on what information they have at their disposal. Results of a risk assessment may indicate a level of risk to a person and may identify the appropriate level of safeguarding activity required to protect them. It must be stressed that risk is an ongoing issue that requires regular reassessment throughout, in order to safeguard those at risk. Whilst the DARA may serve to improve risk assessments, there are unanswered questions around professional judgement and risk beyond obvious times when DASH or DARA is used, such as when deciding upon a DAPN or DAPO requirements, when a perpetrator intervention is utilised, when

[20] Juan Jose Medina Ariza, Amanda Robinson, and Andy Myhill, 'Cheaper, faster, better: Expectations and achievements in police risk assessment of domestic abuse' (2016) 10(4) *Policing: A Journal of Policy and Practice* 341, 342.

[21] Laura Richards, DASH Risk Checklist (2009) https://www.dashriskchecklist.co.uk/wp-content/uploads/2021/12/DASH-2009.pdf (accessed 21 March 2022).

[22] Andy Myhill and Katrin Hohl, 'The "golden thread": Coercive control and risk assessment for domestic violence' (2019) 34(21–22) *Journal of Interpersonal Violence* 4477.

[23] Her Majesty's Inspectorate of Constabulary. 'Everyone's business: Improving the police response to domestic abuse' (2014) https://www.justiceinspectorates.gov.uk/hmic/publications/improving-the-police-response-to-domestic-abuse/ (accessed 28 March 2022).

[24] See College of Policing, 'Recognising and responding to vulnerability-related risks guidelines' (November 2021) https://assets.college.police.uk/s3fs-public/2021-11/Recognising-responding-vulnerability-related-risks-Evidence-review-part-2.pdf (accessed 21 March 2022).

[25] Julia Wire and Andy Myhill, 'Piloting a new approach to domestic abuse frontline risk assessment, Evaluation Report' College of Policing (2018) https://vdocuments.site/piloting-a-new-approach-to-domestic-abuse-frontline-risk-abuse-support-worker.html (accessed 29 May 2022).

a person is investigated and arrested, and when they are bailed, remanded, released, and convicted. This would extend to cases where a perpetrator is sentenced to imprisonment, when they are released, and how they are managed, and monitored by agencies and how former victims (and current partners where appropriate) are safeguarded. New consistency that the DAA 2021 brings to DAPNs and DAPOs might also assist safeguarding of victims, and victim safety is a strand of police response that is developed by Drive's proposed strategy contribution in addition to stressing the importance of any perpetrator strategy being multi agency-oriented, with all agencies having responsibility for holding perpetrators to account (see further below).[26]

In terms of Part 1(c), a clear perpetrator strategy in relation to prevention and intervention is required. Funding is necessary for perpetrator interventions, even to support behavioural conditions which can be applied under the new DAPOs and bail conditions.[27] It has also been argued that it is essential for perpetrator interventions at all levels of risk to be quality assured,[28] and it appears that already Police Crime Commission (PCC) funding is being utilised to assess quality and effectiveness of perpetrator programmes.[29] The government had already pledged £11.1 million funding for domestic abuse and stalking perpetrator programmes.[30] The Istanbul Convention[31] requires that states must set up programmes to ensure perpetrators desist from violent behaviours, so the obligation to ensure programme guidance exists in a more joined-up way is welcomed.[32]

The government has pledged to link the strategy to other important domestic abuse strategies, indicating a willingness to create a more joined-up and consistent approach.[33] The Home Office states:

The Government will also be publishing a complementary Tackling Violence Against Women and Girls Strategy. The dual strategy approach will allow us to focus on lesser understood violence against women and girls' crimes, whilst a dedicated strategy on domestic abuse, given its high-volume, high-harm nature, will ensure it gets the attention it deserves.[34]

Importantly, during the passage of the Bill Baroness Royall commented on the importance of clear strategy to ensure a joined-up approach to assessing and managing risk: She stated:

---

[26] Drive, 'Building a robust response to perpetrators: recommendations for the new Domestic Abuse Strategy' (September 2021) http://driveproject.org.uk/wp-content/uploads/2021/09/Building-a-robust-response-to-perpetrators-recommendations-for-the-new-Domestic-Abuse-Strategy-080921.pdf (accessed 28 March 2022).

[27] ibid 10.

[28] Report of the Joint Committee on the Draft Domestic Abuse Bill' (June 2019) para 18 https://publicati ons. parliament.uk/pa/jt201719/jtselect/jtddab/2075/2075.pdf' (accessed 21 March 2022).

[29] Todd (n 6).

[30] Home Office Policy Paper, 'Tackling violence against women and girls strategy' (updated November 2021) https://www.gov.uk/government/publications/tackling-violence-against-women-and-girls-strategy/tackling-violence-against-women-and-girls-strategy (accessed 27 March 2022).

[31] Istanbul Convention, art 16 https://www.coe.int/en/web/istanbul-convention/home.

[32] Note that the UK is a signatory to the Convention, but has not yet ratified it, although it has signalled an intention to do so; HM Government, 'Ratification of the Council of Europe convention on combating violence against women and domestic violence: progress report' (2020) https://www.gov.uk/government/publi cations/ratification-of-the-council-of-europe-convention-on-combating-violence-against-women-and-domes tic-violence-progress-report-2020 (accessed 21 March 2022).

[33] Todd (n 6).

[34] ibid.

I have outlined details of the perpetrator strategy which must be an integral part of the policy relating to the database. There must be a statutory requirement for police, prison and probation services to risk assess and manage perpetrators, in partnership with domestic abuse and stalking services. Unless this is mandatory, the key professionals will not always come to the table, and their participation is vital.[35]

The Drive project called for better working together and education and training of practitioners to ensure perpetrators can be held to account, and identified this (multi-agency working) as one of five separate but key elements that a perpetrator strategy should contain.[36] Other strands of the perpetrator strategy should include proven perpetrator interventions at all levels and an effective education and awareness programme of perpetrator behaviours (availability and awareness), quality assured interventions supported by ongoing research, appropriate funding to support the strategy, and leadership. In terms of ongoing research, this would be useful for all of the developments discussed within this section, including effectiveness of perpetrator criminal justice outcomes, police investigations, risk assessments and management of perpetrators, and the use of DAPN and DAPO to help minimise risk.

2. SECTION 76 POLYGRAPH CONDITIONS FOR OFFENDERS RELEASED ON LICENCE

i. Context and Background

Section 76 of the Domestic Abuse Act (DAA) 2021 specifies requirements to be met for domestic abuse offenders to receive conditions for mandatory polygraph tests as part of their release on licence. The section builds on Part 3 of the Offender Management Act 2007, section 28, which specifies the equivalent provisions for sex offenders with various amendments. These are primarily focused on establishing the sentenced offence as 'more serious', by specifying a minimum sentence term of twelve months and a range of offence categories relating to domestic abuse as defined by section 1 of the DAA 2021 and as set out in section 76(4)3C (murder, offences under the Protection from Harassment Act 1997, and specified violent offences such as grievous bodily harm and coercive and controlling behaviour).

Post-conviction sex offender testing (PCSOT) has been widely used in the United States for over a decade.[37] Following a pilot of tests on a voluntary basis in ten English probation areas,[38] and a non-randomised trial of mandatory tests in the East and West Midlands probation regions,[39] mandatory polygraph testing was introduced as a licence condition for all serious sexual offenders in 2014.[40] Prior research on PCSOT has consistently identified patterns

[35] Baroness Royall, House of Lords, Domestic Abuse Bill, vol 811, debated on Wednesday 24 March 2021 https://hansard.parliament.uk/lords/2021-03-24/debates/D7FA1B25-208B-4A89-974D-982C78A4B250/DomesticAbuseBill (accessed 27 March 2022).

[36] Drive (n 26) 9.

[37] Robert McGrath and others,, 'Current practices and emerging trends in sexual abuser management' The Safer Society 2009 North American Survey (2010).

[38] Don Grubin, 'A trial of voluntary polygraphy testing in 10 English probation areas' (2010) 22(3) *Sexual Abuse* 266.

[39] Theresa Gannon and others, 'An evaluation of mandatory polygraph testing for sexual offenders in the United Kingdom' (2014) 26(2) *Sexual Abuse* 178.

[40] Home Office, 'Mandatory polygraph tests factsheet' (2022) https://www.gov.uk/government/publications/domestic-abuse-bill-2020-factsheets/mandatory-polygraph-tests-factsheet (accessed 3 March 2022).

of increased rates of disclosure of information pertinent to the risk assessment concerning the test subjects. The nature of these disclosures is inherently subjective but can relate to behaviour or thoughts and feelings. Until now, however, no randomised trial has taken place to establish a direct cause and effect relationship.

Polygraph tests involve the measurement of physiological responses, including heart rate, blood pressure, and breathing. A trained examiner monitors changes in these measurements to assess the truthfulness of statements made by the person being tested. Analyses of multiple polygraph studies have claimed the accuracy of results to be in the region of 80–90 per cent,[41] but the controversy around the use of the technique endures, maintained by competing positions in politics, science, and law. Some scholars make the case that polygraph testing should no longer be permitted for use in the penal system.[42] The primary factor in this position is that the polygraph procedure is unscientific, with no single physiological indicator of truth (or deception) in existence. Other research identifies consistent findings of new information arising from polygraph tests.[43] The use of polygraph in the management of sex offenders began in the United States in the 1990s and the American Polygraph Association's model policy informed the development of UK legislation in 2009.[44] The utility of post-conviction testing is less clear, however. Most studies of PCSOT report increases in information disclosure but not in reoffending. Few studies have involved comparison groups and none, to date, has been evaluated with a causal design.

The use of post-conviction polygraph testing for domestic abuse offenders has never been undertaken. The DAA is the first piece of legislation in the world to include such a condition. Accordingly, the UK government is conducting a three-year pilot of its use of the new legislation in four probation areas (all in the North of England). The Ministry of Justice has appointed independent researchers to conduct a randomised controlled trial to measure the impact of the pilot. Nationwide implementation of the new legislation is contingent upon the results of this trial, which will be laid before Parliament around 2025.

a. *Who is eligible for a polygraph licence condition?*

Under the new Act, licence conditions for mandatory polygraph tests are only applicable for eligible offenders, as specified in subsections 2, 3A, 3B, and 3C. To be eligible, offenders must have been convicted for a domestic abuse-related offence (defined as set out in Part 1 of the Act) with a sentence of twelve months or more (for example: homicide, attempted homicide, coercive and controlling behaviour, grievous bodily harm with intent). Offenders with concurrent sentences over twelve months, but for which the domestic abuse related component is less than twelve months, are ineligible.

Only specific crime classifications are eligible for the licence condition. Sexual offences that meet the new statutory definition are eligible but are excluded from the pilot if the offender would otherwise be subject to a mandatory polygraph condition under the Offender Management Act 2007. Breaches of a domestic abuse protection order or a restraining order

---

[41] Mike Gougler and others, 'Meta-analytic survey of criterion accuracy of validated polygraph techniques' (2011) 40(4) *Polygraph* 194.

[42] Kyriakos Kotsoglou and Marion Oswald, 'Not "Very English": on the Use of the Polygraph by the Penal System in England and Wales' (2021) 85(3) *The Journal of Criminal Law* 189

[43] Don Grubin, 'The case for polygraph testing of sex offenders' (2008) 13(2) *Legal and Criminological Psychology* 177.

[44] Don Grubin and others 'Post-conviction polygraph testing of sex offenders' (2019) 31(2) *International Review of Psychiatry* 141.

or offences of homicide, types of violent crime specified in Part 1 of Schedule 15 to the Criminal Justice Act 2003, and coercive and controlling behaviour are also eligible. The Ministry of Justice has further stated that it will only consider individuals to be eligible for the licence condition if they are over 18 (in accordance with Part 3 s 28(2b) of the Offender Management Act 2007) and have been assessed as very high or high risk by a nationally accredited risk assessment tool.[45]

b. *What does a polygraph licence condition entail?*

Polygraph tests are administered by probation practitioners, recruited and trained specifically for the purpose of conducting polygraph tests. For the period of the Ministry of Justice's pilot, each of the four probation regions has an assigned polygraph examiner. Examinations are carried out to standards set by the American Polygraph Association. Polygraph tests are administered at set intervals during the period of an offender's licence. The first test is given three months after release and the frequency of subsequent tests is dependent on the results of that first test. Tests can have three broad categories of result: (1) a 'significant response' is recorded, in which the test indicates a deception; (2) no significant response is recorded; or (3) no result is possible. If the outcome is (1), then another test is scheduled for three months after the first. If the outcome is (2), a test is scheduled for six months later and, if the outcome is (3), then a test is scheduled for the following month.

While administering a polygraph test, the examiner will conduct a series of pre-test questions. Previous research has suggested that many disclosures relevant to risk assessment are made during this part of the process[46] rather than the test itself. Such disclosures may include information about new relationships or risky thoughts and feelings on the part of the person on probation. The entire process takes several hours, after which a report is compiled and submitted to the probation staff member responsible for the management of the offender. The content of the test is not admissible in court and a 'deception indicated' outcome (1) cannot directly result in the offender being recalled to prison. However, the nature of disclosures made during the process may lead to a change in risk assessment or uncovering of the breach of another licence condition and these may result in a recall. Equally, refusal to undertake the test is considered a breach of licence. In these senses, the polygraph process is a potential deterrent measure in itself, entirely separate to discourse about the accuracy of the testing process.

c. *How is the legislation being used?*

A randomised controlled trial design has been implemented to assess the impact of the licence condition relative to eligible cases without the licence condition. The research has been designed and administered by the Cambridge Centre for Evidence-Based Policing[47] to a standard of rigour sufficient to draw robust inferences about cause and effect. The experiment involves the random assignment of eligible offenders to two conditions: intervention (in which the mandatory polygraph test condition is added to the licence) or control (in which it is not). The assignment is applied by algorithm to both determinate and indeterminate sentence individuals and, once made, the assignment persists for the duration of the licence.

[45] See Mandatory polygraph test factsheet (n 40).
[46] Gannon and others (n 39).
[47] See https://www.cambridge-ebp.co.uk (accessed 25 April 2022).

A dedicated trial manager ensures compliance with the assignment and will track the administration of the tests over the full course of the pilot's three years.

The evaluation will draw conclusions on a range of impact measures including: (1) the prevalence, frequency, and severity of reoffending among the participants; (2) the rate of recall to prison; and (3) the number and nature of risk-relevant disclosures recorded by probation. The pilot will be able to report robust findings on the effect of the mandatory polygraph licence condition on these outcomes by virtue of its random assignment design, which enables researchers to control for potential confounding factors.[48]

The pilot of the new legislation began in July 2021 and will conclude in June 2024. The final reports will be laid before Parliament to facilitate decisions on the future use of post-conviction polygraph testing for domestic abuse offenders.

ii. Critical Commentary

The utility of mandatory post-conviction polygraph testing on domestic abuse perpetrators is unknown and this section of the DAA will bring about the first experimental evidence on polygraph testing anywhere in the world. Whatever the results of the three-year pilot, one's perceptions of the impact of the licence condition is likely to depend on individual perspective. It is entirely feasible that this legislation will result in increased information available to probation practitioners for the purposes of risk assessment with little or no observed change in recidivism because there are many factors that may influence offender management strategy between the undertaking of a polygraph test and the recall to prison or successful reintegration of a person on probation. At the same time, probation and other criminal justice professionals might view the conditions as a worthwhile source of potential information in the same circumstances.

All possibilities remain open. At the time of writing, more than 500 individuals have entered the pilot in just over six months. It is likely that the final intake at the end of the three-year pilot will exceed that of any prior polygraph study and the results will provide the Ministry of Justice with tangible evidence on which to make future decisions regarding the use of the legislation. This section of the legislation is specifically aimed at reducing the risk of harm that offenders pose, and the Act should lead to definitive answers to the question of whether mandatory polygraph licence conditions fulfil this purpose.

3. SECTION 77 GUIDANCE ABOUT DISCLOSURE OF INFORMATION BY UK POLICE FORCES

i. Context and Background

The disclosure of previous criminal acts of a perpetrator to parties, with a view to protect putative victims, has generally been catered for under the common law in the form of a reasonableness and necessity test of a 'pressing need' to disclose.[49] Disclosure in this and other contexts has been deemed essential for public protection, for example, in relation to sexual

---

[48] Barek Ariel, Matthew Bland, and Alex Sutherland,. *Experimental Designs* (Sage 2022).

[49] Jamie Grace, *Domestic Abuse Disclosure Schemes* (Kindle edn, Springer International Publishing 2022) 235.

offenders against children in the light of the murder of Sarah Payne in 2000.[50] In that case, it was discovered that killer Roy Whiting lived in the locality, unknown to members of the community. They were in no position to be able to find out about his existence, whereabouts, or past offending, which Sarah's mother suggested might have helped to save Sarah's life had she known.[51] As a result, there were calls to adopt in relation to child sex offenders 'Megan's law', a US scheme that allowed public knowledge of the identity and whereabouts of offenders (i.e., addresses). The scheme in the USA was, however, controversial, because such public knowledge allowed vigilantism to occur, causing serious harm and death to those 'outed', threats made to their lives, and people being victims of arson and having to flee their homes. These developments arguably led convicted sexual offenders in the community to go underground, effectively more remote from the authorities than before the laws were enacted.[52]

The UK government piloted (and then rolled out nationally) the Child Sex Offender Disclosure Scheme (CSODS), allowing members of the public to report concerns to the police about people in contact with children (either as a parent or any other concerned party).[53] This involved police in ensuring that the person reporting was genuine, checking intelligence around the subject of the request, and then carefully considering and managing disclosure in defined circumstances. The scheme ensured that the disclosee signed a confidentiality agreement, and that any such disclosure was only given to people in a position to protect children.[54] Therefore, a person who alerted the police to concerns would not necessarily receive disclosure unless they were the person in a position to protect any relevant child.[55]

Following the murder of Clare Wood by her former partner,[56] a campaign was launched by Clare's father to have a formal process in place to allow the previous violent history of individuals to be disclosed so that cases like Clare's could be prevented in future.[57] The suggestion was that a scheme could be created where individuals could ask the police if their partner had any history of domestic violence or abuse, and the police would make inquiries and disclose in appropriate circumstances. There was a wealth of support for these proposals and. given the assumed success of CSODS,[58] it was felt that a similar scheme would provide a means by which actual or potential victims could find out about perpetrator history. In 2014, the

---

[50] *Re Whiting (application under para 3 of Sch 22 to the Criminal Justice Act 2003)* [2010] All ER (D) 23 (Jun), [2010] EWHC 1329 (QB).

[51] Home Office, 'Child sex offender review' (2007); Kristen M Zgoba and Devin Cowan, 'Sexual offense legislation across the pond: A review of community sentiment toward the United Kingdom's implementation of Sarah's Law' (2020) 32(4) *Sexual Abuse* 477.

[52] Jill S Levenson and Leo P Cotter, 'The Effect of Megan's Law on Sex Offender Reintegration' (2005) 21 *J Contemp Crim Just* 49.

[53] Terry Thomas and Daniel J Marsh, *The Sex Offender Register: Politics, Policy and Public Opinion* (1st edn, Routledge 2021) 144–52; HM Government, Child sexual offender disclosure scheme guidance document (2010) 2 https://assets.publishing.service.gov.uk/government/uploads/system/uploads/attachment_data/file/118125/disclosure-scheme-guidance.pdf (accessed 25 April 2022).

[54] ibid.

[55] Zgoba and Cowan (n 51).

[56] Home Office, 'Domestic Violence Disclosure Scheme (DVDS) Guidance' (December 2016) 4 https://assets.publishing.service.gov.uk/government/uploads/system/uploads/attachment_data/file/575361/DVDS_guidance_FINAL_v3.pdf (accessed 25 April 2022).

[57] Marian Duggan, 'Reflections on the domestic violence disclosure scheme (England and Wales)' (2019) 3(2) *Journal of Gender-based Violence* 249.

[58] Hazel Kemshall, Gill Kelly, and Bernadette Wilkinson, 'Child Sex Offender Public Disclosure Scheme: The views of applicants using the English pilot disclosure scheme' (2012) 18(2) *Journal of Sexual Aggression* 164.

Domestic Violence Disclosure Scheme (DVDS) was piloted in four police services, including Greater Manchester Police (GMP), where Clare was killed. GMP were criticised for systemic and individual failings in their response to Clare's reports of violence preceding her murder, including their knowledge of undisclosed information about previous history, which could have informed a risk assessment.[59] The scheme, like the Child Sex Disclosure Scheme, was not created by statute, an issue that has received subsequent criticism.[60] The nature of the scheme is described:

Within existing legislation and common law, police have the power to disclose information to an individual, if it might help protect them, about previous violent offending by their partner. The DVDS pilot aimed to introduce a consistent process for this. The pilot tested two processes for disclosing this information, 'Right to Ask' where a disclosure request is triggered by a member of the public directly contacting the police about a partner, and 'Right to Know' where a disclosure request is triggered by police or partner agencies based on information that an individual is at risk of harm from their partner.[61]

The creation, implementation, and effectiveness of the scheme has been criticised for a number of reasons. Whilst described as a public relations success for the police, it was argued that early guidance on the DVDS gave insufficient attention to procedural rights of subjects, particularly in relation to Articles 6 and 8 of the European Convention on Human Rights (ECHR) as incorporated in the Human Rights Act 1998, with regard to right to fair trial, privacy and consultation, notification, and proportionality.[62] The pilot assessment recommended improvements in aspects of the scheme, including training for police officers to ensure understanding of the process and to develop consistency in disclosure decisions, multi-agency support for non-disclosures, and actions to raise awareness of the scheme locally.[63] It has also been argued that the scheme places too much emphasis upon victim engagement and self-regulation (of themselves and their vulnerable children),[64] when such people are vulnerable and in need of support through the process.[65] This enables a potential blame culture described as 'responsibilisation' of victims.[66] Support for victims through the process is often absent due to poor resourcing. Other problematic issues relate to the inconsistent use throughout England and Wales,[67] fragmentation of information since existing information

---

[59] IPCC, Independent Investigation: Greater Manchester Police contact with Clare Wood prior to her death (2011) https://webarchive.nationalarchives.gov.uk/ukgwa/20101224054721/http:/www.ipcc.gov.uk/clare_wood_report_final_10_march.pdf (accessed 12 April 2022).

[60] Vanessa Bettinson, 'Adding to the domestic abuse criminal law framework: the Domestic Abuse Act 2021' (2022) 2 *Crim LR* 88.

[61] Home Office, Domestic Violence Disclosure Scheme (DVDS) Pilot Assessment (2015) 2 https://assets.publishing.service.gov.uk/government/uploads/system/uploads/attachment_data/file/260894/DVDS_assessment_report.pdf (accessed 25 April 2022).

[62] Jamie Grace, 'Clare's Law, or the national Domestic Violence Disclosure Scheme: the contested legalities of criminality information sharing' (2015) 79(1) *The Journal of Criminal Law* 36, 45.

[63] Home Office (n 61) 5.

[64] Katerina Hadjimatheou, '"Social care told me I had to": Empowerment and Responsibilisation in the Domestic Violence Disclosure Scheme' (2021) 62(2) *The British Journal of Criminology* 320.

[65] Grace (n 49) 235.

[66] Marian Duggan, 'Victim hierarchies in the domestic violence disclosure scheme' (2018) 24(2) *International Review of Victimology* 199, 206; Sophia Graca, 'Domestic violence policy and legislation in the UK: A discussion of immigrant women's vulnerabilities' (2017) 23(1) *European Journal of Current Legal Issues* 1.

[67] Grace (n 49) 232.

(including from other agencies) is often not available, and the potential for either false positives or false negatives to be a product of the scheme (false positives could relate to inaccurate prediction of risk due to incomplete or error prone intelligence,[68] whilst false negatives could mean incomplete intelligence being gathered and a low level of risk inaccurately predicted, when in fact the risk is higher). False negatives are particularly concerning, because this may provide a false sense of security for actual or potential victims.[69]

ii. The Section

Section 77 of the DAA provides:

(1) The Secretary of State must issue guidance to chief officers of police about the disclosure of police information by police forces for the purposes of preventing domestic abuse.

'Police information' means information held by a police force.

(2) Each chief officer of police of a police force must have regard to any guidance issued under this section.

(3) The Secretary of State may from time to time revise any guidance issued under this section.

The Act does not place the DVDS on a statutory footing and opportunity to codify the process has been lost, which has been criticised.[70] What the Act does is mandate the Home Secretary to issue statutory guidance to chief officers on the disclosure of information for prevention purposes, although section 77(2) does not mandate the chief officer of a Home Office police service (or British Transport Police) to follow the guidance.[71] It states that the chief officer must *have regard* to any such guidance, and can only depart from it with good reason.[72] The government suggested that the statutory guidance would also ensure the visibility of the scheme and encourage greater use of it.[73] There is opportunity to create up to date and relevant guidance and it is expected that this will be available within a year of enactment. On a positive note, the government intends to provide examples on issues such as minimum levels of practitioner knowledge and experience effectively to discharge functions under the scheme, timescales under each route, minimum standards of investigation into applicant information and intelligence gathering, multi-agency engagement, risk assessments, the disclosure decision and example wording, and guidance on the term 'reasonable and proportionate' in line with Human Rights Act (HRA) 1998, Data Protection Act (DPA) 1998, and General Data Protection Regulation (GDPR) 2018 considerations.[74] If effective, this could reduce the level of inconsistency that the scheme has been criticised for in the past.[75] There have been particular concerns about the low use the police make of the 'right to know' route

[68] ibid 70.

[69] ibid 230.

[70] Bettinson (n 60) 11.

[71] DAA (n 8) 55 [369] https://www.legislation.gov.uk/ukpga/2021/17/pdfs/ukpgaen_20210017_en.pdf?msclkid=0591f460c4a511ecbf42b1bff149a0ab (accessed 25 April 2022).

[72] ibid.

[73] Home Office, 'Transforming the Response to Domestic Abuse: Consultation Response and Draft Bill' (January 2019) https://assets.publishing.service.gov.uk/government/uploads/system/uploads/attachment_data/file/772202/CCS1218158068-Web_Accessible.pdf (accessed 28 March 2022).

[74] DAA (n 8) [372].

[75] Home Office (n 24) [134]; Bettinson (n 60) 89.

in the scheme[76] and this is an area where clear and unambiguous guidance could help. When issuing guidance or revised guidance, the Secretary of State must consult with the Domestic Abuse Commissioner, the National Police Chiefs Council (NPCC), and any other relevant parties unless any subsequent changes are considered to be minimal.[77] Unsurprisingly, the guidance and subsequent amendments must be published.[78]

iii. Critical Commentary

There are still concerns around the potential effectiveness of the scheme despite the changes provided for in the new Act. For instance:

Lucy Hadley, of Women's Aid, hoped it would also improve consistency across police forces in the use of the DVDS. She told us, however, that the DVDS was not a 'silver bullet' because 'most survivors will not bring criminal convictions or criminal proceedings, therefore their perpetrator will not be known to the police, so that perpetrator will never show up on the disclosure scheme'.[79]

In further response to the Draft Bill, there was strong criticism of the government's wish to increase the use of the DVDS because evidence of its utility is absent.[80] There was particular criticism of the length of time for disclosure to take place, which can take up to six weeks.[81] The addition of minimum timescales in the statutory guidance may go some way to alleviating this criticism, although adherence to the timescales assumes resources commensurate with the volume of requests. In addition, the paucity of requests and disclosures since the DVDS's inception in 2014, measured against the number of rising domestic abuse incidents reported every year, suggests there may be significant problems of knowledge of the scheme, lack of take-up (for multiple reasons), poor implementation of the scheme by the police, or a lack of effectiveness of the scheme in general.[82] Of concern too is the suggestion that use of the scheme can in fact increase the risk to victims.[83] It has been argued that the scheme should provide for monitoring of cases following disclosures under the scheme in order to ensure greater protection for actual or potential victims.[84] Ongoing risk assessment by the police in these cases is a crucial aspect which requires more careful consideration.

[76] House of Lords, House of Commons, Joint Committee on the Draft Domestic Abuse Bill Draft Domestic Abuse Bill First Report of Session 2017–19 [143] https://publications.parliament.uk/pa/jt201719/jtselect/jtddab/2075/2075.pdf (accessed 25 April 2022).

[77] DAA 2021, s 77(4), (5).

[78] ibid s 77(6).

[79] DAA (n 8) [134].

[80] Written evidence from Professor Sandra Walklate (Liverpool and Monash Universities) and Dr Kate Fitz-Gibbon (Monash University) (DVB0012), House of Lords, House of Commons, Joint Committee on the Draft Domestic Abuse Bill, First Report of Session 2017–19; Joint Committee (n 76) [135].

[81] Joint Committee (n 76) [135].

[82] ibid [137].

[83] Duggan (n 66).

[84] ibid.

16
HOMELESSNESS, TENANCY AND CHARGING (SECTIONS 78–80)

Stephanie Harrison KC and Marina Sergides, Susan Edwards*

1. SECTIONS 78–79

i. Context and Background

Sections 78 and 79 of the Domestic Abuse Act (DAA) 2021 is the response to many years of campaigning on behalf of domestic abuse survivors who, needing to flee domestic abuse, were deterred by the risk of homelessness and finding themselves in a disadvantaged housing position. Until the DAA, there was no obligation on local housing authorities to provide refuges in their borough[1] and, upon making a homelessness application, there was no certainty that accommodation would be provided at all.

The DAA made some important changes, increasing a survivor's access to housing support and greater security of tenure in some circumstances. But many campaigners argue that the changes did not go far enough. Data from the Department for Levelling Up, Housing and Communities shows that, between July and September 2021, the second most common reason for those owed a duty to accommodate was domestic abuse[2] and none of the changes

* Sections 78–79 by Stephanie Harrison KC and Marina Sergides, section 80 by Susan Edwards.

[1] By way of s 57(1)(a) of the DAA, each relevant local authority in England must now assess, or make arrangements for the assessment of, the need for accommodation -based support in its area. That 'accommodation-based support' means support, in relation to domestic abuse, provided to victims of domestic abuse, or their children, who reside in relevant accommodation.

[2] https://assets.publishing.service.gov.uk/government/uploads/system/uploads/attachment_data/file/1050291/Statutory_Homelessness_Stats_Release_July-September_2021.pdf (accessed 25 April 2022).

Stephanie Harrison KC and Marina Sergides, Susan Edwards, *Homelessness, Tenancy and Charging (Sections 78–80)* In: *Blackstone's Guide to the Domestic Abuse Act 2021*. Edited by Susan Edwards, David Malone, and Gillian Jones KC, Oxford University Press.
 DOI: 10.1093/oso/9780192870513.003.0016

introduced by the DAA apply to those survivors with a prohibition on recourse to public funds[3] because of their immigration status.

At the time of writing, two further consultations have been announced:

The first[4] will consider removing the 'local connection' requirement for domestic abuse victims, which prevents survivors from applying for social housing if they do not have a local connection to the area.[5] This often forces survivors to live in the same communities as their perpetrators and prevents them from living in a place that is suitable to their overall needs. It is proposed that the local connection requirements are removed for abuse survivors who are living in refuges, social housing, the private rented sector, and privately owned accommodation.[6]

The second[7] will consider whether and how to change current rules that make it difficult for survivors to remove their perpetrators from joint tenancies. Currently, a perpetrator can terminate a joint tenancy by serving a notice to quit on the landlord, leaving the remaining tenant (the survivor) with no tenancy.[8] The impact of this is that survivors can feel forced to stay in their home or are at risk of being made homeless by their abuser. The consultations closed on 10 May 2022.

ii. Section 78 (Amending sections 177 and 189 of the Housing Act 1996)

Before the introduction of section 78 DAA, a person fleeing domestic abuse who sought housing assistance as homeless under Part VII of the 1996 Housing Act, would only be owed a section 193 'main housing duty'[9] by the local housing authority if they were homeless,[10]

[3] Solace, Women's Aid, and others have called for the protections afforded by the DAA to be extended to survivors with no recourse to public funds https://www.solacewomensaid.org/policy-campaigns/domestic-abuse-act. See further Part III of this Guide.

[4] https://www.gov.uk/government/consultations/consultation-on-local-connection-requirements-for-social-housing-for-victims-of-domestic-abuse/local-connection-requirements-for-social-housing-for-victims-of-domestic-abuse (accessed 25 April 2022).

[5] By way of the Housing Act 1996, s 166A(5)(c), the local connection category enables discrimination in a housing allocation scheme, among those within the reasonable preference categories, in favour of local applicants. Accordingly, some local housing authorities still require applicants to have a 'local connection' before they can be considered within their allocation scheme under Part 6 of the 1996.

[6] On 25 January 2022, the Secretary of State for Housing, Communities and Local government published guidance on what local authorities should have regard to in exercising their functions under Part 6. At para 29 the guidance states: 'Paragraphs 19 and 20 above should ensure that those who need to move between local authority districts in order to escape domestic abuse are not disadvantaged by the residency or local connection test'. See Statutory Guidance improving access to social housing for victims of domestic abuse (Updated 25 January 2022) https://www.gov.uk/government/publications/improving-access-to-social-housing-for-victims-of-domestic-abuse/improving-access-to-social-housing-for-victims-of-domestic-abuse (accessed 25 April 2022).

[7] Open consultation: Consultation on the impacts of joint tenancies on victims of domestic abuse https://www.gov.uk/government/consultations/consultation-on-the-impacts-of-joint-tenancies-on-victims-of-domestic-abuse (accessed 25 April 2022).

[8] *Hammersmith & Fulham LBC v Monk* [1991] UKHL 6.

[9] Section 193(2) of the 1996 Act. This is the highest duty to secure accommodation that can be owed under the 1996 Act and will only be owed where a person is homeless, eligible for assistance, have not become homeless intentionally and have a priority need and the 'relief duty' (owed to the applicant under s 189B(2) of the 1996 Act has come to an end.

[10] Sections 175–78 of the 1996 Act: The legal definition of 'homeless' is contained in these four interrelated sections. By way of s 177 of the 1996, a person is homeless if it is 'not reasonable for a person to continue to occupy accommodation if it is probable that this will lead to violence or domestic abuse against him,

eligible,[11] in priority need[12] and unintentionally homeless.[13] Each of these components has its own statutory meaning.

Section 78 of the DAA makes several important changes that will entitle survivors of domestic abuse to the main housing duty without having to prove separately they are *vulnerable* by virtue of the abuse they have suffered (assuming all other components are met).

a. *Amendment to section 189 of the 1996 Act: section 189 before the amendments introduced by section 78 of the Act*

Before the amendment introduced by section 78, a person was in priority need if they fell within one of the prescribed four categories of people in section 189 of the 1996 Housing Act or within one of the further six categories of people within the Homelessness (Priority Need for Accommodation) (England) Order 2002[14] (2002 Order). Article 6 of the 2002 Order conferred a priority need to: '(6) A person who is vulnerable as a result of ceasing to occupy accommodation by reason of violence from another person or threats of violence from another person which are likely to be carried out'.

In these circumstances, the local authority would have to be satisfied that:

(a) the person ceased to occupy accommodation *as a result* of violence from another person or threats of violence from another person that were likely to be carried out, *and*

(b) the person was *vulnerable, and*

(c) the person was vulnerable *as a result* of having ceased to occupy accommodation *because* of violence from another or threats of violence that were likely to be carried out.

There was no statutory definition of domestic violence in the housing jurisdiction and the Housing Act 1996 was concerned with domestic 'violence', not 'abuse'. Children were also not recognised as survivors of domestic abuse in their own right. In *Yemshaw v London Borough of Hounslow*,[15] Baroness Hale quoting the Practice Direction (Residence and Contact Orders) (No 2)[16] said, 'domestic violence includes physical violence, threatening or intimidating behaviour and any other form of abuse which, directly or indirectly, may give rise to the risk of harm'.[17] Although the intention was to benefit those fleeing domestic violence, the provision related to all forms of violence.[18]

Importantly, to qualify for the local authority's full housing duty, a survivor had to also be 'vulnerable,' as a result of that violence. This meant that the local housing authority had to ask the question set out in *Panayiotou v Waltham Forest London Borough Council, Smith v*

---

or against (a) a person who normally resides with him as a member of his family or (b) any other person who might reasonably be expected to reside with him'. The reference to 'domestic abuse' in s 177 of the 1996 Act is an amendment introduced by s 78 of the DAA.

[11] Section 185 of the 1996 Act: 'eligibility' normally (but not exclusively) depends on the immigration status of the person seeking assistance.

[12] Section 189 of the 1996 Act.

[13] ibid s 191.

[14] SI 2002/2051, Appendix 2.

[15] [2011] UKSC 3, [2011] 1 WLR 433, [2011] HLR 16, (SC).

[16] 1 WLR 251.

[17] *Yemshaw* (n 15) [28].

[18] See *Hussain v Waltham Forest London Borough Council* [2015] EWCA Civ, [2015] HLR 16 (CA), where the Court of Appeal held that the extended definition of 'violence' in *Yemshaw* (n 15) extended to people fleeing from violence that was not domestic violence.

Haringey London Borough Council, namely 'whether, compared to an ordinary person if made homeless, the applicant, in consequence of a characteristic within section 189(1)(c), would suffer or be at risk of suffering harm or detriment which the ordinary person would not suffer or be at risk of suffering such that the harm or detriment would make a noticeable difference to his ability to deal with the consequences of homelessness'.[19]

Previous versions of the Homelessness Code of Guidance for Local Authorities[20] gave guidance on what local housing authorities had to consider when determining whether an applicant was 'vulnerable' as a result of having to leave accommodation because of violence from another person, or threats that are likely to be carried out. This included whether the applicant had any existing support networks (family and friends) and whether there was a continuing threat from the perpetrator. This left much to the evaluative assessment of the local housing authority and, in practical terms, survivors of domestic abuse would often have to persuade local authorities of their vulnerability. Whilst the duty to make inquiries remained with the local housing authority, survivors would often be in a position where they would have to present evidence that the violence, they had suffered was likely to cause them 'harm' or be at 'risk of harm' as defined by *Panayiotou*, often requiring them to obtain evidence from social workers, refuge workers or any other independent evidence that would support their application.

Furthermore, Article 6 of the 2002 Order required that a survivor 'ceased to occupy' their accommodation before the local authority could consider whether they were vulnerable. In leaving their accommodation, survivors would place themselves in a precarious position—the possibility that the local housing authority would not find them to be either a victim of domestic violence or not vulnerable because of it, but whilst having left the accommodation risked rendering themselves homeless. Accordingly, section 189 and the 2002 Order were often seen as creating unnecessary obstacles for survivors of domestic abuse facing homelessness and in need of accommodation.

b. *Amendment to section 189 of the 1996 Act: section 189 after the amendments introduced by section 78 of the Act*

Section 78(5) of the DAA amends section 189(1) of the 1996 Housing Act and inserts a fifth and entirely new category of priority need. A person will now have priority need for accommodation if they are: '(e) A person who is homeless as a result of that person being a victim of domestic abuse'.[21] 'Domestic abuse' has the meaning given by section 1 of the Act[22] and children are now recognised as survivors of domestic abuse in their own right.

This significant amendment simplifies the position and brings English law into line with the law in Wales.[23] It means that survivors of domestic abuse no longer need to establish they are 'vulnerable' before a full housing duty is owed, and local housing authorities no longer have to carry out the evaluative assessment. They simply must answer two questions to ascertain

[19] *Panayiotou v Waltham Forest London Borough Council, Smith v Haringey London Borough Council* [2017] EWCA Civ 1624, [2017] HLR 48 (CA) [64].

[20] The Homelessness Code of Guidance for Local Authorities is issued by the Secretary of State for the Department of Levelling up, Housing and Communities in accordance with s 182 of the 1996 Housing Act (February 2018) https://assets.publishing.service.gov.uk/media/607970e9d3bf7f401659fdda/Homelessness_code_of_guidance_31_Dec_2020_to_18_Apr_2021.pdf (accessed 25 April 2022).

[21] See s 189(e) of the 1996 Act.

[22] See s 78(5) of the 2021 Act.

[23] Housing (Wales) Act 2014, s 70.

the relevant facts: (a) is the person a victim of domestic abuse? and if so, (b) is the applicant homeless as a result?

The most recent Homelessness Code of Guidance was updated on 12 October 2021 and reflects the changes introduced by section 78 of the 2021 Act.[24] Chapter 21 gives extensive guidance to local housing authorities and social housing providers on the issue of domestic abuse and should be considered in its entirety.[25] It provides guidance on the definition of domestic abuse, how it affects the lives of victims, identifying abuse and preventing homelessness, the factors to have regard to when carrying out their inquiries (in particular, the need to carry out investigations in a safe manner) and suitability. The guidance emphases the need to address each application on a case-by-case basis, recognising that local housing authorities need to be flexible in the way in which they accept homeless applications and how they communicate with victims.

Article 6 of the 2002 Order remains in force but has, as a consequence the specific provision in section 78, been amended so that the reference to 'violence' does not include violence that is domestic abuse (where 'domestic abuse' has the meaning given by section 1 of the DAA[26]).

c. *Referrals*

By virtue of section 198 of the 1996 Act, where a local housing authority is subject to a duty under sections 189B or 193 of the 1996 Act but considered that the conditions for referral to another local authority were met, they could notify the other local authority of their opinion.

However, before amendments introduced by section 78 of the DAA, the conditions for referral would not be met if neither the applicant nor any person who might reasonably be expected to reside with them will run the risk of domestic violence in that other district.[27]

The conditions under section 198(2) of the 1996 Act are amended by the DAA so that a local connection referral can only be made if the applicant, or any person who lives with them, will not be at risk of '*domestic abuse*' in the other local housing authority's district.

d. *Amendment to section 177 of the 1996 Act*

By virtue of section 175 of the 1996 Act, a person shall not be treated as having accommodation (i.e., homeless) unless it is accommodation which it would be 'reasonable for that person to continue to occupy'. Before its amendment by section 78 of the DAA, section 177(1) of the 1996 Act provided that it was 'not reasonable for a person to continue to occupy' accommodation if it was *probable* that this would lead to domestic violence or other violence against them, or against a person who normally resides with them as a member of their family, or any other person who might reasonably be expected to reside with them'.

Violence meant violence from another person or threats of violence that were likely to be carried out, and violence was domestic violence if it was from a person associated[28] with the victim.[29]

---

[24] Chapter 21 of the Homelessness Code of Guidance 2021. See also recent updates https://www.gov.uk/guidance/homelessness-code-of-guidance-for-local-authorities/updates (most recent update March 2022) (accessed 25 April 2022).

[25] Housing authorities are required to have regard to this statutory guidance in exercising their functions relating to homelessness and prevention of homelessness, including their functions under Part 7 of the 1996 Act, in accordance with s 182(1) of the 1996 Act.

[26] See s 78(8) of the DAA.

[27] Section 198(2)(c) of the 1996 Act.

[28] 'Associated person' defined by ibid s 178.

[29] ibid s 177.

Section 78 of the Act brings the law broadly in line with the case law and amends section 177(1) of the 1996 Act such that it is now not reasonable for a person to continue to occupy accommodation if it is 'probable that this will lead to violence or domestic abuse against him, or against a person who normally resides with him as a member of his family or any other person who might reasonably be expected to reside with him'. Domestic abuse has the meaning given by section 1 of the DAA.

'Probable' means more likely than not.[30] It is not necessary to show that domestic abuse *has* occurred or that it *will* occur in the future. For survivors of domestic abuse, this is a relatively low threshold to overcome. It must be 'probable' that a single incident of one of the abusive behaviours set out in section 1 of the DAA will occur.

Where the duty to inquire into priority need arises, the legal obligation is on the local housing authority to make 'such inquiries as are necessary' (s 184(1) of the 1996 Act). Chapter 21 of the Homelessness Code of Guidance for Local Authorities[31] sets what local housing authorities should consider when identifying whether someone is or has been the victim of domestic abuse. At paragraph 21.24, local housing authorities are warned that their 'inquiries do not provoke further violence and abuse' and they should 'not approach the alleged perpetrator'. They should also not have a blanket approach toward domestic abuse which requires corroborative or police evidence to be provided.

iii. Section 79 of the Domestic Abuse Act 2021 (Introducing section 81ZA Housing Act 1985)

In 2017, the government made a manifesto commitment to ensure 'that victims who have lifetime tenancies and flee violence are able to secure a new lifetime tenancy automatically' and section 79 gives effect to that promise. Section 79 amends Part 4, Housing Act 1985 (secure tenants and rights of secure tenants) by inserting a new section 81ZA (the 1985 Act).

Section 81ZA provides that where a local authority offers a tenancy to a person who is or was previously a 'qualifying tenant' *and* the new tenancy is granted to a person who has been a victim of domestic abuse *and* the new tenancy is granted for reasons connected with that abuse, the local authority must grant a lifetime secure tenancy. In this instance, a local authority cannot offer a flexible tenancy[32] (as it would otherwise be entitled to do) even if the local authority normally operates a flexible tenancy policy.

'Abuse' has the same meaning as it does in section 1 of the DAA.[33] The local housing authority must be satisfied that the person to whom the tenancy is granted, or a member of

---

[30] *Bond v Leicester City Council* [2001] EWCA Civ 1544, [2002] HLE 6 (CA).

[31] Homelessness Code of Guidance for Local Authorities (20 March 2022) https://assets.publishing.service.gov.uk/media/5ef9d8613a6f4023cf12fc67/current_Homelessness_Code_of_Guidance.pdf (accessed 25 April 2022).

[32] A flexible tenancy is a form of fixed-term secure tenancy that carries a mandatory right to repossession at the end of the term; Localism Act 2011, s 154; Housing Act 1985, s 107A.

[33] See s 81ZA(4). Section 1 of the 2021 Act defines behaviour of a person ('A') towards another person ('B') as domestic abuse if (a) A and B are each aged 16 or over and are personally connected to each other, and (b) the behaviour is abuse. By way of s 3 1 (3) behaviour is abusive if it consists of (a) physical or sexual abuse; (b) violent or threatening behaviour; (c) controlling or coercive behaviour; (d) economic abuse (see subs (4)); psychological, emotional, or other abuse and it does not matter whether the behaviour consists of a single incident or a course of conduct. By way of s 1(4) 'Economic abuse' means any behaviour that has a substantial adverse effect on B's ability to (a) acquire, use, or maintain money or other property, or (b) obtain goods or services. By way of s 1(5) for the purposes of this Act A's behaviour may be behaviour 'towards' B, despite the fact that it consists of conduct directed at another person (eg B's child).

the person's household, is or has been the victim of domestic abuse.[34] The reference to 'has been' ensures that there is no time restriction on when the domestic abuse occurred, so long as the new tenancy is granted for 'reasons connected' with that abuse.

A person's 'household' would include those who normally reside with that person or who might reasonably be expected to reside with them.[35]

a. *Qualifying tenancies*

A 'qualifying tenancy' is either a secure tenancy[36] which is provided by a local housing authority[37] and is not a flexible tenancy,[38] or an assured tenancy[39] which is not an assured shorthold tenancy, and which is provided by a private registered provider of social housing, by the Regulator of Social Housing or by a housing trust which is a charity.

Secure (non-flexible) tenancies have no fixed end date and can only be brought to an end by the landlord obtaining a possession order on one of the specified grounds for possession set out in Schedule 2 of the 1985 Act. Accordingly, secure (non-flexible) tenancies, often referred to as 'lifelong' tenancies, offer the strongest security of tenure that a social landlord can provide. By contrast, flexible tenancies are granted for a fixed term of no less than two years and are usually granted for five years. Currently, it is for the local housing authority to decide which type of tenancy to grant and in what circumstances they will grant flexible tenancies. Section 79 (amending Part 4 of the Housing Act 1985, s 81 (81ZA)) seeks to remove that discretion for local housing authorities when accommodating *some* victims of domestic abuse.

Furthermore, the qualifying tenancy can be held in sole or joint names, and it does not matter if, at the point at which the local housing authority grants a secure tenancy under section 81ZA(1), the person continues to reside at their previous property or that they have moved out.[40]

The local housing authority merely must be satisfied that the person had a 'qualifying tenancy', is or has been a victim of domestic abuse (or a member of their household) and that the new secure (non-flexible) tenancy is being granted for reasons connected to that abuse.

b. *Critical Commentary*

Whilst the changes introduced by section 81ZA are significant, they have limits. Section 81ZA does not impose an obligation upon local authorities to offer secure (non-flexible) tenancies[41] to those who are survivors of domestic abuse *irrespective* of the status of their previous tenancy. The DAA also does not amend the way in which local authorities discharge their homelessness duties towards homeless applicants generally. The consequence is that there is no obligation upon local housing authorities to discharge their 'main' homelessness

---

[34] See s 81ZA(2)(b).

[35] Homelessness Code of Guidance (October 2021) para 17.3; HA 1996, s 176(a); H(W)A 2014, s 56(1)(a).

[36] Section 79 of the 1985 Act.

[37] ibid s 80.

[38] See n 32.

[39] Housing Act 1988, s 1.

[40] Section 81ZA(2)(a) states that the local authority '[m]ust grant a secure tenant that is not a flexible tenancy if—(a) the tenancy is offered to a person who is *or was* a tenant of some other dwelling—house under a qualifying tenancy'. Accordingly, the obligation under s 81ZA still applies where a survivor has fled the property or even surrendered the qualifying tenancy.

[41] Or 'lifetime' tenancies.

duty under Part VII of the 1996 Act[42] towards victims of domestic abuse by way of a guaranteed secure (non-flexible) tenancy under Part VI of the 1996 Act in all cases. Accordingly, where a survivor of domestic abuse *did not* have a qualifying tenancy, they may still be offered accommodation by in the private rented sector, rather than a secure (non-flexible) tenancy.[43] However, local authorities continue to have a *discretion* to grant secure (non-flexible) tenancies by way of an allocation under Part VI of the 1996 Act.[44]

Furthermore, section 81ZA will have effect only until schedule 7 to the Housing and Planning 2016 Act is brought into force on 2 November 2022. Schedule 7 to the 2016 Act,[45] when enacted, will phase out life-time secure tenancies such that all new tenancies will be for fixed terms. Schedule 7 seeks to amend the Housing Act 1985 and contains measures to prevent local authorities in England from offering secure tenancies for life, except in limited circumstances.[46] However, it is worth noting that the Housing and Planning Act 2016 includes a power for the Secretary of State to prescribe in regulations the circumstances in which a local authority may still grant secure (non-flexible) lifelong tenancies[47]. Furthermore, the Secure Tenancies (Victims of Domestic Abuse) Act 2018 (2018 Act) seeks to amend Schedule 7 to the Housing and Planning Act to require local housing authorities to grant secure (non-flexible) tenancies to survivors of domestic abuse who have a qualifying tenancy.[48] Schedule 7 the Housing and Planning Act and the 2018 Act are not yet in force and the government has not indicated a time for implementation.[49]

Chapter 21 of the Homelessness Code of Guidance for Local Authorities, and the guidance issued by the SSHCLG in respect of Part 6 of the 1996, shows that there is a greater understanding of the impact of domestic abuse on survivors and their families and the complexities of it. There is a greater emphasis and recognition of the importance of 'joint working' and there is some recognition that tenants who have suffered domestic abuse may wish to remain in their home (or return to it) if the perpetrator can be removed. But whilst there are efforts in improving the decision-maker's ability better to identify the traumas caused by domestic abuse and that accommodation is central to a survivor's ability to flee, it is difficult to predict what impact the DAA will have in reality. Not only does the 2021 Act not address some of the major obstacles affecting survivors (partly identified by the consultations set out above), but there remains enormous pressure on available social housing, refuges, or other suitable—particularly 'women only'—emergency accommodation and funding.

---

[42] Section 193 of the 1996 Act.

[43] See Domestic Abuse Act 2021: overarching factsheet, updated on 22 November 2021 https://www.gov.uk/government/publications/domestic-abuse-bill-2020-factsheets/domestic-abuse-bill-2020-overarching-factsheet and the Explanatory Notes https://www.legislation.gov.uk/ukpga/2021/17/pdfs/ukpgaen_20210017_en.pdf (accessed 25 April 2022).

[44] Accordingly, where a survivor of domestic abuse did not have a secure (non-flexible) tenancy, it remains open to the local authority to allocate a flexible tenancy, or an introductory tenancy (pursuant to s 124 of the Housing Act 1996) or a secure (non-flexible) tenancy. It is also open the local authority in these circumstances to make a nomination to a private registered provider or registered social landlord through allocation schemes under Pt VI, s 159 of the 1996 Act.

[45] Para 4, sch 7 of the Housing and Planning Act seeks to insert s 81A and s 81B into the 1985 Act.

[46] See para 4 of Sch 7 and the proposed insertion of s 81B to the 1985 Act.

[47] The government has stated that there will be exemptions for those who escape violence PQ 42408 https://questions-statements.parliament.uk/written-questions/detail/2016-07-11/42408.

[48] Section 2 of the 2018 Act reflects the wording of s 81ZA.

[49] Explanatory Notes to the DAA (n 43) 15 [65].

2. SECTION 80 MEDICAL EVIDENCE OF DOMESTIC ABUSE

Section 80 DAA ends the postcode lottery of discretionary charging by health care professionals for letters of evidence of domestic abuse required by victim survivors in their application for legal aid. Under the Legal Aid, Sentencing and Punishment of Offenders Act 2012 (LASPO) legal aid is available for private family law matters if the applicant is a victim of domestic abuse, subject to the applicant passing a statutory means and merits test, and providing evidence of the domestic abuse or risk of domestic abuse (this can include an evidence letter from a GP). Until section 80, it was a matter for the discretion of an individual GP practice or other relevant health care professionals whether to charge for such letters and, if so, how much to charge. This placed an additional financial burden on vulnerable victims, many of whom were unable to pay for the corroborative evidence they needed to pursue protection. Lord Wolfson of Tredegar pressed for this amendment at the Bill stage.[50]

This amendment would prevent certain health care professionals who either assess a patient under an NHS contract or provide services wholly or mainly under an NHS contract, from charging victims of domestic abuse for the provision of evidence of their injuries in order to support a claim for civil legal aid.[51]

Section 80(1) and (2) will prevent charges in general practice for letters of evidence to access legal aid for domestic abuse claims for vulnerable patients where the person providing the letter

(a) [is] a health professional who has been asked by a patient to provide a letter supporting an application for legal aid in instances of domestic abuse and who mostly or wholly provide services under an NHS GP contract; and/or

(b) [is] a health professional who has been requested to provide a letter supporting an application for legal aid in instances of domestic abuse who has assessed the patient in the course of providing services under an NHS GP contract. This provision also ensures patients cannot be charged for these letters by a GP practice in its capacity as a company or partnership'.[52]

Subsection (3) 'relevant evidence', in relation to an individual, means—(a) evidence that the individual is, or is at risk of being, a victim of domestic abuse. Subsection (4) 'relevant health professional' means (a) a medical practitioner licensed to practise by the General Medical Council; (b) a health professional registered to practise in the United Kingdom by the Nursing and Midwifery Council; (c) a paramedic registered to practise in the United Kingdom by the Health and Care Professions Council.

Subsection (3)(b) enables the Secretary of State to make regulations to extend the prohibitions to any other evidence letters or reports provided by relevant health professionals to demonstrate domestic abuse for purposes other than to obtain legal aid, and subsection (6) enables the Secretary of State in relation to England and the Welsh Ministers in relation

[50] Domestic Abuse Bill, Hansard, UK Parliament, cols 30–35 https://hansard.parliament.uk/Lords/2021-03-15/debates/4ECEFBDB-E347-4F76-8DFF-604EFC5A618B/DomesticAbuseBill (accessed 25 April 2022).

[51] ibid col 30.

[52] https://www.gov.uk/government/publications/domestic-abuse-bill-2020-factsheets/prohibition-on-charging-for-the-provision-of-medical-evidence-of-domestic-abuse (accessed 25 April 2022).

to Wales to make regulations to amend the definitions of 'relevant health professional' and 'qualifying medical services contract'.[53]

Baroness Burt of Solihull said:

> In my view, it is a scandal that it ever had to come to this. What hard-hearted group of medical practitioners ever made the decision to charge money for evidence that a woman has been subjected to violence as a qualifying condition for legal aid? I suppose that is what happens when you try to marketise the NHS.[54]

[53] Explanatory Notes (n 43) [385]–[386].

[54] Domestic Abuse Bill (n 50) col 34.

17
IMMIGRATION, CONTACT CENTRES, POWERS OF SECRETARY OF STATE (SECTIONS 81–91)

Pragna Patel and Janaya Walker, Fazeela Ishmael and Rob George, Susan Edwards*

1. SECTIONS 81–82 DATA PROCESSING FOR IMMIGRATION PURPOSES

i. Context and Background

During the passage of the Domestic Abuse Act (DAA) 2021 in Parliament in 2021, women's campaigners, led by the Latin American Women's Rights Service (LAWRS), made a concerted effort to introduce amendments to alleviate some of the harsher outcomes of the government's hard-line immigration laws and policies on migrant survivors of abuse. A key focus of the campaign was the practice of data sharing between the Home Office and the police, as well as social services, health professionals, and others that prevent migrant survivors from accessing vital public services for fear of being arrested, detained, and deported. As

* Sections 81–82 by Pragna Patel and Janaya Walker, section 83 by Fazeela Ishmael and Rob George, sections 84–91 by Susan Edwards.

Pragna Patel and Janaya Walker, Fazeela Ishmael and Rob George, Susan Edwards, *Immigration, Contact Centres, Powers of Secretary of State (Sections 81–91)* In: *Blackstone's Guide to the Domestic Abuse Act 2021*. Edited by Susan Edwards, David Malone, and Gillian Jones KC, Oxford University Press.
DOI: 10.1093/oso/9780192870513.003.0017

a consequence, on 26 April 2021,[1] in the final stages of Act, two new sections were inserted by the government in the form of amendments (ss 40D and 40E).

This discussion provides an overview of the struggle to institute a firewall or safe reporting mechanisms between public services, in particular the police, and the Home Office. We consider briefly the findings of a police super-complaint into data-sharing practices, and the response to it by the Home Office (which undertook a review of the practices) and, more broadly, the government that eventually led to the following amendments to the Act.

Section 81 of the Domestic Abuse Act 2021 inserted a provision for the Home Secretary to 'review the processing of domestic abuse data carried out by specified public authorities for immigration purposes', and to lay the published findings before Parliament.

Section 82 states that: 'The Secretary of State may issue a code of practice relating to the processing of domestic abuse data for immigration purposes.'

These insertions represented last ditch concessions obtained from the government and were cautiously welcomed by LAWRS and others[2] in the hope that the outcome of an ongoing Home Office review (the review) on data sharing between the police and immigration enforcement and plans for creating safe reporting mechanisms or a firewall for migrant survivors of abuse would be brought back to Parliament for further scrutiny and debate. Although the House of Lords had passed an original amendment put forward by LAWRS calling for the creation of a 'firewall' for survivors of domestic abuse with insecure immigration status only three days before the Act received its royal assent, there were clear indications that it they would be rejected by the government. For this reason, with support from the Domestic Abuse Commissioner and the Parliamentary Joint Committee that had earlier scrutinised the draft legislation, these compromise amendments were introduced.

a. *The campaign against data sharing between the police and immigration authorities*

For a number of years, LAWRS has been co-ordinating the Step Up Migrant Women campaign, bringing together a coalition of over fifty organisations to advocate for the right of migrant women to access protection from abuse without fear of private or state retribution.[3] In campaigning for a firewall and/or safe reporting mechanisms, LAWRS drew on its front-line experience of working with migrant women subject to abuse, and to research that it had commissioned from King's College at London University the findings published in a report entitled 'Right to Be Believed' (June 2019)[4] outlining the multiple barriers faced by migrant women when attempting to escape abuse. (See Part III for more information.) It contains many first-hand accounts (cited below) of women who were unable to report abuse due to fears that they would be reported to the police and immigration authorities by their perpetrators and deported.

I was scared that they might take my children, that's why I didn't want to call them [police]. Because my husband is British, my children are British, so I'm the odd one out, and this is what they made me feel.

[1] Domestic Abuse Bill (2021) Commons disagreements, amendments in lieu and reason https://bills.parliament.uk/Publications/41274/Documents/173/5801194.pdf (accessed 25 April 2022).

[2] https://twitter.com/lawrsuk/status/1386959968709005312.

[3] See Step Up Migrant Women: https://stepupmigrantwomen.org/about-sumw/ (accessed 25 April 2022).

[4] King's College London, Latin American Women's Rights Service, 'Right to be Believed: Migrant women facing violence against women and girls (VAWG) in the 'hostile immigration' environment in London' (2019) https://www.researchgate.net/publication/333648520_THE_RIGHT_TO_BE_BELIEVED_Migrant_women_facing_Violence_Against_Women_and_Girls_VAWG_in_the_'hostile_immigration_environment'_in_London (accessed 25 April 2022).

My husband and in-laws were always controlling, and they treated me like a slave ... They threaten me if I said anything about reporting them to social services; they will deport me to my country and take my daughter from me.

After he cancelled my [spousal] visa, he booked my ticket, he called me and said, 'don't come to my house, I cancelled your visa, you are illegal in this country'.

The research found that more than half of the women feared that they would not be believed by the police because of their immigration status (54 per cent) or that the police or the Home Office would support the perpetrator over them (52 per cent).

b. *The police super-complaint on data sharing*

The research findings echoed submissions made in the first ever police super-complaint[5] by the civil liberty organisation Liberty and Southall Black Sisters in December 2018 regarding the practice of systematic sharing of victim data between the police and immigration authorities. The super-complaint, consisting of almost fifty pages of evidence, showed that such data sharing prevented victims of crime, particularly migrant women, from reporting abuse to the police and as a result placed them at greater risk of serious forms of abuse and exploitation. The submission also made clear that there is in fact no legal duty on the police mandating them to share information on a victim's immigration status with the Home Office. Even if such a 'duty' could be identified, it argues that it may well conflict with the state's obligations under the European Convention on Human Rights (ECHR) to protect victims and punish perpetrators of serious crimes. For example, Articles 2 and 3 ECHR guarantees the right to life and the right not to be subjected to torture and inhuman and degrading treatment. They impose substantive obligations on the State to ensure that there is protection from a violation of these rights and to conduct an effective investigation in cases where these rights have been violated. Similarly, Article 4 ECHR prohibits slavery, servitude, and forced labour. Similarly, the state has a positive obligation to prevent trafficking of human beings, which includes penalising and prosecuting traffickers. The super complaint concluded that the police play a central role in ensuring that the UK discharges the burden of its positive obligations under Articles 2, 3, and 4 ECHR and part of its role is to receive and investigate reports of serious crimes which would fall within the ambit of those Articles. If that is not done effectively, the UK will be in breach of its positive obligations under Articles 2, 3, and 4 ECHR. In addition, the super-complaint also pointed out that data sharing between the police and Immigration Enforcement constitutes a potential breach of Article 8 (the right to respect for private and family life) and Article 14 (the right not to be discriminated against in the enjoyment of Convention rights). It made clear that the sharing of victims' or witnesses' data on the basis of a 'suspicion' that they may be in the UK illegally (or that they may be 'foreign') is likely to lead to unlawful discrimination.

Following an investigation into the super-complaint, the police inspectorates, and regulatory bodies, namely His Majesty's Inspectorate of Constabulary and Fire & Rescue Services (HMICFRS), the College of Policing (CoP), and the Independent Office for Police Conduct (IOPC) published its findings in December 2020. It concluded that the law and policy in relation to data sharing needed to be reviewed by the Home Office to provide clarity on police priorities. It recommended the establishment of 'safe reporting pathways informed by the realities of victims' experiences ... that reflect existing laws on everyone's right to data protection'. Much to the surprise of the campaigners, the outcome of the super-complaint in

[5] Southall Black Sister and Liberty, Super-complaint prepared by Liberty and Southall Black Sisters (2018) https://assets.publishing.service.gov.uk/government/uploads/system/uploads/attachment_data/file/767396/Super-complaint_181218.pdf (accessed 25 April 2022).

respect of victims of domestic abuse was far reaching insofar as it made a clear recommendation for 'a separation between the police response to a victim's report of domestic abuse and the handling of their immigration status'. This was justified on the basis that:

[V]ictims should have every confidence in approaching the police for protection. They should expect and receive protection at times when they are vulnerable and so desperately need the assistance of the agents of the state. Victims should never be in a position where they fear that the actions of the police could unintentionally but severely intensify their vulnerability, and thereby strengthen the hands of organised criminals and others whose motives and objectives are to inspire fear and do them harm.

Significantly, the findings supported the view that data sharing between the police and immigration enforcement acted as a deterrent to victims engaging with the police and reporting crime; did not constitute 'safeguarding' and caused 'significant harm to the public interest' because of victims' inability to seek protection or justice. It called for chief constables to put an immediate stop to the practice of data sharing with the Home Office as a temporary measure in cases involving domestic abuse pending the outcome of a Home Office review of 'the legal framework and policy' behind data sharing. It also called for safe reporting mechanisms for all migrant victims and witnesses to be established, with a progress update from the Home Office within six months of its review.[6]

c. *The government's position*

During debates on the DAA in Parliament, the government dismissed the findings of the super-complaint including the recommendation that a temporary firewall be put in place pending the outcome of the Home Office review into the matter. Instead, the government claimed that far from deterring victims, data sharing was necessary to 'safeguard' victims, although no evidence was presented to show exactly how immigration enforcement officers performed a 'safeguarding' function. Justifying the government's position and pointing to the Home Office review into data sharing, Victoria Atkins, the then Home Office Minister for Safeguarding, rejected further amendments tabled in the House of Lords, by stating:

We remain concerned that the revised Lords amendments regarding data firewalls still pre-empt the outcome of the review recommended by the independent policing inspectorate in response to the super-complaint. We need to undertake that review without any preconceptions as to its outcome. To provide further reassurance on that point, Government amendments 40D to 40J introduce two new clauses.[7]

However, due to growing pressure from campaigners, the government agreed to amendment sections 40D and 40E, as set out above. Section 40D sought to put the review undertaken by the Home Office on a statutory footing, which means that there will be further scrutiny of the review by Parliament when it is concluded.[8] Section 40E gives the Secretary of State the opportunity to issue a 'code of practice' relating to data processing for immigration purposes; any such code to be prepared or revised in consultation with the Domestic Abuse and Information Commissioners and be brought back to Parliament.[9]

---

[6] College of Policing, HMICFRS, IOPC, 'Safe to Share? Report on Liberty and Southall Black Sisters' super-complaint on policing and immigration status' (2020) https://assets.publishing.service.gov.uk/government/uploads/system/uploads/attachment_data/file/945314/safe-to-share-liberty-southall-black-sisters-super-complaint-policing-immigration-status.pdf (accessed 25 April 2022).

[7] HC (26 April 2021) vol 693, col 117 https://hansard.parliament.uk/commons/2021-04-26/debates/05E7E125-ADAE-4293-A313-6694F2788EF4/DomesticAbuseBill (accessed 25 April 2022).

[8] HL Bill 124, Domestic Abuse Bill: Commons Disagreement, Amendments in Lieu and in Reason https://bills.parliament.uk/Publications/41274/Documents/173/5801194.pdf (accessed 25 April 2022).

[9] ibid.

d. *The Home Office review*

Following the conclusion of the DAA, on Wednesday 15 December 2021, the government announced the outcome of the Home Office review on data sharing between the police and Immigration Enforcement (IE) concerning migrant victims and witnesses of crime.[10] Disappointingly, it rejected the recommendations made by LAWRS and the Domestic Abuse Commissioner for the implementation of safe reporting mechanisms for victims of domestic abuse. Instead, flying in the face of all existing evidence, and of the findings of the police super-complaint, it concluded:

> Current data sharing practices between the police and the Home Office are essential in protecting those most vulnerable and enforcing the UK's immigration laws. Proposals to cease or delay data sharing between the police and the Home Office on migrant victims and witnesses of crime with irregular immigration status would be harmful to both the safeguarding of those victims and witnesses and the public interest.

The review states that far from having a deterrent and therefore discriminatory effect, data sharing between the police and IE in relation to vulnerable migrant victims is useful since the IE plays a vital safeguarding role. It adds that the problem is that this role is not 'widely understood'. A series of proposals were therefore made including the creation of an 'IE Migrant Victims Protocol' for migrant victims of crime that are referred to IE by the police. The protocol should state that '[n]o immigration enforcement action will be taken against that victim while investigation and prosecution proceedings are ongoing, and the victim is receiving support and advice to make an application to regularise their stay'.

LAWRS, along with SBS and Liberty (the authors of the police super-complaint) have rejected the findings of the review and its recommendations on the basis that a) they fail to address the continuing deterrence effect of data sharing and the risks and harm that is generated by the practice; b) fail to guarantee safety in reporting to the police without the fear of detention or deportation and c) serves to reinforce the government's hostile immigration policy. Taken together, the findings of the review severely undermine the government's 'moral duty to protect … victims of crime' and its commitment to ensure that 'all victims … feel confident to pursue justice'.[11] As a consequence, these organisations have refused to engage with the Home Office on a Protocol that has no teeth and instead are looking to introduce amendments on data sharing and safe reporting mechanisms in other legislation including the forthcoming Victim's Bill.[12] In the meantime, migrant women with insecure immigration status remain in a precarious position with regards to their ability to report abuse to the police and other statutory services without fear of being removed or deported.

[10] Home Office, 'Review of data sharing: Migrant victims and witnesses of crime' (2021) https://www.gov.uk/government/publications/review-of-data-sharing-migrant-victims-and-witnesses-of-crime (accessed 25 April 2022).

[11] Ministry of Justice (2022) Delivering justice for victims: a consultation on improving victims' experiences of the justice system: https://www.gov.uk/government/consultations/delivering-justice-for-victims-a-consultation-on-improving-victims-experiences-of-the-justice-system/delivering-justice-for-victims-a-consultation-on-improving-victims-experiences-of-the-justice-system (accessed 25 April 2022).

[12] Latin American Women's Rights Service (15 December 2021) Press release, 'Home Office Review on data-sharing on migrant victims is not fit for purpose, say women's rights groups and civil liberties groups'; Latin American Women's Rights Service (2021) Press release, 'Home Office Review on data-sharing on migrant victims is not fit for purpose, say women's rights and civil liberties groups' https://lawrs.org.uk/blog/2021/12/15/press-release-home-office-review-on-data-sharing-on-migrant-victims-is-not-fit-for-purpose-say-womens-rights-and-civil-liberties-groups/ (accessed 25 April 2022).

2. SECTION 83 DOMESTIC ABUSE AND CONTACT CENTRES

i. Context and Background

The court's well-established pro-contact culture,[13] reinforced by section 1(2A) of the Children Act 1989 with its presumption of parental involvement, has led to strongly argued concerns that the risks of further harm, to the child or to the parent or to both, from an abusive parent during formal and informally arranged contact, have not been adequately understood or acted upon.[14] These concerns are seen most dramatically and tragically in cases where children are killed by a parent during contact arrangements.[15] Child contact centres are neutral places offering children of separated parents the opportunity to have contact and develop their relationships with their non-resident parent. Contact centres can be used informally as a result of private arrangements, or in a legally regulated way when ordered by the court in private law children disputes (usually meaning dispute between separated parents). While not all users of contact centres do so because of concerns connected to domestic abuse, it is one of their major functions to offer a space for contact to take place when there are potentially serious risks to adults and children arising from that contact. Inadequate management of those risks, due to absence of regulation, inadequate resources, or insufficient training, leaves adults and children vulnerable. These concerns informed some of the rationale in relation to the Domestic Abuse Act (DAA) 2021, including in the background to section 83.

ii. Section 83

By section 83 of the DAA, the Secretary of State is mandated to prepare a report 'about the extent to which individuals, when they are using contact centres in England, are protected from the risk of domestic abuse or, in the case of children, other harm'. This report must be published within two years of the Act being passed, and for the purposes of the section a 'contact centre' is defined as 'a place that is used for the facilitation of contact between a child and an individual with whom the child is not, or will not be, living (including the handover of the child to that individual)'. While the scope of the review that is mandated by section 83 is clearly broad, the parliamentary debates suggest that a particular concern that led to the enactment of this provision is the lack of regulation of contact centres and how this may impact their management of cases involving actual or alleged domestic abuse.[16]

As we note below, the lack of statutory regulation and inconsistent levels of training and resourcing for contact centres are significant safety concerns. While the review mandated by

[13] Amongst many studies see eg Rebecca Bailey-Harris, Jacqueline Barron, and Julia Pearce, 'From Utility to Rights? The Presumption of Contact in Practice' (1999) 13(2) *International Journal of Law, Policy and the Family* 111.

[14] Women's Aid, *Nineteen Child Homicides* (2016) https://www.womensaid.org.uk/shop/reports/nineteen-child-homicides/ (accessed 19 January 2022).

[15] Women's Aid, *Twenty-Nine Child Homicides: Lessons Still to be Learnt on Domestic Violence and Child Protection* (2004) http://familieslink.co.uk/download/jan07/twenty_nine_child_homicides.pdf (accessed 19 January 2022); Women's Aid (n 14). See also 'Scandal of 63 children killed by parents after officials missed warning signs' *Sunday Mirror* (17 August 2019).

[16] HL Deb (1 February 2021) vol 809, col 1981 https://hansard.parliament.uk/Lords/2021-02-01/debates/3D604C08-7BD7-46DF-A1F6- accessed 19.01. 202271B8A7DB91B5/DomesticAbuseBill?highlight=domestic%20abuse%20contact%20centres#contribution-C2B8B2B2-8BE6-497B-8525-FB0650A6B021 (accessed 19 January 2022).

section 83 is likely to provide helpful information about these issues, without a commitment to action in response to the findings, the report in itself is a limited response to the concerns that led to this section being included in the Act.

a. *NACCC*

The National Association of Child Contact Centres (NACCC) is the registered charity which sets national standards for such contact centres and provides specialist training and an accreditation process. Their mission is to ensure that 'Parenting shouldn't end when relationships do'. There were 318 accredited centres as of 1st April 2021 providing direct contact services.[17] There is no legal requirement for contact centres to be accredited or accountable and therefore the number of unaccredited, unregulated child contact centres is unknown.

Contact sessions at accredited centres will be either 'Supervised Contact' or 'Supported Contact'. The NACCC defines 'Supported Contact' as sessions of contact *where 'direct observations are not made and reports are not written but staff or volunteers will be present to ensure the comfort of those engaging in the service'.*[18] The NACCC recommends such format of contact to be 'suitable for families that are deemed to present minimal risk of violence or abuse.'[19] 'Supervised Contact' is described as ensuring the 'physical safety and emotional well-being of children in a one-to-one observed setting. This form of contact is provided where it is assessed that there might be a higher risk or greater complexity in a family's circumstances. These sessions will be supervised by staff who are experienced in this role. Observations will be made, and reports will be written. It is generally expected that staff will remain within sight and sound of the children at all times'.[20] Such format of contact 'can also be used to reintroduce a child to a parent where there has been a substantial gap in contact'.[21] Around 3,000 volunteers and 1,500 staff run these services.[22] There is a greater availability of supported contact sessions as this is often staffed by volunteers. However, the availability of supervised contact sessions is increasing.[23]

b. *Domestic abuse in private children proceedings, and contact centres*

The evidence suggests that allegations of domestic abuse are present in at least half of private law children proceedings in the family courts, with the most recent Cafcass study finding domestic abuse allegations in 62 per cent of cases.[24] Practice Direction 12J of the Family Procedure Rules 2010 provides detailed guidance when issues of domestic abuse are raised

[17] National Association of Child Contact Centres, 'Annual Report and Unaudited Financial Statements For the Year ended 31 March 2021' https://naccc.org.uk/wp-content/uploads/2021/09/National-Association-of-Child-Contact-Centres-2021.pdf (accessed 16 December 2021).

[18] National Association of Child Contact Centres (NACCC), 'Types of Contact' https://naccc.org.uk/for-parents/types-of-contact/ (accessed 16 December 2021)

[19] National Association of Child Contact Centres, 'About NACCC' https://naccc.org.uk/about-naccc/ (accessed 16 December 2021).

[20] NACCC (n 18).

[21] 'About NACCC' (n 19).

[22] National Association of Child Contact Centres, 'What we do' https://naccc.org.uk/about-naccc/what-we-do/ (accessed 16 December 2021).

[23] National Association of Child Contact Centres, 'Annual Statistics' https://naccc.org.uk/about-naccc/annual-statistics/ (accessed 16 December 2021).

[24] Cafcass and Women's Aid, 'Allegations of domestic abuse in child contact cases' (25 July 2017) https://www.cafcass.gov.uk/wp-content/uploads/2017/12/Allegations-of-domestic-abuse-in-child-contact-cases-2017.pdf (accessed 19 January 2022).

in court applications concerning child arrangements. Where the court gives directions for a fact-finding hearing to determine disputed allegations of domestic abuse, it should not make an interim child arrangements order for contact between a child and the non-resident parent unless (i) it is satisfied that it is in the interests of the child to do so and (ii) the order would not expose the child or the other parent to an unmanageable risk of harm bearing in mind the impact which domestic abuse against a parent can have on the emotional well-being of the child, the safety of the other parent, and the need to protect against domestic abuse.[25]

Where the court is considering whether to make an order for interim contact, one of the factors that the court should consider is the arrangements required to ensure, as far as possible, that any risk of harm to the child and the parent who is at any time caring for the child is minimised and that the safety of the child and the parties is secured, and in particular: (i) whether the contact should be supervised or supported, and if so, where and by whom; and (ii) the availability of appropriate facilities for that purpose.[26] The 'Revised Protocol for Referrals of Families to Child Contact Centres by Judges and Magistrates' of October 2017 requires that when making an order for referral to contact centres or services, regardless of whether there are issues of domestic abuse, judges and magistrates require the centre or service to be accredited.[27]

The NACCC reported that approximately 21 per cent of the total number of referrals to accredited contact centres in 2020–2021 were by either the court or solicitors.[28] It is acknowledged that these figures are probably affected by the Covid-19 pandemic, but these statistics demonstrate that contact centres are clearly an important resource used by the family court.

c. *How do contact centres currently manage issues of domestic abuse?*

The NACCC has a training programme for contact centres as part of their accreditation process, which includes annual safeguarding training of the staff and volunteers in cases concerning domestic abuse.[29] The NACCC also offers enhanced accreditation for supervised contact.[30] In cases of domestic abuse (especially where there have been criminal proceedings or injunctive relief), supervised contact will generally be necessary, at least initially. The accredited contact centres are also required to conduct risk assessments, and the parents may be invited to attend the centre separately to discuss ground rules and any concerns prior to any contact commencing. In respect of the practicalities of arranging contact sessions, contact centres may differ dependent on their resources, but common measures to minimise the interaction between the parents include: liaising with both parents separately to arrange the

[25] FPR 2010 PD12J 25.

[26] ibid 27.

[27] National Association of Child Contact Centres and Sir James Munby, 'Revised Protocol for Referrals of Families to Child Contact Centres by Judges and Magistrates' National Association of Child Contact Centres (October 2017) https://naccc.org.uk/wp-content/uploads/2020/05/JUDICIAL_PROTOCOL_for_Referral_of_Families_to_Child_Contact_Centres_17th_October_2017_FINAL_LINKS1.pdf (accessed 16 December 2021).

[28] National Association of Child Contact Centres, 'NACCC accredited centre statistics data summary' Report Title (naccc.org.uk) (accessed 23 January 2022).

[29] National Association of Child Contact Centres, 'NACCC's National Standards—safeguarding children in domestic abuse situations' Annual Statistics' https://naccc.org.uk/naccc s-national-standards-safeguarding-children-in-domestic-abuse-situations/ (accessed 16 December 2021).

[30] National Association of Child Contact Centres, 'Accreditation and enhanced accreditation' https://naccc.org.uk/about-naccc/accreditation-enhanced-accreditation/ (accessed 16 December 2021).

dates, staggered arrivals and departures of the parents, and taking the child(ren) from one parent in the waiting room to the other parent in the contact room.[31] In supervised contact sessions, both parents will also have the benefit of observation reports from each session which the centre will send to both parents, which would include any safeguarding issues if these arose during sessions.[32]

iii. Critical Commentary

There are a number of areas of potential difficulties with the current contact system. A non-resident parent may self-refer to a contact centre. If there are no court proceedings, involvement from Children Services, or any other professionals involved with the family, the contact centre will be primarily dependent on the referral forms completed by both parents. Referral forms must be completed as fully and accurately as possible to equip the contact centre will all details of any domestic abuse or safeguarding information. However, the parents may make cross-allegations of domestic abuse in these forms. It is not a contact centre's role to determine the allegations, although contact centres should take steps to safeguard a child's welfare if safeguarding concerns in relation to domestic abuse are raised. These issues may be resolved by undertaking a risk assessment and regular reviews of the contact to ensure that the appropriate level of supervision or support is in place.

Another area of concern is in relation to funding. Contact centres are mainly staffed by volunteers, and parents may have to fund contact sessions privately. The price of child contact is often dependent on several factors and the cost can vary significantly. Elements that can affect cost can relate to how the centre is funded, the range of services on offer, the expertise of staff offering a service as well as the cost of all of the usual overheads associated with running a service.[33] On the one hand, situations can arise where victims of domestic abuse, who may already be suffering financial hardship, are burdened by the cost of funding contact sessions where such supervision is only required due to actions of the perpetrator of domestic abuse. However, victims of domestic abuse may feel they have no other realistic option if the only alternative is the perpetrator having unsupervised contact with the children where the risks are unassessed and unknown. On the other hand, an alleged perpetrator of domestic abuse may have to fund such contact sessions at a contact centre where the allegations of domestic abuse are maliciously raised, and vehemently disputed. The parent may not be able to afford the court process to challenge these allegations, or if they do, it may be a number of months before the family court determines the allegations, taking into account the lengthy delays in the court system. Until such time, the alleged perpetrator may be burdened by expensive contact sessions at a contact centre.

The absence of a regulatory framework and legal requirement of accreditation means that anyone can open a child contact centre and they do not need to undertake any training, accreditation process, or be accountable to an independent body. Non-resident parents may self-refer to unregulated contact centres because they are cheaper. The government's

[31] National Association of Child Contact Centres, 'I don't want to see my ex at the centre—how would this work?' https://naccc.org.uk/faq/i-dont-want-to-see-my-ex-at-the-centre-how-would-this-work/ (accessed 16 December 2021).

[32] National Association of Child Contact Centres, 'In supervised contact, who do the contact reports go to?' https://naccc.org.uk/faq/in-supervised-contact-who-do-the-contact-reports-go-to/ (accessed 16 December 2021).

[33] National Association of Child Contact Centres, 'FAQ Non-Resident Parents' https://naccc.org.uk/category/faq-non-resident-parents/ (accessed 16 December 2021).

recent HARM report identified that professionals involved in child arrangement cases 'show a lack of understanding of the different forms that domestic abuse takes, and of the ongoing impacts of abuse on children and victim parents'.[34] Whilst the NACCC requires tailored safeguarding training in respect of domestic abuse in order to achieve accreditation, there is no legal requirement for contact centres to undertake such training and therefore domestic abuse and other issues can be inappropriately handled, which could have long term, detrimental consequences for the children involved. Without a professional contact system which operates to a consistent standard, the issues identified in the HARM report will persist and it is self-evident that such risks will be amplified in child contact centres without oversight.[35]

Whilst the review mandated under section 83 will provide welcome information, without a requirement that the report consider recommendations or a commitment from government to act in response, section 83 in itself is of limited value.

3. SECTIONS 84–91 SECRETARY OF STATE DUTIES AND POWERS AND GUIDANCE

i. Context and Background

The Secretary of State's powers and duties within the DAA are set out in each section concerning what he/she 'must' do regarding his/her responsibilities and duties and what he/she 'may' do.

The Secretary of State's functions and powers have been set out throughout the previous sections of the DAA regarding regulations, guidance, and codes of practice.

In Part One of the DAA the Secretary of State 'must' appoint a Domestic Abuse Commissioner (DAC) and 'may' fund and 'must' appoint staff (s 4(1), ss 5 and 6) to this newly created office. The Secretary of State under section 11 'must' provide a framework document. The Secretary of State 'may' remove any matter from the DAC's reports or advice issued under sections 8(4), 9(6), and 14(4). By regulation, under section 15(4) the Secretary of State 'may' amend, adding, removing, or varying a public authority in respect of this section.

In Part Three regarding domestic abuse protection orders on application, the Secretary of State under section 28(2) 'may' add '(c) a person specified in regulations made by the Secretary of State'. Under section 31(8) regarding domestic abuse protection orders otherwise than on application, 'relevant proceedings' means proceedings of a description specified in regulations made by the Secretary of State.

Under section 37 concerning further provision about electronic monitoring requirements, subsection (7) ('the responsible person') 'must' be of a description specified in regulations made by the Secretary of State. Under section 41(7), the Secretary of State 'may' by regulations specify further notification requirements which a court may impose when making or

[34] Ministry of Justice, 'Assessing Risk of Harm to Children and Parents in Private Law Children Cases' (June 2020) 4. https://assets.publishing.service.gov.uk/government/uploads/system/uploads/attachment_data/file/895173/assessing-risk-harm-children-parents-pl-childrens-cases-report_.pdf (accessed 16 December 2021).

[35] National Association of Child Contact Centres, 'House of Lords debate the Domestic Abuse Bill amendment to require all child contact centres to be accredited' https://naccc.org.uk/house-of-lords-debate-the-domestic-abuse-bill-amendment-to-require-all-child-contact-centres-to-be-accredited/ (accessed 16 December 2021).

varying a domestic abuse protection order. With regard to guidance, the Secretary of State under section 50 'must' issue guidance in respect of domestic abuse notices and orders and under section 51(1), the Secretary of State 'must' issue a code of practice in respect of data from electronic monitoring.

In respect of housing, under section 57(2) 'relevant accommodation' means accommodation of a description specified by the Secretary of State in regulations and under section 57(9) the Secretary of State 'may' by regulations make provision about the preparation and publication of strategies under this section.

Under section 60(1), the Secretary of State 'must' issue guidance relating to the exercise by local authorities in England of functions under this Part.

Under section 75(1), the Secretary of State 'must', prepare and publish a document setting out a strategy for the prosecution and management of offenders and under section 77 (1) 'must' issue guidance about the disclosure of information by police forces for the purposes of preventing domestic abuse.

Section 80 deals with the Secretary of State's responsibility to specify in regulations (ss (3)) what other evidence may constitute 'relevant evidence', in relation to an individual, (B), that the individual is, or is at risk of being, a victim of domestic abuse.

Under section 81(1), the Secretary of State 'must ...(a) review the processing of domestic abuse data carried out by specified public authorities for immigration purposes', and under section 82(1) 'may' issue a code of practice relating to the processing of domestic abuse data for immigration purposes.

ii. Section 84 Guidance

Under section 84 in this Part is found a review of the duties and responsibilities of the Secretary of State in respect to the issuing of guidance. This is important in establishing a clear role for the Secretary of State with regard to the Act itself.

Under section 84(1) the Secretary of State 'may issue guidance' concerning '(a) the effect of any provision made by or under—other sections of the act, which are set out in each of the individual sections'. However, 'may issue guidance' places the responsibility to issue guidance on a slightly different footing as compared with the 'must' requirement.

Section 84(2) creates a stronger requirement on the Secretary of State to issue guidance about any of the provisions in the act that extend to England and Wales and about other matters relating to domestic abuse, but 'must' in particular, issue guidance under this section regarding particular sections of the DAA: '(a) the effect of sections 1 and 2, including guidance as to particular kinds of behaviour that amount to domestic abuse; (b) the effect of domestic abuse on children'. Guidance on the particular kinds of behaviour that amount to domestic abuse is already set out in the statutory guidance.[36] Any guidance about the impact and 'effect' of sections 1 and 2 will require evaluative research on police and prosecutorial practice (see Part I in this Guide), on reporting by victim/survivors and the impact of this and other legislation both on prosecution of domestic abuse related offences and on public confidence to report such incidents and crimes to the police. Analysis of the impact of domestic abuse on children and subsequent guidance will require research on the specific impact of

[36] Domestic Abuse Draft Statutory guidance framework (July 2021) https://assets.publishing.service.gov.uk/government/uploads/system/uploads/attachment_data/file/1007814/draft-da-statutory-guidance-2021-final.pdf (accessed 25 April 2022).

abuse and witnessing abuse on children's health, welfare, and safety. Funding will be needed to enable the necessary research and evaluation of the impact of these particular sections.

Section 84(3) departs from a technical citation of the powers and 'may' and 'must' duties of the Secretary of State and places within the statute itself a recognition of the gendered specificity of domestic abuse. Whilst the DAA does not take into account international conventions, and the eschewing of the Istanbul Convention must surely be considered an omission, subsection (3) states: 'Any guidance issued under this section must, so far as relevant, take account of the fact that the majority of victims of domestic abuse in England and Wales (excluding children treated as victims by virtue of section 3) are female.' This is as far as the Act—which is in essence 'gender neutral'—goes in recognising that the preponderance of abuse and violence is committed by men on women. However, that leaves what is to be done very much to interpretation and there is no further direction of what that 'take account of' might require in giving effect to the subsection.

The government acknowledge in its violence against women and girls' strategy 'Tackling Violence Against Women and Girls'[37] that the majority of those experiencing domestic abuse and domestic violence are women and girls (See Part I of the Guide). Whilst the government does not wish to lose the momentum which has recognised the specificity of violence against women and girls and the institutional failures to respond robustly, merely stating the recognition of the gendered specificity of domestic abuse will not be sufficient. However, the requirement placed on the Secretary of State to report on what is being done and to consult with the DAC is a step towards public transparency and accountability.

iii. Sections 85–91

Sections 85 and 86 concern consequential amendments by regulation, transitional, or saving provisions and are largely self-explanatory.

Under section 87 concerning regulations: '(1) Any power of the Secretary of State, the Lord Chancellor or the Welsh Ministers to make regulations under this Act is exercisable by statutory instrument.'

Regarding financial provision under section 88, 'There is to be paid out of money provided by Parliament

(a) any expenditure incurred by a Minister of the Crown under or by virtue of this Act, and
(b) any increase attributable to this Act in the sums payable under any other Act out of money so provided'.

Under section 89(1), 'Except as set out in the subsections of this section the DAA extends only to England and Wales'.

Section 90 deals with the commencement[38] of the sections of the Act and section 91 deals with the short title—the Domestic Abuse Act 2021.

[37] Tackling violence against women and girls (publishing.service.gov.uk) https://assets.publishing.service.gov.uk/government/uploads/system/uploads/attachment_data/file/1033934/Tackling_Violence_Against_Women_and_Girls_Strategy_-_July_2021.pdf (accessed 25 April 2022).

[38] Domestic Abuse Act 2021 commencement schedule https://www.gov.uk/government/publications/domestic-abuse-act-2021-commencement-schedule (accessed 16 November 2022).

18
SCHEDULES

Martin O'Neill, Susan Edwards, David Malone*,**

1. SCHEDULE 1—FURTHER PROVISION ABOUT REMAND UNDER SECTION 40

Section 40(6) of the Domestic Abuse Act (DAA) 2021 provides that a relevant court has power to remand a person arrested on warrant for breach of a domestic abuse protection order (DAPO) where they do not deal with the matter immediately. 'Relevant court' refers to Family Court, High Court, or county court (s 40(2)) so this relates to where courts are dealing with any breach of an order as a civil rather than a criminal matter. Further provisions

* Schedule 3 has been written with the assistance of David Malone's pupil, Mr Andreas Malekos.
** Schedule 1 by Martin O'Neill, Schedule 2 by Susan Edwards, Schedule 3 by David Malone.

Martin O'Neill, Susan Edwards, David Malone, *Schedules* In: *Blackstone's Guide to the Domestic Abuse Act 2021*. Edited by Susan Edwards, David Malone, and Gillian Jones KC, Oxford University Press.
 DOI: 10.1093/oso/9780192870513.003.0018

under section 40(7) allow for remand in custody or on bail and provide timescales in defined circumstances. The justification for the remand provisions was set out in Parliament:

> Remand would usually only be used in cases where the court considers that the person arrested for breach is at a high risk of either committing further breaches or evading the return hearing. That may include, for example, if the court considers that person a flight risk.[1]

Where the court has power to remand under section 40, it may do so in custody or on bail.[2] In cases where the court decides to remand in custody, the Act provides:

> (2) If remanded in custody, P is to be committed to custody to be brought before the court—
> (a) at the end of the period of remand, or
> (b) at such earlier time as the court may require.[3]

There are a number of reasons why the court may remand in custody, and each has discrete timescales attached. If a person is remanded in custody, and the custody will not exceed three days, they can be placed in the custody of a police constable, presumably so that they are remanded locally.[4] The court may remand a person for the purposes of an examination and report on their medical condition.[5] In such a case, if remanded in custody, this can be for no longer than three weeks at a time. If remanded on bail, then this can be for no longer than four weeks at a time.[6] The Explanatory Notes to the Act describe the additional power of the court to remand in custody where a person is suspected of suffering from a mental disorder:

> Paragraph 5(5) gives the court the same power as it has in respect of an accused person to make an order under section 35 of the Mental Health Act 1983 if it suspects that the perpetrator is suffering from a mental disorder. Section 35 of that Act enables a court to remand an individual to a hospital specified by the court for a report on his mental condition. Such a remand may not be for more than 28 days at a time or for more than 12 weeks in total.[7]

If the court decide to remand for longer than three days, then it can only remand for longer than eight days in two situations. Firstly, if section 5(1) of Schedule 1 applies, or secondly if both the person to be remanded and the original applicant for a warrant for breach of the order to be issued agrees.[8] The second condition is seemingly to allow the original applicant for a warrant for breach of order to have a say in the length of remand of the person, although it is to be noted that the person to be remanded in custody also has to agree to longer than an eight-day remand in custody. Therefore, the parties have to be *ad idem* before a longer remand can be ordered by the court.[9] The original applicant for a warrant for breach of an order may be the police, the person to be protected, or a third party allowed to do so at the

---

1 Alex Chalk, Domestic Abuse Bill Deb (10 June 2020) col 214 https://www.theyworkforyou.com/pbc/2019-21/Domestic_Abuse_Bill/06-0_2020-06-10a.214.5 (accessed 26 April 2022).

2 DAA 2021, sch 1, cl 2(1).

3 ibid cl 2(2).

4 ibid cl 4(2).

5 ibid cl 5(1).

6 ibid cl 5(2). See also Home Office, Ministry of Justice: Explanatory Notes to the Domestic Abuse Act 2021 [181] https://www.legislation.gov.uk/ukpga/2021/17/pdfs/ukpgaen_20210017_en.pdf (accessed 26 April 2022).

7 DAA 2021, Explanatory Notes [182].

8 ibid sch 1, cl 4(1).

9 ibid cl 4(1).

discretion of the court.[10] Quite how much a victim may want to be involved in these decisions is questionable, given reluctance to be involved in processes that could (a) eventually criminalise behaviour, and (b) exacerbate the problem moving forward.[11] It has also been noted that elongation of the process may not serve the best interests of the victim.[12]

There are situations where the court may decide to remand on bail rather than in custody. In these cases, a recognisance can be obtained with or without sureties from either the person to be remanded or other persons capable of providing surety.[13] In addition, the court has power to impose protective conditions:

> The court may, when remanding a person on bail in accordance with this Schedule, require the person to comply, before release on bail or later, with any requirements that appear to the court to be necessary to secure that the person does not interfere with witnesses or otherwise obstruct the course of justice.[14]

The court will have the same powers to remand at subsequent hearings by virtue of the Act.[15] Provisions allow for remand to be extended in the absence of the person remanded, in circumstances where they are unable to attend (i.e., illness or accident).[16]

2. SCHEDULE 2—STRANGULATION OR SUFFOCATION: CONSEQUENTIAL AMENDMENTS

The breadth of consequential amendments is indicative not only of the intention to catch the offence across a broad range of legislation but also the potential reach of the problem of strangulation and suffocation.

Until the DAA section 70 strangulation and suffocation related conduct was only recognised in statute when it was committed prior to the committal of any indictable offence and with the intention of rendering the person unable to resist.

Section 21 of the Offences against the Person Act 1861 provides:

> Whosoever shall, by any means whatsoever, attempt to choke, suffocate, or strangle any other person, or shall by any means calculated to choke, suffocate, or strangle, attempt to render any other person insensible, unconscious, or incapable of resistance, with intent in any of such cases thereby to enable himself or any other person to commit, or with intent in any of such cases thereby to assist any other person in committing, any indictable offence, shall be guilty of felony, and being convicted thereof shall be liable ... to be kept in penal servitude for life.

---

[10] ibid s 40(4).

[11] Roger Bird, *Domestic Abuse: Law and Practice* (8th edn, Lexis Nexis 2020) 37.

[12] House of Commons Joint Committee on the Draft Domestic Abuse Bill Draft Domestic Abuse Bill First Report of Session 2017–19 Report, together with formal minutes relating to the report Ordered by the House of Lords to be printed 11 June 2019 Ordered by the House of Commons to be printed 11 June 2019, 27 https://publications.parliament.uk/pa/jt201719/jtselect/jtddab/2075/2075.pdf?msclkid=04a59b39c53511ecb2e376e2318a8904 (accessed 26 April 2022).

[13] DAA 2021, sch 1, cl 3(1).

[14] ibid cl 4(1).

[15] ibid cl 2(4).

[16] ibid cl 6(1).

However, section 21 rarely formed part of the indictment[17] when committed prior to the index offence as, for example, in cases of rape[18] and robbery.[19] In *R v Fazli*[20] the defendant was proceeded against in relation to several counts of assault against his wife in that he had '[t]hrottled her with a long cotton scarf so that she was unable to breathe and was close to passing out'.[21] The judge in passing sentence for assault occasioning actual bodily harm following committal to the Crown Court for sentence considered the Sentencing Guideline on Domestic Violence and '[e]xpressed surprise that the appellant had not been charged with a more serious offence which would have enabled him to pass a sentence of imprisonment for public protection ... suggest[ing] that a charge of attempting to choke, suffocate or strangle contrary to s. 21 of the Offences against the Person Act 1861 might have been appropriate'.[22]

The Law Commission proposed abolition of section 21 on the grounds that it is little used, taking the view (at the time) that the general sentencing powers of the courts were sufficient to take into account strangulation as an aggravating factor.[23]

The statutory provisions listed below have been amended following the introduction of a stand-alone offence of strangulation and suffocation under section 70 and its incorporation into section 75A of the Serious Crime Act 2015 and demonstrate the wide application and implication across legislation as indicated below.

i. Police and Criminal Evidence Act 1984

1. In section 65A of the Police and Criminal Evidence Act 1984 (qualifying offences for the purposes of Part 5 of that Act which concerns the questioning and treatment of persons by police), in subsection (2), after paragraph (r) insert—

   '(ra) an offence under section 75A of the Serious Crime Act 2015 (strangulation or suffocation).'

ii. Housing Act 1985

2. In Schedule 2A to the Housing Act 1985 (absolute ground for possession for anti-social behaviour: serious offences), after paragraph 14 insert—

   '14A.An offence under section 75A of the Serious Crime Act 2015 (strangulation or suffocation).

[17] *R v F (DR)* [2013] EWCA Crim 1689; *R v Groombridge* [2013] EWCA Crim 274; *R v Moura* [2009] EWCA Crim 1891; *R v Abdroikof* [2007] UKHL 37; [2007] 1 WLR 2679; [2008] 1 Cr App R 21 (p.280); *R v L* [2006] EWCA Crim 1902, [2006] 1 WLR 3092, [2007] 1 Cr App R 1 (at 1); *R v Dempster* [2001] EWCA Crim 571, [2001] Crim LR 567.

[18] *R v Nolan* [2007] EWCA Crim 2410; *R v Doucoure* [2006] EWCA Crim 1814.

[19] *R v Mykoo* [2010] EWCA Crim 989 (strangled lone females walking home and took jewellery); *R v Williams* [2008] EWCA Crim 2886 (strangled and robbed).

[20] *R v Fazli* [2009] EWCA Crim 939 [9], [17].

[21] ibid [9].

[22] ibid [18].

[23] Law Commission, *Reform of Offences against the Person No 361* (2015) para 8.42.

iii. Criminal Justice and Public Order Act 1994

3. In Part 1 of Schedule 7A to the Criminal Justice and Public Order Act 1994 (offences in England and Wales for which cross-border powers of arrest available), for paragraph 24 substitute—

'24 An offence under either of the following provisions of the Serious Crime Act 2015—
(a) section 45 (participating in activities of organised crime group);
(b) section 75A (strangulation or suffocation).'

iv. Crime and Disorder Act 1998

4(1) Section 29 of the Crime and Disorder Act 1998 (racially or religiously aggravated assaults) is amended as follows.

(2) In subsection (1), after paragraph (b) (but before the 'or' following it) insert—
'(ba) an offence under section 75A of the Serious Crime Act 2015 (strangulation or suffocation);'.

(3) In subsection (2), for 'or (b)' substitute ', (b) or (ba)'.

v. Youth Justice and Criminal Evidence Act 1999

5(1) Schedule 1A to the Youth Justice and Criminal Evidence Act 1999 (proceedings in which witnesses are automatically eligible for assistance on grounds of fear or distress about testifying) is amended as follows.

(2) After paragraph 29 insert—
'Serious Crime Act 2015

29A. An offence under section 75A of the Serious Crime Act 2015 (strangulation or suffocation) in a case where it is alleged that—
(a) the accused was carrying a firearm or knife at any time during the commission of the offence, and
(b) a person other than the accused knew or believed at any time during the commission of the offence that the accused was carrying a firearm or knife.'

(3) In paragraph 30, after 'paragraphs 1 to 8' insert 'and 29A'.

vi. Sexual Offences Act 2003

6. In Schedule 5 to the Sexual Offences Act 2003 (cases where sexual harm prevention orders may be made), after paragraph 63B insert—
'63C An offence under section 75A of the Serious Crime Act 2015 (strangulation or suffocation).'

vii. Criminal Justice Act 2003

7. In Part 1 of Schedule 15 to the Criminal Justice Act 2003 (violent offences specified for purposes of certain custodial sentences), before paragraph 63G insert—
'63FA An offence under section 75A of the Serious Crime Act 2015 (strangulation or suffocation).'

viii. Domestic Violence, Crime and Victims Act 2004

8. In section 6A of the Domestic Violence, Crime and Victims Act 2004 (evidence and procedure in cases of serious physical harm: England and Wales), in subsection (2), at the end insert—
   '(c) an offence under section 75A of the Serious Crime Act 2015 (strangulation or suffocation).'

ix. Children Act 2004

9. In section 58 of the Children Act 2004 (reasonable punishment: England), in subsection (2), after paragraph (c) insert—
   '(d) an offence under section 75A of the Serious Crime Act 2015 (strangulation or suffocation).'

x. Criminal Justice and Immigration Act 2008

10. In section 98 of the Criminal Justice and Immigration Act 2008 (violent offender orders), in subsection (3), after paragraph (d) insert—
   '(da) an offence under section 75A of the Serious Crime Act 2015 (strangulation or suffocation);'.

xi. Modern Slavery Act 2015

11. In Schedule 4 to the Modern Slavery Act 2015 (offences to which defence for slavery or trafficking victims under section 45 of that Act does not apply), after paragraph 35 insert—
   'Serious Crime Act 2015

35A. An offence under section 75A of the Serious Crime Act 2015 (strangulation or suffocation).'

xii. Sentencing Act 2020

12(1) The Sentencing Act 2020 is amended as follows.

(2) In section 67 (assaults on emergency workers), in subsection (3), after paragraph (a) insert—
   '(aa) an offence under section 75A of the Serious Crime Act 2015 (strangulation or suffocation);'.

(3) In Part 1 of Schedule 18 (violent offences for which extended sentence of imprisonment available), after paragraph 25 insert—
   'Serious Crime Act 2015

25A. An offence under section 75A of the Serious Crime Act 2015 (strangulation or suffocation).'

3. SCHEDULE 3—AMENDMENTS RELATING TO OFFENCES COMMITTED OUTSIDE THE UK

i. Part 1

The first paragraph of Schedule 3 extends the jurisdiction of the criminal law of England and Wales in relation to the offence of harassment by inserting a new section, section 4B, into the Protection from Harassment Act 1997. This extension of jurisdiction to have extra-territorial effect in relation to this offence was enacted in accordance with Article 34 of the Istanbul Convention, which requires the UK to ensure that the intentional conduct by a UK national, or a habitual resident of the UK, of repeatedly threatening another person or causing them to fear for their safety is criminalised, regardless of where in the world the offence was committed.[24]

Currently under section 4 of the Protection from Harassment Act 1997 it is an offence to cause another to fear on a least two occasions that violence will be used against them where they know or ought to know that their course of conduct will cause the other to fear violence on each occasion. Moreover, section 4A makes it an offence to stalk another and to cause them to fear, on at least two occasions, that violence will be used against them, or cause them serious alarm or distress which has a substantial adverse effect on the person's usual day-to-day activities provided that the perpetrator knows or ought to know that their conduct will cause the other to fear violence on any occasion or cause them such alarm or distress. Prior to the passing of the Domestic Abuse Act 2021, the offences of harassment and stalking were only made out where the relevant conduct took place in the UK. The effect of section 4B is to extend the jurisdiction of the courts of England and Wales to enable offenders to be prosecuted in England and Wales for stalking or harassment committed abroad where three conditions are met. First, the accused's conduct must include conduct committed outside of the UK; secondly, the conduct must constitute an offence under section 4 or 4A (harassment or stalking), and, thirdly, the accused must be a UK national or habitually resident in England or Wales (s 4B(1)).

The second paragraph of Schedule 3 extends the jurisdiction of the criminal law of England and Wales in relation to certain sexual offences. Prior to the passing of this Act, it was, and remains, a criminal offence under section 72 of the Sexual Offences Act 2003 (SOA 2003) to commit offences abroad where those offences are listed in Schedule 2 to the SOA 2003. Before the passing of the DAA 2021, a UK national would be guilty of offences of rape, assault by penetration, sexual assault, and causing a person to engage in sexual activity where the offence was committed outside of the UK provided that the victim was under the age of 18. Schedule 3 extends the extra-territorial jurisdiction of English and Welsh courts to these offences where the victim was 18 or over at the time of the offence by introducing section 1A into Schedule 2.

The third paragraph of Schedule 3 extends the jurisdictional scope of the offence of coercive and controlling behaviour under section 76 Serious Crime Act 2015 via the introduction of section 76A into that Act. Under section 76 Serious Crime Act, it is an offence in England

[24] Istanbul Convention, Council of Europe Convention on preventing and combating violence against women and domestic violence CETS No 210, art 34. https://www.coe.int/en/web/istanbul-convention (accessed 26 May 2022).

and Wales for a person repeatedly or continuously to engage in behaviour towards another, to whom the perpetrator is personally connected, which is controlling or coercive, has a serious effect on the other, and which the perpetrator knows or ought to know that the behaviour would have such an effect. The effect of section 76A is that an offence will be committed in England and Wales regardless of where in the world that behaviour took place, provided that the perpetrator is a UK national or is habitually resident in England and Wales and the offence would constitute an offence under section 76 if it occurred in England and Wales.

ii. Part 2

Part 2 extends the territorial jurisdiction of the offences it sets out via amendments made to the Criminal Procedure (Scotland) Act 1995 and the Sexual Offences (Scotland) Act 2009. First, the territorial jurisdiction of the common law offence of assault is extended to cover the conduct of a UK national or a person habitually resident in Scotland which took place outside of the UK. In order for this extra-territorial jurisdiction to be conferred, the conduct must amount to the crime of assault if it were committed in Scotland, and it must also constitute an offence under the law of the country in which the conduct was committed, however that offence may ultimately be described. The introduction of section 11(2C) of the Criminal Procedure (Scotland) Act 1995 creates a presumption that conduct amounting to the crime of assault in Scotland will also constitute an offence under the law of the country in which the offence was committed. This presumption can be rebutted if the accused serves a notice on the prosecutor setting out grounds in support of the accused's opinion that the conduct would not constitute an offence in the country in which it was committed and requiring the prosecutor to prove otherwise.[25] The offence of stalking contrary to section 39 of the Criminal Justice and Licensing (Scotland) Act 2010 is afforded extra-territorial jurisdiction by the introduction of section 39A, which enables a UK national or habitual resident of Scotland to be prosecuted in Scotland for the offence of stalking provided that their course of conduct would constitute the offence of stalking if it occurred in Scotland.

Paragraph 5 inserts section 54D into the Sexual Offences (Scotland) Act 2009. This extends the territorial jurisdiction of Scottish courts in relation to certain sexual offences including rape, sexual assault by penetration, sexual assault, and sexual coercion to cover offences committed against an individual who was aged 18 or over at the time of the offence provided that the accused is a habitual resident of Scotland, and the conduct would constitute an offence in the country in which it was committed. Scottish courts already have this extraterritorial jurisdiction over these offences where they have been committed against an individual under the age of 18 by virtue of section 55 of the 2009 Act.[26]

Due to the territorial jurisdiction of sheriff courts, in order for an offence committed outside of the sheriffdom to be tried in a sheriff court, extraterritorial jurisdiction must be expressly provided for by way of a statutory provision.[27] Such extra-territorial jurisdiction is conferred on sheriff courts where the accused is alleged to have committed an offence under section 54(D) of the Sexual Offences (Scotland) Act 2009; in such cases, the accused may be tried in the sheriff court district in which the accused is apprehended or is in custody, or in

---

[25] Criminal Procedure (Scotland) Act 1995, s 11(2C).

[26] DAA 2021 Explanatory Notes, sch 3 'Amendments relating to offences committed outside the UK' [353] https://www.legislation.gov.uk/ukpga/2021/17/pdfs/ukpgaen_20210017_en.pdf. (accessed 26 May 2022).

[27] ibid [6].

any sheriff court district selected by the Lord Advocate (s 54D(8)). Such extraterritorial jurisdiction is also conferred by section 39A(2) of the Criminal Justice and Licensing (Scotland) Act 2010.

iii. Part 3

Part 3 relates to Northern Ireland and confers extraterritorial jurisdiction to cover the offence of harassment set out in Article 6 of the Protection from Harassment Order (Northern Ireland) 1997 ('the 1997 Order') by inserting Article 6A into the Order. Consequently, where a UK national or resident in Northern Ireland undertakes a course of conduct in a country, partially or wholly, outside the UK which would constitute an offence under Article 6 of the 1997 Order, they may be prosecuted in Northern Ireland of that offence. Part 3 also inserts paragraph 76(10A) into Article 76 of the Sexual Offences (Northern Ireland) Order 2008. This paragraph confers extraterritorial jurisdiction upon the court to try a person accused of rape, assault by penetration, sexual assault, and causing a person to engage in sexual activity without consent where the conduct was committed by a UK national, or UK resident, outside of the UK against a victim aged 18 or over at the time of the offence provided that the conduct would constitute an offence in the country where it was committed.

PART III OF GUIDE

OMISSIONS FROM THE DOMESTIC ABUSE ACT 2021

19

THE DOMESTIC ABUSE ACT 2021 AND MIGRANT WOMEN

Pragna Patel and Janaya Walker

1. INTRODUCTION

The Domestic Abuse Act (DAA) 2021 received royal assent on 29 April 2021. Hailed as 'long overdue' and 'landmark legislation', then Home Secretary Priti Patel stated that it would 'provide further protections to the millions of people who experience domestic abuse' and 'transform the support we offer *across society*' (emphasis added).[1] But this legislation was not a cause for celebration for all. Despite immense efforts by women's organisations like Southall Black Sisters (SBS) and the Latin American Women's Rights Service (LAWRS) to amend the law to ensure protection and support for migrant women who have insecure immigration status which heightens their risk of gender-related abuse, the government resolutely refused to include this cohort of survivors within the scope of the legislation.

Insecure immigration status as a risk factor for abuse is reflected in the government's 'Controlling or Coercive Behaviour Statutory Guidance'[2] and in the draft

[1] UK Government, 'Landmark Domestic Abuse Bill receives Royal Assent' (29 April 2021) https://www.gov.uk/government/news/landmark-domestic-abuse-bill-receives-royalassent (accessed 17 April 2022).

[2] Home Office, 'Controlling or Coercive Behaviour in an Intimate or Family Relationship: Statutory Guidance Framework' (2015) https://assets.publishing.service.gov.uk/government/uploads/system/uploads/attachment_data/file/482528/Controlling_or_coercive_behaviour_-_statutory_guidance.pdf (accessed 17 April 2022).

Pragna Patel and Janaya Walker, *The Domestic Abuse Act 2021 and Migrant Women* In: *Blackstone's Guide to the Domestic Abuse Act 2021*. Edited by Susan Edwards, David Malone, and Gillian Jones KC, Oxford University Press.
 DOI: 10.1093/oso/9780192870513.003.0019

statutory guidance framework for the DAA.[3] It has also been recognised by the College of Policing[4] and other government departments and in policy documents. Yet the government's failure to incorporate protective measures for migrant women in the Act in recognition of this, only serves to entrench discriminatory processes within immigration law that produce a double whammy for abused migrant women: they are not only excluded from state protection but are also actually subject to state complicity in the violence that they experience, at the hands of their abusers. Far from featuring in the government's vision of 'society', abused migrant women join a growing group of migrants that continue to be treated by the government, at best, as undeserving of equality and justice and, at worst, as disposable. It is a position that consolidates a two-tier discriminatory system of protection for survivors of abuse based on their immigration status and violates international human rights law.

In this chapter, we briefly outline the dire circumstances and challenges faced by migrant survivors of abuse in the UK and examine the government's justification for rejecting amendments put forward during the passage of the Act in order to alleviate the problems faced by migrant women. We conclude with some reflections on developments since the Act came into force, highlighting the need for conformity and a growing need to include immigration status as a protected characteristic in the Equality Act 2010.

2. NO RECOURSE TO PUBLIC FUNDS AND THE 'HOSTILE ENVIRONMENT'

In recent decades, considerable progress has been made in advancing the rights of women and girls subject to all forms of gender-based violence (GBV) in the UK. However, over the same period, a succession of deeply hostile, anti-immigration legislation and policies have created fertile ground for the abuse and exploitation of migrant women. As it stands, migrant women are at disproportionate risk of GBV including suicide and homicide[5] in the UK and yet they have the most limited access to protection and support.[6] There are two principal factors that lie behind the high proportion of migrant women trapped in domestic abuse: the 'no recourse to public funds' (NRPF) condition and the Home Office's 'hostile environment'.

The NRPF is a condition imposed on almost everyone in the UK subject to immigration controls as defined at section 115 of the Immigration and Asylum Act 1999.

(9)' A person subject to immigration control' means a person who—
- (a) requires leave to enter or remain in the United Kingdom but does not have it;
- (b) has leave to enter or remain in the United Kingdom which is subject to a condition that he does not have recourse to public funds;

[3] Home Office, 'Domestic Abuse Draft Statutory Guidance Framework' (2020) https://assets.publishing.service.gov.uk/government/uploads/system/uploads/attachment_data/file/896640/Draft_statutory_guidance_July_2020.pdf (accessed 17 April 2022).

[4] College of Policing's APP on Major Investigations and Public Protection https://www.app.college.police.uk/app-content/major-investigation-and-public-protection/domestic-abuse/risk-and-vulnerability/ (accessed 17 April 2022).

[5] See Hannana Siddiqui, and Meena Patel, 'SBS: Safe and Sane' (2010) http://www.southallblacksisters.org.uk/reports/safe-and-sane-report/ and Mayor of London 'The way forward taking action to end violence against women and girls: Final Strategy 2010–2013' (2010) https://www.london.gov.uk/sites/default/files/the_way_forward_-_strategy.pdf (accessed 17 April 2022).

[6] Mayor of London (n 5).

(c) has leave to enter or remain in the United Kingdom given as a result of a maintenance undertaking; or
(d) has leave to enter or remain in the United Kingdom only as a result of paragraph 17 of Schedule 4.

This means they are prohibited from accessing the majority of welfare benefits such as universal credit and social housing and child tax credit.[7] Prohibiting such access has always formed part of the Home Office's immigration control policies, but the NRPF condition was explicitly introduced in 1999 to restrict migrants from accessing the welfare safety net. In tandem with other hostile immigration environment policies, the NRPF condition has had the effect of institutionalising exclusion and racial profiling within statutory and, increasingly, the private sectors, that are incentivised to block those perceived as 'non-British' from accessing resources.[8]

Many specialist Black and Minority Ethnic (BME) women's NGOs supporting migrant women state that at least 60 per cent of the women they support are subject to GBV *and* have insecure immigration status.[9] Many arrive in the UK as the partner or spouse of a British national or through other immigration routes, such as student visas and as dependents of those on work visas and visitor visas. A large proportion is subject to NRPF.

In contexts of domestic abuse, the NRPF condition effectively forces women to make a dangerous choice between enduring abuse or facing destitution, detention, and further harm if they exit abuse. In most cases, the abuse that women experience escalates over time and is exacerbated by their insecure immigration status and the NRPF condition. Many abusers also deliberately jeopardise women's immigration status, for example by supplying them with false information, withholding essential documentation, and interfering with their application to regularise their stay. This results in many women becoming 'overstayers' and undocumented as a result of the abuse. Women are also therefore vulnerable to higher rates of destitution, poverty, indebtedness, trauma, and mental illness.

i. Challenges Supporting Migrant Survivors

In these circumstances, migrant survivors with NRPF and those supporting them face immense challenges in accessing welfare services to facilitate their protection. What little change that has occurred has been entirely due to campaigns waged by groups like SBS for many years. In 2002, SBS successfully campaigned for the introduction of the domestic violence (DV) rule, allowing women on spousal visas a route to apply for indefinite leave to remain if their relationship breaks down due to domestic violence. Further campaigning and lobbying led to the creation of the destitution and domestic violence (DDV) concession in 2012; this gives spousal visa DV rule applicants access to limited state benefits and emergency housing pending their applications under the DV rule. Whilst these are welcome developments, countless abused migrant women continue to be excluded from such

[7] Free Movement, 'What is the no recourse to public funds condition?' (2019) https://www.freemovement.org.uk/what-is-the-no-recourse-to-public-funds-condition/ (accessed 17 April 2022).

[8] This discrimination is typified by the right to rent scheme, which was found by the Court of Appeal to cause racial discrimination. See *R (Joint Council for the Welfare of Immigrants) v Secretary of State for the Home Department* [2020] EWCA Civ 542.

[9] Southall Black Sisters, 'The Domestic Abuse Bill & Migrant Women: Briefing Paper 2' (2020) https://southallblacksisters.org.uk/wp-content/uploads/2021/01/DA-Bill-Briefing-Paper-2.pdf (accessed 17 April 2022).

protection. Evidence from Women's Aid, for example, has found that over a one-year period, two-thirds of their users with NRPF were not eligible for statutory support because they were on non-spousal visas and had NRPF.[10]

Whilst local authorities have a legal duty to safeguard vulnerable adults and children, this duty often remains unmet due to the combination of cuts in services and anti-immigration policies. Section 17 of the Children Act 1989 sets out local authority duties towards vulnerable and destitute women with children, including those subject to NRPF. Under this duty, local authorities are obliged to provide accommodation and financial support, but they regularly fail to do so. There is no statutory guidance regarding supporting vulnerable families with NRPF and there is considerable inconsistency of practice across the UK towards migrant women and children with NRPF, who are often left facing severe hardships and trauma.

Migrant women also face difficulties in obtaining access to women's refuges mainly because refuges are unable to meet the costs of their housing and other subsistence costs and lack the resources to assist with what are often complex immigration matters.[11]

3. PROPOSED AMENDMENTS TO THE DOMESTIC ABUSE ACT FOR MIGRANT WOMEN

It is against this backdrop that SBS together with other organisations put forward a package of three amendments to the Domestic Abuse Act to assist migrant survivors. The first sought to extend the DV rule and the DDV concession to a broader cohort of abused migrant women, and to extend the time limit of the DDVC from three to six months.[12] The second presented by the Latin American Women's Rights Service (LAWRS) sought to introduce a safe reporting mechanism for survivors to enable them to access the police and other public services without fear of being subject to immigration enforcement.[13] The third,[14] submitted by the End Violence Against Women (EVAW) coalition sought to introduce a principle of non-discrimination on the basis of migrant status in accessing public services in line with Article 4(3) of the Istanbul Convention (a landmark treaty of the Council of Europe for preventing and combating violence against women and domestic violence).[15] Throughout

---

[10] Women's Aid, 'Nowhere to Turn: Findings from the first year of the No Women Turned Away project' (2017) https://www.womensaid.org.uk/no-woman-turned-away/ (accessed 16 November 2022).

[11] In 2020–21, only 6.3 per cent of refuge spaces on Routes to Support were accessible to women with NRPF. See Women's Aid, 'The Domestic Abuse Report 2022: The Annual Audit' (2022) https://www.womensaid.org.uk/evidence-hub/research-and-publications/the-domestic-abuse-report/ (accessed 12 April 2022).

[12] See NC26, 'Recourse for Public Funds for domestic abuse survivors' and NC26: 'Victims of domestic abuse: leave to remain' in House of Commons (Monday 6 July 2020) Consideration of Bill (Report Stage) https://publications.parliament.uk/pa/bills/cbill/58-01/0141/amend/domestic_daily_rep_0703.pdf (accessed 12 April 2022).

[13] See NC27, 'Victims of domestic abuse: data-sharing for immigration purposes' in House of Commons (Monday 6 July 2020) Consideration of Bill (Report Stage): https://publications.parliament.uk/pa/bills/cbill/58-01/0141/amend/domestic_daily_rep_0703.pdf. See also Step Up Migrant Women (undated) Resources https://stepupmigrantwomen.org/resources/ (accessed 12 April 2022).

[14] See NC25, 'Effective protection and support for all victims of domestic abuse' in House of Commons (Monday 6 July 2020) Consideration of Bill (Report Stage): https://publications.parliament.uk/pa/bills/cbill/58-01/0141/amend/domestic_daily_rep_0703.pdf.

[15] Council of Europe, *The Council of Europe Convention on Preventing and Combating Violence against Women and Domestic Violence* (November 2014) https://www.refworld.org/docid/548165c94.html (accessed 12 April 2022).

the passage of the Act, SBS, LAWRS, and EVAW worked collaboratively to present these amendments, give evidence to relevant parliamentary committees, and to provide briefings to MPs and peers in the House of Lords.

i. Parliamentary Debates

The absence of protection for migrant women was consistently raised throughout the passage of the Bill. In January 2019, a Joint Committee on the draft Domestic Abuse bill (Joint Committee) was formed with members across the political spectrum to scrutinise the Bill. In its final report, published on 14 June 2019, it emphatically stated that the draft Bill represented:

> [a] missed opportunity to address the needs of migrant women who have no recourse to public funds and recommended that the Government explore '[w]ays to extend the temporary concessions available under the DV Rule and DDV Concession to support migrant survivors of abuse'.[16]

The Joint Committee made clear recommendations to the government to remedy the crisis faced by migrant women, but the government rejected this and all other recommendations on safe reporting mechanisms and compliance with the non-discrimination principle of the Istanbul Convention (see s 81 of DAA in Part II). Instead, it reiterated its NRPF policy,[17] and referred to funds that had been provided to SBS via the Tampon Tax Fund to cover the cost of temporary housing and basic needs of abused migrant women, even though it was also conceded that not all of them had access to this support. Under pressure, it also made reference to a review on migrant women that was underway by then.

During the Second Reading of the Bill on 2 October 2019, the issue of migrant women was raised twenty-three times by a selection of cross-party MPs. Conservative MP (and former Immigration Minister) Caroline Nokes urged the Under-Secretary of State for the Home Office, Victoria Atkins, to: '[d]o what she can to make sure that we are doing more for migrant women'.[18] Atkins responded by reiterating a review that was under way, and stated that, if necessary, changes were needed, they could be made without primary legislation.[19]

However, during the passage of the Bill, the government gave three primary reasons to justify its position, namely, first, that a 'migrant review' was already in place; secondly, there was a lack of evidence on the needs of migrant women; and, thirdly, the need to protect the immigration system from 'exploitation' by migrants remained a top priority.

On the question of the review, SBS amongst others had already expressed considerable disquiet about the flawed process and lack of transparency. It contained no terms of reference, did not meaningfully engage with the evidence submitted by key specialist organisations, and eventually produced poor and misleading analysis and conclusions. SBS and the LAWRS

[16] House of Lords House of Commons Joint Committee on the Draft Domestic Abuse Bill (11 June 2019) Draft Domestic Abuse Bill First Report of Session 2017–2019 https://publications.parliament.uk/pa/jt201719/jtselect/jtddab/2075/2075.pdf (accessed 12 April 2022).

[17] See para 147 of the government response to the report from the Joint Committee on the Draft Domestic Abuse Bill (July 2019) https://assets.publishing.service.gov.uk/government/uploads/system/uploads/attachment_data/file/817556/CCS0619467038-001_Domestic_Abuse_Bill_Print_WEb_Accessible.pdf (accessed 12 April 2022).

[18] HC Deb (2 October 2019) vol 664, col 1283 https://hansard.parliament.uk/commons/2019-10-02/debates/C3488538-CFEC-4670-9299-732672E2BE67/DomesticAbuseBill (accessed 12 April 2022).

[19] ibid HC Deb Victoria Atkins col 1331.

published a detailed formal response to the review in September 2020, outlining serious concerns about its methodology, scope, and analysis.[20] This was sent to the Home Office and to the Minister for Safeguarding, Victoria Atkins. No response was received.

The final report of the review was eventually published by the Home Office on Friday 3 July 2020 and was used by the government simply to restate its decision (first announced on 28 April 2020) to commission a pilot project for migrant women which was launched in autumn 2020. However, there remained much scepticism as to its effectiveness in guaranteeing adequate long-term protection for abused migrant women on non-spousal visas.

The government's second stated reason for not deviating from its position was the purported lack of evidence to support any legislative change. The Home Office's Review stated: '[w]e need a better evidence base before we can make robust policy decisions'.[21] This was the basis on which Victoria Atkins announced £1.5 million for a pilot fund to cover the cost of support for migrant women with NRPF in refuge accommodation, stating that the pilot would be used 'to better assess the level of need and to inform longer-term funding'.[22] Similarly, in the Lords, Baroness Williams of Trafford stated that '[t]here is currently a lack of robust data to demonstrate which cohorts of migrant victims are likely to be in most need of support'.[23] The claim that there was insufficient evidence was made against a backdrop of copious research and evidence that already existed into the circumstances and needs of migrant women, much of it having been provided to the Home Office and Parliament during the course of the review and throughout the passage of the DAA.

At the later stages of the Bill, Conservative MPs in particular acknowledged the poor circumstances of migrant survivors, whilst voting against SBS' amendment on the basis of the government's claim that there was a lack of evidence and that a pilot scheme was required to inform long-term changes.[24] On 6 July 2020, clause 22 concerning the extension of eligibility for the DV rule and the DDVC lost the vote in the House of Commons, by 330 votes against versus 207 in favour.[25]

There was a cruel irony in the government's rejection of SBS' amendments on the basis of 'insufficient evidence' when the very government policies that create the conditions of entrapment for migrant women such as the NRPF condition or data sharing between the police and the Home Office, were themselves introduced without any 'specific evidence base to support the effectiveness of these measures'. This conclusion came from a report by the National Audit Office (NAO), the UK's independent public spending watchdog.[26]

---

[20] Southall Black Sisters and Latin American Women's Rights Service, 'Migrant Victims of Domestic Abuse Review Findings: A response by Southall Black Sisters and Latin American Women's Rights Service' (September 2020) https://southallblacksisters.org.uk/wp-content/uploads/2021/01/SBS-and-LAWRS-joint-response-to-the-Migrant-Victims-of-Domestic-Violence-Review.pdf (accessed 12 April 2022).

[21] ibid para 57.

[22] HC Deb (28 April 2020) vol 675, col 299 https://hansard.parliament.uk/commons/2020-04-28/debates/AABF0D9C-D3BC-40C5-830A-52073E09ED35/DomesticAbuseBill (accessed 12 April 2022).

[23] HL Deb (5 January 2021) vol 809, col 126 https://hansard.parliament.uk/lords/2021-01-05/debates/1384371F-73F4-40BC-A44A-B0358CF839B6/DomesticAbuseBill (accessed 12 April 2022).

[24] See Maria Miller MP, HC Deb (6 July 2020) vol 678, col 728 https://hansard.parliament.uk/Commons/2020-07-06/debates/CEAE6941-5DC8-4F76-9377-3DE3ED0F3553/DomesticAbuseBill (accessed 12 April 2022).

[25] UK Parliament (6 July 2020) 'Domestic Abuse Bill: Report Stage: New Clause 22' https://votes.parliament.uk/Votes/Commons/Division/814 (accessed 12 April 2022).

[26] National Audit Office 'Report by the Comptroller and Auditor General: Home Office immigration enforcement' (June 2020) https://www.nao.org.uk/report/immigration-enforcement/ (accessed 12 April 2022).

The third justification given by the government as to why protection for migrant women should not be enshrined in the Act was its fear that extending eligibility for the DV rule and the DDVC would usurp immigration control objectives. During discussions on the NRPF amendment in the Commons, Victoria Atkins stated that survivors on non-spousal visas were not eligible for the DV rule and the DDVC, unlike the spouses of British nationals or those settled in the UK, migrant women who had a 'legitimate expectation of staying in the country'.[27]

SBS pointed out that this was an inaccurate position given that the DV rule and the DDVC do not extend to *all* migrant women who also have a legitimate expectation of settlement in the UK. There was no recognition of the fact that there are many women on other types of visas who for various reasons have expectations of settlement who are deprived of routes to settlement by their abusers. Others have real and justified fears of returning to their country of origin where they may be at greater risk from their abuser and/or wider family in the form of reprisals. Yet others include survivors who have deliberately had documents withheld and applications tarnished by abusers, so that they become 'undocumented' or 'overstayers'. This includes women who may have previously been financially independent prior to coming to the UK but who become destitute in the course of an abusive relationship.

Nonetheless, the government remained opposed to any extension of the DV rule and the DDV concession on the basis that it would 'undermine the specific purpose that gave rise to them' and, further, 'might lead to more exploitation of vulnerable migrants or, indeed, of our immigration system'.[28]

The government did not provide any evidence to substantiate these claims. It is unclear why it would be in an abuser's interest to 'exploit' his partner/spouse by helping her to regularise her status through the DV rule. Indeed, such a move would risk implicating the abuser, exposing him to criminal and legal proceedings, whilst providing his partner/spouse with a route by which to access protection and independence. On the matter of potential exploitation of the immigration system, it is worth reflecting here on the political context in which the legislation was being debated, under the then Home Secretary Priti Patel. One month before the Domestic Abuse Act became law, the Home Office published its 'New Plan for Immigration', the antecedent to the Nationality and Borders Bill, which revealed a fixation on the apparent 'exploitation' and frequent 'open gaming' of the asylum (and immigration) system.[29] This was perhaps the most troubling reason presented by the government, since it confirmed the view that immigration enforcement remains a priority irrespective of migrant women's need for protection.

4. FINAL REFLECTIONS

On 15 March 2021, the Lord Bishop of Gloucester, with considerable cross-party support in the House of Lords, successfully moved SBS' amendment to a vote, which inserted a new clause to allow victims of domestic abuse leave to remain in the UK and to extend the

[27] HC Deb (17 June 2020) col 417 https://hansard.parliament.uk/commons/2020-06-17/debates/56d8cf25-5197-4301-b4f3-e872ae712acb/DomesticAbuseBill(EleventhSitting (accessed 12 April 2022).

[28] ibid.

[29] HM Government, 'New Plan for Immigration Policy Statement' (March 2021) https://assets.publishing.service.gov.uk/government/uploads/system/uploads/attachment_data/file/972517/CCS207_CCS0820091708-001_Sovereign_Borders_Web_Accessible.pdf (accessed 12 April 2022).

DDV concession. It was passed by 318 votes to 269.[30] However, when the Bill subsequently returned to the Commons, SBS' amendment to extend eligibility for the DV rule and the DDVC was once again rejected in the Commons (with 352 against versus 270 in favour).[31] In view of the government's intransigence, SBS put forward a compromise amendment calling on the government to lift the NRPF temporarily for one year as part of the pilot project, to allow more women to come forward and seek support and to allow for a greater analysis of need. This was again moved by the Lord Bishop of Gloucester and accepted in the House of Lords, by a vote of 292 in favour and 233 against.[32] However, this too was ultimately rejected by the House of Commons by 352 versus 270 votes.[33]

Eventually, the Bill received royal assent a few days later without including anything of substance for the protection of migrant women. As a result, migrant women risk being excluded even from the new provisions in the legislation intended to improve the response to domestic abuse victims, such as the introduction of a new statutory duty (see ss 57 and 58 in Part II of this guide) on tier 1 local authorities to provide safe accommodation (with associated funding) for victims of domestic abuse, and their children.[34] Since coming into force in April 2021, frontline NGOs report that migrant victims and survivors are often regarded by local authorities as remaining outside the scope of the duty. Similarly, whilst the Act recognises children as victims of domestic abuse in their own right,[35] it remains unclear whether this development has mitigated against the effect of hostile policies such as the NRPF towards the children of migrant survivors.[36]

All of the above takes on even greater significance when we consider that the cohort of women with insecure immigration status and subject to NRPF has likely to have expanded since the UK exited the European Union. It is highly probable that local authorities will see an increase in victims of domestic abuse from the European Economic Area (EEA) requiring support, particularly considering the economic impact of the Covid-19 pandemic.[37] The Nationality and Borders Bill also contains proposals which will subject even more victims and survivors to the NRPF condition.[38]

---

[30] Amendment 70, 'Victims of domestic abuse: leave to remain and the destitution domestic violence concession (DDVC)' in UK Parliament (15 March 2021) Domestic Abuse Bill https://votes.parliament.uk/votes/lords/division/2484 (accessed 12 April 2022).

[31] HC (15 April 2021) Domestic Abuse Bill Division 258 https://hansard.parliament.uk/Commons/2021-04-15/division/9DD5DDB8-427B-4FD1-9E3A-744A18871636/DomesticAbuseBill?outputType=Names (accessed 12 April 2022).

[32] UK Parliament, Domestic Abuse Bill Division 3 (21 April 2021) https://votes.parliament.uk/votes/lords/division/2510 (accessed 12 April 2022).

[33] UK Parliament, Domestic Abuse Bill: motion to disagree with Lords Amendment 41B: Division 275 (26 April 2021) https://votes.parliament.uk/Votes/Commons/Division/1017 (accessed 12 April 2022).

[34] Home Office Policy Paper 'Local authority support for victims of domestic abuse and their children within safe accommodation fact sheet' (2020) https://www.gov.uk/government/publications/domestic-abuse-bill-2020-factsheets/local-authority-support-for-victims-of-domestic-abuse-and-their-children-within-safe-accommodation-factsheet (accessed 12 April 2022).

[35] Domestic Abuse Act 2021, s 3: Commentary on provisions of Act https://www.legislation.gov.uk/ukpga/2021/17/notes/division/6/index.htm (accessed 12 April 2022).

[36] See Project 17, 'Not Seen, Not Heard: Children's Experiences of the Hostile Environment' (2019); Children's Society, 'A Lifeline for All Children and Families with No Recourse to Public Funds' (May 2020).

[37] NRPF Network, 'Councils likely to incur costs providing safety-net support to EEA nationals after free movement ends' (December 2020) https://www.nrpfnetwork.org.uk/news/eea-nationals-dec-2020 (accessed 12 April 2022).

[38] Home Office Policy paper, Nationality and Borders Bill: A differentiated approach factsheet: (undated) https://www.gov.uk/government/publications/nationality-and-borders-bill-differentiation-factsheet/nationality-and-borders-bill-differentiation-factsheet (accessed 12 April 2022).

The exclusion of migrant survivors from the DAA is profoundly disappointing. But we take hope from the fact we won the moral battle if not the legal battle. We have been greatly heartened by the groundswell of cross-party support that was garnered in both Houses of Parliament, albeit in varying degrees. Our efforts also received wider public support including from the Domestic Abuse Commissioner, the Victim's Commissioner, the London Victim's Commissioner, leading organisations in the Violence Against Women and Girls (VAWG) sector, the Equality and Human Rights Commission, children's charities, and many other organisations and policy-makers, as well attracting considerable media coverage. At almost every stage of the Bill's progression through Parliament, the government was challenged on its treatment of migrant survivors of abuse, leading Baroness Williams to remark that 'practically the whole House talked about the needs of migrant victims'[39] at the Second Reading in the House of Lords. Six months after the Act became law, the Domestic Abuse Commissioner (DAC) dedicated her first report to migrant victims, identified as a priority for her office.[40]

We consider that the continuing exclusion of migrant women from protection amounts to a breach of the UK's obligations under domestic and international human rights law, in particular the European Convention on Human Rights (ECHR), the Convention on the Elimination of All Forms of Discrimination against Women (CEDAW) and the Council of Europe Convention on Preventing and Combating Violence against Women and Domestic Violence 2011 (IC).

The failure to include proper protection for migrant women law and policy amounts to potential breaches of ECHR Article 2 (right to life), Article 3 (right to be free from inhuman/degrading treatment), and Article 8 (right to private and family life including physical and moral personal integrity), especially when taken together with Article 14 (non-discrimination in the enjoyment of Convention rights).

In its concluding observations, the 2019 CEDAW Committee also called on the UK to 'ensure that asylum-seeking and migrant women and women with insecure immigration status are able to seek effective protection and support services without fear of having their immigration status reported to authorities'.[41] For this reason, the focus must now be two-pronged. First, there is a need to compel the government to ratify the IC, signed a decade ago. The IC makes it explicit that all survivors of abuse must be protected without discrimination which means the enjoyment of Convention Rights on the basis of, for example, migrant or refugee status. Any policy which prevents migrant women accessing protection from abuse, or which discourages migrant women from reporting and penalises them when they do, must be seen to be depriving migrant victims of abuse (as opposed to citizens/those with settled status) of the full enjoyment of their rights and protections. Secondly, taking a leave from the IC, there is a compelling case for inserting migrant status as a specific protected

[39] Hansard HL Deb (5 January 2021) col 126https://hansard.parliament.uk/lords/2021-01-05/debates/1384371F-73F4-40BC-A44A-B0358CF839B6/DomesticAbuseBill (accessed 12 April 2022).

[40] 'Safety Before Status' provided a series of recommendations to provide a 'clear and universal pathway to support for victims of domestic abuse with insecure immigration status'. The DAC has since commissioned further research seeking to build the evidence base to make the case for support. See Domestic Abuse Commissioner, 'Safety Before Status: Improving pathways to support for migrant victims of domestic abuse' (October 2021) https://domesticabusecommissioner.uk/wp-content/uploads/2021/10/Safety-Before-Status-Report-2021.pdf (accessed 12 April 2022).

[41] https://tbinternet.ohchr.org/_layouts/15/treatybodyexternal/Download.aspx?symbolno=CEDAW/C/GBR/CO/8&Lang=En (accessed 12 April 2022).

characteristic into the Equality Act 2010. This is necessary to prevent direct discrimination and to extend the government's general commitment to equality to refugees and migrants. At present, discrimination on the basis of colour, nationality, and ethnic origins can be invoked but restrictions written into immigration laws themselves are likely to nullify the Equality Act provisions.

The year 2020–21 was a year in which the government repeatedly asserted its commitment to addressing GBV, in part due to widespread coverage of women killed by men in public spaces. Whilst the government continues to claim that GBV is a priority, it is incumbent on all of us committed to ending GBV to be relentless in ensuring that protection is provided without discrimination. As long as migrant survivors remain excluded from support on the basis of their immigration status, our vision for a different world for women and girls will remain out of reach.

20

LIMITATIONS OF THE DOMESTIC ABUSE ACT 2021: DEFENCES FOR VICTIMS WHO OFFEND OR ALLEGEDLY OFFEND IN THE CONTEXT OF DOMESTIC ABUSE

Katy Swaine Williams

1. INTRODUCTION

This chapter discusses how failings in criminal law and practice can lead to unjust treatment of victims accused of offences that result from their experience of domestic abuse. It describes two new statutory defences that were put forward for inclusion in the DAA 2021—the first replicating the householder defence for victims of domestic abuse who use force against their abuser, and the second replicating the statutory defence available to victims of trafficking who are compelled to offend, making the same protection available to victims of domestic abuse in the same circumstances. It argues that the government's rejection of those proposals at the Bill stage, mainly based on their belief that existing defences are adequate, was a missed opportunity to help ensure just outcomes in these cases.

Katy Swaine Williams, *Limitations of the Domestic Abuse Act 2021: Defences for Victims Who Offend or Allegedly Offend in the Context of Domestic Abuse* In: *Blackstone's Guide to the Domestic Abuse Act 2021*. Edited by Susan Edwards, David Malone, and Gillian Jones KC, Oxford University Press. © Katy Swaine Williams 2023. DOI: 10.1093/oso/9780192870513.003.0020

Based on government data, nearly 60 per cent of women in prison and under community supervision are victims of domestic abuse.[1] Of 173 women screened at HMP Drake Hall, 64 per cent reported a history indicative of brain injury and for most this was caused by domestic violence.[2] It is widely recognised, including by government, that women's offending is often directly linked to their experience of domestic abuse.[3] There is substantial agreement amongst legal and domestic abuse experts, including the Domestic Abuse Commissioner and Victims' Commissioner, that new statutory defences, replicating the householder defence and the trafficking victims' defence, with a surrounding policy and practice framework, are needed to help prevent unjust outcomes for victims of domestic abuse accused of offending.[4]

The Centre for Women's Justice (CWJ) put forward two proposed new statutory defences during the passage of the Domestic Abuse Bill.[5] The first addresses deficiencies in the law on self-defence, giving victims who use force against their abuser the same protection as householders who use force against an intruder (the 'self-defence proposal'). The second offers victims who are coerced into offending the same protection that already exists for victims of trafficking who are compelled to offend as part of, or as a direct result of, their exploitation (the 'coercion (compulsion) defence proposal'). Despite being passed by the House of Lords, these new defences were opposed by the government and left out of the Act.

2. HOW VICTIMS OF DOMESTIC ABUSE ARE CRIMINALISED

There are many ways in which victims of domestic abuse find themselves criminalised.[6] This may result from their use of force against their abuser in self-defence, or from being coerced by their abuser into committing crimes such as theft, fraud, handling of stolen goods and possession of controlled substances. Male perpetrators of domestic abuse may use the criminal justice system as an additional means of exerting power, while for some women, physical retaliation may be part of an attempt to survive their victimisation.[7] Police officer perpetrators of abuse may use their powers or contacts to criminalise their victims.[8]

---

[1] Ministry of Justice, 'Female Offender Strategy' (2018) 11 https://www.gov.uk/government/publications/female-offender-strategy (accessed 17 December 2021).

[2] The Disabilities Trust Making the Link Female Offending and Brain Injury https://www.headway.org.uk/media/6461/making-the-link-female-offending-and-brain-injury-brief-report.pdf (accessed 17 December 2021).

[3] See Prison Reform Trust, 'There's a reason we're in trouble: Domestic abuse as a driver to women's offending' (2017); see also Ministry of Justice,, 'Transforming the Response to Domestic Abuse Consultation Response and Draft' (2019) Bill.https://assets.publishing.service.gov.uk/government/uploads/system/uploads/attachment_data/file/772247/Transforming_the_response_to_domestic_abuse_-_consultation_response_and_draft_bill_-print.pdf (accessed 17 December 2021).

[4] Centre for Women's Justice, 'Domestic Abuse Bill—legal protection for survivors who offend due to abuse' (2021) https://static1.squarespace.com/static/5aa98420f2e6b1ba0c874e42/t/5fdc843c9d30181faffbb1f5/1608287293168/CWJ+DA+Bill+short+briefing+Dec+2020.pdf (accessed 17 December 2021).

[5] ibid.

[6] Prison Reform Trust (n 3).

[7] Jo Roberts, '"It was do or die": how women's offending can occur as a by-product of attempting to survive domestic abuse' (2019) 3(3) *Journal of Gender-Based Violence* 283. See also Marianne Hester, 'Who does what to whom? Gender and Domestic Violence Perpetrators' (2009) 10(5) *European Journal of Criminology* 1.

[8] HM Inspectorate of Police and Fire & Rescue Services Police super-complaints: force response to police perpetrated domestic abuse https://www.gov.uk/government/publications/police-super-complaints-force-response-to-police-perpetrated-domestic-abuse ((accessed 17 December 2021)).

3. DEFICIENCIES IN LAW AND PROPOSED STATUTORY DEFENCES

There is widespread agreement amongst legal and domestic abuse experts that the existing defences available to victims of domestic abuse who use force against their abuser, or who are coerced by their abuser into offending, lag far behind the modern understanding of domestic abuse as reflected in section 76 of the SCA 2015 (which introduced the criminal offence of controlling or coercive behaviour in an intimate or family relationship) and section 1 of the DAA 2021 (which introduced a statutory definition of domestic abuse, including coercive and controlling conduct), and that they require legislative reform.[9]

Working with experts including the Victims' Commissioner, the Domestic Abuse Commissioner, and the Criminal Bar Association, the CWJ argued for two new statutory defences to be included in the Domestic Abuse Act.[10] These were tabled in the House of Commons by Jess Phillips MP and Peter Kyle MP, and in the House of Lords by Baroness Helena Kennedy KC. In a survey of thirty-one criminal defence lawyers, more than two-thirds believed that the self-defence proposal would provide a more effective defence in this context than the current law, while three-quarters considered that the coercion defence proposal would be more effective than the law of duress, where offending results from domestic abuse.[11] The proposals were voted into the Bill by the House of Lords, but were opposed by the government and fell in the Bill's final stages.[12]

i. The Self-defence Proposal

The law on self-defence allows the use of reasonable force but has proved very difficult for women defendants to rely upon regarding use of force against their abuser. As Susan Edwards explains:[13]

> [f]ear of being abused by a domestic abuser (experienced largely by women) is not always understood, considered reasonable or within common sense knowledge, and is often contested as insufficient to excuse violent defensive conduct.

---

9 See eg Prison Reform Trust (n 3); Criminal Bar Association of England and Wales, 'Defences available for women defendants who are victims/survivors of domestic abuse' (2017) CBA-domestic-violence-briefing.pdf (prisonreformtrust.org.uk) http://www.prisonreformtrust.org.uk/wp-content/uploads/2022/02/CBA-domestic-violence-briefing.pdf (accessed 16 November 2022). See also CWJ (n 4).

10 See amendments 37, 38, and 83 in House of Lords (2021) Domestic Abuse Bill: Marshalled list of motions to be moved on consideration of Commons disagreement, amendments in lieu and reasons https://bills.parliament.uk/publications/41155/documents/154 (accessed 17 December 2021).

11 PRT conducted a short survey of criminal defence lawyers in summer 2020 to seek their views on the adequacy of defences available to individuals who offend due to their experience of domestic abuse, including coercion. Further details are available from CWJ on request.

12 Hansard (Thursday 15 April 2021) vol 692, cols 583–91, https://hansard.parliament.uk/commons/2021-04-15/debates/0E322BD7-571C-4DC5-A8C8-7B29806DE067/DomesticAbuseBill (accessed 17 December 2021).

13 Susan Edwards, 'Recognising the Role of the Emotion of Fear in Offences and Defences' (2019) 83(6) *The Journal of Criminal Law* 450, 461. See also Susan Edwards, '"Demasculinising" the defences of Self-Defence, the "Householder Defence" and Duress' (2022) 2 *Crim LR* 111.

Women who kill their abusers are rarely acquitted on the grounds of self-defence, and there are multiple barriers to relying successfully on self-defence even where there is evidence of severe contextual domestic abuse.[14] The CWJ's research found that most prosecutions of women who kill their abuser lead to convictions for murder or manslaughter and that most women used a weapon. The use of a weapon has been historically understood as a disproportionate response. In 2004, the Law Commission explained how the law of self-defence had been criticised for failing to assist '[t]he abused child, or adult, who fears further physical abuse at the hands of a serial abuser, who perceives no prospect of escape and who is well aware that there is such a physical mismatch that to respond directly and proportionately to an attack or an imminent attack will be futile and dangerous. Such a person, who uses disproportionate force ... is unassisted by the law of self-defence'. In this way, the objective requirement of reasonableness applied to the amount of force used in response to an attack, or threat of attack, fails adequately to reflect cases in which a gross discrepancy in physical strength may force the person being abused to defend themselves with a weapon, which may be considered excessive.[15]

Further barriers include factors undermining defendants' credibility and character, including defendants' initial false accounts of the killing, traumatic memory loss, and harmful myths and stereotypes regarding how victims should behave. There are also failures to take account of the history of abuse, rather than only the events immediately surrounding the killing:[16]

> Accurately interpreting reasonableness relies heavily on the insight of judges and juries into the defendant's beliefs at the time of the killing. In domestic abuse cases, this requires both an understanding of domestic abuse, including coercive control, and a full picture of the factual context faced by the defendant at the time of the killing and her relevant past experiences ... The absence of such understanding, and the frequent use of a weapon in these cases which, at face value, may suggest disproportionality, may help to explain why self-defence is so rarely successful in this context.

Many of these barriers would apply equally in relation to non-lethal use of force.

Case study: Ioanna

Ioanna[17] was convicted for attacking her abusive partner with a knife, having been subject to long-term coercion and control by him. When he became threatening during an argument at home, she grabbed a knife lying nearby in the kitchen and raised it towards him. He tried to catch the knife and in the process received a small cut on his finger. He contacted the police. Ioanna received a community order.

---

[14] Sophie Howes, Katy Swaine Williams, and Harriet Wistrich, 'Women who kill: why self-defence rarely works for women who kill their abuser' (2021) 11 *Crim LR* 945.

[15] Law Commission (2004) Partial defences to murder: Final Report 77–78 https://lawcom.gov.uk/app/uploads/2015/03/lc290_Partial_Defences_to_Murder.pdf (accessed 25 April 2022).

[16] Howes and others (n 14).

[17] Centre for Women's Justice Home Office Violence Against Women and Girls (VAWG) Strategy 2021–2024: Call for Evidence—Submission for the Centre for Women's Justice: Section 4—ending the unjust criminalisation of survivors of domestic abuse and other forms of VAWG (2021) 10. Note that Ioanna is not the real name of the subject of this case study. See https://static1.squarespace.com/static/5aa98420f2e6b1ba0c874e42/t/60377bbbbffc9b26ef5b62be/1614248893718/CWJ+VAWG+response_section4_criminalisation.pdfl (accessed 17 December 2021).

The law on self-defence has been clarified by section 76 of the CJIA 2008. Subsection 76(5A) of the 2008 Act allows householders—unlike other defendants—to use disproportionate (but not grossly disproportionate) force when defending themselves against intruders in the home, provided the degree of force was reasonable in the circumstances as the householder believed them to be. Nicola Wake highlights the similarities between victims of domestic abuse who offend and the householder protecting themselves from an intruder and argues that the disparity in protection cannot be justified.[18]

The self-defence proposal is intended to address this disparity and make it easier for domestic abuse victims to rely on self-defence, by replicating the householder defence for victims who are accused of using force against their abuser.[19] Although the householder defence has been found to be of only marginal benefit in law, it would be useful to see research on whether it has an impact on decisions to prosecute.[20]

ii. The Coercion Defence Proposal

The only defence available to domestic abuse victims who are coerced into offending is the common law defence of duress, but this 'remains largely inaccessible to abused women'.[21] This is because:[22]

- Duress does not reflect the complexities of domestic abuse and does not recognise psychological, sexual, or financial abuse, all of which are included in the new statutory definition of domestic abuse in section 1, DAA 2021 and already exist under coercive and controlling behaviour in section 76, SCA 2015.
- For the defence of duress to succeed, the threat of physical harm must be imminent. This fails to recognise the 'typically entrenched, unpredictable and random' nature of domestic abuse.[23]
- The defendant must establish 'relevant characteristics' including 'battered woman syndrome' and 'learned helplessness', as was attempted unsuccessfully in the case of *R v C (GA)*.[24] These concepts are now discredited for their artificiality in attempting to reflect what might rather be considered a natural response to extreme circumstances, rather than relying on an effective defence for the actual circumstances. This approach also requires the production of medical evidence which is not usually practicable.

Case study: YS

YS[25] is charged with driving whilst disqualified, driving with excess alcohol, driving without insurance, and dangerous driving. An officer noticed a vehicle with its brake lights

[18] Nicola Wake, 'Battered Women, Startled Householders and Psychological Self-Defence: Anglo-Australian perspectives' (2013) 77(5) *The Journal of Criminal Law* 433.

[19] Marshalled list (n 10) amendment 37.

[20] Howes and others (n 14) 1.

[21] Edwards, 'Recognising the Role of the Emotion of Fear in Offences and Defences' (n 13) 462.

[22] Criminal Bar Association (n 9). See also Janet Loveless, 'Domestic Violence, Coercion and Duress' (2010) *Crim LR* 93.

[23] Loveless (n 22) 98.

[24] *R v C (GA)* [2013] EWCA Crim 1472 [9], [26].

[25] Case study provided by Paramjit Ahluwalia of Lamb Building, taken from factual matrix within *R v YS* [2017] EWHC 2839.

permanently illuminated and swerving from side to side. He activated the siren, indicating for the vehicle to stop. The vehicle did not stop, and a chase continued for five minutes. In the driving seat was a woman, YS.

YS explained she had been dragged from her home partially dressed by her partner, forced to drive, and that he threatened to kill her if she did not drive on. The partner was screaming at her throughout, punching her in the ribs and trying to grab the steering wheel.

The police stop the vehicle and YS is prosecuted. Despite running duress, and despite her being viewed as credible, she is convicted. Her conviction is upheld on appeal to the High Court.

The coercion defence proposal would provide a new statutory defence for victims who are compelled to offend as part of, or as a direct result of, their experience of domestic abuse. The proposal is closely modelled on the defence provided in section 45 of the MSA 2015 for victims of human trafficking or modern slavery who are compelled to offend as part of, or as a direct result of, their exploitation.[26] The section 45 defence requires proactive, early case management and allows all agencies to become more adept at recognising and responding to circumstances which indicate there is no public interest in prosecuting a case, or where the statutory defence is likely to apply. The proposed new coercion defence would provide the same benefits to victims of domestic abuse.

4. NEED FOR PRACTICE REFORM

Improvements in practice could significantly improve victims' access to justice in these cases, even without legislative reform. In many cases public interest considerations could properly lead to a decision not to prosecute or to divert from the criminal justice system under the current law. In practice, all too often, contextual domestic abuse is not properly taken into account—leading to unfair arrests, cautions, convictions, and sentencing for victims.[27]

Marianne Hester's research found that women were three times more likely to be arrested than their male partners in cases involving counter-allegations, often for violence used to protect themselves from further harm from their abuser.[28] Recent research highlights the over-use of arrests of women for use of force in the context of domestic abuse, followed by later release without charge (in other words, cases in which they should not have been arrested at all).[29] The CWJ's case work reveals many cases in which decisions by the Police and Crown Prosecution Service to arrest or pursue charges against victims appear to have

[26] Marshalled list (n 10) amendments 38 and 83.

[27] CWJ (n 17).

[28] Marianne Hester, 'Portrayal of Women as Intimate Partner Domestic Violence Perpetrators' (University of Bristol in association with the Northern Rock Foundation 2012). Professor Hester studied the following three sample groups: (1) All women recorded by the police as sole domestic violence perpetrator in a heterosexual relationship (N=32); (2) a random sample of sole male perpetrators; and (3) a random sample involving 32 cases where both partners were recorded at some time as perpetrator. These different sets of cases were then compared to assess differences and similarities in the rate of arrest where allegations were made. Analysis showed that an arrest was three times more likely to follow where the allegations were made against a woman, than where they were made against a man.

[29] APPG on Women in the Penal System, 'Arresting the entry of women into the criminal justice system: Briefing 2' (2020) https://howardleague.org/wp-content/uploads/2020/09/APPG-on-Women-in-the-Penal-System-briefing-2-FINAL.pdf (accessed 29 May 2022).

been made without any proper consideration of the context of domestic abuse in which the incident took place.[30]

College of Policing Authorised Professional Practice (APP) guidance addresses the need for police officers to identify the primary perpetrator in the event of counter-allegations,[31] with a linked section on dual arrests providing that these should be avoided where possible. Documents provided to the CWJ by some police forces in response to Freedom of Information Act requests indicate that local police force guidance is inconsistent in relation to counter-allegations and dual arrest, with some running contrary to the APP provisions and others not addressing the issue in their policies and procedures on domestic abuse. Crown Prosecution Service legal guidance on domestic abuse also addresses the handling of counter-allegations.[32] However, the CWJ's case work indicates that practice on the ground is inconsistent. No specific guidance is provided on the broader need to consider contextual domestic abuse in relation to other offences. However, both the Police and the CPS should consider this when assessing the evidence of an offence having been committed by the victim, and the public interest in their arrest or prosecution.

Sally Challen's successful appeal against her murder conviction in 2019 helped to improve public understanding of coercive control and, to some extent, the links between domestic abuse and women's offending.[33] Following the introduction of controlling or coercive behaviour as a criminal offence in 2015,[34] the appellant put forward expert evidence on coercive control. This gave the court a better understanding of the context in which the offence took place, contributing to the replacing of her murder conviction with one for manslaughter on the grounds of diminished responsibility.[35] However, the courts generally remain reluctant to accept expert evidence on domestic abuse, considering that this should be within the knowledge of the jury. The impact of the context of domestic abuse often remains poorly understood, including the need to consider the impact of domestic abuse over time rather than only focusing on the events immediately surrounding the offence, and failings in criminal justice practice mean it is not properly taken into account.[36]

These failings are experienced in distinct ways by certain groups. This includes black, Asian, minoritized, and migrant women, who are over-represented in the criminal justice system[37] and subject to additional barriers to justice and unequal outcomes.[38] Young women's

---

[30] CWJ (n 17).

[31] College of Policing First Response para 3.5 https://www.app.college.police.uk/app-content/major-investigation-and-public-protection/domestic-abuse/first-response/#determining-the-primary-perpetrator-and-dealing-with-counter-allegations (accessed 17 December 2021).

[32] See 'Self defence and counter-allegations' https://www.cps.gov.uk/legal-guidance/domestic-abuse-guidelines-prosecutors (accessed 17 December 2021).

[33] David Challen, 'My mother, Sally Challen, was branded a cold-blooded killer. At last, she has justice' *The Guardian* (8 June 2019) https://www.theguardian.com/society/2019/jun/08/my-mother-sally-challen-killed-my-father-finally-justice (accessed 17 December 2021).

[34] Serious Crime Act 2015, s 76.

[35] *R v Challen* [2019] EWCA Crim 916 (CA).

[36] Howes and others (n 14).

[37] 'Female Offender Strategy' (n 1) 13.

[38] Prison Reform Trust, 'Still No Way Out: Foreign national women in the criminal justice system' (2018) https://prisonreformtrust.org.uk/publication/still-no-way-out-foreign-national-women-and-trafficked-women-in-the-criminal-justice-system/ (accessed 16 November 2022); Prison Reform Trust, 'Counted Out: Black, Asian and minority ethnic women in the criminal justice system' (2017) http://www.prisonreformtrust.org.uk/Portals/0/Documents/Counted%20Out.pdf; Agenda/Women in Prison, 'Double disadvantage: the experiences of Black, Asian and Minority Ethnic women in the criminal justice system' (2017) https://weareagenda.org/wp-content/uploads/2017/03/Double-disadvantage-FINAL.pdf; Ministry of Justice,

experiences of violence, abuse, and exploitation can drive them into the criminal justice system in distinct ways.[39] Young women with experience of local authority care may be more vulnerable to violence and abuse, and less able to access support.[40] Most women convicted under the law of joint enterprise are convicted in relation to serious violent offences despite not having taken part in any violence, and often despite being marginal to the violent event or not even present at the scene. These women are constructed as the facilitators of violence and severely punished, often without taking account of the context of domestic abuse in which they existed at the time, and the impact of this on their actions or omissions.[41] Women with learning disabilities may be particularly vulnerable to domestic abuse and consequent criminalisation.[42]

Research has identified multiple failings in practice that can lead to injustice in these cases and makes detailed recommendations for reform.[43] This includes addressing barriers to women's disclosure of contextual abuse. Even where the context of domestic abuse is known about, barriers in the system mean that it is frequently not properly taken into account. This includes a lack of procedural safeguards to facilitate disclosure of abuse and allow victim suspects and defendants to give their best evidence; police failures to investigate contextual abuse by reviewing their own records and gathering evidence from the victim and third parties; and prosecutors' failure to instruct the police to gather contextual evidence rigorously, and then to take proper account of it. Criminal defence lawyers require expertise, time, and resources to discern and effectively put across evidence of contextual domestic abuse and its relevance to the offence, which may be unrealistic on criminal legal aid fees. Judges and juries may have limited understanding of the dynamics of domestic abuse and may be susceptible to myths and stereotypes that negatively influence their perceptions of the victim defendant. For example, in Emma-Jane Magson's appeal against her conviction for the murder of her abusive partner, prosecutors made reference to her as a typical estate girl who had experienced 50 one-night stands. These slurs helped to discredit Magson's character and therefore undermine her account of the abuse she had experienced, thereby weakening her defence.[44]

Already traumatised women may plead guilty rather than go through a distressing trial and face the risk of a harsher sentence, particularly those who are primary carers of children.

'The Lammy Review: an independent review into the treatment of, and outcomes for, Black, Asian and minority ethnic individuals in the criminal justice system' (2017) https://assets.publishing.service.gov.uk/government/uploads/system/uploads/attachment_data/file/643001/lammy-review-final-report.pdf (accessed 25 April 2022).

[39] Agenda & Alliance for Youth Justice, '"I wanted to be heard": Young women in the criminal justice system at risk of violence, abuse and exploitation' (2021) https://weareagenda.org/i-wanted-to-be-heard/.

[40] ibid.

[41] Becky Clarke and Kathryn Chadwick, 'Stories of Injustice: The criminalisation of women convicted under joint enterprise laws' (2020) https://barrowcadbury.org.uk/project/stories-of-injustice-the-criminalisation-of-women-convicted-under-joint-enterprise-laws/ (accessed 25 April 2022).

[42] Prison Reform Trust and KeyRing, 'Out of the shadows: women with learning disabilities in contact with or on the edges of the criminal justice system' (2018) Layout 1 (prisonreformtrust.org.uk) (accessed 25 April 2022).

[43] Naima 'Sakande, 'Righting Wrongs: What are the barriers faced by women seeking to overturn unsafe convictions or unfair sentences in the Court of Appeal (Criminal Division)? (2020) https://www.thegriffinssociety.org/righting-wrongs-what-are-barriers-faced-women-seeking-overturn-unsafe-convictions-or-unfair (accessed 25 April 2022).

[44] Howes and others (n 14) 953.

5. CONCLUSION

For all its strengths, the DAA 2021 offers no protection to victims who are criminalised as a consequence of their experience of abuse. The government advocates a whole system approach to women's offending, recognising in a suite of recent policy papers the links between women's offending and their experience of domestic abuse, and the need for victims involved in offending to be identified as victims and to receive support.[45] Yet neither a whole system approach to women's offending, nor domestic abuse law and policy aimed at protecting victims, can be effective if they largely fail to address what happens when a victim becomes an 'offender' as a consequence of their abuse.

It is hoped that the DAA statutory guidance and Domestic Abuse Strategy will address some of the failings in practice outlined above and be supported by investment in frontline criminal justice services. Yet without effective defences, victims accused of offending will continue to face unjust outcomes. Introducing new statutory defences—and a surrounding policy framework to support their implementation—would offer vital protection to domestic abuse victims, just as legislation has previously been used to protect householders facing an intruder, and victims of trafficking who are compelled to offend.

During the final stages of the Domestic Abuse Bill's passage through Parliament, Baroness Helena Kennedy KC proposed that an independent review should be established into the effectiveness of existing defences in these cases. The government rejected this proposal but has since commissioned an independent review of sentencing in domestic homicide cases. This review is considering a narrower question, namely the use of current defences to charges of murder when used by domestic abuse victims who kill their abuser, and outcomes in those cases.[46] It is hoped that this will prove to be a step towards legal reform, potentially through the Victims' Bill, of defences rather than just sentencing, and not only relating to homicide but also offering protection to the much greater number of victims accused of other offences resulting from their experience of domestic abuse.

[45] 'Female Offender Strategy' (n 1).

[46] Ministry of Justice, 'Domestic Homicide Sentencing Review: Terms of reference' (2021) https://www.gov.uk/government/publications/domestic-homicide-sentencing-review-terms-of-reference/domestic-homicide-sentencing-review-terms-of-reference (accessed 25 April 2022).

Appendix

Domestic Abuse Act 2021

2021 CHAPTER 17

An Act to make provision in relation to domestic abuse; to make provision for and in connection with the establishment of a Domestic Abuse Commissioner; to make provision for the granting of measures to assist individuals in certain circumstances to give evidence or otherwise participate in civil proceedings; to prohibit cross-examination in person in family or civil proceedings in certain circumstances; to make further provision about orders under section 91(14) of the Children Act 1989; to provide for an offence of threatening to disclose private sexual photographs and films with intent to cause distress; to provide for an offence of strangulation or suffocation; to make provision about circumstances in which consent to the infliction of harm is not a defence in proceedings for certain violent offences; to make provision about certain violent or sexual offences, and offences involving other abusive behaviour, committed outside the United Kingdom; and for connected purposes. [29th April 2021]

BE IT ENACTED by the Queen's most Excellent Majesty, by and with the advice and consent of the Lords Spiritual and Temporal, and Commons, in this present Parliament assembled, and by the authority of the same, as follows:—

PART 1

DEFINITION OF "DOMESTIC ABUSE"

1 Definition of "domestic abuse"

(1) This section defines "domestic abuse" for the purposes of this Act.

(2) Behaviour of a person ("A") towards another person ("B") is "domestic abuse" if—
   (a) A and B are each aged 16 or over and are personally connected to each other, and
   (b) the behaviour is abusive.

(3) Behaviour is "abusive" if it consists of any of the following—
   (a) physical or sexual abuse;
   (b) violent or threatening behaviour;
   (c) controlling or coercive behaviour;
   (d) economic abuse (see subsection (4));
   (e) psychological, emotional or other abuse;

   and it does not matter whether the behaviour consists of a single incident or a course of conduct.

(4) "Economic abuse" means any behaviour that has a substantial adverse effect on B's ability to—
(a) acquire, use or maintain money or other property, or
(b) obtain goods or services.

(5) For the purposes of this Act A's behaviour may be behaviour "towards" B despite the fact that it consists of conduct directed at another person (for example, B's child).

(6) References in this Act to being abusive towards another person are to be read in accordance with this section.

(7) For the meaning of "personally connected", see section 2.

Commencement Information

I1 S. 1 in force at 5.7.2021 for specified purposes by S.I. 2021/797, **reg. 2(1)**

I2 S. 1 in force at 1.10.2021 in so far as not already in force by S.I. 2021/1038, **reg. 2(a)**

2 Definition of "personally connected"

(1) For the purposes of this Act, two people are "personally connected" to each other if any of the following applies—
(a) they are, or have been, married to each other;
(b) they are, or have been, civil partners of each other;
(c) they have agreed to marry one another (whether or not the agreement has been terminated);
(d) they have entered into a civil partnership agreement (whether or not the agreement has been terminated);
(e) they are, or have been, in an intimate personal relationship with each other;
(f) they each have, or there has been a time when they each have had, a parental relationship in relation to the same child (see subsection (2));
(g) they are relatives.

(2) For the purposes of subsection (1)(f) a person has a parental relationship in relation to a child if—
(a) the person is a parent of the child, or
(b) the person has parental responsibility for the child.

(3) In this section—
"child" means a person under the age of 18 years;
"civil partnership agreement" has the meaning given by section 73 of the Civil Partnership Act 2004;
"parental responsibility" has the same meaning as in the Children Act 1989 (see section 3 of that Act);
"relative" has the meaning given by section 63(1) of the Family Law Act 1996.

Commencement Information

I3 S. 2 in force at 5.7.2021 for specified purposes by S.I. 2021/797, **reg. 2(1)**

I4 S. 2 in force at 1.10.2021 in so far as not already in force by S.I. 2021/1038, **reg. 2(b)**

3 Children as victims of domestic abuse

(1) This section applies where behaviour of a person ("A") towards another person ("B") is domestic abuse.

(2) Any reference in this Act to a victim of domestic abuse includes a reference to a child who—
  (a) sees or hears, or experiences the effects of, the abuse, and
  (b) is related to A+ or B.

(3) A child is related to a person for the purposes of subsection (2) if—
  (a) the person is a parent of, or has parental responsibility for, the child, or
  (b) the child and the person are relatives.

(4) In this section—
"child" means a person under the age of 18 years;
"parental responsibility" has the same meaning as in the Children Act 1989 (see section 3 of that Act);
"relative" has the meaning given by section 63(1) of the Family Law Act 1996.

Commencement Information

I5 S. 3 in force at 1.10.2021 for specified purposes by S.I. 2021/1038, **reg. 2(c)**

I6 S. 3 in force at 1.11.2021 for specified purposes by S.I. 2021/1038, **reg. 3(a)**

I7 S. 3 in force at 31.1.2022 in so far as not already in force by S.I. 2022/73, **reg. 2**

PART 2

THE DOMESTIC ABUSE COMMISSIONER

Domestic Abuse Commissioner

4 Appointment of Commissioner

(1) The Secretary of State must appoint a person as the Domestic Abuse Commissioner ("the Commissioner").

(2) The Commissioner is to hold and vacate office in accordance with the terms and conditions of the Commissioner's appointment.

(3) The Commissioner is not to be regarded as the servant or agent of the Crown or as enjoying any status, immunity or privilege of the Crown.

Commencement Information

I8 S. 4 in force at 1.11.2021 by S.I. 2021/1038, **reg. 3(b)**

5 Funding

(1) The Secretary of State may make payments to the Commissioner out of money provided by Parliament for the purpose of enabling the Commissioner to meet expenditure incurred in the exercise of the Commissioner's functions.

(2) Payments are to be made at such times, and subject to any such conditions, as the Secretary of State considers appropriate.

(3) The Secretary of State may pay, or make provision for paying, to or in respect of the Commissioner—
  (a) remuneration;
  (b) allowances;
  (c) sums by way of or in respect of pensions.

Commencement Information

I9 S. 5 in force at 1.11.2021 by S.I. 2021/1038, **reg. 3(b)**

6 Staff etc

(1) The Secretary of State must provide the Commissioner with—
  (a) such staff, and
  (b) such accommodation, equipment and other facilities,

  as the Secretary of State considers necessary for the carrying out of the Commissioner's functions.

(2) Before providing any staff, the Secretary of State must—
  (a) consult the Commissioner, and
  (b) obtain the Commissioner's approval as to the persons to be provided as staff.

(3) The Secretary of State must consult the Commissioner before providing any accommodation, equipment or other facilities.

Commencement Information

I10 S. 6 in force at 1.11.2021 by S.I. 2021/1038, **reg. 3(b)**

Functions of Commissioner

7 General functions of Commissioner

(1) The Commissioner must encourage good practice in—
  (a) the prevention of domestic abuse;
  (b) the prevention, detection, investigation and prosecution of offences involving domestic abuse;
  (c) the identification of—
    (i) people who carry out domestic abuse;
    (ii) victims of domestic abuse;
    (iii) children affected by domestic abuse;
  (d) the provision of protection and support to people affected by domestic abuse.

(2) The things that the Commissioner may do in pursuance of the general duty under subsection (1) include—
  (a) assessing, monitoring, and publishing information about, the provision of services to people affected by domestic abuse;
  (b) making recommendations to any public authority about the exercise of its functions;
  (c) undertaking or supporting (financially or otherwise) the carrying out of research;
  (d) providing information, education or training;
  (e) taking other steps to increase public awareness of domestic abuse;
  (f) consulting public authorities, voluntary organisations and other persons;
  (g) co-operating with, or working jointly with, public authorities, voluntary organisations and other persons, whether in England and Wales or outside the United Kingdom.

(3) Subject to subsection (4), the Commissioner may not do anything in pursuance of the general duty under subsection (1) that—
  (a) relates to a devolved Welsh authority, or
  (b) otherwise relates to Welsh devolved matters.

(4) Subsection (3) does not prevent the Commissioner from—
  (a) doing anything falling within subsection (2)(c), (d) or (e), to the extent that the thing done does not relate to Welsh devolved matters;
  (b) doing anything falling within subsection (2)(f) or (g);
  (c) disclosing information to a devolved Welsh authority, or information which relates to Welsh devolved matters, under section 18.

(5) For the purposes of this section something relates to Welsh devolved matters so far as it relates to—
  (a) any matter provision about which would be within the legislative competence of Senedd Cymru if it were contained in an Act of Senedd Cymru, or
  (b) (so far as it is not within paragraph (a)), any matter functions with respect to which are exercisable by the Welsh Ministers, the First Minister for Wales, the Counsel General to the Welsh Government or the Senedd Commission.

(6) In this section—
"devolved Welsh authority" has the meaning given by section 157A of the Government of Wales Act 2006;
"public authority" means any public authority within the meaning of section 6 of the Human Rights Act 1998, other than a court or tribunal.

Commencement Information

I11 S. 7 in force at 1.11.2021 by S.I. 2021/1038, **reg. 3(b)**

8 Reports

(1) The Commissioner may report to the Secretary of State on any matter relating to domestic abuse.

(2) The Commissioner must publish every report made under this section.

(3) Before publishing a report under this section, the Commissioner must send a draft of the report to the Secretary of State.

(4) The Secretary of State may direct the Commissioner to omit material from any report under this section before publication if the Secretary of State thinks the publication of that material—
  (a) might jeopardise the safety of any person, or
  (b) might prejudice the investigation or prosecution of an offence.

(5) The Secretary of State must consult the Commissioner before making any direction under subsection (4).

(6) The Commissioner must arrange for a copy of any report published under this section to be laid before Parliament.

Commencement Information

I12 S. 8 in force at 1.11.2021 by S.I. 2021/1038, **reg. 3(b)**

9 Advice and assistance

(1) The Commissioner may provide the Secretary of State with any advice or assistance that the Secretary of State may request.

(2) The Commissioner may, at the request of any other person, provide the person with advice or assistance relating to the exercise of any of the person's functions, or the carrying out of any activities by the person, in relation to people affected by domestic abuse.

(3) The Commissioner may charge a person for providing the person with advice or assistance under subsection (2).

(4) The Commissioner must publish any advice given to a person under subsection (2).

(5) Before publishing any advice given under this section, the Commissioner must send a draft of what is proposed to be published to the Secretary of State.

(6) The Secretary of State may direct the Commissioner to omit anything contained in the advice before publication if the Secretary of State thinks the publication of that material—

(a) might jeopardise the safety of any person, or

(b) might prejudice the investigation or prosecution of an offence.

(7) The Secretary of State must consult the Commissioner before making any direction under subsection (6).

Commencement Information

I13 S. 9 in force at 1.11.2021 by S.I. 2021/1038, **reg. 3(b)**

10 Incidental powers

(1) The Commissioner may do anything which the Commissioner considers will facilitate, or is incidental or conducive to, the carrying out of the Commissioner's functions.

(2) But the Commissioner may not borrow money.

Commencement Information

I14 S. 10 in force at 1.11.2021 by S.I. 2021/1038, **reg. 3(b)**

Framework document

11 Framework document

(1) The Secretary of State must issue a document (a "framework document") that deals with matters relating to the Commissioner.

(2) The matters that may be dealt with by a framework document include (among other things)—

(a) matters relating to governance, funding and staffing;

(b) matters relating to the exercise of functions of the Commissioner;

(c) matters relating to scrutiny of the Commissioner's activities by Parliament or by Senedd Cymru.

(3) The Commissioner must have regard to the framework document when exercising any of the Commissioner's functions.

(4) The Secretary of State must have regard to the framework document when exercising any functions in relation to the Commissioner.

(5) The Secretary of State—

(a) must keep the framework document under review, and
(b) may issue a revised framework document.

(6) The Secretary of State—
(a) must consult the Commissioner in preparing or revising a framework document, and
(b) may not issue a framework document without the agreement of the Commissioner.

(7) The Secretary of State must consult the Welsh Ministers before issuing—
(a) the first framework document under this section, or
(b) any other framework document which is, in the opinion of the Secretary of State, significantly different from the framework document it replaces.

(8) The Secretary of State must—
(a) arrange for any framework document issued under this section to be published in the manner which the Secretary of State considers appropriate,
(b) send a copy of the framework document to the Welsh Ministers, and
(c) lay a copy of the framework document before Parliament.

(9) The Welsh Ministers must lay before Senedd Cymru a copy of any framework document sent to them under subsection (8)(b).

Commencement Information

I15 S. 11 in force at 1.11.2021 by S.I. 2021/1038, **reg. 3(b)**

Advisory Board

12 Advisory Board

(1) The Commissioner must establish an Advisory Board ("the Board") for the purposes of providing advice to the Commissioner about the exercise of the Commissioner's functions.

(2) The Board is to consist of not fewer than six and not more than ten members appointed by the Commissioner.

(3) Each member of the Board is to hold and vacate office in accordance with the terms and conditions of the member's appointment.

(4) The members of the Board must include—
(a) at least one person appearing to the Commissioner to represent the interests of victims of domestic abuse;
(b) at least one person appearing to the Commissioner to represent the interests of charities and other voluntary organisations that work with victims of domestic abuse in England;
(c) at least one person appearing to the Commissioner to represent the interests of persons who provide, or have functions relating to, health care services in England;
(d) at least one person appearing to the Commissioner to represent the interests of persons who provide, or have functions relating to, social care services in England;
(e) at least one person appearing to the Commissioner to represent the interests of persons with functions relating to policing or criminal justice;
(f) at least one person appearing to the Commissioner to have academic expertise in relation to domestic abuse.

(5) The Commissioner may pay such remuneration or allowances to members of the Board as the Commissioner may determine.

(6) In this section—

"health care services" means services relating to health care (within the meaning of section 9 of the Health and Social Care Act 2008);

"social care services" means services relating to social care (within the meaning of that section).

Commencement Information

I16 S. 12 in force at 1.11.2021 by S.I. 2021/1038, **reg. 3(b)**

Strategic plans and annual reports

13 Strategic plans

(1) The Commissioner must, as soon as reasonably practicable after the Commissioner's appointment, prepare and publish a strategic plan.

(2) A strategic plan is a plan setting out how the Commissioner proposes to exercise the Commissioner's functions in the period to which the plan relates, which must be not less than one year and not more than three years.

(3) A strategic plan must in particular—
- (a) state the Commissioner's objectives and priorities for the period to which the plan relates;
- (b) state any matters on which the Commissioner proposes to report under section 8 during that period;
- (c) state any other activities the Commissioner proposes to undertake during that period in the exercise of the Commissioner's functions.

(4) The Commissioner must, before the end of the period to which a strategic plan relates ("the current period")—
- (a) prepare a strategic plan for a period immediately following the current period, and
- (b) publish that plan.

(5) At any time during the period to which a strategic plan relates, the Commissioner—
- (a) may revise the strategic plan, and
- (b) must publish any revised plan.

(6) In preparing or revising a strategic plan, the Commissioner must consult—
- (a) the Secretary of State,
- (b) the Advisory Board established under section 12, and
- (c) such other persons as the Commissioner considers appropriate.

(7) The Commissioner must arrange for a copy of any plan (or revised plan) published under this section to be laid before Parliament.

Commencement Information

I17 S. 13 in force at 1.11.2021 by S.I. 2021/1038, **reg. 3(b)**

14 Annual reports

(1) As soon as reasonably practicable after the end of each financial year, the Commissioner must submit to the Secretary of State an annual report on the exercise of the Commissioner's functions during the year.

(2) The annual report must include—
- (a) an assessment of the extent to which the Commissioner's objectives and priorities have been met in that year;

(b) a statement of the matters on which the Commissioner has reported under section 8 during the year;

(c) a statement of the other activities the Commissioner has undertaken during the year in the exercise of the Commissioner's functions.

(3) The Commissioner must arrange for a copy of every annual report under this section to be laid before Parliament (but see subsection (4)).

(4) The Secretary of State may direct the Commissioner to omit material from any report under this section before it is laid before Parliament if the Secretary of State thinks the publication of that material—

(a) might jeopardise the safety of any person, or

(b) might prejudice the investigation or prosecution of an offence.

(5) The Secretary of State must consult the Commissioner before making any direction under subsection (4).

(6) In this section "financial year" means—

(a) the period beginning with the day on which the first Domestic Abuse Commissioner takes office and ending with the following 31 March, and

(b) each successive period of 12 months.

Commencement Information

I18 S. 14 in force at 1.11.2021 by S.I. 2021/1038, **reg. 3(b)**

Duties of public authorities in relation to Commissioner

15 Duty to co-operate with Commissioner

(1) The Commissioner may request a specified public authority to co-operate with the Commissioner in any way that the Commissioner considers necessary for the purposes of the Commissioner's functions.

(2) A specified public authority must, so far as reasonably practicable, comply with a request made to it under this section.

(3) In this section "specified public authority" means any of the following—

(a) a chief officer of police of a police force maintained for a police area in England and Wales;

(b) a local policing body;

(c) the Chief Constable of the British Transport Police Force;

(d) the British Transport Police Authority;

(e) the Ministry of Defence Police;

(f) an immigration officer or other official of the Secretary of State exercising functions in relation to immigration or asylum;

(g) the Crown Prosecution Service;

(h) the Parole Board;

(i) the Criminal Cases Review Commission;

(j) an English local authority;

(k) an NHS body in England;

(l) Her Majesty's Inspectors of Constabulary;

(m) Her Majesty's Chief Inspector of the Crown Prosecution Service;

(n) Her Majesty's Chief Inspector of Education, Children's Services and Skills;

(o) a body approved as an independent inspectorate under section 106 of the Education and Skills Act 2008 (inspection of registered independent educational institutions);
(p) the Care Quality Commission;
(q) Monitor.

(4) The Secretary of State may by regulations amend this section so as to—
(a) add a public authority as a specified public authority for the purposes of this section;
(b) remove a public authority added by virtue of paragraph (a);
(c) vary any description of a public authority.

(5) Before making regulations under subsection (4) the Secretary of State must consult the Commissioner.

(6) Regulations under subsection (4) may not contain provision adding a devolved Welsh authority as a specified public authority for the purposes of this section.

(7) In this section—
"devolved Welsh authority" has the meaning given by section 157A of the Government of Wales Act 2006;
"English local authority" means—
(a) a county council or district council in England,
(b) a London borough council,
(c) the Greater London Authority,
(d) the Common Council of the City of London in its capacity as a local authority, or
(e) the Council of the Isles of Scilly;
"immigration officer" means a person appointed as an immigration officer under paragraph 1 of Schedule 2 to the Immigration Act 1971;
"NHS body in England" means—
(a) a National Health Service trust in England established under section 25 of the National Health Service Act 2006,
(b) an NHS foundation trust within the meaning given by section 30 of that Act,
(c) the National Health Service Commissioning Board,
(d) a clinical commissioning group established under section 14D of that Act, or
(e) the National Health Service Trust Development Authority;
"public authority" means any public authority within the meaning of section 6 of the Human Rights Act 1998, other than a court or tribunal.

Commencement Information

I19 S. 15 in force at 1.11.2021 by S.I. 2021/1038, **reg. 3(b)**

16 Duty to respond to Commissioner's recommendations

(1) This section applies where the Commissioner publishes a report under section 8 containing recommendations in relation to—
(a) any public authority that is a specified public authority for the purposes of section 15;
(b) any government department in the charge of a Minister.

(2) The relevant person must prepare comments on the report.

(3) In this section "the relevant person" means—
(a) the public authority, or
(b) the Minister in charge of the government department, as the case may be.

(4) The comments must include, in respect of each recommendation made in the report, an explanation of—

(a) the action which the relevant person has taken, or proposes to take, in response to the recommendation, or

(b) why the relevant person has not taken, or does not propose to take, any action in response.

(5) The relevant person must arrange for the comments to be published in such manner as the person considers appropriate.

(6) The comments must be published before the end of the period of 56 days beginning with the day on which the report is published.

(7) The relevant person must send a copy of anything published under subsection (5) to—

(a) the Commissioner, and

(b) where the relevant person is a specified public authority for the purposes of section 15, the Secretary of State.

Commencement Information

I20 S. 16 in force at 1.11.2021 by S.I. 2021/1038, **reg. 3(b)**

17 Duty to send conclusions of domestic homicide review to Commissioner

(1) Section 9 of the Domestic Violence, Crime and Victims Act 2004 (establishment and conduct of domestic homicide reviews) is amended as follows.

(2) After subsection (3A) insert—

"(3B) A person or body within subsection (4)(a) that establishes a domestic homicide review (whether or not held pursuant to a direction under subsection (2)) must send a copy of any report setting out the conclusions of the review to the Domestic Abuse Commissioner.

(3C) The copy must be sent as soon as reasonably practicable after the report is completed."

Commencement Information

I21 S. 17 in force at 1.11.2021 by S.I. 2021/1038, **reg. 3(b)**

Disclosure of information

18 Disclosure of information

(1) The Commissioner may disclose to a person any information received by the Commissioner in connection with the Commissioner's functions if the disclosure is made for a purpose connected with a function of the Commissioner.

(2) A person may disclose any information to the Commissioner if the disclosure is made for the purposes of enabling or assisting the Commissioner to exercise any function.

(3) A disclosure of information authorised by this section does not breach—

(a) any obligation of confidence owed by the person making the disclosure in relation to that information, or

(b) any other restriction on the disclosure of information (however imposed).

(4) But nothing in this Part requires or authorises any of the following—

(a) the disclosure of any patient information (see subsection (5));

(b) the making of a disclosure which, although made in the exercise of a function under this Part, would contravene the data protection legislation (see subsection (6));

(c) the making of a disclosure which is prohibited by any of Parts 1 to 7 or Chapter 1 of Part 9 of the Investigatory Powers Act 2016.

(5) "Patient information" means information (however recorded) which—
   (a) relates to—
      (i) the physical or mental health or condition of an individual,
      (ii) the diagnosis of an individual's condition, or
      (iii) an individual's care or treatment,
   or is (to any extent) derived directly or indirectly from information relating to any of those matters, and
   (b) identifies the individual or enables the individual to be identified (either by itself or in combination with other information).

(6) In this section "the data protection legislation" has the same meaning as in the Data Protection Act 2018 (see section 3 of that Act).

(7) This section does not affect any power to disclose that exists apart from this section.

Commencement Information

I22 S. 18 in force at 1.11.2021 by S.I. 2021/1038, **reg. 3(b)**

Miscellaneous and supplementary

19 Restriction on exercise of functions in individual cases

(1) The Commissioner may not exercise any function in relation to an individual case.

(2) But subsection (1) does not prevent the Commissioner considering individual cases and drawing conclusions about them for the purpose of, or in the context of, considering a general issue.

Commencement Information

I23 S. 19 in force at 1.11.2021 by S.I. 2021/1038, **reg. 3(b)**

20 Duty to report on domestic abuse services in England

(1) The Commissioner must, before the end of the relevant period, prepare and publish a report under section 8 on—
   (a) the need for domestic abuse services in England, and
   (b) the provision of such services.

(2) But subsection (1) does not require the Commissioner to report on the need for, or provision of, services provided to people who reside in relevant accommodation (within the meaning of section 57(2)).

(3) In subsection (1)—
   "domestic abuse services" means any advice, advocacy or counselling services provided, in relation to domestic abuse, to victims of domestic abuse or their children;
   "the relevant period" means the period of 12 months beginning with the day on which this section comes into force (but see subsection (4)).

(4) The Secretary of State, with the agreement of the Commissioner, may by regulations extend the relevant period for a further period of up to 6 months.

(5) The power conferred by subsection (4) may be exercised only once.

Commencement Information

I24 S. 20 in force at 1.11.2021 by S.I. 2021/1038, **reg. 3(b)**

21 Amendments relating to Commissioner

(1) In Part 3 of Schedule 1 to the House of Commons Disqualification Act 1975 (offices disqualifying for membership), at the appropriate place insert— " Domestic Abuse Commissioner. "

(2) In Part 6 of Schedule 1 to the Freedom of Information Act 2000 (other public bodies and offices: general), at the appropriate place insert— " The Domestic Abuse Commissioner. "

(3) In section 37 of the Government of Wales Act 2006 (power of the Senedd to call witnesses etc), after subsection (6A) insert—

"(6B) Subsection (1) applies in relation to things done by the Domestic Abuse Commissioner by virtue of section 7(4)(b) or (c) of the Domestic Abuse Act 2021 (functions exercisable in relation to devolved Welsh authorities etc) as it applies in relation to the exercise by the Welsh Ministers of their functions."

Commencement Information

I25 S. 21 in force at 1.11.2021 by S.I. 2021/1038, **reg. 3(b)**

PROSPECTIVE
PART 3

POWERS FOR DEALING WITH DOMESTIC ABUSE

Domestic abuse protection notices

22 Power to give a domestic abuse protection notice

(1) A senior police officer may give a domestic abuse protection notice to a person ("P") if conditions A and B are met.

(2) A domestic abuse protection notice is a notice prohibiting P from being abusive towards a person aged 16 or over to whom P is personally connected.

(Section 23 contains further provision about the provision that may be made by notices.)

(3) Condition A is that the senior police officer has reasonable grounds for believing that P has been abusive towards a person aged 16 or over to whom P is personally connected.

(4) Condition B is that the senior police officer has reasonable grounds for believing that it is necessary to give the notice to protect that person from domestic abuse, or the risk of domestic abuse, carried out by P.

(5) It does not matter whether the abusive behaviour referred to in subsection (3) took place in England and Wales or elsewhere.

(6) A domestic abuse protection notice may not be given to a person who is under the age of 18.

(7) A domestic abuse protection notice has effect in all parts of the United Kingdom.

(8) In this Part—

"senior police officer" means a member of a relevant police force who is a constable of at least the rank of inspector;

"relevant police force" means—

(a) a force maintained by a local policing body;
(b) the British Transport Police Force;
(c) the Ministry of Defence Police.

23 Provision that may be made by notices

(1) A domestic abuse protection notice may provide that the person to whom the notice is given ("P")—
  (a) may not contact the person for whose protection the notice is given;
  (b) may not come within a specified distance of any premises in England or Wales in which that person lives.

  "Specified" means specified in the notice.

(2) If P lives in premises in England or Wales in which the person for whose protection the notice is given also lives, the notice may also contain provision—
  (a) prohibiting P from evicting or excluding that person from the premises;
  (b) prohibiting P from entering the premises;
  (c) requiring P to leave the premises.

24 Matters to be considered before giving a notice

(1) Before giving a domestic abuse protection notice to a person ("P"), a senior police officer must, among other things, consider the following—
  (a) the welfare of any person under the age of 18 whose interests the officer considers relevant to the giving of the notice (whether or not that person and P are personally connected);
  (b) the opinion of the person for whose protection the notice would be given as to the giving of the notice;
  (c) any representations made by P about the giving of the notice;
  (d) in a case where the notice includes provision relating to premises lived in by the person for whose protection the notice would be given, the opinion of any relevant occupant as to the giving of the notice.

(2) In subsection (1)(d) "relevant occupant" means a person other than P or the person for whose protection the notice would be given—
  (a) who lives in the premises, and
  (b) who is personally connected to—
    (i) the person for whose protection the notice would be given, or
    (ii) if P also lives in the premises, P.

(3) The officer must take reasonable steps to discover the opinions mentioned in subsection (1).

(4) It is not necessary for the person for whose protection a domestic abuse protection notice is given to consent to the giving of the notice.

25 Further requirements in relation to notices

(1) A domestic abuse protection notice must be in writing.

(2) A domestic abuse protection notice given to a person ("P") must state—
  (a) the grounds on which it has been given,
  (b) that a constable may arrest P without warrant if the constable has reasonable grounds for believing that P is in breach of the notice,
  (c) that an application for a domestic abuse protection order under section 28 will be heard by a magistrates' court within 48 hours of the time of giving the notice (disregarding any days mentioned in section 29(3)) and a notice of the hearing will be given to P,
  (d) that the notice continues in effect until that application has been determined or withdrawn, and
  (e) the provision that a magistrates' court may include in a domestic abuse protection order.

(3) The notice must be served on P personally by a constable.

(4) On serving the notice on P, the constable must ask P for an address at which P may be given the notice of the hearing of the application for the domestic abuse protection order.

(5) Subsection (6) applies where—

(a) a senior police officer gives a domestic abuse protection notice to a person ("P") who the officer believes is a person subject to service law in accordance with sections 367 to 369 of the Armed Forces Act 2006,

(b) the notice includes provision by virtue of section 23(2) prohibiting P from entering premises, or requiring P to leave premises, and

(c) the officer believes that the premises are relevant service accommodation.

(6) The officer must make reasonable efforts to inform P's commanding officer of the giving of the notice.

(7) In this section—

"commanding officer" has the meaning given by section 360 of the Armed Forces Act 2006;

"relevant service accommodation" means premises which fall within paragraph (a) of the definition of "service living accommodation" in section 96(1) of that Act.

26 Breach of notice

(1) If a constable has reasonable grounds for believing that a person is in breach of a domestic abuse protection notice, the constable may arrest the person without warrant.

(2) A person arrested by virtue of subsection (1) must be held in custody and brought before the appropriate magistrates' court—

(a) before the end of the period of 24 hours beginning with the time of the arrest, or

(b) if earlier, at the hearing of the application for a domestic abuse protection order against the person (see section 28(3)).

(3) In subsection (2) "the appropriate magistrates' court" means the magistrates' court which is to hear the application mentioned in subsection (2)(b).

(4) In calculating when the period of 24 hours mentioned in subsection (2)(a) ends, the following days are to be disregarded—

(a) any Sunday,

(b) Christmas Day,

(c) Good Friday, and

(d) any day which is a bank holiday in England and Wales under the Banking and Financial Dealings Act 1971.

(5) If the person is brought before the court as mentioned in subsection (2)(a), the court may remand the person.

(For power to remand a person brought before the court as mentioned in subsection (2) (b), see section 29(8).)

(6) In the application of section 128(6) of the Magistrates' Courts Act 1980 to remand under subsection (5) above, the reference to the "other party" is to be read as a reference to the senior police officer who gave the notice.

(7) The court may, when remanding the person on bail, require the person to comply, before release on bail or later, with any requirements that appear to the court to be necessary to secure that the person does not interfere with witnesses or otherwise obstruct the course of justice.

[F1(8) The requirement in subsection (2) to bring a person before the court is satisfied if the person appears before the court through a live video link or live audio link (within the meaning given by section 56 of the Criminal Justice Act 2003).]

(9) In section 17(1) of the Police and Criminal Evidence Act 1984 (entry for purpose of arrest etc), after paragraph (c) insert—

"(cza) of arresting a person who the constable has reasonable grounds for believing is in breach of a domestic abuse protection notice given under section 22 of the Domestic Abuse Act 2021;".

Textual Amendments

F1 S. 26(8) substituted (28.6.2022) by Police, Crime, Sentencing and Courts Act 2022 (c. 32), s. 208(5) (y), **Sch. 20 para. 9**

Domestic abuse protection orders

27 Meaning of "domestic abuse protection order"

(1) In this Part a "domestic abuse protection order" is an order which, for the purpose of preventing a person ("P") from being abusive towards a person aged 16 or over to whom P is personally connected—
  (a) prohibits P from doing things described in the order, or
  (b) requires P to do things described in the order.

(2) A domestic abuse protection order may be made—
  (a) on application (see section 28), or
  (b) in the course of certain proceedings (see section 31).

(3) Section 32 sets out the conditions for making a domestic abuse protection order.

28 Domestic abuse protection orders on application

(1) A court may make a domestic abuse protection order under this section against a person ("P") on an application made to it in accordance with this section.

(2) An application for an order under this section may be made by—
  (a) the person for whose protection the order is sought;
  (b) the appropriate chief officer of police (see subsection (4));
  (c) a person specified in regulations made by the Secretary of State;
  (d) any other person with the leave of the court to which the application is to be made.

(3) Where P is given a domestic abuse protection notice by a member of a relevant police force under section 22, the chief officer of police in relation to that force must apply for a domestic abuse protection order against P.

(For further provision about such applications, see section 29.)

(4) The appropriate chief officer of police is—
  (a) in a case where subsection (3) applies, the chief officer of police referred to in that subsection;
  (b) in any other case, any of the following—
    (i) the chief officer of police of the force maintained for any police area in which P resides;
    (ii) the chief officer of police of any other force maintained for a police area who believes that P is in that police area or is intending to come to it;
    (iii) the Chief Constable of the British Transport Police Force;

(iv) the Chief Constable of the Ministry of Defence Police.

(5) An application for an order under this section must be made to the family court, except where subsection (6) or (7) applies.

(6) An application made by a chief officer of police for an order under this section must be made by complaint to a magistrates' court.

(7) In a case where—

(a) P, and the person for whose protection the order is sought, are parties to any family or civil proceedings, and

(b) the court would have power to make a domestic abuse protection order under section 31 in those proceedings without an application being made,

an application for an order under this section may be made in those proceedings by the person for whose protection the order is sought.

(8) Where an application is made to a magistrates' court in accordance with this section—

(a) the magistrates' court may adjourn the hearing of the application;

(b) on the hearing of the application, section 97 of the Magistrates' Courts Act 1980 (summons to witness and warrant for arrest) does not apply in relation to the person for whose protection the order is sought, except where the person has given oral or written evidence at the hearing.

29 Applications where domestic abuse protection notice has been given

(1) This section applies where, as a result of a person ("P") being given a domestic abuse protection notice under section 22, a chief officer of police is required by section 28(3) to apply for a domestic abuse protection order against P.

(2) The application must be heard by the magistrates' court not later than 48 hours after the notice was given to P.

(3) In calculating when the period of 48 hours mentioned in subsection (2) ends, the following days are to be disregarded—

(a) any Sunday,

(b) Christmas Day,

(c) Good Friday, and

(d) any day which is a bank holiday in England and Wales under the Banking and Financial Dealings Act 1971.

(4) P must be given a notice of the hearing of the application.

(5) The notice under subsection (4) is to be treated as having been given if it has been left at the address given by P under section 25(4).

(6) But if the notice has not been given because P did not give an address under section 25(4), the court may hear the application if satisfied that the chief officer of police has made reasonable efforts to give P the notice.

(7) If the court adjourns the hearing of the application, the domestic abuse protection notice continues in effect until the application has been determined or withdrawn.

(8) If—

(a) P is brought before the court at the hearing of the application as a result of P's arrest by virtue of section 26(1) (arrest for breach of domestic abuse protection notice), and

(b) the court adjourns the hearing,

the court may remand P.

30 Remand under section 29(8) of person arrested for breach of notice

(1) This section applies where—

(a) as a result of a person being given a domestic abuse protection notice under section 22, a chief officer of police has applied for a domestic abuse protection order against the person, and

(b) the magistrates' court remands the person under section 29(8).

(2) In the application of section 128(6) of the Magistrates' Courts Act 1980 to such remand, the reference to the "other party" is to be read as a reference to the chief officer of police who applied for the order.

(3) If the court has reason to suspect that a medical report will be required, the power to remand the person may be exercised for the purpose of enabling a medical examination to take place and a report to be made.

(4) If the person is remanded in custody for that purpose, the adjournment may not be for more than 3 weeks at a time.

(5) If the person is remanded on bail for that purpose, the adjournment may not be for more than 4 weeks at a time.

(6) If the court has reason to suspect that the person is suffering from mental disorder within the meaning of the Mental Health Act 1983, the court has the same power to make an order under section 35 of that Act (remand to hospital for report on accused's mental condition) as it has under that section in the case of an accused person (within the meaning of that section).

(7) The court may, when remanding the person on bail, require the person to comply, before release on bail or later, with any requirements that appear to the court to be necessary to secure that the person does not interfere with witnesses or otherwise obstruct the course of justice.

31 Domestic abuse protection orders otherwise than on application

(1) A court may make a domestic abuse protection order under this section in any of the cases set out below.

Family proceedings

(2) The High Court or the family court may make a domestic abuse protection order against a person ("P") in any family proceedings to which both P and the person for whose protection the order would be made are parties.

Criminal proceedings

(3) Where a person ("P") has been convicted of an offence, the court dealing with P for that offence may (as well as sentencing P or dealing with P in any other way) make a domestic abuse protection order against P.

(4) But subsection (3) does not apply where the Court of Appeal is dealing with a person for an offence.

(5) A court by or before which a person is acquitted of an offence may make a domestic abuse protection order against the person.

(6) Where the Crown Court allows a person's appeal against a conviction for an offence, the Crown Court may make a domestic abuse protection order against the person.

Civil proceedings

(7) The county court may make a domestic abuse protection order against a person ("P") in any relevant proceedings to which both P and the person for whose protection the order would be made are parties.

(8) In subsection (7) "relevant proceedings" means proceedings of a description specified in regulations made by the Secretary of State.

32 Conditions for making an order

(1) The court may make a domestic abuse protection order under section 28 or 31 against a person ("P") if conditions A and B are met.

(2) Condition A is that the court is satisfied on the balance of probabilities that P has been abusive towards a person aged 16 or over to whom P is personally connected.

(3) Condition B is that the order is necessary and proportionate to protect that person from domestic abuse, or the risk of domestic abuse, carried out by P.

(4) It does not matter—
- (a) whether the abusive behaviour referred to in subsection (2) took place in England and Wales or elsewhere, or
- (b) whether it took place before or after the coming into force of this section.

(5) A domestic abuse protection order may not be made against a person who is under the age of 18.

33 Matters to be considered before making an order

(1) Before making a domestic abuse protection order against a person ("P"), the court must, among other things, consider the following—
- (a) the welfare of any person under the age of 18 whose interests the court considers relevant to the making of the order (whether or not that person and P are personally connected);
- (b) any opinion of the person for whose protection the order would be made—
  - (i) which relates to the making of the order, and
  - (ii) of which the court is made aware;
- (c) in a case where the order includes provision relating to premises lived in by the person for whose protection the order would be made, any opinion of a relevant occupant—
  - (i) which relates to the making of the order, and
  - (ii) of which the court is made aware.

(2) In subsection (1)(c) "relevant occupant" means a person other than P or the person for whose protection the order would be made—
- (a) who lives in the premises, and
- (b) who is personally connected to—
  - (i) the person for whose protection the order would be made, or
  - (ii) if P also lives in the premises, P.

(3) It is not necessary for the person for whose protection a domestic abuse protection order is made to consent to the making of the order.

34 Making of orders without notice

(1) A court may, in any case where it is just and convenient to do so, make a domestic abuse protection order against a person ("P") even though P has not been given such notice of the proceedings as would otherwise be required by rules of court.

(2) Subsection (1) does not apply in relation to the making of an order under section 28 on an application made in accordance with subsection (3) of that section (see instead section 29(4) to (6)).

(3) In deciding whether to exercise its powers under subsection (1), the court must have regard to all the circumstances, including—
 (a) any risk that, if the order is not made immediately, P will cause significant harm to the person for whose protection the order would be made,
 (b) in a case where an application for the order has been made, whether it is likely that the person making the application will be deterred or prevented from pursuing the application if an order is not made immediately, and
 (c) whether there is reason to believe that—
  (i) P is aware of the proceedings but is deliberately evading service, and
  (ii) the delay involved in effecting substituted service will cause serious prejudice to the person for whose protection the order would be made.

(4) If a court makes an order against a person by virtue of subsection (1), it must give the person an opportunity to make representations about the order—
 (a) as soon as just and convenient, and
 (b) at a hearing of which notice has been given to all the parties in accordance with rules of court.

35 Provision that may be made by orders

(1) A court may by a domestic abuse protection order impose any requirements that the court considers necessary to protect the person for whose protection the order is made from domestic abuse or the risk of domestic abuse.

"Requirement" includes any prohibition or restriction.

(2) The court must, in particular, consider what requirements (if any) may be necessary to protect the person for whose protection the order is made from different kinds of abusive behaviour.

(3) Subsections (4) to (6) contain examples of the type of provision that may be made under subsection (1), but they do not limit the type of provision that may be so made.

(4) A domestic abuse protection order may provide that the person against whom the order is made ("P")—
 (a) may not contact the person for whose protection it is made;
 (b) may not come within a specified distance of any premises in England or Wales in which that person lives;
 (c) may not come within a specified distance of any other specified premises, or any other premises of a specified description, in England or Wales.

"Specified" means specified in the order.

(5) If P lives in premises in England or Wales in which the person for whose protection the order is made also lives, the order may contain provision—
 (a) prohibiting P from evicting or excluding that person from the premises;
 (b) prohibiting P from entering the premises;
 (c) requiring P to leave the premises.

(6) A domestic abuse protection order may require P to submit to electronic monitoring in England and Wales of P's compliance with other requirements imposed by the order.

In this Part a requirement imposed by virtue of this subsection is referred to as an "electronic monitoring requirement".

(7) Sections 36 and 37 contain further provision about the requirements that may be imposed by a domestic abuse protection order.

36 Further provision about requirements that may be imposed by orders

(1) Requirements imposed on a person by a domestic abuse protection order must, so far as practicable, be such as to avoid—
  (a) conflict with the person's religious beliefs;
  (b) interference with the person's work or with the person's attendance at an educational establishment;
  (c) conflict with the requirements of any other court order or injunction to which the person may be subject.

(2) A domestic abuse protection order that imposes a requirement to do something on a person ("P") must specify the person who is to be responsible for supervising compliance with that requirement.

(3) Before including such a requirement in a domestic abuse protection order, the court must receive evidence about its suitability and enforceability from the person to be specified under subsection (2).

(4) Subsections (2) and (3) do not apply in relation to electronic monitoring requirements (see instead section 37(3) to (6)).

(5) It is the duty of a person specified under subsection (2)—
  (a) to make any necessary arrangements in connection with the requirements for which the person has responsibility (the "relevant requirements");
  (b) to promote P's compliance with the relevant requirements;
  (c) if the person considers that—
    (i) P has complied with all the relevant requirements, or
    (ii) P has failed to comply with a relevant requirement, to inform the appropriate chief officer of police.

(6) In subsection (5)(c) the "appropriate chief officer of police" means—
  (a) the chief officer of police of the force maintained for the police area in which it appears to the person specified under subsection (2) that P resides,
  (b) if it appears to that person that P resides in more than one police area, whichever one of the relevant chief officers of police the person thinks it most appropriate to inform, or
  (c) if it appears to the person specified under subsection (2) that P does not reside in any police area, the chief officer of police of the force maintained for the police area in which the court that made the order is situated.

(7) A person ("P") who is subject to a requirement imposed by a domestic abuse protection order—
  (a) must keep in touch with the person specified under subsection (2) in relation to that requirement, in accordance with any instructions given by that person from time to time;
  (b) if P changes home address, must notify the person specified under subsection (2) of the new home address;
  (c) if P ceases to have any home address, must notify the person specified under subsection (2) of that fact.

These obligations have effect as requirements of the order.

37 Further provision about electronic monitoring requirements

(1) Subsections (2) to (4) apply for the purpose of determining whether a court may impose an electronic monitoring requirement on a person ("P") in a domestic abuse protection order.

(2) The requirement may not be imposed in P's absence.

(3) If there is a person (other than P) without whose co-operation it would be impracticable to secure the monitoring in question, the requirement may not be imposed without that person's consent.

(4) The court may impose the requirement only if—

(a) it has been notified by the Secretary of State that electronic monitoring arrangements are available in the relevant area, and

(b) it is satisfied that the necessary provision can be made under the arrangements currently available.

(5) In subsection (4)(a) "the relevant area" means—

(a) the local justice area in which it appears to the court that P resides or will reside, and

(b) in a case where it is proposed to include in the order—

(i) a requirement that P must remain, for specified periods, at a specified place, or

(ii) a provision prohibiting P from entering a specified place or area, the local justice area in which the place or area proposed to be specified is situated.

"Specified" means specified in the order.

(6) A domestic abuse protection order that includes an electronic monitoring requirement must specify the person who is to be responsible for the monitoring.

(7) The person specified under subsection (6) ("the responsible person") must be of a description specified in regulations made by the Secretary of State.

(8) Where a domestic abuse protection order imposes an electronic monitoring requirement on a person, the person must (among other things)—

(a) submit, as required from time to time by the responsible person, to—

(i) being fitted with, or the installation of, any necessary apparatus, and

(ii) the inspection or repair of any apparatus fitted or installed for the purposes of the monitoring,

(b) not interfere with, or with the working of, any apparatus fitted or installed for the purposes of the monitoring, and

(c) take any steps required by the responsible person for the purpose of keeping in working order any apparatus fitted or installed for the purposes of the monitoring.

These obligations have effect as requirements of the order.

38 Duration and geographical application of orders

(1) A domestic abuse protection order takes effect on the day on which it is made. This is subject to subsection (2).

(2) If, on the day on which a domestic abuse protection order ("the new order") is made against a person, the person is subject to another domestic abuse protection order ("the previous order"), the new order may be made so as to take effect on the previous order ceasing to have effect.

(3) A domestic abuse protection order has effect—

(a) for a specified period,

(b) until the occurrence of a specified event, or

(c) until further order.

"Specified" means specified in the order.

(4) A domestic abuse protection order may also specify periods for which particular requirements imposed by the order have effect.

(5) But a domestic abuse protection order may not provide for an electronic monitoring requirement to have effect for more than 12 months.

(6) Subsection (5) is subject to any variation of the order under section 44.

(7) A requirement imposed by a domestic abuse protection order has effect in all parts of the United Kingdom unless expressly limited to a particular locality.

39 Breach of order

(1) A person who is subject to a domestic abuse protection order commits an offence if without reasonable excuse the person fails to comply with any requirement imposed by the order.

(2) In a case where the order was made against the person without that person being given notice of the proceedings, the person commits an offence under this section only in respect of behaviour engaged in at a time when the person was aware of the existence of the order.

(See also section 45(8) and (9), which makes similar provision where an order has been varied.)

(3) Where a person is convicted of an offence under this section in respect of any behaviour, that behaviour is not punishable as a contempt of court.

(4) A person may not be convicted of an offence under this section in respect of any behaviour which has been punished as a contempt of court.

(5) A person guilty of an offence under this section is liable—
  (a) on summary conviction—
    (i) to imprisonment for a term not exceeding 12 months (or 6 months, if the offence was committed before [F22 May 2022]), or
    (ii) to a fine, or both;
  (b) on conviction on indictment, to imprisonment for a term not exceeding 5 years or to a fine, or both.

(6) If a person is convicted of an offence under this section, it is not open to the court by or before which the person is convicted to make, in respect of the offence, an order under section 80 of the Sentencing Code (conditional discharge).

(7) If a person is convicted of an offence under section 42 of the Armed Forces Act 2006 as respects which the corresponding offence under the law of England and Wales (within the meaning given by that section) is an offence under this section, it is not open to the service court that convicted the person to make, in respect of the offence, an order under section 185 of that Act (conditional discharge).

In this subsection "service court" means the Court Martial or the Service Civilian Court.

(8) In proceedings for an offence under this section, a copy of the original domestic abuse protection order, certified by the proper officer of the court that made it, is admissible as evidence of its having been made and of its contents to the same extent that oral evidence of those matters is admissible in those proceedings.

Textual Amendments

F2 Words in s. 39(5)(a)(i) substituted (28.4.2022) by The Criminal Justice Act 2003 (Commencement No. 33) and Sentencing Act 2020 (Commencement No. 2) Regulations 2022 (S.I. 2022/500), regs. 1(2), 5(1), **Sch. Pt. 1**

40 Arrest for breach of order

(1) This section applies where a relevant court has made a domestic abuse protection order against a person ("P").

(2) In this section "relevant court" means—
  (a) the High Court,
  (b) the family court, or
  (c) the county court.

(3) A person mentioned in subsection (4) may apply to the relevant judge for the issue of a warrant for P's arrest if the person considers that P has failed to comply with the order or is otherwise in contempt of court in relation to the order.

(4) The persons referred to in subsection (3) are—
  (a) the person for whose protection the order was made;
  (b) where the order was made under section 28, the person who applied for the order (if different);
  (c) any other person with the leave of the relevant judge.

(5) The relevant judge may issue a warrant on an application under subsection (3) only if—
  (a) the application is substantiated on oath, and
  (b) the relevant judge has reasonable grounds for believing that P has failed to comply with the order or is otherwise in contempt of court in relation to the order.

(6) If—
  (a) P is brought before a relevant court as a result of a warrant issued under this section, and
  (b) the court does not immediately dispose of the matter, the court may remand P.

(7) Schedule 1 contains further provision about remand under this section.

(8) In this section "the relevant judge" means—
  (a) where the order was made by the High Court, a judge of that court;
  (b) where the order was made by the family court, a judge of that court;
  (c) where the order was made by the county court, a judge of that court.

(9) For the power of a constable to arrest P without warrant for breach of a domestic abuse protection order, see section 24 of the Police and Criminal Evidence Act 1984.

41 Notification requirements

(1) Subsections (2) to (6) apply where a person is subject to a domestic abuse protection order.

(2) The person must, within the period of three days beginning with the day on which the order is made, notify the police of the information in subsection (3).

(3) The information referred to in subsection (2) is—
  (a) the person's name and, if the person uses one or more other names, each of those names;
  (b) the person's home address.

(4) If the person uses a name which has not been notified under this section, the person must, within the period of three days beginning with the day on which the person first uses that name, notify the police of that name.

(5) If the person changes home address, the person must, before the end of the period of three days beginning with the day on which that happens, notify the police of the new home address.

(6) If the person ceases to have any home address, the person must, before the end of the period of three days beginning with the day on which that happens, notify the police of that fact.

(7) The Secretary of State may by regulations specify further notification requirements which a court may impose when making or varying a domestic abuse protection order.

In this subsection a "notification requirement" is a requirement for the person against whom the order is made to provide specified information to the police.

(8) The requirements imposed by subsections (2) to (6) do not apply where—
  (a) the person is subject to another domestic abuse protection order (and accordingly those requirements already apply), or
  (b) the person is subject to notification requirements under Part 2 of the Sexual Offences Act 2003 or section 9 of the Stalking Protection Act 2019.

(9) If on any day the person ceases to be subject to any notification requirements as mentioned in subsection (8)(a) or (b), the requirements imposed by subsections (2) to (6) apply to the person on and after that day, but as if the reference in subsection (2) to the day on which the order was made were a reference to that day.

(10) For provision about how to give a notification under subsection (2), (4), (5) or (6), see section 42.

42 Further provision about notification under section 41

(1) A person gives a notification under section 41(2), (4), (5) or (6) by—
  (a) attending at a police station in the appropriate police area, and
  (b) giving an oral notification to—
    (i) a police officer, or
    (ii) any person authorised for the purpose by the officer in charge of the station.

(2) In subsection (1) "the appropriate police area", in relation to a person, means—
  (a) if the person's home address is in England and Wales, the police area in which that home address is situated;
  (b) if the person does not have a home address in England and Wales, the police area in which the court that last made a domestic abuse protection order against the person is situated.

(3) In a case of a person giving a notification under section 41(5), any reference in subsection (2) to the person's home address is a reference to the person's home address at the time of giving the notification.

(4) A notification given in accordance with this section must be acknowledged—
  (a) in writing, and
  (b) in the form directed by the Secretary of State.

(5) When a person ("P") gives a notification under section 41, P must, if requested to do so by the person to whom notification is given, allow that person to do any of the following things—
  (a) take P's fingerprints;
  (b) photograph, or otherwise produce an image of, P or any part of P.

(6) The power in subsection (5) is exercisable for the purpose of verifying P's identity.

43 Offences relating to notification

(1) A person ("P") commits an offence if P—
  (a) fails, without reasonable excuse, to comply with a requirement imposed by or under section 41, or
  (b) notifies the police, in purported compliance with such a requirement, of any information which P knows to be false.

(2) A person who fails, without reasonable excuse, to comply with section 42(5) commits an offence.

(3) A person guilty of an offence under subsection (1) or (2) is liable—
  (a) on summary conviction—
    (i) to imprisonment for a period not exceeding 12 months (or 6 months, if the offence was committed before the [F32 May 2022]), or
    (ii) to a fine, or both;
  (b) on conviction on indictment, to imprisonment for a term not exceeding 5 years or to a fine, or both.

(4) A person commits an offence under subsection (1)(a) on the day on which the person first fails, without reasonable excuse, to comply with a requirement imposed by or under section 41.

(5) The person continues to commit the offence throughout any period during which the failure continues.

(6) But the person may not be prosecuted more than once in respect of the same failure.

Textual Amendments

F3 Words in s. 43(3)(a)(i) substituted (28.4.2022) by The Criminal Justice Act 2003 (Commencement No. 33) and Sentencing Act 2020 (Commencement No. 2) Regulations 2022 (S.I. 2022/500), regs. 1(2), 5(1), **Sch. Pt. 1**

44 Variation and discharge of orders

(1) A court may vary or discharge a domestic abuse protection order made by that or any other court.

This is subject to section 45.

(2) A court may vary or discharge a domestic abuse protection order under this section—
  (a) on the application of a person mentioned in subsection (3), or
  (b) in any case in which it could make a domestic abuse protection order under section 31.

(3) The persons referred to in subsection (2)(a) are—
  (a) the person for whose protection the order was made;
  (b) the person against whom the order was made ("P");
  (c) where the order was made under section 28, the person who applied for the order;
  (d) the chief officer of police of the force maintained for any police area in which P resides;
  (e) the chief officer of police of any other force maintained for a police area who believes that P is in that police area or is intending to come to it.

(4) Before deciding whether to vary or discharge an order under this section, the court must hear from—
  (a) any relevant chief officer of police who wishes to be heard, and
  (b) in a case where the person for whose protection the order was made is seeking to discharge the order, or to remove or make less onerous any requirement imposed by the order, the person for whose protection it was made.

(5) For the purposes of subsection (4)(a) each of the following is a "relevant chief officer of police"—
  (a) where the order was made on an application by a chief officer of police, that chief officer;
  (b) the chief officer of police of the force maintained for any police area in which P resides;
  (c) the chief officer of police of any other force maintained for a police area who believes that P is in that police area or is intending to come to it.

(6) Section 33 (matters to be considered before making an order) applies in relation to the variation or discharge of a domestic abuse protection order as it applies in relation to the making of such an order, but as if references to the person for whose protection the order would be made were references to the person for whose protection the order was made.

(7) Section 34 (making of orders without notice) applies in relation to the variation of a domestic abuse protection order as it applies in relation to the making of such an order, but as if—
  (a) references to the person for whose protection the order would be made were references to the person for whose protection the order was made,
  (b) subsection (2) were omitted, and
  (c) the reference in subsection (4) to making representations about the order were a reference to making representations about the variation.

(8) The court may make any order varying or discharging a domestic abuse protection order that it considers appropriate.

This is subject to subsections (9) to (13).

(9) The court may include an additional requirement in the order, or extend the period for which the order, or a requirement imposed by the order, has effect, only if it is satisfied that it is necessary to do so in order to protect the person for whose protection the order was made from domestic abuse, or the risk of domestic abuse, carried out by P.

(10) The court may not extend the period for which an electronic monitoring requirement has effect by more than 12 months at a time.

(11) The court may remove any requirement imposed by the order, or make such a requirement less onerous, only if satisfied that the requirement as imposed is no longer necessary to protect the person for whose protection the order was made from domestic abuse, or the risk of domestic abuse, carried out by P.

(12) If it appears to the court that any conditions necessary for a requirement to be imposed are no longer met, the court—
  (a) may not extend the requirement, and
  (b) must remove the requirement.

(13) The court may discharge the order only if satisfied that the order is no longer necessary to protect the person for whose protection it was made from domestic abuse, or the risk of domestic abuse, carried out by P.

45 Variation and discharge: supplementary

(1) Any application to vary or discharge a domestic abuse protection order under section 44 must be made to the court that made the order.

This is subject to subsections (2) and (3).

(2) Where the order was made by a magistrates' court, an application to vary or discharge the order may be made to any other magistrates' court acting in the local justice area in which that court acts.

(3) Where—
  (a) the order was made under section 31 on an appeal in relation to a person's conviction or sentence for an offence, or
  (b) the order was made by a court under that section against a person committed or remitted to that court for sentencing for an offence,

any application to vary or discharge the order must be made to the court by or before which the person was convicted (but see subsection (4)).

(4) Where the person mentioned in subsection (3)(b) was convicted by a youth court, the reference in subsection (3) to the court by or before which the person was convicted is to be read as a reference to a magistrates' court acting in the local justice area in which the youth court acts.

(5) Except as provided for by subsection (3), a domestic abuse protection order made by the Crown Court may be varied or discharged under section 44 only by the Crown Court.

(6) A domestic abuse protection order made by the High Court may be varied or discharged under section 44 only by the High Court.

(7) An order that has been varied under section 44 remains an order of the court that first made it for the purposes of any further application under that section.

(8) Subsection (9) applies in a case where—

(a) an order made against a person is varied under section 44 so as to include an additional requirement, or to extend the period for which the order, or a requirement imposed by the order, has effect, and

(b) the person was not given notice of the proceedings.

(9) The person commits an offence under section 39 only if—

(a) the behaviour constituting the offence was engaged in at a time when the person was aware of the making of the variation, and

(b) the behaviour would not have constituted an offence under that section in the absence of the variation.

46 Appeals

(1) A person listed in subsection (2) may appeal against any decision of a court on an application for a domestic abuse protection order under section 28 (to the extent that it would not otherwise be so appealable).

(2) The persons referred to in subsection (1) are—

(a) the person for whose protection the order was sought,

(b) the person who applied for the order (if different), and

(c) where the court made a domestic abuse protection order under section 28, the person against whom it was made.

(3) A person against whom a domestic abuse protection order is made under subsection (3), (5) or (6) of section 31 may appeal against the making of the order (to the extent it would not otherwise be so appealable) as if it were a sentence passed on the person for the offence referred to in that subsection (assuming, in a case within section 31(5) or (6), that the person had been convicted of the offence).

(4) A person against whom a domestic abuse protection order is made may appeal against a variation of the order under section 44 that is made in a case within subsection (3), (5) or (6) of section 31 (to the extent it would not otherwise be so appealable) as if the varied order were a sentence passed on the person for the offence referred to in that subsection (assuming, in a case within section 31(5) or (6), that the person had been convicted of the offence).

(5) A person listed in subsection (6) may appeal against any decision of a court under section 44 in relation to a domestic abuse protection order (to the extent it would not otherwise be so appealable, whether under subsection (4) or otherwise).

(6) The persons referred to in subsection (5) are—

(a) the person for whose protection the order was made;

(b) the person against whom the order was made ("P");

(c) where the order was made under section 28, the person who applied for the order;

(d) the chief officer of police of the force maintained for any police area in which P resides;
(e) the chief officer of police of any other force maintained for a police area who believes that P is in that police area or is intending to come to it.

(7) An appeal arising by virtue of subsection (1) or (5)—
(a) in the case of a decision made by a magistrates' court, is to be made to the Crown Court;
(b) in the case of a decision made by the Crown Court, is to be made to the Court of Appeal.

For the powers of the Crown Court or Court of Appeal on such an appeal, see section 47(4).

(8) If, in the case of an appeal arising by virtue of subsection (1) or (5) in respect of a decision made by the High Court, the family court or the county court, the person making the appeal was not a party to the proceedings in that court, the person is to be treated for the purposes of that appeal as if the person had been a party to those proceedings.

(9) For further provision about appeals, see (in particular)—
(a) section 31K of the Matrimonial and Family Proceedings Act 1984 (appeals from the family court),
(b) section 16(1) of the Senior Courts Act 1981 (appeals from the High Court),
(c) section 77 of the County Courts Act 1984 (appeals from the county court),
(d) section 108(3) of the Magistrates' Courts Act 1980 (appeals against orders made on conviction in a magistrates' court),
(e) section 50(1) of the Criminal Appeal Act 1968 (appeals against orders made on conviction in the Crown Court), and
(f) rules of court.

47 Further provision about appeals

(1) Before determining any appeal relating to a domestic abuse protection order (whether or not an appeal under section 46), the court must hear from any relevant chief officer of police who wishes to be heard.

(2) For the purposes of subsection (1) each of the following is a "relevant chief officer of police"—
(a) where the order was made on an application by a chief officer of police, that chief officer;
(b) the chief officer of police of the force maintained for any police area in which the person ("P") against whom the order was made, or (in the case of an appeal against the decision of a court not to make an order under section 28) against whom it was sought, resides;
(c) the chief officer of police of any other force maintained for a police area who believes that P is in that police area or is intending to come to it.

(3) Subsection (4) applies to—
(a) an appeal made to the Crown Court by virtue of section 46(7)(a);
(b) an appeal made to the Court of Appeal by virtue of section 46(7)(b).

(4) On an appeal to which this subsection applies, the court may, on a review of the decision appealed against—
(a) confirm, vary or revoke any part of the decision;
(b) refer the matter back to the court that made the decision with a direction to reconsider and make a new decision in accordance with its ruling;
(c) make any order which the court that made the decision appealed against could have made;
(d) make any incidental or consequential orders that appear to it to be just.

(5) For the purposes of section 45 (variation and discharge: supplementary)—

(a) a domestic abuse protection order that has been confirmed or varied on an appeal (whether under subsection (4)(a) or otherwise) remains an order of the court that first made it, and
(b) a domestic abuse protection order made by a court on an appeal (whether under subsection (4)(c) or otherwise) is to be treated as an order made by the court whose decision was appealed against.

48 Nature of certain proceedings under this Part

(1) Proceedings before a court arising by virtue of section 31(3), (5) or (6), and proceedings before a court arising by virtue of section 44(2)(b) in any case within section 31(3), (5) or (6), are civil proceedings (like proceedings before a magistrates' court under section 28 or 44(2)(a)).
(2) The court is not restricted in the proceedings to considering evidence that would have been admissible in the criminal proceedings in which the person concerned was convicted or (as the case may be) acquitted.
(3) The court may adjourn any proceedings arising by virtue of section 31(3), (5) or (6), or any proceedings arising by virtue of section 44(2)(b) in any case within section 31(3), (5) or (6), even after sentencing or acquitting the person concerned or allowing the person's appeal.
(4) A domestic abuse protection order may be made or varied in addition to an order discharging the person conditionally or absolutely in spite of anything in sections 79, 80 and 82 of the Sentencing Code (which relate to orders discharging a person conditionally or absolutely and their effect).

49 Special measures for witnesses

(1) Chapter 1 of Part 2 of the Youth Justice and Criminal Evidence Act 1999 (special measures directions in case of vulnerable and intimidated witnesses) applies to relevant proceedings under this Part as it applies to criminal proceedings, but with—
 (a) the omission of the provisions of that Act mentioned in subsection (2) (which make provision only in the context of criminal proceedings), and
 (b) any other necessary modifications.
(2) The provisions are—
 (a) section 17(4) to (7);
 (b) section 21(4C)(e);
 (c) section 22A;
 (d) section 32.
(3) Rules of court made under or for the purposes of Chapter 1 of Part 2 of that Act apply to relevant proceedings under this Part—
 (a) to the extent provided by rules of court, and
 (b) subject to any modifications provided by rules of court.
(4) Section 47 of that Act (restrictions on reporting special measures directions etc) applies with any necessary modifications—
 (a) to a direction under section 19 of that Act as applied by this section;
 (b) to a direction discharging or varying such a direction.

 Sections 49 and 51 of that Act (offences) apply accordingly.
(5) In this section "relevant proceedings under this Part" means—
 (a) proceedings under section 28, 31(2) or (7), 40 or 44(2)(a);
 (b) proceedings arising by virtue of section 31(3), (5) or (6);

(c) proceedings arising by virtue of section 44(2)(b) in any case within section 31(3), (5) or (6);

(d) proceedings on an appeal relating to a domestic abuse protection order (whether or not an appeal under section 46).

Notices and orders: supplementary

50 Guidance

(1) The Secretary of State must issue guidance relating to the exercise by relevant persons of functions under or by virtue of this Part.

(2) In this section "relevant person" means—

(a) a constable;

(b) a person specified in regulations under subsection (2)(c) of section 28 for the purpose of making applications for orders under that section.

(3) A relevant person must have regard to any guidance issued under this section when exercising a function to which the guidance relates.

(4) The Secretary of State may from time to time revise any guidance issued under this section.

(5) Before issuing or revising guidance under this section, the Secretary of State must consult—

(a) the Domestic Abuse Commissioner, and

(b) such other persons as the Secretary of State considers appropriate.

(6) Subsection (5) does not apply in relation to any revisions of guidance issued under this section if the Secretary of State considers the proposed revisions of the guidance are insubstantial.

(7) The Secretary of State must publish—

(a) any guidance issued under this section, and

(b) any revisions of that guidance.

51 Data from electronic monitoring: code of practice

(1) The Secretary of State must issue a code of practice relating to the processing of data gathered in the course of electronic monitoring of individuals under electronic monitoring requirements imposed by domestic abuse protection orders.

(2) A failure to act in accordance with a code issued under this section does not of itself make a person liable to any criminal or civil proceedings.

52 Powers to make other orders in proceedings under this Part

(1) In section 8 of the Children Act 1989 (child arrangements orders and other orders with respect to children), in subsection (4), at the end insert—

"(k) Part 3 of the Domestic Abuse Act 2021, where the proceedings are in the family court or the Family Division of the High Court."

(2) In Part 4 of the Family Law Act 1996 (family homes and domestic violence), in section 63(2) (definition of "family proceedings"), after paragraph (j) insert—

"(k) Part 3 of the Domestic Abuse Act 2021, where the proceedings are in the family court or the Family Division of the High Court."

53 Proceedings not to be subject to conditional fee agreements

In section 58A of the Courts and Legal Services Act 1990 (conditional fee agreements: supplementary), in subsection (2), after paragraph (fd) (but before the "and" following it) insert—

"(fe) proceedings under Part 3 of the Domestic Abuse Act 2021 (proceedings for domestic abuse protection order), where the proceedings are in the family court or the Family Division of the High Court;".

54 Consequential amendments of the Sentencing Code

(1) The Sentencing Code is amended as follows.

(2) In section 80 (order for conditional discharge), in subsection (3), at the end insert—

"(f) section 39(6) of the Domestic Abuse Act 2021 (breach of domestic abuse protection order)."

(3) In Chapter 6 of Part 11 (other behaviour orders), before section 379 (but after the heading "Other orders") insert—

"378A Domestic abuse protection orders

See Part 3 of the Domestic Abuse Act 2021 (and in particular section 31(3) of that Act) for the power of a court to make a domestic abuse protection order when dealing with an offender for an offence."

55 Repeal of provisions about domestic violence protection notices and orders

(1) In the Crime and Security Act 2010, omit sections 24 to 33 (which make provision for domestic violence protection notices and domestic violence protection orders).

(2) In consequence of the repeal made by subsection (1), omit the following provisions—

(a) in Schedule 8 to the Crime and Courts Act 2013, paragraph 179;

(b) in Schedule 14 to the Policing and Crime Act 2017, paragraph 7(g).

56 Interpretation of Part 3

(1) In this Part—

"chief officer of police" means—

(a) in relation to a police force maintained by a local policing body, the chief officer of police of that force;

(b) in relation to the British Transport Police Force, the Chief Constable of the Force;

(c) in relation to the Ministry of Defence Police, the Chief Constable of the Ministry of Defence Police;

"domestic abuse protection notice" has the meaning given by section 22(2); "domestic abuse protection order" has the meaning given by section 27(1);

"electronic monitoring requirement" has the meaning given by section 35(6);

"family proceedings" means—

(a) proceedings in the family court (other than proceedings under or by virtue of this Part), and

(b) family proceedings within the meaning of Part 5 of the Matrimonial and Family Proceedings Act 1984;

"home address", in relation to a person, means—

(a) the address of the person's sole or main residence in the United Kingdom, or

(b) if the person has no such residence—

(i) the address or location of a place in the United Kingdom where the person can regularly be found;

(ii) if there is more than one such place, the address or location of whichever one of those places the person selects;

"relevant police force" has the meaning given by section 22(8);

"requirement", in relation to a domestic abuse protection order, is to be read in accordance with section 35(1);

"senior police officer" has the meaning given by section 22(8).

(2) Any reference to a member of a police force includes, in the case of a police force maintained by a local policing body, a reference to a special constable appointed by the chief officer of police of that force.

(3) Any reference to changing home address includes a reference to a case where—

(a) a person acquires a home address at any time, and

(b) immediately before that time, the person did not have a home address.

(4) See also—

(a) section 1 (definition of "domestic abuse");

(b) section 2 (definition of "personally connected").

PART 4

LOCAL AUTHORITY SUPPORT

57 Support provided by local authorities to victims of domestic abuse

(1) Each relevant local authority in England must—

(a) assess, or make arrangements for the assessment of, the need for accommodation-based support in its area,

(b) prepare and publish a strategy for the provision of such support in its area, and

(c) monitor and evaluate the effectiveness of the strategy.

(2) For the purposes of subsection (1)—

"accommodation-based support" means support, in relation to domestic abuse, provided to victims of domestic abuse, or their children, who reside in relevant accommodation;

"relevant accommodation" means accommodation of a description specified by the Secretary of State in regulations.

(3) A relevant local authority that publishes a strategy under this section must, in carrying out its functions, give effect to the strategy.

(4) Before publishing a strategy under this section, a relevant local authority must consult—

(a) the domestic abuse local partnership board appointed by the relevant local authority under section 58,

(b) any local authority for an area within the relevant local authority's area, and

(c) such other persons as the relevant local authority considers appropriate.

(5) A relevant local authority that publishes a strategy under this section—

(a) must keep the strategy under review,

(b) must keep under review any effect of the strategy on the provision of other local authority support in its area,

(c) may alter or replace the strategy, and

(d) must publish any altered or replacement strategy.

(6) In this section "other local authority support", in relation to a local authority, means support, in relation to domestic abuse, that—

(a) is provided to victims of domestic abuse or their children, and

(b) is provided or funded by the local authority,

other than accommodation-based support (within the meaning of subsection (2)).

(7) A relevant local authority may request any local authority for an area within the relevant local authority's area to co-operate with it in any way that the relevant local authority considers necessary for the purposes of its functions under this section.

(8) A local authority must, so far as reasonably practicable, comply with a request made to it under subsection (7).

(9) The Secretary of State may by regulations make provision about the preparation and publication of strategies under this section.

(10) The power to make regulations under subsection (9) may, in particular, be exercised to make provision about—
- (a) the procedure to be followed by a relevant local authority in preparing a strategy;
- (b) matters to which a relevant local authority must have regard in preparing a strategy;
- (c) how a relevant local authority must publish a strategy;
- (d) the date by which a relevant local authority must first publish a strategy;
- (e) the frequency with which a relevant local authority must review its strategy or any effect of the strategy on the provision of other local authority support in its area.

(11) Before making regulations under this section, the Secretary of State must consult—
- (a) the Domestic Abuse Commissioner,
- (b) relevant local authorities, and
- (c) such other persons as the Secretary of State considers appropriate.

Modifications etc. (not altering text)

C1 S. 57(2) modified (1.10.2021) by The Domestic Abuse Support (Relevant Accommodation and Housing Benefit and Universal Credit Sanctuary Schemes) (Amendment) Regulations 2021 (S.I. 2021/991), regs. 1(2), **2**

Commencement Information

I26 S. 57 in force at 1.10.2021 by S.I. 2021/1038, **reg. 2(e)**

58 Domestic abuse local partnership boards

(1) A relevant local authority in England must appoint a domestic abuse local partnership board for the purposes of providing advice to the authority about—
- (a) the exercise of the authority's functions under section 57, and
- (b) the provision of other local authority support in the authority's area.

(2) The members of the domestic abuse local partnership board must include—
- (a) a representative of the relevant local authority;
- (b) at least one person appearing to the authority to represent the interests of local authorities for areas within its area;
- (c) at least one person appearing to the authority to represent the interests of victims of domestic abuse;
- (d) at least one person appearing to the authority to represent the interests of children of domestic abuse victims;
- (e) at least one person appearing to the authority to represent the interests of charities and other voluntary organisations that work with victims of domestic abuse in its area;
- (f) at least one person appearing to the authority to represent the interests of persons who provide, or have functions relating to, health care services in its area;
- (g) at least one person appearing to the authority to represent the interests of persons with functions relating to policing or criminal justice in its area.

(3) In this section—

"health care services" means services relating to health care (within the meaning of section 9 of the Health and Social Care Act 2008);

"other local authority support" has the same meaning as in section 57.

Commencement Information

I27 S. 58 in force at 1.10.2021 by S.I. 2021/1038, **reg. 2(e)**

59 Annual reports

(1) As soon as reasonably practicable after the end of each financial year, a relevant local authority in England must submit to the Secretary of State an annual report in relation to the exercise of the authority's functions under this Part during the year.

(2) The Secretary of State may by regulations make provision about—

(a) the form of the report, and

(b) the content of the report.

(3) In this section "financial year" means—

(a) the period beginning with the day on which this section comes into force and ending with the following 31 March, and

(b) each successive period of 12 months.

Commencement Information

I28 S. 59 in force at 1.10.2021 by S.I. 2021/1038, **reg. 2(e)**

60 Guidance

(1) The Secretary of State must issue guidance relating to the exercise by local authorities in England of functions under this Part.

(2) Local authorities in England must have regard to the guidance when exercising a function to which the guidance relates.

(3) The Secretary of State may from time to time revise any guidance issued under this section.

(4) Before issuing or revising guidance under this section, the Secretary of State must consult—

(a) the Domestic Abuse Commissioner,

(b) local authorities, and

(c) such other persons as the Secretary of State considers appropriate.

(5) Subsection (4) does not apply in relation to any revisions of guidance issued under this section if the Secretary of State considers the proposed revisions of the guidance are insubstantial.

(6) The Secretary of State must publish—

(a) any guidance issued under this section, and

(b) any revisions of that guidance.

Commencement Information

I29 S. 60 in force at 1.10.2021 by S.I. 2021/1038, **reg. 2(e)**

61 Interpretation of Part 4

In this Part—

"local authority" means—

(a) a relevant local authority;

(b) a district council for an area for which there is a county council;

(c) a London borough council;
(d) the Common Council of the City of London in its capacity as a local authority;
"relevant local authority" means—
(a) a county council;
(b) a district council for an area for which there is no county council;
(c) the Greater London Authority;
(d) the Council of the Isles of Scilly.

Commencement Information

I30 S. 61 in force at 1.10.2021 by S.I. 2021/1038, **reg. 2(e)**

PART 5

PROTECTION FOR VICTIMS, WITNESSES, ETC IN LEGAL PROCEEDINGS

Special measures

62 Special measures in criminal proceedings for offences involving domestic abuse

(1) Chapter 1 of Part 2 of the Youth Justice and Criminal Evidence Act 1999 (giving of evidence or information for purposes of criminal proceedings: special measures directions in case of vulnerable and intimidated witnesses) is amended as follows.

(2) In section 17 (witnesses eligible for assistance on grounds of fear or distress about testifying)—
(a) in subsection (4), for "a sexual offence or an offence under section 1 or 2 of the Modern Slavery Act 2015" substitute " an offence listed in subsection (4A) ";
(b) after subsection (4) insert—
"(4A) The offences are—
(a) a sexual offence;
(b) an offence under section 1 or 2 of the Modern Slavery Act 2015;
(c) any other offence where it is alleged that the behaviour of the accused amounted to domestic abuse within the meaning of the Domestic Abuse Act 2021 (see section 1 of that Act)."

(3) In section 25(4)(a) (evidence given in private), for "a sexual offence or an offence under section 1 or 2 of the Modern Slavery Act 2015" substitute " an offence listed in section 17(4A) ".

Commencement Information

I31 S. 62 in force at 19.5.2022 for specified purposes by S.I. 2022/553, regs. 1(2), **2(1)(a)**

63 Special measures in family proceedings: victims of domestic abuse

(1) This section applies where rules of court provide that the court may make a special measures direction in relation to a person ("P") who is a party or witness in family proceedings.

(2) Rules of court must provide that where P is, or is at risk of being, a victim of domestic abuse carried out by a person listed in subsection (3), it is to be assumed that the following matters are likely to be diminished by reason of vulnerability—
(a) the quality of P's evidence;
(b) where P is a party to the proceedings, P's participation in the proceedings.

(3) The persons referred to in subsection (2) are—
(a) a party to the proceedings;
(b) a relative of a party to the proceedings (other than P);
(c) a witness in the proceedings.

(4) Rules of court may provide for an exception to the provision made by virtue of subsection (2) where P does not wish to be deemed to be eligible for the making of a special measures direction by virtue of that subsection.

(5) In this section—
"family proceedings" has the meaning given by section 75(3) of the Courts Act 2003;
"relative" has the meaning given by section 63(1) of the Family Law Act 1996;
"special measures" means such measures as may be specified by rules of court for the purpose of assisting a person to give evidence or participate in proceedings;
"special measures direction" means a direction by the court granting special measures.

Commencement Information

I32 S. 63 in force at 1.10.2021 by S.I. 2021/1038, **reg. 2(d)**

64 Special measures in civil proceedings: victims of domestic abuse etc

(1) Rules of court must make provision enabling the court to make a special measures direction in relation to a person who is a party or witness in civil proceedings where that person—
(a) is, or is at risk of being, a victim of domestic abuse;
(b) is the victim, or alleged victim, of a specified offence.

(2) Rules made by virtue of subsection (1) must, in particular, provide for the court to consider—
(a) whether—
(i) the quality of the person's evidence, or
(ii) where the person is a party to the proceedings, the person's participation in the proceedings,
is likely to be diminished by reason of vulnerability, and
(b) if so, whether it is necessary to make one or more special measures directions.

(3) For the purposes of this section—
(a) a person is the victim of a specified offence if another person has been convicted of, or given a caution for, the offence;
(b) a person is the alleged victim of a specified offence if another person has been charged with the offence.

(4) In this section—
"civil proceedings" means—
(a) proceedings in the county court,
(b) proceedings in the High Court, other than—
(i) proceedings in the Family Division of the High Court which are business assigned, by or under section 61 of (and Schedule 1 to) the Senior Courts Act 1981, to that Division of the High Court and no other, and
(ii) proceedings in the exercise of its jurisdiction under the Extradition Act 2003, and
(c) proceedings in the civil division of the Court of Appeal;
"special measures" means such measures as may be specified by rules of court for the purpose of assisting a person to give evidence or participate in proceedings;
"special measures direction" means a direction by the court granting special measures;
"specified offence" means an offence which is specified, or of a description specified, in regulations made by the Lord Chancellor.

Commencement Information

I33 S. 64 in force at 14.6.2022 by S.I. 2022/553, regs. 1(2), 4

PROSPECTIVE

Prohibition of cross-examination in person

65 Prohibition of cross-examination in person in family proceedings
In the Matrimonial and Family Proceedings Act 1984, after Part 4A insert—

"PART 4B

FAMILY PROCEEDINGS: PROHIBITION OF CROSS-EXAMINATION IN PERSON

31Q Prohibition of cross-examination in person: introductory In this Part—

"family proceedings" means—
(a) proceedings in the family court,
(b) proceedings in the Family Division of the High Court which are business assigned, by or under section 61 of (and Schedule 1 to) the Senior Courts Act 1981, to that Division of the High Court and no other, and
(c) proceedings in the civil division of the Court of Appeal arising out of proceedings within paragraph (a) or (b);
"witness", in relation to any proceedings, includes a party to the proceedings.

31R Prohibition of cross-examination in person: victims of offences

(1) In family proceedings, no party to the proceedings who has been convicted of or given a caution for, or is charged with, a specified offence may cross-examine in person a witness who is the victim, or alleged victim, of that offence.

(2) In family proceedings, no party to the proceedings who is the victim, or alleged victim, of a specified offence may cross-examine in person a witness who has been convicted of or given a caution for, or is charged with, that offence.

(3) Subsections (1) and (2) do not apply to a conviction or caution that is spent for the purposes of the Rehabilitation of Offenders Act 1974, unless evidence in relation to the conviction or caution is admissible in, or may be required in, the proceedings by virtue of section 7(2), (3) or (4) of that Act.

(4) Cross-examination in breach of subsection (1) or (2) does not affect the validity of a decision of the court in the proceedings if the court was not aware of the conviction, caution or charge when the cross-examination took place.

(5) In this section—
"caution" means—
(a) in the case of England and Wales—
(i) a conditional caution given under section 22 of the Criminal Justice Act 2003,
(ii) a youth conditional caution given under section 66A of the Crime and Disorder Act 1998, or

(iii) any other caution given to a person in England and Wales in respect of an offence which, at the time the caution is given, the person has admitted;

(b) in the case of Scotland, anything corresponding to a caution falling within paragraph (a) (however described) which is given to a person in respect of an offence under the law of Scotland;

(c) in the case of Northern Ireland—

(i) a conditional caution given under section 71 of the Justice Act (Northern Ireland) 2011, or

(ii) any other caution given to a person in Northern Ireland in respect of an offence which, at the time the caution is given, the person has admitted;

"conviction" means—

(a) a conviction by or before a court in England and Wales, Scotland or Northern Ireland;

(b) a conviction in service disciplinary proceedings (in England and Wales, Scotland, Northern Ireland, or elsewhere), including—

(i) in the case of proceedings in respect of a service offence, anything that under section 376(1) and (2) of the Armed Forces Act 2006 (which relates to summary hearings and the Summary Appeal Court) is to be treated as a conviction for the purposes of that Act, and

(ii) in the case of any other service disciplinary proceedings, a finding of guilt in those proceedings;

(c) a finding in any criminal proceedings (including a finding linked with a finding of insanity) that the person concerned has committed an offence or done the act or made the omission charged;

and "convicted" is to be read accordingly;

"service disciplinary proceedings" means—

(a) any proceedings (whether or not before a court) in respect of a service offence (except proceedings before a civilian court within the meaning of the Armed Forces Act 2006);

(b) any proceedings under the Army Act 1955, the Air Force Act 1955, or the Naval Discipline Act 1957 (whether before a court-martial or before any other court or person authorised under any of those Acts to award a punishment in respect of an offence);

(c) any proceedings before a Standing Civilian Court established under the Armed Forces Act 1976;

"service offence" means—

(a) a service offence within the meaning of the Armed Forces Act 2006, or

(b) an SDA offence within the meaning of the Armed Forces Act 2006 (Transitional Provisions etc) Order 2009 (S.I. 2009/1059);

"specified offence" means an offence which is specified, or of a description specified, in regulations made by the Lord Chancellor.

(6) The following provisions (which deem a conviction of a person discharged not to be a conviction) do not apply for the purposes of this section to a conviction of a person for an offence in respect of which an order has been made discharging the person absolutely or conditionally—

(a) section 14 of the Powers of Criminal Courts (Sentencing) Act 2000;

(b) section 82 of the Sentencing Code;

(c) section 187 of the Armed Forces Act 2006 or any corresponding earlier enactment.

(7) For the purposes of this section "offence" includes an offence under a law that is no longer in force.

31S Prohibition of cross-examination in person: persons protected by injunctions etc

(1) In family proceedings, no party to the proceedings against whom an on-notice protective injunction is in force may cross-examine in person a witness who is protected by the injunction.

(2) In family proceedings, no party to the proceedings who is protected by an on-notice protective injunction may cross-examine in person a witness against whom the injunction is in force.

(3) Cross-examination in breach of subsection (1) or (2) does not affect the validity of a decision of the court in the proceedings if the court was not aware of the protective injunction when the cross-examination took place.

(4) In this section "protective injunction" means an order, injunction or interdict specified, or of a description specified, in regulations made by the Lord Chancellor.

(5) For the purposes of this section, a protective injunction is an "on-notice" protective injunction if—

(a) the court is satisfied that there has been a hearing at which the person against whom the protective injunction is in force asked, or could have asked, for the injunction to be set aside or varied, or

(b) the protective injunction was made at a hearing of which the court is satisfied that both the person who applied for it and the person against whom it is in force had notice.

31T Prohibition of cross-examination in person: evidence of domestic abuse

(1) In family proceedings, where specified evidence is adduced that a person who is a witness has been the victim of domestic abuse carried out by a party to the proceedings, that party to the proceedings may not cross-examine the witness in person.

(2) In family proceedings, where specified evidence is adduced that a person who is a party to the proceedings has been the victim of domestic abuse carried out by a witness, that party may not cross-examine the witness in person.

(3) In this section—

"domestic abuse" has the meaning given by section 1 of the Domestic Abuse Act 2021;

"specified evidence" means evidence specified, or of a description specified, in regulations made by the Lord Chancellor.

(4) Regulations under subsection (3) may provide that any evidence which satisfies the court that domestic abuse, or domestic abuse of a specified description, has occurred is specified evidence for the purposes of this section.

31U Direction for prohibition of cross-examination in person: other cases

(1) In family proceedings, the court may give a direction prohibiting a party to the proceedings from cross-examining (or continuing to cross-examine) a witness in person if—

(a) none of sections 31R to 31T operates to prevent the party from cross-examining the witness, and

(b) it appears to the court that—

(i) the quality condition or the significant distress condition is met, and

(ii) it would not be contrary to the interests of justice to give the direction.

(2) The "quality condition" is met if the quality of evidence given by the witness on cross-examination—

(a) is likely to be diminished if the cross-examination (or continued cross-examination) is conducted by the party in person, and
(b) would be likely to be improved if a direction were given under this section.

(3) The "significant distress condition" is met if—
(a) the cross-examination (or continued cross-examination) of the witness by the party in person would be likely to cause significant distress to the witness or the party, and
(b) that distress is likely to be more significant than would be the case if the witness were cross-examined other than by the party in person.

(4) A direction under this section may be made by the court—
(a) on an application made by a party to the proceedings, or
(b) of its own motion.

(5) In determining whether the quality condition or the significant distress condition is met in the case of a witness or party, the court must have regard to, among other things—
(a) any views expressed by the witness as to whether or not the witness is content to be cross-examined by the party in person;
(b) any views expressed by the party as to whether or not the party is content to cross-examine the witness in person;
(c) the nature of the questions likely to be asked, having regard to the issues in the proceedings;
(d) any behaviour by the party in relation to the witness in respect of which the court is aware that a finding of fact has been made in the proceedings or in any other proceedings;
(e) any behaviour by the witness in relation to the party in respect of which the court is aware that a finding of fact has been made in the proceedings or in any other proceedings;
(f) any behaviour by the party at any stage of the proceedings, both generally and in relation to the witness;
(g) any behaviour by the witness at any stage of the proceedings, both generally and in relation to the party;
(h) any relationship (of whatever nature) between the witness and the party.

(6) Any reference in this section to the quality of a witness's evidence is to its quality in terms of completeness, coherence and accuracy.

(7) For this purpose "coherence" refers to a witness's ability in giving evidence to give answers which—
(a) address the questions put to the witness, and
(b) can be understood, both individually and collectively.

31V Directions under section 31U: supplementary

(1) A direction under section 31U has binding effect from the time it is made until the witness in relation to whom it applies is discharged.

(2) But the court may revoke a direction under section 31U before the witness is discharged, if it appears to the court to be in the interests of justice to do so, either—
(a) on an application made by a party to the proceedings, or
(b) of its own motion.

(3) The court may revoke a direction under section 31U on an application made by a party to the proceedings only if there has been a material change of circumstances since—
(a) the direction was given, or
(b) if a previous application has been made by a party to the proceedings, the application (or the last application) was determined.

(4) The court must state its reasons for—
   (a) giving a direction under section 31U;
   (b) refusing an application for a direction under section 31U;
   (c) revoking a direction under section 31U;
   (d) refusing an application for the revocation of a direction under section 31U.

31W Alternatives to cross-examination in person

(1) This section applies where a party to family proceedings is prevented from cross-examining a witness in person by virtue of any of sections 31R to 31U.

(2) The court must consider whether (ignoring this section) there is a satisfactory alternative means—
   (a) for the witness to be cross-examined in the proceedings, or
   (b) of obtaining evidence that the witness might have given under cross-examination in the proceedings.

(3) If the court decides that there is not, the court must—
   (a) invite the party to the proceedings to arrange for a qualified legal representative to act for the party for the purpose of cross-examining the witness, and
   (b) require the party to the proceedings to notify the court, by the end of a period specified by the court, of whether a qualified legal representative is to act for the party for that purpose.

(4) Subsection (5) applies if, by the end of the period specified under subsection (3)(b), either—
   (a) the party has notified the court that no qualified legal representative is to act for the party for the purpose of cross-examining the witness, or
   (b) no notification has been received by the court and it appears to the court that no qualified legal representative is to act for the party for the purpose of cross-examining the witness.

(5) The court must consider whether it is necessary in the interests of justice for the witness to be cross-examined by a qualified legal representative appointed by the court to represent the interests of the party.

(6) If the court decides that it is, the court must appoint a qualified legal representative (chosen by the court) to cross-examine the witness in the interests of the party.

(7) A qualified legal representative appointed by the court under subsection (6) is not responsible to the party.

(8) For the purposes of this section—
   (a) a reference to cross-examination includes a reference to continuing to conduct cross-examination;
   (b) "qualified legal representative" means a person who, for the purposes of the Legal Services Act 2007, is an authorised person in relation to an activity which constitutes the exercise of a right of audience (within the meaning of that Act) in family proceedings.

31X Costs of legal representatives appointed under section 31W(6)

(1) The Lord Chancellor may by regulations make provision for the payment out of central funds of sums in respect of—
   (a) fees or costs properly incurred by a qualified legal representative appointed under section 31W(6), and
   (b) expenses properly incurred in providing such a person with evidence or other material in connection with the appointment.

(2) The regulations may provide for sums payable under subsection (1) to be determined by the Lord Chancellor or such other person as the regulations may specify.

(3) The regulations may provide for sums payable under subsection (1)—
  (a) to be such amounts as are specified in the regulations;
  (b) to be calculated in accordance with—
    (i) a rate or scale specified in the regulations, or
    (ii) other provision made by or under the regulations.

31Y Guidance for legal representatives appointed under section 31W(6)

(1) The Lord Chancellor may issue guidance in connection with the role which a qualified legal representative appointed under section 31W(6) in connection with any family proceedings is to play in the proceedings, including (among other things) guidance about the effect of section 31W(7).

(2) A qualified legal representative appointed under section 31W(6) must have regard to any guidance issued under this section.

(3) The Lord Chancellor may from time to time revise any guidance issued under this section.

(4) The Lord Chancellor must publish—
  (a) any guidance issued under this section, and
  (b) any revisions of that guidance.

31Z Regulations under Part 4B

(1) Any power of the Lord Chancellor to make regulations under this Part—
  (a) is exercisable by statutory instrument,
  (b) includes power to make different provision for different purposes, and
  (c) includes power to make supplementary, incidental, consequential, transitional, transitory or saving provision.

(2) A statutory instrument containing regulations under this Part is subject to annulment in pursuance of a resolution of either House of Parliament."

66 Prohibition of cross-examination in person in civil proceedings
In the Courts Act 2003, after Part 7 insert—

"PART 7A

CIVIL PROCEEDINGS: PROHIBITION OF CROSS-EXAMINATION IN PERSON

85E Prohibition of cross-examination in person: introductory
In this Part—

"civil proceedings" means—
  (a) proceedings in the county court,
  (b) proceedings in the High Court, other than—
    (i) proceedings in the Family Division of the High Court which are business assigned, by or under section 61 of (and Schedule 1 to) the Senior Courts Act 1981, to that Division of the High Court and no other, and
    (ii) proceedings in the exercise of its jurisdiction under the Extradition Act 2003, and
  (c) proceedings in the civil division of the Court of Appeal arising out of civil proceedings within paragraph (a) or (b);

"witness", in relation to any proceedings, includes a party to the proceedings.

85F Prohibition of cross-examination in person: victims of offences

(1) In civil proceedings, no party to the proceedings who has been convicted of, or given a caution for, a specified offence may cross-examine in person a witness who is the victim of that offence.

(2) In civil proceedings, no party to the proceedings who is the victim of a specified offence may cross-examine in person a witness who has been convicted of, or given a caution for, that offence.

(3) Subsections (1) and (2) do not apply to a conviction or caution that is spent for the purposes of the Rehabilitation of Offenders Act 1974, unless evidencein relation to the conviction or caution is admissible in, or may be required in, the proceedings by virtue of section 7(2), (3) or (4) of that Act.

(4) Cross-examination in breach of subsection (1) or (2) does not affect the validity of a decision of the court in the proceedings if the court was not aware of the conviction or caution when the cross-examination took place.

(5) In this section—

"caution" means—

(a) in the case of England and Wales—
   (i) a conditional caution given under section 22 of the Criminal Justice Act 2003,
   (ii) a youth conditional caution given under section 66A of the Crime and Disorder Act 1998, or
   (iii) any other caution given to a person in England and Wales in respect of an offence which, at the time the caution is given, the person has admitted;

(b) in the case of Scotland, anything corresponding to a caution falling within paragraph (a) (however described) which is given to a person in respect of an offence under the law of Scotland;

(c) in the case of Northern Ireland—
   (i) a conditional caution given under section 71 of the Justice Act (Northern Ireland) 2011, or
   (ii) any other caution given to a person in Northern Ireland in respect of an offence which, at the time the caution is given, the person has admitted;

"conviction" means—

(a) a conviction by or before a court in England and Wales, Scotland or Northern Ireland;

(b) a conviction in service disciplinary proceedings (in England and Wales, Scotland, Northern Ireland, or elsewhere), including—
   (i) in the case of proceedings in respect of a service offence, anything that under section 376(1) and (2) of the Armed Forces Act 2006 (which relates to summary hearings and the Summary Appeal Court) is to be treated as a conviction for the purposes of that Act, and
   (ii) in the case of any other service disciplinary proceedings, a finding of guilt in those proceedings;

(c) a finding in any criminal proceedings (including a finding linked with a finding of insanity) that the person concerned has committed an offence or done the act or made the omission charged;

and "convicted" is to be read accordingly;

"service disciplinary proceedings" means—

(a) any proceedings (whether or not before a court) in respect of a service offence (except proceedings before a civilian court within the meaning of the Armed Forces Act 2006);
(b) any proceedings under the Army Act 1955, the Air Force Act 1955, or the Naval Discipline Act 1957 (whether before a court-martial or before any other court or person authorised under any of those Acts to award a punishment in respect of an offence);
(c) any proceedings before a Standing Civilian Court established under the Armed Forces Act 1976;

"service offence" means—
(a) a service offence within the meaning of the Armed Forces Act 2006, or
(b) an SDA offence within the meaning of the Armed Forces Act 2006 (Transitional Provisions etc) Order 2009 (S.I. 2009/1059);

"specified offence" means an offence which is specified, or of a description specified, in regulations made by the Lord Chancellor.

(6) The following provisions (which deem a conviction of a person discharged not to be a conviction) do not apply for the purposes of this section to a conviction of a person for an offence in respect of which an order has been made discharging the person absolutely or conditionally—
(a) section 14 of the Powers of Criminal Courts (Sentencing) Act 2000;
(b) section 82 of the Sentencing Code;
(c) section 187 of the Armed Forces Act 2006 or any corresponding earlier enactment.

(7) For the purposes of this section "offence" includes an offence under a law that is no longer in force.

85G Prohibition of cross-examination in person: persons protected by injunctions etc

(1) In civil proceedings, no party to the proceedings against whom an on-notice protective injunction is in force may cross-examine in person a witness who is protected by the injunction.

(2) In civil proceedings, no party to the proceedings who is protected by an on-notice protective injunction may cross-examine in person a witness against whom the injunction is in force.

(3) Cross-examination in breach of subsection (1) or (2) does not affect the validity of a decision of the court in the proceedings if the court was not aware of the protective injunction when the cross-examination took place.

(4) In this section "protective injunction" means an order, injunction or interdict specified, or of a description specified, in regulations made by the Lord Chancellor.

(5) For the purposes of this section, a protective injunction is an "on-notice" protective injunction if—
(a) the court is satisfied that there has been a hearing at which the person against whom the protective injunction is in force asked, or could have asked, for the injunction to be set aside or varied, or
(b) the protective injunction was made at a hearing of which the court is satisfied that both the person who applied for it and the person against whom it is in force had notice.

85H Prohibition of cross-examination in person: evidence of domestic abuse

(1) In civil proceedings, where specified evidence is adduced that a person who is a witness has been the victim of domestic abuse carried out by a party to the proceedings, that party to the proceedings may not cross-examine the witness in person.

(2) In civil proceedings, where specified evidence is adduced that a person who is a party to the proceedings has been the victim of domestic abuse carried out by a witness, that party may not cross-examine the witness in person.

(3) In this section—
"domestic abuse" has the meaning given by section 1 of the Domestic Abuse Act 2021;
"specified evidence" means evidence specified, or of a description specified, in regulations made by the Lord Chancellor.

(4) Regulations under subsection (3) may provide that any evidence which satisfies the court that domestic abuse, or domestic abuse of a specified description, has occurred is specified evidence for the purposes of this section.

85I Direction for prohibition of cross-examination in person: other cases

(1) In civil proceedings, the court may give a direction prohibiting a party to the proceedings from cross-examining (or continuing to cross-examine) a witness in person if—
   (a) none of sections 85F to 85H operates to prevent the party from cross-examining the witness, and
   (b) it appears to the court that—
      (i) the quality condition or the significant distress condition is met, and
      (ii) it would not be contrary to the interests of justice to give the direction.

(2) The "quality condition" is met if the quality of evidence given by the witness on cross-examination—
   (a) is likely to be diminished if the cross-examination (or continued cross-examination) is conducted by the party in person, and
   (b) would be likely to be improved if a direction were given under this section.

(3) The "significant distress condition" is met if—
   (a) the cross-examination (or continued cross-examination) of the witness by the party in person would be likely to cause significant distress to the witness or the party, and
   (b) that distress is likely to be more significant than would be the case if the witness were cross-examined other than by the party in person.

(4) A direction under this section may be made by the court—
   (a) on an application made by a party to the proceedings, or
   (b) of its own motion.

(5) In determining whether the quality condition or the significant distress condition is met in the case of a witness or party, the court must have regard to, among other things—
   (a) any views expressed by the witness as to whether or not the witness is content to be cross-examined by the party in person;
   (b) any views expressed by the party as to whether or not the party is content to cross-examine the witness in person;
   (c) the nature of the questions likely to be asked, having regard to the issues in the proceedings;
   (d) any charge of which the court is aware in respect of a specified offence alleged to have been committed by the party in relation to the witness;
   (e) any charge of which the court is aware in respect of a specified offence alleged to have been committed by the witness in relation to the party;
   (f) any behaviour by the party in relation to the witness in respect of which the court is aware that a finding of fact has been made in the proceedings or in any other proceedings;
   (g) any behaviour by the witness in relation to the party in respect of which the court is aware that a finding of fact has been made in the proceedings or in any other proceedings;
   (h) any behaviour by the party at any stage of the proceedings, both generally and in relation to the witness;

(i) any behaviour by the witness at any stage of the proceedings, both generally and in relation to the party;
(j) any relationship (of whatever nature) between the witness and the party.

(6) In subsection (5)(d) and (e) "specified offence" means an offence that is a specified offence for the purposes of section 85F.

(7) Any reference in this section to the quality of a witness's evidence is to its quality in terms of completeness, coherence and accuracy.

(8) For this purpose "coherence" refers to a witness's ability in giving evidence to give answers which—
(a) address the questions put to the witness, and
(b) can be understood, both individually and collectively.

85J Directions under section 85I: supplementary

(1) A direction under section 85I has binding effect from the time it is made until the witness in relation to whom it applies is discharged.

(2) But the court may revoke a direction under section 85I before the witness is discharged, if it appears to the court to be in the interests of justice to do so, either—
(a) on an application made by a party to the proceedings, or
(b) of its own motion.

(3) The court may revoke a direction under section 85I on an application made by a party to the proceedings only if there has been a material change of circumstances since—
(a) the direction was given, or
(b) if a previous application has been made by a party to the proceedings, the application (or the last application) was determined.

(4) The court must state its reasons for—
(a) giving a direction under section 85I;
(b) refusing an application for a direction under section 85I;
(c) revoking a direction under section 85I;
(d) refusing an application for the revocation of a direction under section 85I.

85K Alternatives to cross-examination in person

(1) This section applies where a party to civil proceedings is prevented from cross-examining a witness in person by virtue of any of sections 85F to 85I.

(2) The court must consider whether (ignoring this section) there is a satisfactory alternative means—
(a) for the witness to be cross-examined in the proceedings, or
(b) of obtaining evidence that the witness might have given under cross-examination in the proceedings.

(3) If the court decides that there is not, the court must—
(a) invite the party to the proceedings to arrange for a qualified legal representative to act for the party for the purpose of cross-examining the witness, and
(b) require the party to the proceedings to notify the court, by the end of a period specified by the court, of whether a qualified legal representative is to act for the party for that purpose.

(4) Subsection (5) applies if, by the end of the period specified under subsection (3)(b), either—
(a) the party has notified the court that no qualified legal representative is to act for the party for the purpose of cross-examining the witness, or

(b) no notification has been received by the court and it appears to the court that no qualified legal representative is to act for the party for the purpose of cross-examining the witness.

(5) The court must consider whether it is necessary in the interests of justice for the witness to be cross-examined by a qualified legal representative appointed by the court to represent the interests of the party.

(6) If the court decides that it is, the court must appoint a qualified legal representative (chosen by the court) to cross-examine the witness in the interests of the party.

(7) A qualified legal representative appointed by the court under subsection (6) is not responsible to the party.

(8) For the purposes of this section—

(a) a reference to cross-examination includes a reference to continuing to conduct cross-examination;

(b) "qualified legal representative" means a person who, for the purposes of the Legal Services Act 2007, is an authorised person in relation to an activity which constitutes the exercise of a right of audience (within the meaning of that Act) in civil proceedings.

85L Costs of legal representatives appointed under section 85K(6)

(1) The Lord Chancellor may by regulations make provision for the payment out of central funds of sums in respect of—

(a) fees or costs properly incurred by a qualified legal representative appointed under section 85K(6), and

(b) expenses properly incurred in providing such a person with evidence or other material in connection with the appointment.

(2) The regulations may provide for sums payable under subsection (1) to be determined by the Lord Chancellor or such other person as the regulations may specify.

(3) The regulations may provide for sums payable under subsection (1)—

(a) to be such amounts as are specified in the regulations;

(b) to be calculated in accordance with—

(i) a rate or scale specified in the regulations, or

(ii) other provision made by or under the regulations.

85M Guidance for legal representatives appointed under section 85K(6)

(1) The Lord Chancellor may issue guidance in connection with the role which a qualified legal representative appointed under section 85K(6) in connection with any civil proceedings is to play in the proceedings, including (among other things) guidance about the effect of section 85K(7).

(2) A qualified legal representative appointed under section 85K(6) must have regard to any guidance issued under this section.

(3) The Lord Chancellor may from time to time revise any guidance issued under this section.

(4) The Lord Chancellor must publish—

(a) any guidance issued under this section, and

(b) any revisions of that guidance.

85N Regulations under Part 7A

Regulations under this Part may make different provision for different purposes."

Orders under section 91(14) of the Children Act 1989

67 Orders under section 91(14) of the Children Act 1989

(1) The Children Act 1989 is amended as follows.

(2) In section 91 (effect and duration of orders etc.), at the end of subsection (14) insert—
"For further provision about orders under this subsection, see section 91A (section 91(14) orders: further provision)."

(3) After section 91 insert—

"91A Section 91(14) orders: further provision

(1) This section makes further provision about orders under section 91(14) (referred to in this section as "section 91(14) orders").

(2) The circumstances in which the court may make a section 91(14) order include, among others, where the court is satisfied that the making of an application for an order under this Act of a specified kind by any person who is to be named in the section 91(14) order would put—
   (a) the child concerned, or
   (b) another individual ("the relevant individual"), at risk of harm.

(3) In the case of a child or other individual who has reached the age of eighteen, the reference in subsection (2) to "harm" is to be read as a reference to ill-treatment or the impairment of physical or mental health.

(4) Where a person who is named in a section 91(14) order applies for leave to make an application of a specified kind, the court must, in determining whether to grant leave, consider whether there has been a material change of circumstances since the order was made.

(5) A section 91(14) order may be made by the court—
   (a) on an application made—
      (i) by the relevant individual;
      (ii) by or on behalf of the child concerned;
      (iii) by any other person who is a party to the application being disposed of by the court;
   (b) of its own motion.

(6) In this section, "the child concerned" means the child referred to in section 91(14)."

Commencement Information

I34 S. 67 in force at 19.5.2022 by S.I. 2022/553, regs. 1(2), **2(1)(b)**

PART 6

OFFENCES INVOLVING ABUSIVE OR VIOLENT BEHAVIOUR

PROSPECTIVE

Controlling or coercive behaviour

68 Controlling or coercive behaviour in an intimate or family relationship

(1) Section 76 of the Serious Crime Act 2015 (offence of controlling or coercive behaviour in an intimate or family relationship) is amended as follows.

(2) In subsection (1)(b), after "personally connected" insert " (see subsection (6)) ".

(3) Omit subsection (2).

(4) For subsection (6) substitute—

"(6) A and B are "personally connected" if any of the following applies—

(a) they are, or have been, married to each other;

(b) they are, or have been, civil partners of each other;

(c) they have agreed to marry one another (whether or not the agreement has been terminated);

(d) they have entered into a civil partnership agreement (whether or not the agreement has been terminated);

(e) they are, or have been, in an intimate personal relationship with each other;

(f) they each have, or there has been a time when they each have had, a parental relationship in relation to the same child (see subsection (6A));

(g) they are relatives.

(6A) For the purposes of subsection (6)(f) a person has a parental relationship in relation to a child if—

(a) the person is a parent of the child, or

(b) the person has parental responsibility for the child."

(5) In subsection (7), for "subsection (6)" substitute " subsections (6) and (6A) ".

Disclosure of private sexual photographs and films

69 Threats to disclose private sexual photographs and films with intent to cause distress

(1) Section 33 of the Criminal Justice and Courts Act 2015 (disclosing private sexual photographs and films with intent to cause distress) is amended as follows.

(2) In the heading, after "Disclosing" insert " , or threatening to disclose, ".

(3) For subsection (1) substitute—

"(1) A person commits an offence if—

(a) the person discloses, or threatens to disclose, a private sexual photograph or film in which another individual ("the relevant individual") appears,

(b) by so doing, the person intends to cause distress to that individual, and

(c) the disclosure is, or would be, made without the consent of that individual."

(4) In subsection (2)—

(a) after "disclose" insert " , or threaten to disclose, ";

(b) for "the individual mentioned in subsection (1)(a) and (b)" substitute " the relevant individual ".

(5) After subsection (2) insert—

"(2A) Where a person is charged with an offence under this section of threatening to disclose a private sexual photograph or film, it is not necessary for the prosecution to prove—

(a) that the photograph or film referred to in the threat exists, or

(b) if it does exist, that it is in fact a private sexual photograph or film."

(6) In subsection (4)(a), after "disclosure" insert " , or threat to disclose, ".

(7) In subsection (5)—

(a) in paragraph (a), for "the individual mentioned in subsection (1)(a) and (b)" substitute " the relevant individual ";

(b) in paragraph (b), for "the individual mentioned in subsection (1)(a) and (b)" substitute " the relevant individual ".

(8) For subsection (8) substitute—

"(8) A person charged with an offence under this section is not to be taken to have intended to cause distress by disclosing, or threatening to disclose, a photograph or film merely because that was a natural and probable consequence of the disclosure or threat."

(9) In section 35 of that Act (meaning of "private" and "sexual"), in subsection (5)(c), for "the person mentioned in section 33(1)(a) and (b)" substitute " the relevant individual (within the meaning of section 33) ".

(10) In Schedule 8 to that Act (disclosing private sexual photographs or films: providers of information society services)—

(a) in the heading, after "Disclosing" insert " , or threatening to disclose, ";

(b) in paragraph 5 (exception for hosting)—

(i) in sub-paragraph (1), after "sub-paragraph (2)" insert " , (2A) ";

(ii) in sub-paragraph (2), in the words before paragraph (a), after "if" insert " , in the case of information which consists of or includes a private sexual photograph or film, ";

(iii) after sub-paragraph (2) insert—

"(2A) This sub-paragraph is satisfied if, in the case of information which consists of or includes a threat to disclose a privatesexual photograph or film, the service provider had no actual knowledge when the information was provided—

(a) that it consisted of or included a threat to disclose a private sexual photograph or film in which another individual appears,

(b) that the threat was made with the intention of causing distress to that individual, or

(c) that the disclosure would be made without the consent of that individual."

Offences against the person

70 Strangulation or suffocation

(1) In Part 5 of the Serious Crime Act 2015 (protection of children and others), after section 75 insert—

"Strangulation or suffocation

75A Strangulation or suffocation

(1) A person ("A") commits an offence if—

(a) A intentionally strangles another person ("B"), or

(b) A does any other act to B that—

(i) affects B's ability to breathe, and

(ii) constitutes battery of B.

(2) It is a defence to an offence under this section for A to show that B consented to the strangulation or other act.

(3) But subsection (2) does not apply if—

(a) B suffers serious harm as a result of the strangulation or other act, and

(b) A either—

(i) intended to cause B serious harm, or

(ii) was reckless as to whether B would suffer serious harm.

(4) A is to be taken to have shown the fact mentioned in subsection (2) if—

(a) sufficient evidence of the fact is adduced to raise an issue with respect to it, and

(b) the contrary is not proved beyond reasonable doubt.

(5) A person guilty of an offence under this section is liable—

(a) on summary conviction—

(i) to imprisonment for a term not exceeding 12 months (or 6 months, if the offence was committed before the coming into force of paragraph 24(2) of Schedule 22 to the Sentencing Act 2020), or

(ii) to a fine,

or both;

(b) on conviction on indictment, to imprisonment for a term not exceeding 5 years or to a fine, or both.

(6) In this section "serious harm" means—

(a) grievous bodily harm, within the meaning of section 18 of the Offences Against the Person Act 1861,

(b) wounding, within the meaning of that section, or

(c) actual bodily harm, within the meaning of section 47 of that Act.

75B Offences under section 75A committed outside the United Kingdom

(1) If—

(a) a person does an act in a country outside the United Kingdom,

(b) the act, if done in England and Wales, would constitute an offence under section 75A, and

(c) the person is a United Kingdom national or is habitually resident in England and Wales,

the person is guilty in England and Wales of that offence.

(2) In this section—

"country" includes territory;

"United Kingdom national" means an individual who is—

(a) a British citizen, a British overseas territories citizen, a British National (Overseas) or a British Overseas citizen,

(b) a person who under the British Nationality Act 1981 is a British subject, or

(c) a British protected person within the meaning of that Act."

(2) Schedule 2 contains consequential amendments.

Commencement Information

I35 S. 70 in force at 7.6.2022 by S.I. 2022/553, regs. 1(2), **3(a)**

71 Consent to serious harm for sexual gratification not a defence

(1) This section applies for the purposes of determining whether a person ("D") who inflicts serious harm on another person ("V") is guilty of a relevant offence.

(2) It is not a defence that V consented to the infliction of the serious harm for the purposes of obtaining sexual gratification (but see subsection (4)).

(3) In this section—

"relevant offence" means an offence under section 18, 20 or 47 of the Offences Against the Person Act 1861 ("the 1861 Act");

"serious harm" means—

(a) grievous bodily harm, within the meaning of section 18 of the 1861 Act,
(b) wounding, within the meaning of that section, or
(c) actual bodily harm, within the meaning of section 47 of the 1861 Act.

(4) Subsection (2) does not apply in the case of an offence under section 20 or 47 of the 1861 Act where—
(a) the serious harm consists of, or is a result of, the infection of V with a sexually transmitted infection in the course of sexual activity, and
(b) V consented to the sexual activity in the knowledge or belief that D had the sexually transmitted infection.

(5) For the purposes of this section it does not matter whether the harm was inflicted for the purposes of obtaining sexual gratification for D, V or some other person.

(6) Nothing in this section affects any enactment or rule of law relating to other circumstances in which a person's consent to the infliction of serious harm may, or may not, be a defence to a relevant offence.

Offences committed outside the UK

72 Offences against the person committed outside the UK: England and Wales

(1) If—
(a) a person who is a United Kingdom national or is habitually resident in England and Wales does an act in a country outside the United Kingdom,
(b) the act constitutes an offence under the law in force in that country, and
(c) the act, if done in England and Wales, would constitute an offence to which this subsection applies,

the person is guilty in England and Wales of that offence.

(2) The offences to which subsection (1) applies are—
(a) murder;
(b) manslaughter;
(c) an offence under section 18, 20 or 47 of the Offences Against the Person Act 1861 (offences relating to bodily harm or injury);
(d) an offence under section 23 or 24 of that Act (administering poison);
(e) an offence under section 1 of the Infant Life (Preservation) Act 1929 (child destruction).

(3) Subsection (1) does not apply where a person would, in the absence of that subsection, be guilty of an offence of murder or manslaughter under the law of England and Wales.

(4) An act punishable under the law in force in any country constitutes an offence under that law for the purposes of subsection (1)(b) however it is described in that law.

(5) The condition in subsection (1)(b) is to be taken to be met unless, not later than rules of court may provide, the defendant serves on the prosecution a notice—
(a) stating that, on the facts as alleged with respect to the act in question, the condition is not in the defendant's opinion met,
(b) showing the grounds for that opinion, and
(c) requiring the prosecution to prove that it is met.

(6) But the court, if it thinks fit, may permit the defendant to require the prosecution to prove that the condition is met without service of a notice under subsection (5).

(7) In the Crown Court the question whether the condition is met is to be decided by the judge alone.

(8) In this section—
"act" includes a failure to act;
"country" includes territory;
"United Kingdom national" means an individual who is—
(a) a British citizen, a British overseas territories citizen, a British National (Overseas) or a British Overseas citizen,
(b) a person who under the British Nationality Act 1981 is a British subject, or
(c) a British protected person within the meaning of that Act.

73 Offences against the person committed outside the UK: Northern Ireland

(1) If—
(a) a person who is a United Kingdom national or is habitually resident in Northern Ireland does an act in a country outside the United Kingdom,
(b) the act constitutes an offence under the law in force in that country, and
(c) the act, if done in Northern Ireland, would constitute an offence to which this subsection applies,

the person is guilty in Northern Ireland of that offence.

(2) The offences to which subsection (1) applies are—
(a) murder;
(b) manslaughter;
(c) an offence under section 18, 20 or 47 of the Offences Against the Person Act 1861 (offences relating to bodily harm or injury);
(d) an offence under section 23 or 24 of that Act (administering poison);
(e) an offence under section 25 of the Criminal Justice Act (Northern Ireland) 1945 (child destruction).

(3) Subsection (1) does not apply where a person would, in the absence of that subsection, be guilty of an offence of murder or manslaughter under the law of Northern Ireland.

(4) An act punishable under the law in force in any country constitutes an offence under that law for the purposes of subsection (1)(b) however it is described in that law.

(5) The condition in subsection (1)(b) is to be taken to be met unless, not later than rules of court may provide, the defendant serves on the prosecution a notice—
(a) stating that, on the facts as alleged with respect to the act in question, the condition is not in the defendant's opinion met,
(b) showing the grounds for that opinion, and
(c) requiring the prosecution to prove that it is met.

(6) But the court, if it thinks fit, may permit the defendant to require the prosecution to prove that the condition is met without service of a notice under subsection (5).

(7) In the Crown Court the question whether the condition is met is to be decided by the judge alone.

(8) In this section—
"act" includes a failure to act;
"country" includes territory;
"rules of court" means—
(a) in relation to proceedings in a magistrates' court, magistrates' court rules;
(b) in relation to proceedings in the Crown Court, Crown Court rules; "United Kingdom national" means an individual who is—

(a) a British citizen, a British overseas territories citizen, a British National (Overseas) or a British Overseas citizen,
(b) a person who under the British Nationality Act 1981 is a British subject, or
(c) a British protected person within the meaning of that Act.

(9) The Interpretation Act (Northern Ireland) 1954 applies for the purposes of this section as it applies to an Act of the Northern Ireland Assembly.

Commencement Information

I36 S. 73 in force at 21.2.2022 by S.R. 2022/52, **art. 2(a)**

74 Amendments relating to offences committed outside the UK

(1) Part 1 of Schedule 3 contains amendments to provide for extra-territorial jurisdiction over certain other offences under the law of England and Wales.

(2) Part 2 of Schedule 3 contains amendments to provide for extra-territorial jurisdiction over certain offences under the law of Scotland.

(3) Part 3 of Schedule 3 contains amendments to provide for extra-territorial jurisdiction over certain other offences under the law of Northern Ireland.

Commencement Information

I37 S. 74(1) in force at 29.6.2021, see s. 90

I38 S. 74(3) in force at 21.2.2022 by S.R. 2022/52, **art. 2(b)**

PART 7

MISCELLANEOUS AND GENERAL

Prosecution and management of offenders

75 Strategy for prosecution and management of offenders

(1) The Secretary of State must, before the end of the period of 12 months beginning with the day on which this Act is passed, prepare and publish a document setting out a strategy for—
(a) detecting, investigating and prosecuting offences involving domestic abuse,
(b) assessing and managing the risks posed by individuals who commit offences involving domestic abuse, including (among others) risks associated with stalking, and
(c) reducing the risk that such individuals commit further offences involving domestic abuse.

(2) The Secretary of State—
(a) must keep the strategy under review;
(b) may revise it.

(3) If the Secretary of State revises the strategy, the Secretary of State must publish a document setting out the revised strategy.

(4) In preparing or revising a strategy under this section, the Secretary of State must consult—
(a) the Domestic Abuse Commissioner, and
(b) such other persons as the Secretary of State considers appropriate.

(5) Subsection (4) does not apply in relation to any revisions of the strategy if the Secretary of State considers the proposed revisions of the strategy are insubstantial.

(6) In this section, the reference to "risks associated with stalking" is to be read in accordance with section 1(4) of the Stalking Protection Act 2019.

76 Polygraph conditions for offenders released on licence

(1) In Part 3 of the Offender Management Act 2007 (other provisions about the management of offenders), section 28 (application of polygraph condition) is amended as follows.

(2) In subsection (2), for "a relevant sexual offence" substitute " an offence within subsection (3A) ".

(3) In subsection (3)(a), for "for a term of twelve months or more" substitute " that is not for a term of less than twelve months ".

(4) After subsection (3) insert—

"(3A) An offence is within this subsection if it is—

(a) a relevant offence involving domestic abuse (see subsections (3B) and (3C)), or

(b) a relevant sexual offence (see subsection (4)).

(3B) In this section "relevant offence involving domestic abuse" means—

(a) an offence listed in subsection (3C) which involved behaviour by the offender amounting to domestic abuse within the meaning of the Domestic Abuse Act 2021 (see section 1 of that Act);

(b) an offence under section 39 of that Act (breach of domestic abuse protection order).

(3C) The offences are—

(a) murder;

(b) an offence under section 5 of the Protection from Harassment Act 1997 (breach of a restraining order);

(c) an offence specified in Part 1 of Schedule 15 to the Criminal Justice Act 2003 (specified violent offences);

(d) an offence under section 76 of the Serious Crime Act 2015 (controlling or coercive behaviour in an intimate or family relationship)."

Commencement Information

I39 S. 76 in force at 5.7.2021 in relation to specified areas for the specified period by S.I. 2021/797, **reg. 3** (with reg. 4(2))

PROSPECTIVE

Disclosure of information by police

77 Guidance about the disclosure of information by police forces

(1) The Secretary of State must issue guidance to chief officers of police about the disclosure of police information by police forces for the purposes of preventing domestic abuse.
"Police information" means information held by a police force.

(2) Each chief officer of police of a police force must have regard to any guidance issued under this section.

(3) The Secretary of State may from time to time revise any guidance issued under this section.

(4) Before issuing or revising guidance under this section, the Secretary of State must consult—

(a) the Domestic Abuse Commissioner,

(b) the National Police Chiefs' Council, and
(c) such other persons as the Secretary of State considers appropriate.

(5) Subsection (4) does not apply in relation to any revisions of guidance issued under this section if the Secretary of State considers the proposed revisions of the guidance are insubstantial.

(6) The Secretary of State must publish—
(a) any guidance issued under this section, and
(b) any revisions of that guidance.

(7) In this section—
"chief officer of police" means—
(a) in relation to the British Transport Police Force, the Chief Constable of that Force;
(b) in relation to any other police force, the chief officer of police of that force;
"police force" means—
(a) a police force maintained by a local policing body, or
(b) the British Transport Police Force.

Homelessness

78 Homelessness: victims of domestic abuse

(1) Part 7 of the Housing Act 1996 (homelessness: England) is amended as follows.

(2) In section 177 (whether it is reasonable to continue to occupy accommodation)—
(a) in subsection (1), for "domestic violence or other violence" substitute " violence or domestic abuse ";
(b) for subsection (1A) substitute—
"(1A) For this purpose—
(a) "domestic abuse" has the meaning given by section 1 of the Domestic Abuse Act 2021;
(b) "violence" means—
(i) violence from another person; or
(ii) threats of violence from another person which are likely to be carried out."

(3) Omit section 178 (meaning of associated person).

(4) In section 179 (duty of local housing authority in England to provide advisory services), in subsection (5)—
(a) for the definition of "domestic abuse" substitute—
"“domestic abuse" has the meaning given by section 1 of the Domestic Abuse Act 2021;";
(b) omit the definition of "financial abuse".

(5) In section 189 (priority need for accommodation)—
(a) in subsection (1), after paragraph (d) insert—
"(e) a person who is homeless as a result of that person being a victim of domestic abuse.";
(b) after subsection (4) insert—
"(5) In this section "domestic abuse" has the meaning given by section 1 of the Domestic Abuse Act 2021."

(6) In section 198 (referral of case to another local housing authority)—
(a) in subsection (2), in paragraph (c), for "domestic violence" substitute " domestic abuse ";
(b) in subsection (2ZA), in paragraph (b), for "domestic violence" substitute " domestic abuse ";

(c) in subsection (2A), in paragraph (a), for "domestic violence" substitute " violence that is domestic abuse ";

(d) for subsection (3) substitute—

"(3) For the purposes of subsections (2), (2ZA) and (2A)—

(a) "domestic abuse" has the meaning given by section 1 of the Domestic Abuse Act 2021;

(b) "violence" means—

(i) violence from another person; or

(ii) threats of violence from another person which are likely to be carried out."

(7) In section 218 (index of defined expressions: Part 7), in the table, omit the entry relating to section 178.

(8) In article 6 of the Homelessness (Priority Need for Accommodation) (England) Order 2002 (S.I. 2002/2051) (vulnerability: fleeing violence or threats of violence)—

(a) the existing text becomes paragraph (1);

(b) after that paragraph insert—

"(2) For the purposes of this article—

(a) "violence" does not include violence that is domestic abuse;

(b) "domestic abuse" has the meaning given by section 1 of the Domestic Abuse Act 2021."

(9) In consequence of the repeal made by subsection (3), omit the following provisions—

(a) in Schedule 8 to the Civil Partnership Act 2004, paragraph 61;

(b) in Schedule 3 to the Adoption and Children Act 2002, paragraphs 89 to 92.

Commencement Information

I40 S. 78 in force at 5.7.2021 by S.I. 2021/797, **reg. 2(2)** (with reg. 4(1))

Secure tenancies

79 Grant of secure tenancies in cases of domestic abuse

(1) Part 4 of the Housing Act 1985 (secure tenancies and rights of secure tenants) is amended as follows.

(2) After section 81 insert—

"81ZA Grant of secure tenancies in cases of domestic abuse

(1) This section applies where a local housing authority grants a secure tenancy of a dwelling-house in England before the day on which paragraph 4 of Schedule 7 to the Housing and Planning Act 2016 (grant of new secure tenancies in England) comes fully into force.

(2) The local housing authority must grant a secure tenancy that is not a flexible tenancy if—

(a) the tenancy is offered to a person who is or was a tenant of some other dwelling-house under a qualifying tenancy (whether as the sole tenant or as a joint tenant), and

(b) the authority is satisfied that—

(i) the person or a member of the person's household is or has been a victim of domestic abuse carried out by another person, and

(ii) the new tenancy is granted for reasons connected with that abuse.

(3) The local housing authority must grant a secure tenancy that is not a flexible tenancy if—

(a) the tenancy is offered to a person who was a joint tenant of the dwelling-house under a qualifying tenancy, and
(b) the authority is satisfied that—
(i) the person or a member of the person's household is or has been a victim of domestic abuse carried out by another person, and
(ii) the new tenancy is granted for reasons connected with that abuse.

(4) In this section—
"abuse" means—
(a) physical or sexual abuse;
(b) violent or threatening behaviour;
(c) controlling or coercive behaviour;
(d) economic abuse (within the meaning of section 1(4) of the Domestic Abuse Act 2021);
(e) psychological, emotional or other abuse;
"domestic abuse" means abuse carried out by a person who is personally connected to the victim of the abuse (within the meaning of section 2 of the Domestic Abuse Act 2021);
"qualifying tenancy" means a tenancy of a dwelling-house in England which is—
(a) a secure tenancy other than a flexible tenancy, or
(b) an assured tenancy—
(i) which is not an assured shorthold tenancy, and
(ii) which is granted by a private registered provider of social housing, by the Regulator of Social Housing or by a housing trust which is a charity.

(5) For the purposes of this section, a person may be a victim of domestic abuse despite the fact that the abuse is directed at another person (for example, the person's child)."

(3) In section 81B (cases where old-style English secure tenancies may be granted)—
(a) in subsection (2C)—
(i) for the definition of "abuse" substitute—
""abuse" means—
(a) physical or sexual abuse;
(b) violent or threatening behaviour;
(c) controlling or coercive behaviour;
(d) economic abuse (within the meaning of section 1(4) of the Domestic Abuse Act 2021);
(e) psychological, emotional or other abuse;";
(ii) for the definition of "domestic abuse" substitute—
""domestic abuse" means abuse carried out by a person who is personally connected to the victim of the abuse (within the meaning of section 2 of the Domestic Abuse Act 2021);";
(b) after subsection (2C) insert—
"(2D) For the purposes of this section, a person may be a victim of domestic abuse despite the fact that the abuse is directed at another person (for example, the person's child)."

Commencement Information

I41 S. 79 in force at 1.11.2021 by S.I. 2021/1038, **reg. 3(c)**

Medical evidence of domestic abuse

80 Prohibition on charging for the provision of medical evidence of domestic abuse

(1) No person may charge a fee or any other remuneration for the preparation or provision of relevant evidence relating to an assessment of an individual carried out by a relevant health professional in England or Wales under a qualifying medical services contract.

(2) No person may charge a fee or any other remuneration for the preparation or provision of relevant evidence relating to an individual by a relevant health professional in England or Wales if the services provided by the relevant health professional are wholly or mainly services provided under a qualifying medical services contract.

(3) In this section "relevant evidence", in relation to an individual, means—

(a) evidence that the individual is, or is at risk of being, a victim of domestic abuse which is intended to support an application by the individual for civil legal services, or

(b) any other evidence that the individual is, or is at risk of being, a victim of domestic abuse which is of a description specified in regulations made by the Secretary of State.

(4) In this section "relevant health professional" means—

(a) a medical practitioner licensed to practise by the General Medical Council;

(b) a health professional registered to practise in the United Kingdom by the Nursing and Midwifery Council;

(c) a paramedic registered to practise in the United Kingdom by the Health and Care Professions Council.

(5) In this section "qualifying medical services contract" means—

(a) in relation to England—

(i) a general medical services contract made under section 84(2) of the National Health Service Act 2006;

(ii) any contractual arrangements made under section 83(2) of that Act;

(iii) an agreement made under section 92 of that Act;

(b) in relation to Wales—

(i) a general medical services contract made under section 42(2) of the National Health Service (Wales) Act 2006;

(ii) any contractual arrangements made under section 41(2)(b) of that Act;

(iii) an agreement made under section 50 of that Act.

(6) The appropriate national authority may by regulations amend the definition of—

(a) "relevant health professional";

(b) "qualifying medical services contract".

(7) In this section—

"appropriate national authority" means—

(a) in relation to England, the Secretary of State;

(b) in relation to Wales, the Welsh Ministers;

"assessment" includes a consultation, whether in person or otherwise;

"civil legal services" has the meaning given by section 8 of the Legal Aid, Sentencing and Punishment of Offenders Act 2012.

(8) Subsections (1) and (2) do not apply in relation to anything done by a relevant health professional before the coming into force of this section.

Data processing for immigration purposes

81 Review of processing of victims' personal data for immigration purposes

(1) The Secretary of State must, before the end of the relevant period—
  (a) review the processing of domestic abuse data carried out by specified public authorities for immigration purposes,
  (b) prepare and publish a report setting out the findings of the review, and
  (c) lay a copy of the report before Parliament.

(2) In carrying out the review, the Secretary of State must have regard to the recommendations of the HMIC Report.

(3) In subsection (1), the "relevant period" means the period beginning with the day on which this section comes into force and ending with 30 June 2021 (but see subsection (4)).

(4) The Secretary of State may by regulations extend the relevant period by a further period of up to 6 months.

(5) The power conferred by subsection (4) may be exercised only once.

(6) In this section—
"domestic abuse data" means personal data obtained for the purposes of, or in connection with, the provision of support in relation to domestic abuse to victims of domestic abuse or their children;
"the HMIC Report" means the report on Liberty and Southall Black Sisters' super-complaint on policing and immigration status published by Her Majesty's Chief Inspector of Constabulary on 17 December 2020;
"immigration officer" means a person appointed as an immigration officer under paragraph 1 of Schedule 2 to the Immigration Act 1971;
"immigration purposes" means the purposes of—
  (a) the maintenance of effective immigration control, or
  (b) the investigation or detection of activities that would undermine the maintenance of effective immigration control;
"personal data" has the meaning given by section 3(2) of the Data Protection Act 2018;
"processing" has the meaning given by section 3(4) of that Act;
"specified public authority" means—
  (a) a chief officer of police of a police force maintained for a police area in England and Wales;
  (b) the chief constable of the Police Service of Scotland;
  (c) the Chief Constable of the Police Service of Northern Ireland;
  (d) the Chief Constable of the British Transport Police Force;
  (e) the Chief Constable of the Ministry of Defence Police;
  (f) an immigration officer or other official of the Secretary of State exercising functions in relation to immigration or asylum.

PROSPECTIVE

82 Code of practice

(1) The Secretary of State may issue a code of practice relating to the processing of domestic abuse data for immigration purposes.

(2) A code of practice issued under this section—
(a) must be kept under review;
(b) may be revised or replaced.

(3) A person to whom a code of practice issued under this section applies must have regard to it in processing domestic abuse data for immigration purposes.

(4) In preparing, revising or replacing a code, the Secretary of State must consult—
(a) the Domestic Abuse Commissioner,
(b) the Information Commissioner, and
(c) such other persons as the Secretary of State considers appropriate.

(5) Before issuing a code (or a revised code) under this section, the Secretary of State must lay the code before Parliament.

(6) If, within the 40-day period, either House of Parliament resolves not to approve the code—
(a) the code is not to be issued, and
(b) the Secretary of State may prepare another code.

(7) If no such resolution is passed within the 40-day period, the Secretary of State may issue the code.

(8) In this section, the "40-day period" is the period of 40 days beginning with the day on which the code is laid before Parliament (or, if it is not laid before each House of Parliament on the same day, the later of the 2 days on which it is laid).

(9) In calculating the 40-day period, no account is to be taken of any period during which Parliament is dissolved or prorogued or during which both Houses are adjourned for more than 4 days.

(10) In this section—
"domestic abuse data" has the same meaning as in section 81;
"immigration purposes" has the same meaning as in section 81;
"personal data" has the meaning given by section 3(2) of the Data Protection Act 2018;
"processing" has the meaning given by section 3(4) of that Act.

Contact centres

83 Report on the use of contact centres in England

(1) The Secretary of State must, before the end of the relevant period, prepare and publish a report about the extent to which individuals, when they are using contact centres in England, are protected from the risk of domestic abuse or, in the case of children, other harm.

(2) "The relevant period" means the period of 2 years beginning with the day on which this Act is passed.

(3) In this section "contact centre" means a place that is used for the facilitation of contact between a child and an individual with whom the child is not, or will not be, living (including the handover of the child to that individual).

Guidance

84 Power of Secretary of State to issue guidance about domestic abuse, etc

(1) The Secretary of State may issue guidance about—
(a) the effect of any provision made by or under—
(i) Parts 1 to 5,

(ii) section 68 or 70,
(iii) section 72 or Part 1 of Schedule 3,
(iv) section 76, 77, 78 or 79, or
(v) section 80 so far as relating to England;

(b) other matters relating to domestic abuse—
(i) in England, and
(ii) so far as not relating to Welsh devolved matters, in Wales.

(2) The Secretary of State must, in particular, issue guidance under this section about—
(a) the effect of sections 1 and 2, including guidance as to particular kinds of behaviour that amount to domestic abuse;
(b) the effect of domestic abuse on children.

(3) Any guidance issued under this section must, so far as relevant, take account of the fact that the majority of victims of domestic abuse in England and Wales (excluding children treated as victims by virtue of section 3) are female.

(4) A person exercising public functions to whom guidance issued under this section relates must have regard to it in the exercise of those functions.

But nothing in this section permits the Secretary of State to issue guidance to a court or tribunal.

(5) The Secretary of State may from time to time revise any guidance issued under this section.

(6) Before issuing or revising guidance under this section, the Secretary of State must consult—
(a) the Domestic Abuse Commissioner,
(b) the Welsh Ministers, so far as the guidance relates to a devolved Welsh authority, and
(c) such other persons as the Secretary of State considers appropriate.

(7) In subsection (6)(b) "devolved Welsh authority" has the meaning given by section 157A of the Government of Wales Act 2006.

(8) Subsection (6) does not apply in relation to any revisions of guidance issued under this section if the Secretary of State considers the proposed revisions of the guidance are insubstantial.

(9) The Secretary of State must publish—
(a) any guidance issued under this section, and
(b) any revisions of that guidance.

(10) For the purposes of this section something relates to Welsh devolved matters so far as it relates to—
(a) any matter provision about which would be within the legislative competence of Senedd Cymru if it were contained in an Act of Senedd Cymru, or
(b) (so far as it is not within paragraph (a)), any matter functions with respect to which are exercisable by the Welsh Ministers, the First Minister for Wales, the Counsel General to the Welsh Government or the Senedd Commission.

Commencement Information

I42 S. 84 in force at 1.11.2021 by S.I. 2021/1038, **reg. 3(d)**

Powers to make consequential or transitional provision, etc

85 Power to make consequential amendments

(1) The Secretary of State may by regulations make provision that is consequential on any provision made by or under—

(a) Parts 1 to 5,
(b) section 68, 69, 70 or 71,
(c) section 72 or Part 1 of Schedule 3, or
(d) section 76, 77, 78, 79, 81 or 82.

(2) The appropriate national authority may by regulations make provision that is consequential on any provision made by or under section 80.

(3) In subsection (2) "the appropriate national authority" means—
(a) in relation to England, the Secretary of State;
(b) in relation to Wales, the Welsh Ministers.

(4) The power of the Secretary of State to make regulations under this section may, in particular, be exercised by amending, repealing, revoking or otherwise modifying any provision made by or under an Act passed before, or in the same session of Parliament as, this Act.

(5) The power of the Welsh Ministers to make regulations under this section may, in particular, be exercised by amending, repealing, revoking or otherwise modifying any provision made by or under primary legislation passed or made before, or in the same session of Parliament as, this Act.

(6) In subsection (5) "primary legislation" means—
(a) an Act of Parliament;
(b) a Measure or Act of the National Assembly for Wales or an Act of Senedd Cymru.

86 Power to make transitional or saving provision

(1) The Secretary of State may by regulations make such transitional or saving provision as the Secretary of State considers appropriate in connection with the coming into force of any provision of—
(a) Parts 1 to 5,
(b) section 68, 69, 70 or 71,
(c) section 72 or 74(1) or Part 1 of Schedule 3, or
(d) any of sections 75 to 79 or 81 to 84.

(2) The appropriate national authority may by regulations make such transitional or saving provision as the authority considers appropriate in connection with the coming into force of section 80.

(3) In subsection (2) "the appropriate national authority" means—
(a) in relation to England, the Secretary of State;
(b) in relation to Wales, the Welsh Ministers.

(4) The Department of Justice in Northern Ireland may by regulations make such transitional or saving provision as the Department considers appropriate in connection with the coming into force of any provision of section 73 or 74(3) or Part 3 of Schedule 3.

(5) Regulations under this section may (among other things) make any adaptations of provisions of this Act mentioned in subsection (1), (2) or (4) (as the case may be) brought into force that appear to be appropriate in consequence of other provisions of this Act not yet having come into force.

Final provisions

87 Regulations

(1) Any power of the Secretary of State, the Lord Chancellor or the Welsh Ministers to make regulations under this Act is exercisable by statutory instrument.

(2) Any power of the Department of Justice in Northern Ireland to make regulations under this Act is exercisable by statutory rule for the purposes of the Statutory Rules (Northern Ireland) Order 1979 (S.I. 1979/1573 (N.I. 12)).

(3) Regulations under this Act may—

(a) make different provision for different purposes or in relation to different areas;

(b) contain supplementary, incidental, consequential, transitional or saving provision.

(4) Subsection (3) does not apply to regulations under section 90 (see instead subsection (7) of that section).

(5) A statutory instrument containing regulations made by the Secretary of State or Lord Chancellor under this Act is subject to annulment in pursuance of a resolution of either House of Parliament, unless the instrument—

(a) is required by subsection (6) or any other enactment to be laid in draft before, and approved by a resolution of, each House of Parliament, or

(b) contains only regulations under section 20(4), 37(7), 81(4), 86 or 90.

(6) A statutory instrument that contains (with or without other provisions)—

(a) regulations under section 41(7),

(b) regulations of the Secretary of State under section 80(6), or

(c) regulations of the Secretary of State under section 85 that amend or repeal any Act,

may not be made unless a draft of the instrument has been laid before, and approved by a resolution of, each House of Parliament.

(7) A statutory instrument containing regulations made by the Welsh Ministers under this Act is subject to annulment in pursuance of a resolution made by Senedd Cymru, unless the instrument—

(a) is required by subsection (8) or any other enactment to be laid before, and approved by a resolution of, Senedd Cymru, or

(b) contains only regulations under section 86.

(8) A statutory instrument that contains (with or without other provisions)—

(a) regulations of the Welsh Ministers under section 80(6), or

(b) regulations of the Welsh Ministers under section 85 that amend or repeal primary legislation (within the meaning of section 85(4)),

may not be made unless a draft of the instrument has been laid before, and approved by a resolution of, Senedd Cymru.

88 Financial provision

There is to be paid out of money provided by Parliament—

(a) any expenditure incurred by a Minister of the Crown under or by virtue of this Act, and

(b) any increase attributable to this Act in the sums payable under any other Act out of money so provided.

89 Extent

(1) Except as set out below, this Act extends to England and Wales only.

(2) Any amendment or repeal made by Part 2 or 3 or Schedule 2 has the same extent within the United Kingdom as the provision amended or repealed.

(3) Section 74(2) and Part 2 of Schedule 3 extend to Scotland only.

(4) Sections 73 and 74(3) and Part 3 of Schedule 3 extend to Northern Ireland only.

(5) The following provisions extend to England and Wales, Scotland and Northern Ireland—

(a) section 39(7),

(b) sections 81 and 82,
(c) sections 85 to 88,
(d) this section, and
(e) sections 90 and 91.

(6) Section 39(7) and this subsection (and sections 85 to 87, 90 and 91, so far as relating to those provisions) extend to—
(a) the Isle of Man, and
(b) the British overseas territories except Gibraltar;

and the power under section 384(2) of the Armed Forces Act 2006 may be exercised so as to modify section 39(7) as it extends to the Isle of Man or a British overseas territory other than Gibraltar.

(7) The power under section 384(1) of the Armed Forces Act 2006 may be exercised so as to extend section 39(7) of this Act to any of the Channel Islands (with or without modifications).

90 Commencement

(1) The following provisions of this Act come into force on the day on which this Act is passed—
(a) section 71;
(b) section 75;
(c) section 81;
(d) section 83;
(e) sections 85 to 89, this section and section 91;
(f) any power to make regulations under or by virtue of this Act.

(2) Sections 69, 72 and 74(1) and Part 1 of Schedule 3 come into force at the end of the period of two months beginning with the day on which this Act is passed.

(3) Section 74(2) and Part 2 of Schedule 3 come into force in accordance with provision contained in regulations made by the Scottish Ministers.

(4) Sections 73 and 74(3) and Part 3 of Schedule 3 come into force in accordance with provision contained in an order made by the Department of Justice in Northern Ireland.

(5) Section 80 comes into force on 1 October 2021.

(6) The remaining provisions of this Act come into force in accordance with provision contained in regulations made by the Secretary of State.

(7) Regulations or an order under this section may make different provision for different purposes or in relation to different areas.

(8) Regulations under this section bringing any provision of Part 3 or section 76 into force only for a specified purpose or in relation to a specified area may—
(a) provide for that provision or section to be in force for that purpose or in relation to that area for a specified period;
(b) make transitional or saving provision relating to that provision or section ceasing to be in force at the end of the specified period.

(9) Regulations containing provision permitted by subsection (8)(a) may be amended by subsequent regulations under this section so as to continue any provision of Part 3 or section 76 in force for the specified purpose or in relation to the specified area for a further specified period.

(10) The power of the Department of Justice in Northern Ireland to make an order under this section is exercisable by statutory rule for the purposes of the Statutory Rules (Northern Ireland) Order 1979 (S.I. 1979/1573 (N.I. 12)).

(11) Any provision which the Department of Justice in Northern Ireland could make by regulations under section 86 may be made by the Department by an order under this section.

91 Short title

This Act may be cited as the Domestic Abuse Act 2021.

SCHEDULES
PROSPECTIVE
SCHEDULE 1

Section 40

FURTHER PROVISION ABOUT REMAND UNDER SECTION 40

Introductory

1 This Schedule a where a court has power to remand a person ("P") under section 40.

Remand in custody or on bail

2 (1) The court may remand P in custody or on bail.

(2) If remanded in custody, P is to be committed to custody to be brought before the court—

(a) at the end of the period of remand, or

(b) at such earlier time as the court may require.

(3) The court may remand P on bail—

(a) by taking from P a recognizance (with or without sureties) conditioned as provided in paragraph 3, or

(b) by fixing the amount of the recognizances with a view to their being taken subsequently in accordance with paragraph 7 and, in the meantime, committing P to custody as mentioned in sub-paragraph (2).

(4) Where P is brought before the court after remand, the court may further remand P.

3 (1) Where P is remanded on bail, the court may direct that P's recognizance be conditioned for P's appearance—

(a) before the court at the end of the period of remand, or

(b) at every time and place to which during the course of the proceedings the hearing may from time to time be adjourned.

(2) Where a recognizance is conditioned for P's appearance as mentioned in sub-paragraph (1)(b), the fixing of a time for P next to appear is to be treated as a remand.

(3) Nothing in this paragraph affects the power of the court at any subsequent hearing to remand P afresh.

4 (1) The court may not remand P for a period exceeding eight clear days unless—

(a) the court adjourns proceedings for the purpose mentioned in paragraph 5(1), or

(b) P is remanded on bail and both P and the person who applied for the warrant under section 40 consent.

This is subject to paragraph 6.

(2) Where the court has power to remand P in custody, P may be committed to the custody of a constable if the remand is for a period not exceeding three clear days.

Remand for medical examination and report

5 (1) If the court has reason to suspect that a medical report will be required, the power to remand a person under section 40 may be exercised for the purpose of enabling a medical examination to take place and a report to be made.

(2) If the person is remanded in custody for that purpose, the adjournment may not be for more than 3 weeks at a time.

(3) If the person is remanded on bail for that purpose, the adjournment may not be for more than 4 weeks at a time.

(4) Sub-paragraph (5) applies if there is reason to suspect that a person who has been arrested under a warrant issued on an application made under section 40 is suffering from mental disorder within the meaning of the Mental Health Act 1983.

(5) The court has the same power to make an order under section 35 of that Act (remand to hospital for report on accused's mental condition) as the Crown Court has under that section in the case of an accused person (within the meaning of that section).

Further remand

6 (1) If the court is satisfied that a person ("P") who has been remanded is unable by reason of illness or accident to appear or be brought before the court at the end of the period of remand, the court may further remand P in P's absence.

(2) The power under sub-paragraph (1) may, in the case of a person who was remanded on bail, be exercised by enlarging the person's recognizance and those of any sureties for the person to a later time.

(3) Where a person ("P") remanded on bail is bound to appear before the court at any time and the court has no power to remand P under sub-paragraph (1), the court may (in P's absence) enlarge P's recognizance and those of any sureties for P to a later time.

(4) The enlargement of P's recognizance is to be treated as a further remand.

(5) Paragraph 4(1) (limit of remand) does not apply to the exercise of the powers conferred by this paragraph.

Postponement of taking of recognizance

7 Where under paragraph 2(3)(b) the court fixes the amount in which the principal and the sureties, if any, are to be bound, the recognizance may afterwards be taken by a person prescribed by rules of court, with the same consequences as if it had been entered into before the court.

Requirements imposed on remand on bail

8 The court may, when remanding a person on bail in accordance with this Schedule, require the person to comply, before release on bail or later, with any requirements that appear to the court to be necessary to secure that the person does not interfere with witnesses or otherwise obstruct the course of justice.

SCHEDULE 2

Section 70

STRANGULATION OR SUFFOCATION: CONSEQUENTIAL AMENDMENTS

Police and Criminal Evidence Act 1984

1 In section 65A of the Police and Criminal Evidence Act 1984 (qualifying offences for the purposes of Part 5 of that Act), in subsection (2), after paragraph (r) insert—

"(ra) an offence under section 75A of the Serious Crime Act 2015 (strangulation or suffocation)."

Commencement Information

I43 Sch. 2 para. 1 in force at 7.6.2022 by S.I. 2022/553, regs. 1(2), **3(b)**

Housing Act 1985

2 In Schedule 2A to the Housing Act 1985 (absolute ground for possession for antisocial behaviour: serious offences), after paragraph 14 insert—

"14A An offence under section 75A of the Serious Crime Act 2015 (strangulation or suffocation)."

Commencement Information

I44 Sch. 2 para. 2 in force at 7.6.2022 by S.I. 2022/553, regs. 1(2), **3(b)**

Criminal Justice and Public Order Act 1994

3 In Part 1 of Schedule 7A to the Criminal Justice and Public Order Act 1994 (offences in England and Wales for which cross-border powers of arrest available), for paragraph 24 substitute—

"24 An offence under either of the following provisions of the Serious Crime Act 2015—

(a) section 45 (participating in activities of organised crime group);

(b) section 75A (strangulation or suffocation)."

Commencement Information

I45 Sch. 2 para. 3 in force at 7.6.2022 by S.I. 2022/553, regs. 1(2), **3(b)**

Crime and Disorder Act 1998

4 (1) Section 29 of the Crime and Disorder Act 1998 (racially or religiously aggravated assaults) is amended as follows.

(2) In subsection (1), after paragraph (b) (but before the "or" following it) insert—

"(ba) an offence under section 75A of the Serious Crime Act 2015 (strangulation or suffocation);".

(3) In subsection (2), for "or (b)" substitute " , (b) or (ba) ".

Commencement Information

I46 Sch. 2 para. 4 in force at 7.6.2022 by S.I. 2022/553, regs. 1(2), **3(b)**

Youth Justice and Criminal Evidence Act 1999

5 (1) Schedule 1A to the Youth Justice and Criminal Evidence Act 1999 (proceedings in which witnesses are automatically eligible for assistance on grounds of fear or distress about testifying) is amended as follows.

(2) After paragraph 29 insert—

"Serious Crime Act 2015

29AAn offence under section 75A of the Serious Crime Act 2015 (strangulation or suffocation) in a case where it is alleged that—

(a) the accused was carrying a firearm or knife at any time during the commission of the offence, and

(b) a person other than the accused knew or believed at any time during the commission of the offence that the accused was carrying a firearm or knife."

(3) In paragraph 30, after "paragraphs 1 to 8" insert " and 29A ".

Commencement Information

I47 Sch. 2 para. 5 in force at 7.6.2022 by S.I. 2022/553, regs. 1(2), **3(b)**

Sexual Offences Act 2003

6 In Schedule 5 to the Sexual Offences Act 2003 (cases where sexual harm prevention orders may be made), after paragraph 63B insert—

"63C An offence under section 75A of the Serious Crime Act 2015 (strangulation or suffocation)."

Commencement Information

I48 Sch. 2 para. 6 in force at 7.6.2022 by S.I. 2022/553, regs. 1(2), **3(b)**

Criminal Justice Act 2003

7 In Part 1 of Schedule 15 to the Criminal Justice Act 2003 (violent offences specified for purposes of certain custodial sentences), before paragraph 63G insert—

"63FA An offence under section 75A of the Serious Crime Act 2015 (strangulation or suffocation)."

Commencement Information

I49 Sch. 2 para. 7 in force at 7.6.2022 by S.I. 2022/553, regs. 1(2), **3(b)**

Domestic Violence, Crime and Victims Act 2004

8 In section 6A of the Domestic Violence, Crime and Victims Act 2004 (evidence and procedure in cases of serious physical harm: England and Wales), in subsection (2), at the end insert—

"(c) an offence under section 75A of the Serious Crime Act 2015 (strangulation or suffocation)."

Commencement Information

I50 Sch. 2 para. 8 in force at 7.6.2022 by S.I. 2022/553, regs. 1(2), **3(b)**

Children Act 2004

9 In section 58 of the Children Act 2004 (reasonable punishment: England), in subsection (2), after paragraph (c) insert—

"(d) an offence under section 75A of the Serious Crime Act 2015 (strangulation or suffocation)."

Commencement Information

I51 Sch. 2 para. 9 in force at 7.6.2022 by S.I. 2022/553, regs. 1(2), **3(b)**

Criminal Justice and Immigration Act 2008

10 In section 98 of the Criminal Justice and Immigration Act 2008 (violent offender orders), in subsection (3), after paragraph (d) insert—

"(da) an offence under section 75A of the Serious Crime Act 2015 (strangulation or suffocation);".

Commencement Information

I52 Sch. 2 para. 10 in force at 7.6.2022 by S.I. 2022/553, regs. 1(2), **3(b)**

Modern Slavery Act 2015

11 In Schedule 4 to the Modern Slavery Act 2015 (offences to which defence for slavery or trafficking victims under section 45 of that Act does not apply), after paragraph 35 insert—

"Serious Crime Act 2015

35A An offence under section 75A of the Serious Crime Act 2015 (strangulation or suffocation)."

Commencement Information

I53 Sch. 2 para. 11 in force at 7.6.2022 by S.I. 2022/553, regs. 1(2), **3(b)**

Sentencing Act 2020

12 (1) The Sentencing Act 2020 is amended as follows.

(2) In section 67 (assaults on emergency workers), in subsection (3), after paragraph (a) insert—

"(aa) an offence under section 75A of the Serious Crime Act 2015 (strangulation or suffocation);".

(3) In Part 1 of Schedule 18 (violent offences for which extended sentence of imprisonment available), after paragraph 25 insert—

"Serious Crime Act 2015

25A An offence under section 75A of the Serious Crime Act 2015 (strangulation or suffocation)."

Commencement Information

I54 Sch. 2 para. 12 in force at 7.6.2022 by S.I. 2022/553, regs. 1(2), **3(b)**

SCHEDULE 3

Section 74

AMENDMENTS RELATING TO OFFENCES COMMITTED OUTSIDE THE UK

PART 1

ENGLAND AND WALES

Protection from Harassment Act 1997

1 In the Protection from Harassment Act 1997, after section 4A insert—

"4B Offences under sections 4 and 4A committed outside the United Kingdom

"4B "4B Offences under sections 4 and 4A committed outside the United Kingdom

(1) If—

(a) a person's course of conduct consists of or includes conduct in a country outside the United Kingdom,

(b) the course of conduct would constitute an offence under section 4 or 4A if it occurred in England and Wales, and

(c) the person is a United Kingdom national or is habitually resident in England and Wales,

the person is guilty in England and Wales of that offence.

(2) In this section—

"country" includes territory;

"United Kingdom national" means an individual who is—

(a) a British citizen, a British overseas territories citizen, a British National (Overseas) or a British Overseas citizen,

(b) a person who under the British Nationality Act 1981 is a British subject, or

(c) a British protected person within the meaning of that Act."

Sexual Offences Act 2003

2 (1) The Sexual Offences Act 2003 is amended as follows.

(2) In section 72 (offences outside the United Kingdom)—

(a) in subsections (1)(b) and (2)(c), for "section" substitute " subsection ";

(b) in subsection (3)(c), for "section" substitute " subsection ";

(c) in subsection (10), for "this section applies" substitute " subsections (1) to

(3) apply ".

(3) In Schedule 2 (sexual offences to which section 72 applies)—

(a) in the heading, for "section 72" substitute " section 72(1) to (3) ";

(b) in paragraph 1, in the opening words, for "section 72 applies" substitute " subsections (1), (2) and (3) of section 72 apply ";

(c) after paragraph 1 insert—

"1A In relation to England and Wales, subsections (1) and (2) of section 72 also apply to an offence under any of sections 1 to 4 where the victim of the offence was 18 or over at the time of the offence.";

(d) in paragraph 3, after "paragraph 1" insert " or 1A ".

Serious Crime Act 2015

3 In the Serious Crime Act 2015, after section 76 (controlling or coercive behaviour in an intimate or family relationship) insert—

"76A Offences under section 76 committed outside the United Kingdom

"76A "76A Offences under section 76 committed outside the United Kingdom

(1) If—
 (a) a person's behaviour consists of or includes behaviour in a country outside the United Kingdom,
 (b) the behaviour would constitute an offence under section 76 if it occurred in England and Wales, and
 (c) the person is a United Kingdom national or is habitually resident in England and Wales,

 the person is guilty in England and Wales of that offence.

(2) In this section—
 "country" includes territory;
 "United Kingdom national" means an individual who is—
  (a) a British citizen, a British overseas territories citizen, a British National (Overseas) or a British Overseas citizen,
  (b) a person who under the British Nationality Act 1981 is a British subject, or
  (c) a British protected person within the meaning of that Act."

PART 2

SCOTLAND

Criminal Procedure (Scotland) Act 1995

4 (1) Section 11 of the Criminal Procedure (Scotland) Act 1995 (certain offences committed outside Scotland) is amended as follows.

(2) In subsections (1) and (2), for "British citizen or British subject" substitute " relevant person ".

(3) After subsection (2) insert—
 "(2A) Any relevant person who in a country outside the United Kingdom does any act which—
  (a) constitutes an offence under the law in force in that country, and
  (b) if done in Scotland would constitute the crime of assault,

  is guilty of the same crime and subject to the same punishment as if the act had been done in Scotland.

 (2B) For the purposes of subsection (2A)(a), an act punishable under the law in force in the country is an offence under that law however it is described in that law.

 (2C) The condition specified in subsection (2A)(a) is to be taken as satisfied unless, not later than such time as may be prescribed by Act of Adjournal, the accused serves on the prosecutor a notice—
  (a) stating that, on the facts as alleged with respect to the act in question, the condition is not in the accused's opinion satisfied,
  (b) setting out the grounds for the accused's opinion, and
  (c) requiring the prosecutor to prove that the condition is satisfied.

(2D) But the court, if it thinks fit, may permit the accused to require the prosecutor to prove that the condition is satisfied without the prior service of a notice under subsection (2C).

(2E) In proceedings on indictment, the question whether the condition is satisfied is to be determined by the judge alone.

(2F) For the purposes of subsections (1) to (2B)— "country" includes territory;

"relevant person" means a person who is a United Kingdom national or is habitually resident in Scotland;

"United Kingdom national" means an individual who is—

(a) a British citizen, a British overseas territories citizen, a British National (Overseas) or a British Overseas citizen,

(b) a person who under the British Nationality Act 1981 is a British subject, or

(c) a British protected person within the meaning of that Act."

Sexual Offences (Scotland) Act 2009 (asp 9)

5 (1) The Sexual Offences (Scotland) Act 2009 is amended as follows.

(2) After section 54C insert—

"54D Offences committed outside the United Kingdom: adult victims

"54D "54D Offences committed outside the United Kingdom: adult victims

(1) If—

(a) a person who is a UK national does an act in a country outside the United Kingdom, and

(b) the act, if done in Scotland, would constitute an offence to which this subsection applies,

then the person commits that offence.

(2) If—

(a) a person who is habitually resident in Scotland does an act in a country outside the United Kingdom,

(b) the act constitutes an offence under the law in force in that country, and

(c) the act, if done in Scotland, would constitute an offence to which this subsection applies,

then the person commits that offence.

(3) The offences to which subsections (1) and (2) apply are offences under any of sections 1 to 4 where the victim of the offence was 18 or over at the time of the offence.

(4) For the purposes of subsection (2)(b), an act punishable under the law in force in the country is an offence under that law however it is described in that law.

(5) The condition specified in subsection (2)(b) is to be taken as satisfied unless, not later than such time as may be prescribed by Act of Adjournal, the accused serves on the prosecutor a notice—

(a) stating that, on the facts as alleged with respect to the act in question, the condition is not in the accused's opinion satisfied,

(b) setting out the grounds for the accused's opinion, and

(c) requiring the prosecutor to prove that the condition is satisfied.

(6) But the court, if it thinks fit, may permit the accused to require the prosecutor to prove that the condition is satisfied without the prior service of a notice under subsection (5).

(7) In proceedings on indictment, the question whether the condition is satisfied is to be determined by the judge alone.

(8) A person may be prosecuted, tried and punished for an offence by virtue of this section—

(a) in any sheriff court district in Scotland in which the person is apprehended or is in custody, or

(b) in such sheriff court district as the Lord Advocate may determine, as if the offence had been committed in that district; and the offence is, for all purposes incidental to or consequential on trial or punishment, to be deemed to have been committed in that district.

(9) In this section—

"country" includes territory;

"sheriff court district" is to be construed in accordance with section 307(1) of the Criminal Procedure (Scotland) Act 1995 (interpretation);

"UK national" means an individual who is—

(a) a British citizen, a British overseas territories citizen, a British National (Overseas) or a British Overseas citizen,

(b) a person who under the British Nationality Act 1981 is a British subject, or

(c) a British protected person within the meaning of that Act."

(3) In the heading of section 55, at the end insert " : child victims ".

(4) For the heading of section 56 substitute " Section 55: continuity of law ".

Criminal Justice and Licensing (Scotland) Act 2010 (asp 13)

6 In the Criminal Justice and Licensing (Scotland) Act 2010, after section 39 insert—

"39A Offence of stalking committed outside the United Kingdom

"39A "39A Offence of stalking committed outside the United Kingdom

(1) If—

(a) a person's course of conduct consists of or includes conduct in a country outside the United Kingdom,

(b) the course of conduct would constitute the offence of stalking if it occurred in Scotland, and

(c) the person is a United Kingdom national or is habitually resident in Scotland,

then the person commits that offence.

(2) If a person's course of conduct consists entirely of conduct in a country outside the United Kingdom—

(a) the person may be prosecuted, tried and punished for an offence of stalking by virtue of this section—

(i) in any sheriff court district in Scotland in which the person is apprehended or is in custody, or

(ii) in such sheriff court district as the Lord Advocate may determine,

as if the offence had been committed entirely in that district, and

(b) the offence is, for all purposes incidental to or consequential on trial or punishment, to be deemed to have been committed entirely in that district.

(3) In this section—

"country" includes territory;

"sheriff court district" is to be construed in accordance with section 307(1) of the Criminal Procedure (Scotland) Act 1995 (interpretation);

"United Kingdom national" means an individual who is—

(a) a British citizen, a British overseas territories citizen, a British National (Overseas) or a British Overseas citizen,

(b) a person who under the British Nationality Act 1981 is a British subject, or
(c) a British protected person within the meaning of that Act."

PART 3

NORTHERN IRELAND

Protection from Harassment (Northern Ireland) Order 1997 (S.I. 1997/1180 (N.I. 9))

7 In the Protection from Harassment (Northern Ireland) Order 1997, after Article 6 insert—

"Offences under Article 6 committed outside the United Kingdom

6A (1) If—

(a) a person's course of conduct consists of or includes conduct in a country outside the United Kingdom,
(b) the course of conduct would constitute an offence under Article 6 if it occurred in Northern Ireland, and
(c) the person is a United Kingdom national or is resident in Northern Ireland,

the person is guilty in Northern Ireland of that offence.

(2) In this Article—

"country" includes territory;

"United Kingdom national" means an individual who is—

(a) a British citizen, a British overseas territories citizen, a British National (Overseas) or a British Overseas citizen,
(b) a person who under the British Nationality Act 1981 is a British subject, or
(c) a British protected person within the meaning of that Act."

Commencement Information

I55 Sch. 3 para. 7 in force at 21.2.2022 by S.R. 2022/52, **art. 2(c)**

Sexual Offences (Northern Ireland) Order 2008 (S.I. 2008/1769 (N.I. 2))

8 In Article 76 of the Sexual Offences (Northern Ireland) Order 2008 (offences outside the United Kingdom)—

(a) in paragraphs (1)(b) and (2)(c), for "Article" substitute " paragraph ";
(b) in paragraph (3)(c), for "Article" substitute " paragraph ";
(c) in paragraph (10), for "this Article applies" substitute " paragraphs (1), (2) and (3) apply ";
(d) after paragraph (10) insert—
"(10A) Paragraphs (1) and (2) also apply to an offence under any provision of Part 2 where the victim of the offence was 18 or over at the time of the offence.";
(e) in paragraphs (11) and (12), after "paragraph (10)" insert " or (10A) ".

Commencement Information

I56 Sch. 3 para. 8 in force at 21.2.2022 by S.R. 2022/52, **art. 2(c)**

STATUS

This version of this Act contains provisions that are prospective.

CHANGES TO LEGISLATION:

Domestic Abuse Act 2021 is up to date with all changes known to be in force on or before 08 July 2022. There are changes that may be brought into force at a future date. Changes that have been made appear in the content and are referenced with annotations.

View outstanding changes

CHANGES AND EFFECTS YET TO BE APPLIED TO :

– s. 15(3)(q) omitted by 2022 c. 31 Sch. 5 para. 103
– s. 15(7) words omitted by 2022 c. 31 s. 36(4)
– s. 15(7) words substituted by 2022 c. 31 Sch. 1 para. 38
– s. 15(7) words substituted by 2022 c. 31 Sch. 4 para. 239
– s. 80(5)(a)(ii) substituted by 2022 c. 31 Sch. 3 para. 58

Index

For the benefit of digital users, indexed terms that span two pages (e.g., 52–53) may, on occasion, appear on only one of those pages.